Patterns of Empire

The British and American Empires, 1688 to the Present

Patterns of Empire comprehensively examines the two most powerful empires in modern history: the United States and Britain. Challenging the popular theory that the American empire is unique, *Patterns of Empire* shows how the policies, practices, forms, and historical dynamics of the American empire repeat those of the British, leading up to the present climate of economic decline, treacherous intervention in the Middle East, and overextended imperial confidence. A critical exercise in revisionist history and comparative social science, this book also offers a challenging theory of empire that recognizes the agency of non-Western peoples, the impact of global fields, and the limits of imperial power.

Julian Go is an Associate Professor of Sociology at Boston University. He is also a Faculty Affiliate in Asian Studies and New England and American Studies at Boston University, editor of the journal *Political Power and Social Theory*, and former Academy Scholar at Harvard University's Academy for International and Area Studies. His first book, *American Empire and the Politics of Meaning: Elite Political Cultures in the Philippines and Puerto Rico during U.S. Colonialism*, won the Mary Douglas Prize for Best Book from the American Sociological Association and was a finalist for a Philippines National Book Award. His other books include *The American Colonial State in the Philippines: Global Perspectives*, which he coedited.

Patterns of Empire

The British and American Empires, 1688 to the Present

JULIAN GO

Boston University

CAMBRIDGE
UNIVERSITY PRESS

CAMBRIDGE UNIVERSITY PRESS
Cambridge, New York, Melbourne, Madrid, Cape Town,
Singapore, São Paulo, Delhi, Mexico City

Cambridge University Press
32 Avenue of the Americas, New York, NY 10013-2473, USA

www.cambridge.org
Information on this title: www.cambridge.org/9781107600782

First published 2011
Reprinted 2012, 2013

A catalog record for this publication is available from the British Library.

Library of Congress Cataloging in Publication Data

Go, Julian, 1970–
Patterns of empire : the British and American empires, 1688 to the present / Julian Go.
    p. cm.
Includes bibliographical references and index.
ISBN 978-1-107-01183-0 (hardback) – ISBN 978-1-107-60078-2 (paperback)
1. United States – Foreign relations. 2. Great Britain – Foreign relations. 3. Imperialism –
History. 4. United States – Territorial expansion. 5. Great Britain – Territorial expansion.
I. Title.
E183.7.G6 2011
327.73 – dc23   2011017075

ISBN 978-1-107-01183-0 Hardback
ISBN 978-1-107-60078-2 Paperback

For my parents, Heide and Julian, Jr.

Contents

Preface and Acknowledgments

This book is about the American and the British empires. In the tradition of macro-comparative historical sociology, it puts the two empires under a critical comparative lens. But this book is also meant as an assault. It is an assault against a way of thinking called "exceptionalism." Exceptionalism presumes that the United States is special and especially benign. It assumes that the United States has a unique and essential character. It assumes that the United States exemplifies the most perfect liberal democracy in the world. It assumes that understanding what the United States does abroad only depends on understanding what happens within the United States. It also assumes that the United States and its people are the sole agents of history – whether for ill or for good.

Exceptionalism is the North American counterpart to Eurocentrism. It silently structures thought. And it has helped to create and sustain empire. It does this not only by heralding the American empire as unique, but also by assuming the United States and its people have the privilege of directing history. Any analysis of the American empire must therefore confront exceptionalist thought.

This book's comparative analysis is hereby motivated. Comparison is mobilized to confront exceptionalism. For this task, the tools of comparative-historical sociology help. However, in its challenge to exceptionalism, the analysis also derives much of its inspiration from postcolonial theory. Sociologists do not often peddle in postcolonial theory. This book barely cites any. Yet this book's critique of exceptionalism, its associated emphasis on the agency of colonized populations, and its implicit examination of the provinciality of American empire would not be the same without the silent influence of postcolonial theory's critique of imperial knowledge.

Finally, this book might be read as marking a passing. Ten or twenty years from now, to write about the American empire may be akin to writing about the British empire today. It will be about something that has passed. Of course, America's global power is not yet withered. Its imperial manifestations persist. If the comparison with the British empire tells us anything, however, it is that

America's global hegemony is already over. Thus arises one of the sobering if not frightful lessons from the comparison in this book: falling empires, like rising ones, do not behave well. As the American empire falls, it will not go down without a fight.

There are many to thank. Craig Calhoun, Fred Cooper, and Kevin Moore's "Lessons of Empire" conference at New York University provided an important forum for me to explore initial ideas; participants there who gave me valuable criticism and/or support include Matt Connelly, Ann Stoler, Jomo K.S., Stephen Howe, and of course Craig, Fred, and Kevin. An invitation from Bat Sparrow and Sanford Levinson to the University of Texas at Austin Law School permitted me to test some early ideas on U.S. overseas colonialism. I am grateful to them and to Christina Duffy-Burnett who pressed my thoughts in Austin. Roger Owen and Eve Trout Powell invited me to their Imperialism Symposium at the University of Pennsylvania where I got insightful comments from participants there, especially from Robert Vitalis, Engseng Ho, and Robert Tignor. Julia Adams and Phil Gorski at Yale University invited me to their Comparative Research Workshop, where Malik Martin, Jennifer Bair, and Peter Stamatov among other participants offered helpful thoughts. Steve Pincus's invitation to attend his conference on colonialisms at Yale offered another arena to test some ideas and receive helpful criticisms (from Steve and Peter Perdue especially). Alyosha Goldstein hosted a productive visit to the American Studies program at the University of New Mexico. Gurminder Bhambra kindly invited me to give two talks at Warwick, U.K. Other forums included Boston College's Department of Sociology; Brown University's Department of Sociology; the Colloquium on Comparative Research at the Watson Institute and Rich Snyder's and Barbara Stalling's graduate seminar at Brown; and the University of British Columbia. The history group at the Humanities Department at Pompeu Fabra University in Barcelona offered a fantastic place to think, write, and relax; thanks especially to Gloria Cano and Josep Delgado for hosting me.

The indirect and direct guidance of Stephen Howe has been indispensable for this book. In New York City at the "Lessons of Empire" conference, his remarks about the British and U.S. empires helped initiate some of the ideas in this book. And I still think fondly of a lively dinner in his Oxfordshire home with Wm. Roger Louis years ago, an evening that inadvertently served to crystallize some ideas herein. Stephen also read the entire manuscript and provided precise commentary, as did Ian Tyrrell to whom I owe so much. Julia Adams and George Steinmetz continue to nurture and inspire. Phil Gorski perused an initial draft and gave me encouragement when I needed it badly. Many others provided necessary comradeship, encouragement, humor, or helpful suggestions: Nitsan Chorev, Filiz Garip, Neil Gross, Stefan Huemann, Victoria Johnson, Krishan Kumar, Nicholas Hoover Wilson, Michael Mann, Renisa Mawani, Roger Owen, David Swartz, Kathleen Schwartzman, Robert Vitalis, Geneviève Zubrzycki, and my colleagues at Boston University's Sociology Department.

Funding for some of the research for this book was provided by the American Sociological Association/National Science Foundation Funds for the Advancement of the Discipline and by the College of Arts & Sciences at Boston University. A number of students over the years provided much needed research assistance: Cate Boland, Jennifer Childs, Zophia Edwards, Robin Lagorio, Dave McElhattan, Masayo Nishida, Edwin Vargas, and Shirley Wong. Eric Crahan has been a supportive and efficient editor from the start.

My partner, Emily Barman, made writing this book tolerable. My son, Oliver, made it worthwhile. Both of them made research trips to London more fun than they should be (even if the Tube is not amenable to strollers). Finally, I am as ever grateful to my parents, Heide and Julian Go, Jr., for their continued love and support. This book is dedicated to them.

Julian Go
Boston, MA

A note on terminology: With due respect to my Latin American colleagues and my Canadian spouse, I will sometimes use the phrase "American state" or "American empire" to refer to the United States.

List of Tables

List of Figures

Introduction

Empires in Comparison

We covet no territory, and we have no imperialistic ambitions.
        – Sumner Welles, U.S. Secretary of State (1941)

America has never been an empire. We may be the only great power in history that had the chance, and refused.
        – President George W. Bush (2000)

Our nations covet no territory... only a safer world.
        – Donald Rumsfeld on the United States and Britain in Iraq (2003)

America is not the crude stereotype of a self-interested empire. The United States has been one of the greatest sources of progress that the world has ever known. We were born out of revolution against an empire. We were founded upon the ideal that all are created equal, and we have shed blood and struggled for centuries to give meaning to those words – within our borders, and around the world.
        – President Barack H. Obama (2009)

These utterances by America's prominent statesmen represent a longstanding tradition of thought called "exceptionalism." According to this tradition of thought, the United States has always been different from other countries. Unlike European nations, it lacks a feudal past. Born of an anticolonial revolution against a monarchy, it clings interminably to egalitarian, democratic, and liberal ideals. Because of this unique history and national character, the United States has never been an empire, nor could it ever be. George W. Bush's claim that America is "the only great power in history that had the chance [to be an empire] and refused" is one expression among many of this exceptionalist theme. Traditional scholarship on American foreign policy has espoused the same idea, consciously avoiding terms like "imperialism" or "empire," and instead using terms like "diplomacy." "One of the central themes of American historiography," observed the historian William A. Williams in 1955, "is that there is no American empire."[1]

---

[1] Williams (1955).

One goal of this book is to critically reconsider these claims about exceptionalism. On what grounds can we say that the United States has been special, different, or "exceptional"? Can we rightfully assert that the United States has never been an empire? Is exceptionalism a useful way for thinking about America's past and present standing in the world?

In addressing these questions, this book will argue that exceptionalism obscures more than it reveals. As a set of claims about what is or is not, and as a mode of thought, exceptionalism should be rejected. Yet in making this case, the point is not simply to assert exceptionalism's opposite and declare that the United States is and always has been an empire. Such a declaration would not be new. Revisionist historians in the tradition of William A. Williams have already mounted assaults on exceptionalism by unearthing America's real imperial history. Highlighting America's westward expansion, its treatment of Native Americans, the acquisition of overseas colonies like the Philippines, and America's multiple military interventions around the world, these scholars and their successors have already shown us some of the ways in which the United States has been an empire. An additional line of scholarship, which we might think of as "neo-revisionist" scholarship has added further insights, scrutinizing not just America's imperial history, but also how that history has been erased in popular consciousness. According to this scholarship, attempts to deny empire are but predictable manifestations of an "historical amnesia" – a "denial and displacement" of America's indisputable imperial history.[2] Therefore, if there's anything exceptional about America's empire at all, it is only that it is an "empire that dare not speak its name." As Niall Ferguson puts it, "the great thing about the American empire is that so many Americans disbelieve in its existence."[3] Denying empire is simply part of the unique *modus operandi* of American empire itself.

There remain those who still insist that the United States was never a proper "empire."[4] Still, the growing acceptance of revisionist histories means that critiquing exceptionalism by reiterating America's imperial past is not sufficient. Calling the United States an empire does not have the potency it might have once had.[5] In fact, despite the charges of neo-revisionists that America's empire is an empire in denial, popular discourse has become increasingly willing to call a spade a spade. The phrase "American empire" appeared in one thousand news stories over a single six-month period in 2003. During the early years of the Iraq War, the discourse continued, leading the *Atlanta Journal-Constitution* to declare that "the concept of America as world empire, so controversial as to be almost unsayable just a few months ago, is now close to conventional

---

[2] See among others Jacobson (1999), Judis (2004), Kaplan (1993), Kaplan (2003a).
[3] Ferguson (2004).
[4] See Ravenal (2009) and Suri (2009).
[5] "The concept of American-as-imperium, a notion once employed only by scholars of a decidedly revisionist bent or by radical activists . . . has achieved a surprising amount of respectability of late." McMahon (2001), p. 82.

wisdom." Even officials have uttered the once unutterable. In 2003, a senior-level advisor to President George W. Bush stated: "We're an empire now, and when we act, we create our own reality."[6] Nor was this specific to the post-9/11 era. Earlier, in 2000, Richard Haas of the State Department urged Americans to "re-conceive their global role from one of a traditional nation-state to an imperial power."[7]

America's so-called amnesia and denial have abated. Apparently, the United States is not always an empire that dare not speak its name. For these reasons, a passionate declaration that there is an American empire would do little in itself to either critique exceptionalism or enrich our understanding of American power in the world. As the pundit Robert Kaplan wrote in the *Atlantic Monthly*, "It is a cliché these days to observe that the United States now possesses a global empire.... It is time to move beyond statements of the obvious."[8] I agree. A different approach is needed. Accordingly, this book raises and addresses new questions – the very questions invoked by the growing acceptance of revisionist thought. If the United States is and has always been an empire, does this mean that it is exactly the same as other empires? If it is not exactly the same, in what ways has it been distinct? If the United States is no longer an empire that "dare not speak its name," what remains of the notion of American distinctiveness, of something different or unique about America's global power? And what accounts for any similarities or differences we might find?

Revisionist historians have opened up these questions about America's similarity or difference with other empires by alerting us to America's long-standing and widespread imperial practices. But they have not yet answered them. These are *comparative* questions and, a few exceptions aside, comparative investigations of the U.S. empire are remarkably absent. This is a glaring omission. Conventional exceptionalist thought and revisionist criticisms all depend on comparison. To say that the United States is an "exception" is to say that it is an exception to a rule against which American distinctiveness can be measured. Similarly, to insist as revisionists do that the United States is and has always been an empire is to claim that it fits into the rule rather than deviates from it; that it is like or akin to something else. It is to suggest that the United States has exhibited features or enacted policies similar to those of other empires such that it is worthy of being called an empire in the first place. In other words, both exceptionalism and the revisionist critique are predicated on a silent and unstated understanding of other empires. They both depend on asserting an imperial "rule" or pattern against which American distinctiveness is to be measured or rejected. Their claims therefore conjure the need to look beyond the American empire, investigate other empires, and see how they fare in light of each other. Answering *any* questions about what is similar or different about

---

[6] Suskind (2004), p. 44.
[7] Quoted in Bacevich (2002), p. 219.
[8] Kaplan (2003b), p. 66.

the American empire demands a sustained systematic comparison that puts America's empire, both past and present, into a broader frame.[9]

Take, for instance, the British empire.

Turning to Britain

It is well known that Britain forged one of the largest and most powerful empires in the world over the course of the nineteenth century. This was an empire that reached down to Africa and back up to India, across to Hong Kong and down to Australia. Britain was also the world's preeminent military and economic power in the nineteenth century – sending its gunboats, money, and missionaries to do the Crown's bidding. An empire indeed. Still, not all Britons were always ready to utter the words "British empire." Historian Bernard Porter, among others, has shown that most Britons from the early to mid-nineteenth century were either ignorant of their empire or rejected the notion of it.[10] Instead, terms like imperialism and empire in the mid-nineteenth century were most often used to refer to Napoleonic France, not Victorian Britain. Even when it did refer to Victorian Britain, it did not mean empire as we might think of it today. It rather referred to "the United Kingdom of the British Isles and to England in particular." It was "rarely used in connection with topical issues of foreign affairs."[11] Only later, in the late decades of the nineteenth century, did more Britons became cognizant of the British empire and come to freely name it. It was only then, at that specific historical moment, when empire talk among Britons proliferated.

These British perceptions and discourses of empire in the nineteenth century are suggestive in various respects. First, they highlight that repressing, rejecting, or denying empire is not particular to the United States. Even people in the largest and most powerful empire of the time were not always quick to admit that they were part of an empire. In fact, some historians and statesmen have taken up the mantle of denial to suggest that a British empire never *really* existed.[12] Second, the Britons' discourse of empire shows a historical trajectory in imperial consciousness not unlike America's. Britons once denied empire but later began to recognize it, admit it, and talk more about it. This proliferation of empire talk among Britons in the late nineteenth century is akin to the proliferation of American empire talk among Americans in more recent years.

---

[9] Exceptions include Maier (2006) and Porter (2006). These works will be discussed throughout, along with how this book differs significantly from them. A good brief overview comparison between the U.S. and British empires can be found in Howe (2003), and a comparison of historiography can be found in MacDonald (2009). There is an older tradition of comparing British and U.S. imperialism (though this is different from a comparison of "empires"): These include Darby (1987), Liska (1978), Smith (1981), and Winks (1997).

[10] Porter (2004).

[11] Koebner and Schmidt (1964), pp. 145–6.

[12] See Powell (1969), p. 247. Also, historian John Darwin prefaces his recent work, *The Empire Project*, by saying "the British Empire in its heyday was largely a sham." See Darwin (2009), p. xi. Such claims obviously depend on what one means by the word "empire," an issue I take up throughout.

If Americans used to deny empire, they have done so less and less since the late twentieth century, just as Britons did in the late nineteenth century. In short, there has been similarity in empire talk and consciousness between Britain and the United States that would go undetected without an explicit comparative analysis. Without placing discourses of empire in comparative light, we would too easily and wrongly assume that denying empire is a distinctly American phenomenon.

The comparison in the present study is premised on the assumption that a systematic and sustained examination of other aspects of empire might likewise yield insights into matters of exceptionalism and empire. It might reveal similarities between America's and Britain's empire not just in discourse, but also in policies and practices. It might also help to unearth differences between the two empires and ultimately facilitate an *explanation* of whatever similarities or differences we might find.

This sustained comparison is what differentiates the present study from the revisionist historians' earlier work and from more recent examinations of U.S. imperialism. Although forthcoming chapters will indeed follow the revisionists' path and explore U.S. imperial history, the point is not to simply to catalog America's imperial interventions or therapeutically utter empire's name – as if that is all that is needed to attain a critical understanding. Rather, by employing a sustained systematic comparison, this book hopes to ascertain what, if anything at all, is distinctive, unique, or exceptional about American empire. It likewise aims to *explain* whatever differences or similarities arise from the comparison. Finally, this book seeks to raise some informed speculations about America's most recent imperial ventures in the early twenty-first century and where they might go. In 1902, the British critic and early theorist of imperialism J. A. Hobson wrote that "history devises reasons why the lessons of past empire do not apply to ours."[13] At that time, Hobson was criticizing his peers who believed that Britain had nothing to learn from the rise and fall of prior empires like Rome. In regard to the U.S. empire, we might similarly wonder what a consideration of Britain's imperial history has to say about America's imperial present and imperial future – if it has one at all.

First, though, our conceptual apparatus should be laid bare. A large part of what is at stake in our comparison is determining exactly *what it is* that we are comparing. So what exactly is an empire? What about related terms like imperialism or colonialism? After defining these terms, we can better establish the comparison and discuss the theoretical issues underlying it.

"Empire" and its Modalities

Defining terms like empire or imperialism is not a simple task. These terms carry heavy political and emotional baggage. To some, calling the United States an empire is to unfairly charge it with all kinds of wrongdoing and aggression. Another problem is that meanings shift over time. The word empire in the

---

[13] Hobson (1902), p. 234.

twentieth century might signify something different than in the eighteenth. To confuse matters even more, scholars sometimes stretch the terms for their theoretical (or political) purposes. V. I. Lenin defined imperialism as a stage of capitalism. Negri and Hardt conceptualize empire as multifaceted abstract relations of power that encompass the globe. Others have spoken of "cultural imperialism" or "economic imperialism."[14]

Definitions cannot be wrong or right. They can only be useful or not. Accordingly, for the purposes of our analysis, this book offers non-normative definitions that begin with elementary points. The goal is not to hurl accusations. Nor is it to narrow the investigation. The goal is offer a conceptual apparatus that can guide our investigation; to mark out some basic conceptual terrain. The trick is to define our terms widely enough so as to be flexible to the reality of history but narrow enough to be analytically robust.

To begin, *power* must be included in the definition. Empires, in their most basic sense, are sociopolitical formations that are constructed and maintained through the exercise of political power. This is not an arbitrary starting point. The word *empire* derives from the Latin term *imperium*, which roughly translates as "sovereignty" or "rule." During Roman times, *imperium* denoted the capacity to wage war and make laws, thereby describing a sphere of authority.[15] Later, during the early modern period in Europe, the term *imperium* took on added layers of meaning. Some usages rendered empire more or less synonymous with *status* or state. Other usages referred to an emperor or central political authority ruling over a distinct if not distant set of territories.[16] When Charles the Bold, Duke of Burgundy, invaded Lorraine in the fifteenth century, he referred to himself as "Emperor and Augustus" because he had come to rule over two territories rather than one. Empire meant a diversity of territory under a single authority.[17] Later, in 1625, Charles I probably meant something similar when he declared Virginia and New England to be part of "our Royal Empire."[18] In all these instances, at the heart of the meaning of empire was political power.

Most scholars today build on this basic notion of empire. On the one hand, scholars have included various dimensions of empire beyond political power: economic, cultural, religious, and even psychological.[19] On the other hand, despite these possible multiple dimensions, most scholars would recognize political power as the definitive feature. This is not because political power is most important. Some might say the economy determines everything in the last instance. Yet without the exercise of political power, there is no empire. "Power," writes the historian Dominic Lieven, "in its many manifestations is

---

[14] Lenin (1939); Hardt and Negri (2001).

[15] Howe (2002), p. 13; Pagden (1995), p. 12.

[16] Eisenstadt (1968), p. 41; Howe (2002), p. 13.

[17] Pagden (1995), p. 14.

[18] Quoted in ibid. p. 15.

[19] Michael Mann's discussion of America's "incoherent empire," for instance, counts four dimensions of power. See Mann (2003).

the core and essence of empire."[20] Sociologist S. N. Eisenstadt writes: "[T]he term 'empire' has normally been used to designate a political system encompassing wide, relatively centralized territories in which the center, as embodied both in the person of the emperor and in the central political institutions, constituted an autonomous entity."[21] Political scientist David Abernathy defines empire in "political terms as a relationship of domination and subordination.... The distinctive core feature is political control."[22] Empire, adds anthropologist Fernando Coronil, refers to "relatively large geopolitical formations that establish domination by hierarchically differentiating populations across transregional boundaries."[23]

The concept of empire used in the present study follows from these basic definitions. At the risk of sounding overly schematic, this book defines empire as a sociopolitical formation wherein a central political authority (a king, a metropole, or imperial state) exercises unequal influence and power over the political (and in effect the sociopolitical) processes of a subordinate society, peoples, or space. "A kind of basic, consensus definition," Stephen Howe fruitfully summarizes, "would be that an empire is a large political body which rules over territories outside its original political borders. It has a central power or core territory – whose inhabitants usually continue to form the dominant ethnic or national group in the entire system – and extensive periphery of dominated areas."[24] Other terms used in this book follow accordingly. Empires are involved in *imperialism*, which is the process by which they are established, extended, or maintained. They often have *imperial policies*, which are official and stated plans and practices by which power is exercised.[25] And they formulate various *strategies* and deploy multiple *tactics*, *techniques*, or *modalities* – sometimes unstated or unofficial – to realize their policies and extend or sustain themselves.

Keeping these basic definitions in mind is crucial for analytically differentiating empire and imperialism from other phenomena. First, empire is not the same thing as *economic* power. If a private corporation from a country invests in a weaker country and influences its internal affairs, we might call this "economic imperialism." But in the conceptual apparatus here proposed, this is different from the imperialism of a government. Empire entails political exertions of power by a state. Although such exertions might accompany or support a private corporation's economic exploitation, empire implies that a state is the main agent, and that the state directs, manipulates, or decisively influences the political – rather than just economic – processes and policies of a weaker society. Empire is a sociopolitical relation, not just an economic

---

[20] Lieven (2005), p. 128.
[21] Eisenstadt (1968)p. 41.
[22] Abernathy (2000), p. 19.
[23] Coronil (2007), p. 243. See also Tilly (1997), p. 3 and Doyle (1986), p. 19.
[24] Howe (2002), p. 14.
[25] Thornton (1978), p. 3.

one (even though the political operations of empire might entail economic relations).

Empire must also be differentiated from a "great power." A great power is a state with massive military capabilities and/or extensive territory. But such a state would only be an imperial state if the state uses those capabilities to exert influence on other peoples or societies to incorporate them as dependent satellites. A state that has the greatest military in the world but does not use it to construct a hierarchy of power may not necessarily be an empire. The United States may have the greatest military power in the world. It may also cover extensive territory. However, if it does not hold colonial dependencies or does not exert power over other societies, it would not be an empire (this is why the scholar Dominic Lieven, for instance, does not consider the United States today to be an empire, at least in its internal affairs: The "American president does not rule without consent over vast conquered territories and their populations").[26] Of course, states with such internal capabilities, like the United States, often do use their power in imperialistic ways. A state may be a great power and empire at once. The point here is to analytically separate the two. The issue is not whether a state *has* power (like military strength) but *whether* and *how* that power is exercised.[27]

A related distinction is between empire and "hegemony." The concept of hegemony first arose from Marxist theorist Antonio Gramsci to refer to a cultural or ideological process, but many scholars who deploy it today often define it as an economic matter. In this conceptualization, a hegemon is a state that enjoys relative preponderance over the world economy. A state enjoys hegemony when it takes up the largest shares of the world's economic activity (measured by relative share of world GDP, for example).[28] Accordingly, hegemony and empire are not the same. A state can have an empire but not dominate the world economy. Similarly, a state can dominate the world economy without being an empire. Moreover, if we define hegemony as cultural influence, this would not be the same as empire either. We might speak of "cultural imperialism" as a modality of imperial power, but we would not define empire as a state that only wields cultural influence.[29] Hollywood may dominate the global film industry, and its values or meanings may indirectly influence peripheral societies, but if the U.S. government does not meddle in the affairs of weaker countries and aim to control their affairs, the United States would not be an empire in our strict sense of the term.

---

[26] Lieven (2002), p. 79.

[27] Kennedy (1987: 539) defines "great powers" as any "state capable of holding its own against any other nation," a status that in turn depends on the states' relative economic capacities. This is not the same thing as empires and Kennedy states from the outset that his book is not about empires (p. xxi).

[28] This definition derives from world-systems theory, see Arrighi, Silver, and Ahmad (1999), pp. 26–8; Boswell (1995), pp. 2–4; Wallerstein (2002b). There are other ways to define hegemony of course, but for this book's purposes the economic definition will be used.

[29] On "world leaders," see Modelski (1978), Modelski and Thompson (1996).

Empire is analytically distinguishable from great powers, hegemons, and cultural influence, and there is also wide variation across types or forms of empires. Sociological variations are noteworthy. Typically, empires entail internal diversity, with a dominant group residing at the apex of a sociopolitical hierarchy. Perhaps the most common hierarchy is racialized: One race monopolizes political power to rule over other races who reside in the empire's subordinated areas. This is the image typically invoked when one thinks of European colonial empires in Africa during the late nineteenth century. Yet in our conceptualization, an imperial hierarchy need not be racial. It could be ethnic, linguistic, or religious. In the early modern Spanish empire in the Americas, natives subject to Spanish rule were not always conceived as racially different and inferior in the strict phenotypical sense. They were seen as non-Christians, that is, "pagans."[30] Difference was marked here as religious rather than as a matter of biology, blood, or stock. Another example might be the Ottoman empire, which articulated religion with dynasty such that Islam and the Ottoman family ruled Kurd or Turk elites.[31] The Tsarist Russian empire was not even ethnically or religiously differentiated, but class-based.[32]

Another variation arises in *how* political influence is exercised. At stake here are the forms or modalities of imperial power. One common distinction is between *formal* (direct) and *informal* (or indirect) exercises of power. The first, formal imperialism, refers to direct territorial rule. The imperial state annexes foreign land, declares official control over it, and subordinates the local population. The controlled territory then becomes a *colony* or dependency. This dependency is part of the metropolitan state, but its inhabitants do not enjoy the same rights or privileges as the state's citizens. Formal empire is thus the same as *colonial empires* involving the annexation of territory and direct rule over it.[33] This type of empire is often, although not exclusively, obtained by military conquest. During the Roman period, most emperors were victorious military generals. However, direct formal control can also be established "by invitation" rather than conquest.[34] Or it can be established by unequal treaties, as was often the case with early Europeans and Native American tribes. In any case, this type of direct or colonial empire is usually what most people refer to when they speak of empire in popular discourse. It conjures the image of Spain and its colonies in the Americas, France and its possession of Algeria, or Britain and its rule over India or parts of Africa. Flags are raised. Governors are appointed. Policies for governing the natives are formulated and exercised. States are made.

Variations in formal empires follow. We might think of "settler colonialism," whereby the subordinated colony is dominated by emigrants from the

---

[30] Seed (1995).
[31] Barkey (2008).
[32] Lieven (2005), p. 139.
[33] On the concept "colonialism," see Fieldhouse and Emerson (1968) and Osterhammel (1999b).
[34] Howe (2002), p. 13.

home land; or "administrative colonialism," whereby a handful of officials from the home land rule over large native populations. D. K. Fieldhouse goes even further, distinguishing between (1) pure settlement colonies (the majority are settlers from the metropole); (2) mixed colonies (settlers live with a larger indigenous population); (3) plantation colonies (a small settler group managing estates for export); (4) occupation colonies (close to no settlers); and (5) trading settlements or naval bases (small areas of land run by a small group of temporary metropolitans).[35] We may think of other subtypes too, such as land-based as opposed to sea-based empires. Or we might order colonial empires chronologically, attending to differences between early modern empires like Spain's or Portugal's and the modern administrative colonial empires of the late nineteenth century established by Europe in Africa or parts of Asia. Even within any single empire, the legal or juridical status of territories and subjects can be variously named and differentially treated, creating a complex of juridically heterogeneous peripheries.

The overarching point is that formal empires involve direct political control over territory and the subjugation of inhabitants of that territory into a status that is lesser, inferior, or dependent. This is the "rule of colonial difference," as Partha Chatterjee (1993) has aptly named it.[36] By this measure of colonial rule, colonized peoples are treated as inferior to citizens in the metropole, both in practice and in juridical theory or official doctrine. Due to their perceived racial, ethnic, or some other kind of distinction, the colonized are not given the same rights and privileges as the colonizer or citizens in the colonizers' home country. In some ways, it is exactly this subjugated status that differentiates colonial empire from pure democratic nation-states or federal states.[37] Nation-states involve citizens. Empires involve *subjects*, not citizens, and the difference between them is an important marker of empire.[38] For Stoler, McGranahan, and Perdue (2007), it is an essential imperial characteristic: "Uncertain domains of jurisdiction and ad hoc exemptions from the law on the basis of race and cultural difference are guiding and defining imperial principles."[39]

Colonialism, as in formal empire, is only one modality of imperial power – one way of exerting influence over societies. There are others. Robinson and Gallagher (1953) famously chided British historians for thinking of the British empire only in terms of its colonies – those parts of the map painted red – when in fact Britain also exercised influence if not political power over societies that were not officially colonies.[40] Hence the notion of indirect or "informal" empire. This refers to the exercise of power over the internal or external affairs

---

[35] Fieldhouse (1982), p. 11–13.

[36] Chatterjee (1993).

[37] Tilly (1997), p. 7.

[38] As Cooper and Kumar have rightly argued in their own ways, nation-states and empires have not been historically opposed; but here I oppose them as ideal-types only. See Cooper (2005), pp. 153–203 and Kumar (2010).

[39] Stoler, McGranahan, and Perdue (2007).

[40] Robinson and Gallagher (1953).

of nominally independent states through a variety of methods falling shy of annexation. The subordinated periphery in this case does not become a colony but an informal dependency, weak ally, or client. The imperial state keeps these nominally independent territories in line or compels them to meet its interests, but does not declare sovereignty over them. It offers money, protection, access, or other resources in exchange for deference. It might also employ threats of force or actually use force. The methods are thus multiple, the tactics nefarious. They include financial aid or market control, temporary military occupation or deployments of military power, covert operations to topple recalcitrant regimes, or just the threat of military assault.[41] The point is that any or all of these tactics fall short of declarations of sovereignty, even as they facilitate influence.

Classic and premodern imperial formations show early elements of this sort of imperial power. Athens exercised informal control over its allies in the Delian League (478–404 BC). Although nominally independent, the allies were forced to pay contributions (money and ships) to Athens, and Athens was considered to be their informal ruler.[42] Similarly, classic patrimonial empires such as the Egyptian and the Sassanid empires enlisted clients who paid tribute in exchange for protection; those clients then became part of the empires.[43] The modern era has also seen informal imperialism. In modern informal imperialism, nations retain their nominal independence and status as sovereign entities, but a foreign imperial state exercises power over them through various means short of direct rule.

We must not be too stark in our distinctions. Formal and informal empire might be better thought of as two ends of a blurry continuum. In some cases or at some historical moments, the two might become hardened and rigid as distinct types, but not always. The point is that empire can take different forms and have different modalities; and imperial states have a large repertoire of methods, tactics, and techniques by which to establish, extend, or maintain themselves. Imperial states might even mix colonial control and informal methods across different domains, holding an official colony here while establishing an informal client there. Or they might shift modes, decolonizing a territory only to replace formal colonialism with informal control.

There could also be distinctions between tactics or techniques cross-cutting formal or informal modalities. Empires, for instance, might vary in their aggression. At times they can be more indirect or subtle, whereas at other times they might be bolder in exerting power. Declaring sovereignty over foreign territory (i.e., formal imperialism) would be one example of the latter; so, too, would

---

[41] Informal empire is "a situation in which a single state shapes the behavior of others, whether directly or indirectly, partially or completely, by means that can range from the outright use of force through intimidation, dependency, inducement, and even inspiration." Gaddis quoted in McMahon (2001), p. 82.

[42] Doyle (1986), p. 30.

[43] Eisenstadt (1963).

military invasion. In contrast, financial aid, offering protection, or covert operations are more subtle and indirect; they are quieter, more silent, or hidden and thus involve less direct aggression than military invasion. Empires can thus shift between these modalities or tactics, substituting indirect tactics for direct ones, or vice-versa. Or they could mix and mingle them in different places, constituting a complex of strategies dispersed across sites. There are different ways to be imperial. It may be that this diversity contributes to the flexibility, and hence persistence, of empire over time and across different contexts.

In any case, we aim to be alert to these differences; to be aware of the multiplicity of imperial power; and to apprehend them in their possible combinations, shifts, substitutions, or transformations over time. It is for this reason – and due to this complexity and multiplicity – that we would fare well to think of empires not as essences but rather as *imperial formations*: sets of relations and forms involving multiple tactics, policies, practices, and modalities of power; hierarchically ordered formations wherein a state or center exercises control or unequal influence over subordinated territories, peoples, and societies through a variety of means and methods.[44] In this book, the word empire is used as shorthand for these complex formations of relations and practices.

The Task Ahead

The preceding discussion offers an admittedly rudimentary conceptual sketch. Yet it is nonetheless useful as a starting point. For example, with the foregoing definitions in mind, we might ask where and when political control is established and by what means. Formal or informal? We might also ask *why* formal control is established rather than informal, or vice-versa. Furthermore, we can investigate the empire as a whole at any given point in time – its formal territories and informal clients – and consider how the different parts are related or not. We might also consider the expansion or contraction of the imperial formation over time. In other words, we could examine the historical dynamics of empires, looking at moments when imperialistic activity is extended, stable, or retracted; or we could probe degrees of boldness and directness over time, looking for when imperial states become angry aggressors or when they shift to more subtle puppeteering from behind the scenes. Finally, the foregoing conceptual distinctions enable us to *compare* empires or imperial formations; to consider how the preferred strategies and forms are similar or different between the empires under scrutiny.

The main tasks of this book are guided by these conceptual distinctions and comparative questions. First, this book focuses foremost on the actions and operations of the *imperial state*. Although there are many actors involved in imperialism – from corporations to settlers, missionaries, and merchants – and although these actors will be discussed throughout, the primary focus here is the state: the institutional complex wielding resources deployed to establish

---

[44] On "imperial formations," see Stoler, McGranahan, and Perdue (2007).

and maintain its formal sovereignty or informal regimes. This follows from our conceptualization. As noted, empire at base is a matter of political power exerted by a ruling authority, a state. Therefore, an examination of empires can and should begin (but not necessarily end) with a focus on the imperial state. Accordingly, this book explores how the activities of the American state and British state constitute imperialism or not. It then discloses their imperial modalities and methods, policies and practices, and tactics and techniques. Chapters will also explore the activities of each state as they unfolded historically: how they might have expanded or contracted, how modalities in one era might have shifted in another, and the overall configuration of imperial power.

This book also puts imperial states into comparative perspective. To be clear, the comparison is not between British and American hegemony, nor is it about the United States and Britain as "great powers." It is not a comparison of how or why the two nations rose to hegemony; the policies that contributed to their socioeconomic development; or the factors that made them wealthy military powers. It is a comparative analysis of imperial formations. It is a comparison of how and why the two states have (or have not) exercised power over weaker societies, the forms that that exercise has taken, the modalities by which it has occurred, and the dynamics of imperialism over time. The comparison is precisely motivated. Following the implicit methodology of exceptionalist thought so as to better apprehend exceptionalism's operations and limits, the examination aims to illuminate differences and similarities between the two imperial formations. It looks at the modalities of the American imperial state in light of the British imperial state and vice-versa. It examines their respective transformations over time, comparing patterns of emergence, formation, or re-formation. In short, the comparative goal of this book is to better pinpoint what has been different about the American empire from the British empire.

The comparison is undoubtedly large. In taking on the task, this book admittedly runs the risk of overlooking certain complexities, details, and nuances. Multiple studies on these smaller aspects of empires have emerged: studies, for example, of the minute details of the lives of soldiers or settlers, merchants and housewives, travelers and slaves. This book does not purport to be of such caliber. Rather, in the tradition of comparative-historical sociology (and, by the same token, macrosociology and comparative history), it is unabashedly aimed at big comparisons. It looks for overarching patterns and dynamics and underlying forms and features that would otherwise go unnoticed amidst the trees. It is probably true that "empire is in the details" (as one anthropologist puts it), but this book ventures the risk that there might be overarching patterns, modalities, and iterative forms across time and space that warrant investigation too.[45]

---

[45] Lutz (2006). For representative work on the British empire that has paid close attention to the lives of everyday actors, see among others Colley (2003a). Much of this work constitutes new "cultural" or "social" histories of empire that also incorporate studies of gender, sexuality, and emotions. See for the U.S. context, among others, Stoler (2006), Tyrrell (1991b), and Hoganson

The final goal of this book is to *explain* whatever patterns we might find. Rather than only uncovering differences or similarities, this book hopes to account for them. What explains the fact that the U.S. empire has been this way or that way, as opposed to the British empire? Why did the U.S. imperial formation shift in one direction whereas the British formation shifted in the other? These are the sorts of questions that will be addressed as our analysis proceeds. We thereby weave between questions of *what* (What are the differences or similarities?) and *why* (Why the differences or similarities?). And on this matter we return to the issue with which we began: exceptionalism.

Explanation and Exceptionalism

Exceptionalism is relevant for our question of explanation because exceptionalism is more than just a description of the United States. It also has important implications for analyzing it. One implication is that any comparison between the United States and other countries is unfounded. As the United States is exceptional, comparisons to the British empire or any other empire would be misguided at best, misleading at worst. We would be better off rejecting the label empire and discarding "false analogies from a distant past."[46] The other implication has to do with explanation. As the United States has distinct values, cultural traditions, and institutions, whatever it does reflects those values, traditions, and institutions. In other words, America's exceptional history and behavior are caused by its exceptional internal characteristics.

This explanatory regime has been embedded in exceptionalist thought since it was first articulated by Alexis de Tocqueville (and by subsequent writers like Frederick Jackson Turner).[47] The basic theme is twofold. First, as Ian Tyrrell clarifies, American history "has been special and unique, standing as the only example of a true liberal democracy that the rest of the world would emulate."[48] Or as Kammen puts it, "the US has had a unique destiny and history . . . with highly distinctive features or an unusual trajectory."[49] Second, these unique features and trajectory have been caused by America's unique "national character." The United States exhibits special "traits" and "liberal, democratic, individualistic, and egalitarian values," and these traits or values

---

(2000). For macrocomparative studies of empire from which the present book draws inspiration, see Barkey (2008), Cooper and Burbank (2010), and Darwin (2008).

[46] Motyl (2006). One historian recently argues that the "empire" label "obfuscates more than it explains," for it "asserts a core American similarity with historical empires that overrides too many fundamental differences." See Suri (2009), p. 524.

[47] Exceptionalism, as a configuration of thought, has deeper roots. It originates in the discourse of early American settlers, politicians, and clergy who articulated the tenets of republicanism with the view that history is the unfolding of God's millennial plan. After these early stirrings, exceptionalism emerged as a more or less coherent framework influencing historical thinking and scholarship. See Ross (1984), pp. 910–11 and Madsen (1998) for good overviews.

[48] Tyrrell (1991a), p. 1035.

[49] Kammen (1993), p. 6.

account for America's unique features and trajectory.[50] The United States is the way it is (exceptional) because it has avoided the "class conflicts, revolutionary upheaval and authoritarian governments of 'Europe,'" and therefore has distinct values and beliefs that continue to shape it.[51] Social scientists in particular have drawn on these ideas to characterize various aspects of American history and explain features of American political development. Just as some historians claim that "America is a special case in the development of the West," so too do political scientists and sociologists insist that "American political institutions are more open, liberal, and democratic than those of any other major society," and that the American state exhibits "particularities as a liberal state" that cannot be described "as one would describe any other."[52] These social scientists then call on such particularities to understand such things as why the United States has been averse to Communism, why it is the richest country in the world, or why it is more litigious than, say, Canada.[53]

Exceptionalism in this sense has implications for thinking about and explaining empire. In exceptionalist narratives, America's unique values of democracy, liberty, and self-government have led the United States to be a distinctive global power, compelling the American state to behave differently than European powers: America's values and democratic institutions have meant that the United States never constructed an empire. Early expressions on this theme in the 1950s insisted that the United States eschewed empire because the United States was itself "a product . . . of revolt against colonial rule."[54] In the 1970s and 1980s, comparative historians argued that the United States since World War II has had various opportunities to seize colonies, but "deliberately rejected" the opportunities because the United States has been "obliged to conform to the principles which are the unalterable foundation of its political tradition."[55] A more recent commentary puts it simply: Empire is "not in America's DNA."[56]

In short, exceptionalism is not just a set of historical claims. It is a "way of talking about American history and culture," a "form of interpretation with its own language and logic."[57] This way of thinking is deeply entrenched in popular thought. In fact, even some revisionist scholarship critical of exceptionalism runs the risk of reproducing its tenets. As noted, revisionism has examined

---

[50] Huntington (1982), p. 13. Seymour Martin Lipset calls this an "American Creed" consisting of "liberty, egalitarianism, individualism, populism, and laissez-faire" that "reflect the absence of feudal structures, monarchies and aristocracies" [see Lipset (1996), p. 19].

[51] Tyrrell (1991a), p. 1035.

[52] Douglas (1995), p. 3; Huntington (1982), p. 14; Katznelson (2002), p. 84.

[53] The literature is voluminous, but for a recent exemplar, see Lipset (1996) and Shafer (1991). For exceptionalism and foreign policy see Lepgold and McKeown (1995), Ignatieff (1995), and Hoffman (1968). On exceptionalism and law see Koh (2003).

[54] Pratt (1958), p. 114.

[55] Schwabe (1986), p. 30; Liska (1978), p. 153.

[56] Hirsh (2002), p. 43.

[57] Madsen (1998), p. 2.

and reexamined America's global ambitions, its territorial and colonial expansion, and various aspects of American foreign policy that disclose imperial tendencies.[58] Whereas exceptionalism denies empire, this revisionist scholarship shows that empire has been an important feature of American history. Yet even this revisionist scholarship has not completely escaped exceptionalism's assumptions or explanatory models. This might seem odd, considering that the revisionist historians who inaugurated the study of American empire initially pitched their work *against* exceptionalism. Still, it remains the case that exceptional thought's mode of explanation remains a silent shaper of even revisionist thinking.

We can see this in two variants of revisionism. The first of these, which we might call "neo-revisionism" (or "liberal exceptionalism"), is seen in commentaries that emerged in the wake of the 2003 invasion of Iraq.[59] This sort of revisionism approach admits that there has long been an American empire. "Ever since the annexation of Texas and invasion of the Philippines," declares Niall Ferguson, "the United States has systematically pursued an imperial policy."[60] But it also insists that American empire has been special. Giving with one hand while taking from the other, it reinscribes exceptionalism by claiming that America's empire has been unique for its liberal and benign character. Whereas European empires were tyrannical and exploitative, American empire has been selfless, aiming to promote democracy and liberty around the world. "America's imperial goals and *modus operandi* are much more limited and benign than were those of age-old emperors."[61] Whereas European empires suppressed liberty, rights, and democracy, America's empire has been aimed at spreading them. "American imperialists usually moved much more quickly than their European counterparts to transfer power to democratically elected local rulers – as they are attempting to do in Iraq."[62] Traditional exceptionalism represses the word "empire," but this variant of revisionism just proclaims a distinctly American imperialism that ostensibly manifests America's special virtues.

The second variant of revisionism, which might be called "critical revisionism," comes initially from the founding historiography of William A. Williams and harkens back to leftist critiques of imperialism. This approach also insists that the United States has been an empire, but it does not see the American empire as uniquely benign. Rather than praising American empire for its liberal character, it portrays empire as a dangerous exploitative force. How, then, does this critical revisionism reinscribe exceptionalist thought?

---

[58] Bacevich (2002), p. 243.

[59] This includes the work of Niall Ferguson, Max Boot, and others who have been associated with American neoconservativism under George W. Bush's regime.

[60] Quoted in Dowd (2003), p. 27. See also Ferguson (2004) and Raustiala (2003).

[61] Ikenberry (2002), p. 59.

[62] Boot (2003), p. 363.

The reinscription involves two steps. The first is to pinpoint American empire's particularity by saying it has taken on a special form. American empire, in this view, has been indirect and less territorial than other empires. This constitutes a special "American way of empire" that is different from other ways of empire, a unique American brand of informal imperialism. The American empire has been distinct from European empires for its noncolonial character, employing nefarious economic or political means falling short of annexation to manipulate other societies. The second move is to then *explain* this difference (and a host of related ones) by reference to classic exceptionalist themes. If the U.S. empire has been informal rather than colonial, this is because of America's uniquely democratic traditions, beliefs, and values that militate against direct colonial rule and usurpations of sovereignty. Economic exploitation or resource extraction is acceptable, but colonialism is not. As one political scientist argues, the "political ethos and structure of the United States inherently militated against any doctrine other than that of national self-government for foreign peoples. . . . Among the Western democracies, the disinterest in foreign rule, and hence the prejudice in favor of the self-government of others, has been particularly pronounced in the United States."[63] The astute historian Anthony Pagden likewise asserts that colonialism "has never been an option for the United States." In order for the United States to be a colonial empire, "as even the British were at the end of the nineteenth century, the United States would have to change radically the nature of its political culture."[64] Others suggest that America has engaged in informal noncolonial imperialism because of its unique "social system," which has no natural "ruling class."[65] Tocqueville's reckonings here resound in revisionist reinscriptions of imperial exceptionalism.

So both neo-revisionism/liberal exceptionalism and critical revisionism would answer our comparative questions with neo-exceptionalist answers. Has the United States been an empire? Yes, but it has been a different empire than others. Why has the American empire been different? Because of America's special national character, institutions, or political culture.

But if revisionists already have an answer to our comparative questions, what is at stake in this book? Why bother with a comparative analysis? The problem is that the revisionist answers (and exceptionalist ones) remain hypotheses at best. To claim that anything is exceptional about the American empire depends on clarifying the "rule" against which the empire is measured; yet too often the rule is presumed rather than examined. Sustained comparative studies are few and far between. Hence, as long as our claims about what is distinct about the U.S. empire are not put into comparative relief, they remain tentative assertions subject to falsification through systematic comparison. We have already seen how a look at Britons' discourse of empire in the mid-nineteenth

---

[63] Schwabe (1986), p. 30.
[64] Pagden (2005), p. 54–5
[65] Porter (2006), pp. 91–2.

century reveals that the uniqueness of American empire cannot lie in the fact that Americans deny it. And if the specificity of the American empire does not lie in its self-denial, does it actually lie in its so-called reluctance or hesitance to colonize foreign land? Does it lie in the *way* it exerts power? Furthermore, if there are such differences, can they really be attributable to an exceptional or unique "national character" or special liberal-democratic "values"? Only a comparative investigation can properly answer these questions.

In short, exceptionalism and some brands of revisionism provide one perspective for specifying what is unique about the American empire and for explaining that uniqueness. But they do not validate their claims through comparison. Take an example. As noted, one revisionist argument is that the United States' empire has been distinct because, unlike Britain's empire, it has been informal and noncolonial. Presumably, this is due to America's egalitarian social structure and political culture. Because the United States lacks an aristocratic class predisposed to governing from afar, and because its democratically minded populace has supported the principle of self-determination around the world, the American state has been constrained to exert power over other societies in noncolonial, informal ways.[66] So what is wrong with such an argument? On its face, nothing. It *is* the case, for instance, that America has not had the same sort of aristocratic class as England. Yet merely pointing out this difference is not sufficient for validating the causal argument that the lack of an aristocratic class leads to a noncolonial strategy. We would have to trace the causal chain connecting the absence of the class to the absence of colonialism. Furthermore, one could think of various reasons for why a state adopts one imperial strategy rather than another. The presence or absence of an aristocratic governing class would constitute only one possible explanation among a range of alternative explanations. So we would need to consider alternative explanations too.

To be sure, alternative explanations can be formulated. For example, some studies of the British empire have shown that much of what the British empire did and the forms it took had to do with conditions in the *periphery* rather than in the metropole.[67] Similarly, some versions of international relations theory explain what states do by reference to the international system, not to the states' internal culture. Mandlebaum's classic study of states' security policy shows that variations between different states' security policies are "created by variations of the international system itself," such that "two states that are similarly situated in the system but have different domestic orders will tend to pursue similar security policies."[68] Both of these approaches offer

---

[66] Ibid., pp. 91–2; see also pp. 171–2; Schwabe (1986).

[67] This is the classic "peripheral" or "excentric" theory of imperial expansion first espoused in Robinson (1972).

[68] Mandelbaum (1988), p. 2. Within international relations theory, exceptionalist approaches to United States would be considered distinct from "realist" approaches. The latter approaches assume all states are similar (in that they all pursue similar interests), whereas the former assumes that the United States is a particular type of state because of its special values or

different takes on empire than exceptionalism or even revisionism. Rather than explaining what a state does or what type of empire it is by reference to characteristics intrinsic to the state itself, these approaches invite analysts to consider the characteristics of the periphery or the wider geopolitical field in which the state is embedded. Existing assertions of American exceptionalism do not consider these alternative possible explanations. Therefore, the argument that the American empire's distinctiveness is due to national traits or character remains open to justifiable questioning. Further investigation is necessary.

Comparing Empires

The comparative investigation in this book aims to overcome these explanatory limitations of existing scholarship. By adopting a comparative approach, it aims to pinpoint similarities and differences between the two empires. It then examines possible explanations for the variations and assesses them against the weight of evidence. But why use Britain as the key point of comparison? And exactly how should the comparison be conducted?

The British empire is particularly useful. First, popular discourse has often conjured the British empire as providing "lessons" for American empire. This is typical of the recent neoconservative discourse on American empire. "Afghanistan and other troubled lands today," wrote Max Boot in 2003, "cry out for the sort of enlightened foreign administration once provided by self-confident Englishmen in jodhpurs and pith helmets." But the comparisons in popular discourse reach further back. In 1965, an essay in the *New York Times* asked: "Is America an empire? It is a question which no American cares to ask himself and, if you ask it of him, he returns a hasty negative. 'Imperialism is not in our blood. You are still thinking in terms of the British Empire.'"[69] As popular discourse already thinks of Britain as the key reference point, a systematic comparison enables us to better assess these passing comparative claims.

The second reason for using Britain is that it provides a critical entry into the exceptionalism-revisionist debate and its various assertions. Britain is typically used in these debates as a comparative reference point (even if the comparison is usually made in passing reference). More specifically, the case of Britain is implicitly or explicitly invoked to validate cultural values or "national character" as the primary explanation. Britain's monarchical tradition and its aristocratic values are taken as a counterpoint to America's liberal-democratic and more egalitarian character. Comparison with Britain therefore shows America's exceptionalism. The logic is as follows: (1) Britain has different cultural values, political institutions, and traditions than the United States; (2) Britain (ostensibly) constructed an empire whereas the United States did not (or, in the

---

national character. For a good discussion of this in relation to the U.S. empire, see Ciutâ (2006).

[69] Fairlie (1965).

revisionist variant, the United States constructed a different type of empire); therefore (3) what makes the American empire (or lack thereof) different from Britain are America's exceptional cultural values, institutions, and traditions. These implicit comparisons warrant explicit consideration, which is why Britain is analytically useful here.[70]

The final reason for using Britain as a comparative case to the United States has to do with similarities between the two countries rather than differences. Although Britain and the United States have different cultural values and traditions, they share the fact that, of all states in the past centuries, only they have been *hegemonic*. As noted earlier, hegemony is an economic category to refer to a state's relative preponderance over the world economy. During the history of modern capitalism, only the United States and Britain undisputedly fit this category. Britain dominated the world economy in the mid-nineteenth century. It was the banker, baker, and workshop of the world, taking up the largest share of world GDP. The United States in the mid-twentieth century, after the Second World War, then occupied this niche. Of course, their two hegemonies are not exactly the same. There are differences in relative military capacity, economic policies, or the bases of their economic dominance. Yet none of this negates the fact that, when we use measures that scholars use to assess relative economic power in the world, only the United States and Britain have been hegemonic.[71] This similarity is important for adjudicating causal arguments. Working from such similarities, a controlled paired comparison is possible. As political scientist Sidney Tarrow explains, by beginning the comparison with "common foundations," we are less likely to overlook unseen variables that might better explain the outcome under consideration.[72]

To better understand this, consider if we compared the actions of one state with another state. Let's assume that the two states have different "national characters" or cultural values. Let's also say that we happen to find that the states carried out very different imperial strategies. With this sort of comparative method, we might conclude that the difference in imperial strategies can be explained by the different cultural traditions. But consider if the two states differed not just in their cultural values, but also in, say, their hegemonic status: State A dominated the world economy whereas State B did not. If this were the case, it might be that the difference in imperial strategy was not due to cultural difference, but rather to the difference in hegemonic status. Without holding hegemonic status constant – or "controlling" for it, to use social science parlance – it would be more difficult to assess which was the more important

---

[70] For recent calls to more systematically compare the U.S. empire with the British empire, among others, see Hopkins (2007). For a good overview comparison, see Howe (2003).

[71] For the most systematic assessments of economic dominance using statistical measures, see Maddison (2001) and Chase-Dunn, Jorgenson, Reifer, and Lio (2005). There have been debates about whether the United States or England have *really* been hegemonic (see, for example, Strange (1987), Martel (1991), and Schroeder (1994)). But these debates turn on a much broader definition of "hegemony" than the strict economic one used here.

[72] Tarrow (1999).

explanatory factor, culture or hegemonic status. We would not, in short, be able to validate or invalidate our claim that culture was the driving cause of imperialism.

This comparative fallacy underwrites many of the claims made in exceptionalist historiography and social science. For example, one of the ways in which claims about American exceptionalism have been sustained has been by comparing America's post–World War II foreign policy with Britain's imperialism of the late nineteenth century. By this comparison, we might find that the United States did not acquire colonies, whereas Britain in the late nineteenth century did, such as when it took part in the "scramble for Africa." This comparison could then be taken as evidence for an essential American anti-imperial character: The United States did not take new colonies because of its deeply democratic and liberal values. However, the problem here is with the time periods under comparison. Specifically, comparing America's lack of colonial annexations after World War II with Britain's colonial expansion in the late nineteenth century overlooks the very different situations of the two states. In the late nineteenth century, Britain was experiencing new economic competition after enjoying decades of dominance in the world economy. Economic competitors, such as Germany and the United States, were on the rise. This competition might have motivated Britain to seize new colonies. Acquiring new territory might have been an attempt to regain some economic power or, at the very least, prevent rivals from acquiring territory and thereby help thwart the rivals' competitiveness. The context for the United States after World War II, however, was very different. The United States dominated the world economy and faced very little if no economic competition whatsoever. It was in a hegemonic position. This position, not inherent national values or virtues, could plausibly help explain why the United States did not seize new colonies whereas Britain did. Unlike Britain, the United States dominated the world economy and did not face serious economic rivals. It had less of a *need* for overseas colonies.

This is not to say that the reason for the difference was in fact economic need. The point is that, by comparing Britain's and America's imperial activities at time periods when the two were differentially positioned in the world economy, we cannot rule out this alternative explanation. And without ruling out this alternative explanation, the exceptionalist explanation is open to serious question. It would be more persuasive to compare American and British actions in respectively similar historical phases so as to enable some rough controls over possibly confounding explanatory factors (like economic competition and/or hegemonic status).

Accordingly, the method in this book is not just to compare the British and American empires, but also to compare them across comparable historical phases. As both Britain and the United States have been hegemonic, they also experienced similar historical phases, and each of these phases has entailed other similarities. First, both Britain and the United States underwent a period of *hegemonic ascendancy* before they respectively reached hegemonic

TABLE I.I. *Phases in Hegemonic Careers: The United States and Britain*

Phase	Britain	US
Hegemonic Ascent*		
(a) long ascent	(a) 1688–1815	(a) 1776–1945
(b) short ascent	(b) 1763–1815	(b) 1873–1945
Hegemonic Maturity	1816–1872	1946–1973
Competition/Decline	1873–1939	1974-present

* The long ascent is the entire period before the state has reached hegemonic maturity; the short ascent refers to the period within the long ascent when the global system is "multipolar" (i.e., there is no clear hegemon and rivals are battling for hegemony); this period is the same as the "competition/decline" phase.

Sources: Boswell (2004); Chase-Dunn et al. (2005); Wallerstein (1984); Wallerstein (2002b); Wallerstein (1974).

maturity. Britain underwent this phase, roughly, from 1688 to 1815 (and more precisely from 1763 to 1815), and the United States did so from 1776 to 1945 (or from 1873 to 1945). This means that both, although at different times, were similarly positioned in the world system relative to other states. It also means that they shared other characteristics, such as the fact that they were both expanding their economies and internal state capacities. Second, both Britain and the United States then achieved *hegemonic maturity*: Britain from 1815 to 1873 and the United States from 1946 to 1973. In these periods, each state dominated the world's productive capacities (taking up the greatest shares of world GDP). Each also took up the greatest share of military capacities while enjoying relative economic prosperity at home. Finally, both states have experienced *hegemonic decline*: Britain from 1873 to 1939, and the United States from 1974 to the present. This means that both states experienced new economic competition from rivals that they had not experienced during their respective periods of hegemonic maturity. These were also periods, then, when the global system entered a new multipolar or competitive phase (see Table I.1).[73]

By comparing American and British imperial activities during these respective phases, our paired comparison is fulfilled at each step in the analysis. Because hegemony is not defined by imperialism but by relative economic position in the world, the analysis is not circular. Hegemony and empire are not

[73] The dividing line dates typically refer to either world wars, which can be seen as the apex of decline/ascent, or economic events that set off a new economic cycle. The periodization has been worked out by world-systems scholars. See Boswell (2004); Chase-Dunn, Jorgenson, Reifer, and Lio (2005); Wallerstein (1984), Wallerstein (2002b), Wallerstein (1974). The periodization is open to some dispute, but the world-systems literature convincingly demonstrates that if we follow our strict definition of hegemony as preponderance over the world economy, the periodization roughly holds. Other periodizations are available, but these are based on different definitions of hegemony. See, for example, Modelski (1978), Modelski and Thompson (1996).

the same thing; hence we can use the former to ground our comparisons of the latter. This, then, is not to presume that hegemonic phase actually determines imperial actions. It is merely to allow for a controlled comparison to better assess which possible factors might explain imperial actions. The point is to be more methodologically conscious about our comparisons and therefore maximize the validity of our claims.

There are obvious limitations to our method. The first is the "small-N" problem. This means that not all explanations can be properly tested. We would need additional cases beyond the United States and Britain in order to adjudicate more explanations. The second problem is that world developments might confound our attempt to control for variation. As we will see, for instance, the global context during America's period of hegemonic maturity (roughly 1946–1970s) was not exactly the same as the global context when Britain was hegemonic (in the mid-nineteenth century). The world system had itself changed, and this is a factor that must be considered when comparing the two states during those time periods. The final problem is that the comparison depends on analytically separating the two empires from each other when, in reality, they were not separated. When the United States was undergoing hegemonic ascent in the early twentieth century, Britain was undergoing hegemonic decline, and we cannot presume that the two processes were disconnected. In fact, as we will see, the U.S. empire made good use of Britain's existing empire to realize some of its ends. The two empires were often intertwined and entangled.

Despite these problems, this book stakes the claim that the comparative approach is still worthwhile. First, there is no doubt that the small-N problem is an endemic weakness of paired comparison. However, this weakness is exchanged for strength on other counts. Comparing many empires rather than just two may help overcome the small-N problem, but makes it more difficult to conduct a detailed concrete analysis. A very wide lens allows one to see more than a small lens, but not always as clearly. Therefore, although comparing Britain and the United States alone has its limitations, it also enables our study "to combine analytical leverage with in-depth knowledge."[74] Furthermore, even this small-N problem can be compensated for by examining not only the two empires at comparable historical phases, but also by bringing in their other historical phases as comparative reference points. For example, we can compare the United States and Britain during their respective periods of hegemonic maturity, and we can also bring into the comparison an analysis of the two states during their other historical periods, such as their respective periods of hegemonic ascent. This expands the comparative cases by comparing across empires *and* across time.

Second, whereas restricting our comparison to specific historical phases between the two states cannot control for world developments across the time periods, we can at least control for some possibly confounding factors where

[74] Tarrow (1999), p. 9. See also Steinmetz (2004).

we would otherwise not be able to. One is economic capacity. States undergoing the hegemonic maturity phase have more economic resources than when they are undergoing the ascendancy phase, which would in turn give the state more resources. This was indeed the case for both Britain and the United States, as we will see. Therefore, by comparing the two states during their respective stages of hegemonic ascendancy, we can control not just for relative position in the world economy, but also the factor of state capacity. In short, although no comparative method would be perfect, our approach offers one way – hitherto underutilized – to better explain whatever variations or similarities in imperial dynamics or forms that we might find.

There is a final value to tracking and comparing imperial activity by hegemonic phase: It offers a systematic way of considering a possible "natural history" of hegemonic empires. As hegemons rise, mature, and decline, what types of imperial activity do they engage in? Are there differences in their imperial practices or modalities depending on phase? And across the two hegemons analyzed here (Britain and the United States), are there common patterns of imperial activity in conjunction with hegemonic phase? Or are there fundamental differences in their imperial careers? Using hegemonic phases as a guide facilitates a properly *historical* analysis that considers sequence and process. This is a critical issue for analyzing empires in general. Any analysis of empires must take history seriously, in the sense that we must not presume a singular entity – for example, the British empire – that remains constant or unchanged over time.[75] Using hegemonic phases as an analytic guide focuses our attention on imperial formations in history – that is, multifaceted entities of power in the process of formation or reformation, disarticulation or dissolution, expansion, stability, or contraction. Whether or not such imperial processes correspond to hegemonic phases is one question we will want to consider.

What Lies Ahead

The book is organized in loose chronological and comparative fashion. Chapters proceed by comparing British and American imperial activities during their comparable phases of global power (ascent, maturity, decline) with some explanatory sections inserted within and between. Chapter 1, "Imperial Paths to Power," scrutinizes the two states' activities during their respective periods of hegemonic ascent: Britain from 1688 to 1815, and the United States from 1776 to 1945. Both states in these periods were economically ascendant. Both, too, developed their state capacities. The chapter shows that these similarities were also concomitant with certain similarities in imperialism that have been too often overlooked in existing scholarship. As both states developed their economies and capacities, both also embarked on territorial expansion. They also crafted similar forms of imperial rule and ideological self-conceptions. In

[75] Lieven (2005), p. 129.

fact, America's westward expansion entailed colonial rule over new territories that were not only similar to but also modeled on the colonial regimes Britain had previously constructed for the thirteen colonies. The idea of a special liberty-loving American empire was first forged amidst this process, but this had precedents in Britain's previous settler empire in the Americas. Finally, the United States constructed an overseas colonial empire around the turn of the twentieth century – encompassing such places as Puerto Rico, Hawaii, the Philippines, Guam, Samoa, and the Virgin Islands. This reveals that the United States has not shied away from formal administrative colonialism.

Some exceptionalist narratives might admit that America's expansion had imperialistic characteristics, but they would then insist that American imperialism was fundamentally different from other types of imperialism. Some exceptionalist commentaries, for instance, acknowledge that the United States took the Philippines as a colony, but they insist that the *way* in which the United States practiced colonialism was unique. Expressed as America's own exceptional political culture of democracy, U.S. colonialism in the Philippines was a benign form of rule, uniquely aimed at teaching Filipinos the ways of democracy. This renders America's empire a special empire, unmatched by others for its democratizing tendencies. Chapter 2, "Colonial Rules," tackles this assertion from the standpoint of comparative colonialisms. Looking at U.S. colonialism in the Philippines, Puerto Rico, Guam, and Samoa and comparing it with British colonialism in India and Fiji, the comparison unearths more similarities with British colonialism than has been disclosed in existing studies. It also shows that America's "national character" had little to do with the forms of rule the United States enacted in its colonies. America's colonial regimes – just like Britain's colonial regimes in Fiji and India – reflected local conditions rather than national values or metropolitan political institutions. This chapter thereby offers a theory of colonial forms, suggesting that colonial policies and institutions are determined not by the characteristics or character of the colonizer but by the complexities and contingencies of the colonial situation.

Chapter 3, "Hegemonies and Empires," compares the two imperial formations during their respective phases of hegemonic maturity: Britain from 1815 to 1873 and the United States from 1946 to 1973. The chapter shows that whereas the period of ascent was marked by relatively constant territorial expansion, the period of hegemonic maturity was marked by a relative contraction. After the United States seized the former Japanese-mandated territories in the aftermath of World War II, its territorial expansion halted. After the Napoleonic Wars, Britain's expansion similarly slowed. Direct control over territory became less prominent, and instead informal exercises of power took precedence. Both states preferred indirect nonterritorial rule over peripheral areas, creating empires of clients and subordinated allies. Attendant with both imperial formations, too, were a discourse and partial realization of open trading policies over and against the mercantilism of previous years. The enlargement of commercial space along with informal networks of imperial power thus trumped formal territorial domination. Sporadic military interventions, the establishment of military outposts, and clientelistic relations with weaker states became the preferred tactics of imperial power.

Whereas previous chapters disclose fundamental similarities across the empires during their respective periods of hegemonic ascent and maturity, Chapter 4, "Imperial Forms, Global Fields," addresses one glaring difference between the U.S. and British empires. That is, whereas Britain mixed both formal and informal imperialism during its period of hegemonic maturity, the United States relied primarily on the informal mode of imperialism after taking the Japanese territories in the wake of World War II. During their respective periods of hegemony, both Britain and the United States *preferred* informal empire, but Britain nonetheless added some territorial holdings amidst its pursuit of informal empire whereas the American state did not. This remains a crucial difference that some existing commentaries have seized upon to show how the United States has been exceptional. The United States, it has been claimed, did not seize colonies after World War II because of its liberal democratic character. However, as we will see in this chapter, the reason why the United States did not in fact expand its territorial holdings had little to do with its exceptional political culture. Instead it had to do with the character of the global field after World War II that differed significantly from the field Britain engaged during its comparable period of hegemony. Whereas Britain faced an open field ripe for colonization, the United States faced a global field populated by allied empires and rising anticolonial nationalism. Only because of these features of the field, not because of America's national character, did the United States turn away from formal territorial rule.

Chapter 5, "Weary Titans: Declining Powers, New Imperialisms," brings us closer to the current era. It compares Britain's and America's imperial activities amidst their respective periods of hegemonic decline. These are periods when each state, although previously enjoying unqualified dominance over the world economy, faced unprecedented competitors (Britain circa 1873–1939; the United States circa 1973–present). The chapter shows that as both states experienced decline, so too did they intensify and/or extend their imperialistic activity compared with the previous period of hegemony. Both states, in short, embarked on new imperialisms, apparently replaying the imperial follies of their youth. For Britain, this was manifest primarily in its expansion of formal empire; for the United States, it was manifest in a range of new military interventions and temporary occupations (the assaults on Iraq in 1991 and 2003 were only tips of the iceberg: There were other deployments and occupations). Finally, this chapter reveals *why* both states embarked on new imperialisms during their respective periods of economic decline. The chapter will reveal that similarities between the states' imperialistic activities amidst decline are not coincidental but lie in deeper structural forces.

Chapter 6, "The Dynamics of Imperialism," takes a longer view of the two empires. Previous chapters examined specific phases in each imperial state's career, but this chapter puts them all together. It reveals that both empires followed similar historical dynamics over the long *durée*. Specifically, they each followed a pattern of expansion, abatement, and reassertion constituting distinct waves of imperial aggression. The "new imperialism," in other words, was only one phase in a larger dynamic. The chapter then explains the pattern. It shows that the pattern is best understood by considering global competition. The overarching point is not different from the point of other chapters: In order to understand the two imperial formations, their practices and policies, and modalities and methods, we are better off eschewing exceptionalist explanations that focus on national character and instead consider wider fields of interaction and struggle.

Ultimately, this book compares the U.S. and British empires and interrogates the exceptionalist thesis, but it also carries larger lessons. In particular, it allows us to arrive at a larger theory of empires. The theory is simple enough, but it could be too easily ignored in both scholarship and popular discourse. And its implications are important. That is: Empires, rather than omnipotent powers that easily make and remake their subjects and spaces, and rather than entities shaped from within, must be understood as adaptive dynamic entities that are shaped and reshaped by foreign societies as much as they strive to control them. Empires are defined by power, but the modalities of power are crafted, limited, formed, and re-formed through the very relations power seeks to harness. This banality of imperial power, as we will see, is a far cry from exceptionalist portrayals of American empire.

I

Imperial Paths to Power, 1688–1939

Behold! Behold! An Empire rise!
  – Francis Hopkinson, from an ode distributed on July 4, 1788, Philadelphia[1]

[I]t is safe to assume, as a rule, that Americans are actuated by much the same ideas, instincts, motives, and modes of thought as their fellow-kinsmen in the Old World.

  – Edward Dicey (1898)[2]

Expansion has ever been the instinct of the United States. The very symbol of the Union is an Eagle and the Eagle is a bird that spreads its wings.... Compared with the Eagle the British Lion treads mother earth like a tortoise. And no Eagle has ever flown further afield than the American Eagle.

  – P. W. Wilson (1925)[3]

When the average American thinks of "colonialism", or of the Colonial Powers, he is apt to confine his thoughts to European "colonialism".... Not many Americans stop to think that Puerto Rico was conquered from Spain (as the British captured Jamaica); that the Virgin Islands were bought from Denmark ... that Alaska was bought from Russia and Louisiana from the French in the same way; that the Panama Canal Zone was acquired in the twentieth century by methods which would have been condemned if indulged by a European Power at a much earlier period.

  – Sir Alan Burns (1957)[4]

The so-called long eighteenth century from 1688 to 1815 was a formative period for Britain. Up to that point, Britain had been a small island monarchy, a minor player on the European scene. The Glorious Revolution in 1688, however, marked a new era. After establishing representative government, the little

[1] Quoted in Burstein (1999), p. 150.
[2] Dicey (1898), p. 491.
[3] Wilson (1925), p. SM7.
[4] Burns (1957), p. 124.

island slowly shored up its military strength and became increasingly involved in interstate affairs. It defeated its enemies and grew in strength. It expanded its domestic economy and partook of a widening world economic system. It outproduced and outsold its rivals and built its economic infrastructure. By the end of the Napoleonic Wars in 1815, Britain emerged as the world's pre-eminent power. It became a global hegemon, a foe to be feared or a friend to be flattered. Later, the United States followed a similar path. It began as a comparably small series of settlements on the east coast of North America. After World War II, it became the world's new economic mammoth, taking up the role that Britain had held previously. As the years 1688–1815 for Britain marked the path toward world power, so did the years 1776–1945 for the United States.

Scholars have noted these similar paths. But what about the *imperial* dimensions of Britain's and America's respective ascendancies? For Britain the answer might seem obvious. It is well established that Britain's rise to world hegemony was accompanied by the construction of a massive overseas empire. As historian P. J. Marshall notes, the years 1689–1815 marked an important phase in British imperial expansion: "By 1815 Britain's global trade totally eclipsed that of her European rivals and she was the possessor of the only Empire of any consequence."[5] For the United States, however, the imperial issue is more opaque. Was America's long rise to global hegemony over the nineteenth and early twentieth centuries also attended by imperialism and the construction of an "empire"? If so, exactly how similar or different was it from Britain's imperialism in the long eighteenth century?

At first glance, a comparison between Britain in the long eighteenth century and the United States in the nineteenth century would not seem tenable. These histories transpired in very different times and worlds. But the similarities merit attention. First, these were times when the relative capacities of the two states were similar. Both states were still rising to world power, engaging in regional interstate affairs while building their economies, and both ended their respective periods by attaining global hegemony. Second, both states began their ascendancies with similar political characteristics. Both were comparably weak, decentralized polities compared to the stronger, more authoritarian states on the European continent. Both were initially averse to the idea of strong armies controlled by a monarch or executive power, and both lacked powerful centralized bureaucracies.[6] These similarities are notable in themselves. The question explored here is whether they also entailed similarities in imperial practices or forms.

This chapter begins by sketching the processes and dynamics of British and U.S. *state territorial* expansion during their respective periods of ascent. State

---

[5] Marshall (1998), pp. 1–2.
[6] On the comparably "weak" English state, see Stone (1994); on the American state, see Skowronek (1982), cf. Katznelson (2002). This chapter will modify these views of the two states.

territorial expansion is different from the expansion of nonstate entities or social groups like settlers, capitalists, or corporations. It refers to the acquisition and incorporation of new territory by a state such that the new territory becomes subject to that state's sovereignty. This type of expansion cuts to the heart of "empire" as we have defined it in this book. There can be no empire without the exercise of power over a territory, and in this case, no formal empire without a state that annexes territory to rule it. When considering questions of empire, we should first look at state territory.

Although an examination of state territorial expansion is the necessary first step toward considering the imperial dimensions of the two states' pre-hegemonic histories, it is only the beginning. Territorial expansion is a precondition for empire but does not in itself constitute it. Territories can be acquired, but whether they end up as subordinate units of an imperial formation or as equal polities within a nation is another matter entirely. The former is empire building; the latter is nation building. Therefore, after sketching the dynamics and logics of territorial expansion, this chapter considers whether the two states' respective territorial expansions might qualify as *imperial* expansions and, if so, exactly how.

Comparative Expansions

Dynamics of British Expansion, 1688–1815

The diplomat and poet Mathew Prior returned to Britain from Paris in 1699. In December of that year, he gave one of his most elaborate odes, the "Carmen Seculare for the year 1700." Through forty-two stanzas, he praised King William III, extolling him as Britain's savior who would perpetuate Britain's glories around the world. Britain was bound to "calm the earth, and vindicate the sea." He continued:

> Our prayers are heard, our master's fleets shall go
> As far as winds can bear, or waters flow,
> New lands to make, new Indies to explore,
> In worlds unknown to plant Britannia's power.[7]

Britain had only emerged from the Glorious Revolution a couple of decades earlier. Yet the homage was a portent. Over the course of the long eighteenth century, Britain indeed pushed as far as winds could bear, expanding outward to take new foreign land abroad. Of course, Britain had already taken steps beyond its shores before Prior's homage. Explorers and enterprisers had established small outposts on the eastern seaboard of North America, landing on points in Newfoundland, Massachusetts, and Virginia. Backed by royal companies seeking tobacco and cod, these outposts had populations of about 260,000 by the early eighteenth century.[8] In the 1650s, other enterprises were

---

[7] Koebner (1961), pp. 73–4.
[8] Marshall (1998), p. 2.

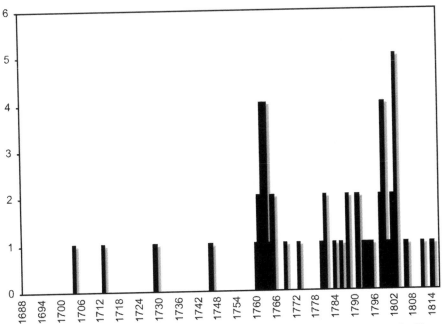

FIGURE 1.1. Britain's Territorial Expansion: Number of Colonial Annexations by Year, 1688–1815. *Source:* See Appendix: Notes on Data.

established in Barbados, the Leeward Islands, and Jamaica; they would become vital for tobacco, sugar, and the slave trade. The British East India Company had also taken some path-breaking steps. A nominally private company under the English monarch's charter, it had established a foothold in small spots of Mughal India.

This earlier period of expansion was seminal: It "laid down the pattern for all that was to come."[9] But the subsequent territorial expansion through the long eighteenth century remains important. This period saw new developments on various registers, all of which were part and parcel of Britain's rise to global hegemony. For the purposes of our comparison, these developments warrant attention.

The first development was territorial growth. British agents, explorers, and settlers moved far beyond England's initial settlements and scattered outposts. The growth came in two distinct phases, with the Seven Years' War (1756–1763) serving as a sort of watershed (see Figure 1.1). The first phase, from 1688 to the 1750s, saw new acquisitions at a relatively slow rate, largely in the Americas. In the north, Britain acquired Acadia (Nova Scotia) and Newfoundland, and it consolidated early settlements in Georgia. In the Caribbean, Britain made the Bahamas (initially settled in 1647) a Crown Colony in 1718 and took the Mosquito Coast in 1740. The second phase saw continued territorial growth

---

[9] Lloyd (1996), p. 3.

in the Americas (Britain added the Windward Islands, Trinidad and Tobago, St. Lucia, and British Guiana, among others) but differed in other respects. Foremost, the growth occurred at a faster rate, and there was a new geographical orientation: The East India Company became more deeply entrenched in India and moved outward; explorers paved the way for trading ports in Western Africa; Captain Arthur Phillip led a settlement in New South Wales; and enterprisers set up a small settlement in Penang.[10]

The second development was emigration and population growth. By 1750, the white population of the North American colonies had reached 1.2 million.[11] The number of persons in the North American colonies and the West Indies together grew from 412,000 in 1700 to 2,762,000 by 1771. Meanwhile, Britain's population in 1771 was 6,448,000.[12] Additionally, by 1811, there were some 10,000 British subjects living in New South Wales, with a further 1,500 in Van Diemen's Land (Tasmania).[13] This growth abroad was matched, if not propelled, by population growth at home. The population of Britain nearly trebled from 1550 to 1820, whereas at the same time France's population grew only by about 79 percent.[14]

The third development had to do with the *character* of expansion. During the seventeenth century, overseas expansion had been driven by explorers, settlers, or merchants. The Crown sometimes sanctioned these initiatives but did not play an active role. However, as the eighteenth century progressed, "government rather than the subject was responsible for extending the empire."[15] For one thing, the British state negotiated the acquisition of colonies from rivals and articulated how the territories fit into wider strategic and economic goals. By enacting the Navigation Acts, along with other measures to eliminate competition from rival powers, it signaled that the economics of the territories were to be subordinated to the state's economic plans. For another, the state took administrative charge from chartered companies and increasingly intervened in territorial affairs overseas. Parliament revoked or modified early royal charters to give London more direct control. Beginning in the 1740s, the Crown increasingly vetoed laws passed by colonial legislatures. The Board of Trade, at this time in charge of most colonial matters, tried to increase the powers

---

[10] On this growth, see Marshall (1998), p. 1–2 and Bayly (1998). Since Harlow (1952), it has been typical to speak of a "first" and "second" British empire, with the latter referring to a new geographical orientation toward Asia. The division must not be exaggerated; even after the American Revolution, Britain maintained a presence in the Caribbean and small American possessions, and before 1763, the British East India Company had probed parts of Asia. But it is true that Britain reached to Asia in new ways by the late 1700s.

[11] Brewer (1994), p. 65.

[12] Horn (1998), p. 100.

[13] Marshall (1998), p. 4.

[14] Colley (2003b), p. 6. The new expansion and population growth came at a high cost for the native inhabitants. Between 1600 and 1750, the natives of New England probably lost close to ten thousand people resulting from wars with colonists. Historians have estimated a death rate from exposure to alien diseases of about 75 percent. See Merrell (1991), p. 122.

[15] Fieldhouse (1982), p. 75, 84–5.

of the London-appointed colonial governors over their respective jurisdictions and local legislatures. Not all of these assertions of authority were successful (as we will see later), but they nonetheless represented the metropolitan state's increased role in colonial governance. Whereas the state had been "slender and enabling rather than interventionist," it now centralized administration and began to form "a coherent, London-directed British Empire in America."[16]

In addition to taking and administering territories, the British state took increasing charge of colonial trade, security, and defense. Throughout the first half of the eighteenth century, it constructed a "maritime-imperial system" whereby London could promote and protect the commercial activities of private interests in the New World in exchange for loyalty and customs revenues. Whereas it had not before, it sent naval squadrons to the Caribbean to help protect commerce and suppress piracy.[17] The British state became active on land as well. Parliament set up new administrative agencies in North America for protecting frontiers against Native Americans and for handling native affairs. In the early 1700s, provincial governors in North America had been in charge of Indian diplomatic matters, but in the 1750s London created its own regional superintendents directly responsible to Whitehall.[18] Fittingly, total expenses of the British home government for army, navy, colonial administration, and other minor activities in North America increased fourfold during the period from 1740 to 1775.[19]

This increasing state involvement was part of a larger transformation in the British state itself. Prior to the long eighteenth century, Britain's engagement with Europe had been relatively limited and sporadic. But during the 1700s, it became increasingly enmeshed in European affairs. Between 1680 and 1780, Britain fought four major wars with European powers and engaged in a slew of smaller conflicts and military deployments.[20] In turn, these unprecedented foreign entanglements demanded military power and new domestic fiscal arrangements to cultivate it. Accordingly, there was a twofold development in British state formation in this period. On the one hand, Britain's domestic state capacities were comparably weak. After 1688, "the powers of central government were devolved on the localities and diluted by a spoils system which provided income and office for the scions of the landed classes."[21] On the other hand, the British state's external capacities were enhanced. Even as the British state's "despotic" power at home was weak, its power for engagements abroad grew, leading to a strong "fiscal-military state." As historian John Brewer's seminal work shows, the military became "the most important single factor in

---

[16] First quote from Colley (2003b), p. 155; referred to in Webster (2006), p. 16; second from Johnson (1998), p. 295. For all of these developments, see Greene (1986), pp. 13–17, 50; Marshall (2005), p. 76.

[17] Baugh (1994), p. 194.

[18] Milner (1981), p. 139.

[19] Gwyn (1980), p. 77.

[20] Brewer (1989), pp. 29–31, 57.

[21] Ibid., p. xvii.

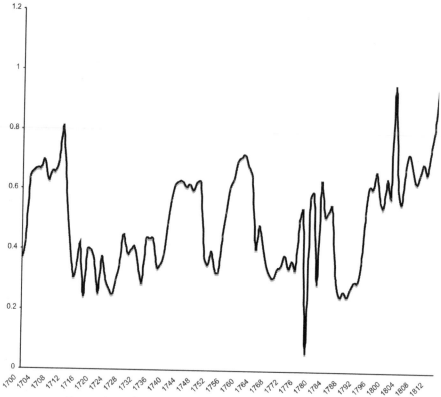

FIGURE 1.2. Proportion of Expenditures Devoted to Military Spending, U.K., 1700–1814. *Source:* From data in Mitchell (1988).

the domestic economy: the largest borrower and spender, as well as the largest single employer. Public spending, fuelled by military costs, rose by leaps and bounds. The civilian administration supporting the military effort burgeoned; taxes and debts increased. Britain acquired a standing army and navy. She became, like her main rivals, a fiscal-military state, one dominated by the task of waging war."[22] Military spending thus grew some 450 percent between the 1720s and the 1820s (see Figure 1.2).[23]

Britain's territorial expansion was inextricably entangled with these developments. Interstate war in the European theater meant that the New World became a site of engagement. During the Nine Years' War, the French tried to divert Britain's resources from Europe by attacking Britain's New England and

[22] Ibid., p. 26. See also Stone (1994).

[23] The trend is partly attributable to the overall growth in state spending in the period, but military spending still took a disproportionate share over civil government and debt spending. This was the case even during peacetime, when military spending was between three to four times greater than spending on civil government. See Harling and Mandler (1993), p. 49; see also Brewer (1989), p. 30; O'Brien (1988b).

New York territories; this led to various battles that deployed Indian allies.[24] During the War of Spanish Succession, the British state feared that a Bourbon prince on the Spanish throne would enable the French to dominate the Spanish Indies, which would in turn threaten Britain's holdings and trade. In response, Britain sent fleets to the West Indies and engaged in yet more battles in North America (where the War of Spanish Succession was better known as Queen Anne's War).[25] Territorial expansion needed a more powerful state to protect the new territorial network.

The final development in imperial matters over the long eighteenth century had to do with identity and ideology: The term *empire* became increasingly part of the vocabulary and also took on new meanings. Before the mid-1700s, the vast collection of overseas colonies, plantations, or dominions were not typically unified under the category "British empire." The term rather signified the Crown's power as distinct from the authority of any external power (it thus maintained the original Latin meaning of *imperium* as "sovereignty").[26] But around 1743, according to the historian P. J. Marshall, a shift occurred and the idea of a single British empire consisting of its territorial holdings surfaced. And by the 1760s (after Britain's victories over France), it became "conventional to speak and write of a single British Empire" that included all of Britain's overseas territories, plantations, and colonies.[27] This discourse of a single empire was especially potent among the Anglophone inhabitants of the New World, who began for the first time "to habitually describe their community as the 'British Empire.'"[28] As we will see later, the meaning would be submerged in the mid-nineteenth century, only to be conjured again in the late nineteenth century. But whatever the later usages and shifts of "empire," the long eighteenth century remains transformative: It saw the first development of the empire concept distinct from its Latin roots."[29]

Contours of American Expansion, 1776–1898

How does the ascendance of the United States compare to these British developments? Surely it also saw territorial growth: From 1803 to 1853, the United States expanded its territorial holdings by more than two million square miles. By the time it acquired Alaska and Hawaii, its territory had expanded almost fourfold from the territory of the original thirteen colonies. The U.S. government thereby became "one of the great landlords of world

---

[24] McLay (2006); Lenman (1998), pp. 152–6.

[25] Lenman (1998), pp. 154–5.

[26] Armitage (2000): 11, p. 11; Lloyd (1996), p. 8; Pocock (1988), pp. 68–9; Koebner (1952), pp. 85–92. It was also used to refer, not to rule over territory, but to the island Britannia or, in more extreme instances, to "power or dominant interests outside Britain." Koebner (1961), p. 61.

[27] Marshall (1998), p. 7.

[28] Armitage (2000): 171, p. 171.

[29] Koebner (1961), p. 60.

history."[30] This territorial expansion came with population growth, just as Britain's had. In 1850, the population in the territories newly opened to colonization (which exceeded half a million square miles) numbered about 10 million souls.[31] This was 44 percent of the nation's total, which was more than that of Britain's earlier Atlantic empire. In 1700, for example, the percentage of the total population of Britain and its North American and West Indies colonies that lived in the colonies was only 7 percent; at most, it reached 21 percent in 1750.[32]

Given the immensity of expansion, it is appropriate that contemporaries did not hesitate to think of the United States as an expanding empire. Founding statesmen referred to their expanding country as an "American empire" and a "rising empire." This was an easy appropriation from British discourse. Given "the coming of Revolution and the welding of the Thirteen Colonies into a new sovereign nation, the substitution of the phrase 'American Empire' for British came easily and naturally."[33] To be sure, Reverend Thomas Brockaway in 1784 scripted America's new imperium as but a continuation of the British imperium: "Empire, learning, and religion have in past ages been traveling from east to west, and this continent is their last western state. Here then is God erecting a stage on which to exhibit the great things of his kingdom."[34] At least until the Civil War, this self-identification of empire was not uncommon. The word empire to refer to the United States remained a dominant part of political discourse.[35]

In short, not unlike Britain's expansion earlier, U.S. expansion involved territorial growth, population growth, and ideological developments. But what about state involvement? It is here that popular narratives of U.S. history would stop us from making comparisons. In these narratives, U.S. expansion was led by self-reliant settlers who conquered an empty wilderness.[36] Expansion was a private affair rather than a process led by an aggressive and aggrandizing state. This is how the "West has come to stand for independence, self-reliance, and individualism."[37] The narrative also entails long-standing social science claims about the so-called weakness of the American state. Tocqueville claimed that Americans "did not have any neighbors, and consequently no great wars, and neither ravages nor conquest to fear," thus they did not need "a numerous army, nor great generals."[38] Many social scientists similarly claim that the U.S. state before 1877 was weak and devoid of a strong centralized government.[39]

---

[30] Sylla (1996), p. 494.
[31] Meinig (1993), II, p. 223.
[32] Calculated from data in Horn (1998), p. 100.
[33] Van Alstyne (1960), p. 2.
[34] Quoted in Stephanson (1995), p. 19.
[35] Van Alstyne (1960), p. 6.
[36] This image pervades much existing scholarship, serving as a vital element in exceptionalist narratives. See Rodgers (1998), p. 36.
[37] White (1991), p. 57.
[38] Quoted in Zolberg (2002), p. 24.
[39] Skowronek (1982).

Supposedly, even if the state *wanted* to play a part in expansion, it did not have the capacities to do so.

But these are misconceptions. First, expansion did not unfold into an empty wilderness. Nearly all of the territories the United States eventually annexed had been populated and/or governed by rival powers. After independence, the eastern colonies and the Northwest Territory, which was organized in 1787, were bounded by Spanish Florida in the south, Spanish Louisiana to the immediate west, and British Canada to the north. After the Louisiana Purchase, Spain still had territory in Florida, and its Mexico territory bordered the southwest, whereas British territory flanked the young United States from the north and northwest. Second, along these borders, across them, and within them were diverse populations. The Northwest Territory already had 60,000 inhabitants in 1796. Previously, in the trans-Applachian region, the resistance of the Choctaw, Creek, Miami, and other tribes had frustrated the early founders' dreams of easy expansion. In other territories, not only were there multiple Native American groups but also various non-Anglo populations. Creoles, free blacks (many from Santo Domingo), and Cajuns populated the Louisiana territory. Peoples of Hispano, Mexican, and Spanish-Indian descent populated the Spanish-held territories. Few if any of these groups were easily reconciled to U.S. intrusion.[40]

It follows that the American state *had* to take a part in expansion.[41] "The frontier," notes historian Peter Onuf, "required the exercise of authority . . . by a strong national government."[42] The state was needed first of all to explore and survey land. Although images of valiant individual explorers like Lewis and Clark permeate America's consciousness, in fact the U.S. Army led most expeditions throughout the continent.[43] Furthermore, the state had to induce or otherwise attract settlement. The Oregon Donation Act of 1850 offered settlers generous land grants to persuade them to move in.[44] Also, the state was necessary as a coercive force to pacify land. From 1820 to the beginning of the Civil War, fifty-seven military forts were established in Alabama to subdue resistance from Native Americans. By 1868, the U.S. Army had more troops stationed in the West than in the South (even before the end of Reconstruction).[45] Subduing Indians was America's "central military task throughout the nineteenth century."[46]

---

[40] Sparrow (2006): 17, p. 17, 21–35; Ball (2002): 8, p. 8.

[41] For work that has challenged the characterization of the American state in the nineteenth century as "weak," see Balogh (2009), Katznelson (2002), and Novak (2008). On westward expansion and state capacity, see especially Heumann (2009).

[42] Onuf (1987), p. xiii.

[43] Goetzmann (1959). See also, for one of the best examinations of the federal state's involvement and the military's role in land acquisition and conquest, Heumann (2009).

[44] Limerick (1988), p. 45.

[45] Rauchway (2006), p. 132.

[46] On Alabama, Katznelson (2002), p. 90; quote from p. 96; on land sales pp. 98–99. Not only did military force facilitate settlement, it also contributed to the economy. It was by the hand of the federal government, through its military power and direct appropriation of land, that

Moreover, whereas military power was necessary for subduing native populations, it was likewise necessary for fending off international rivals and facilitating territorial acquisitions. Consider how Florida was won. Although it is true that some East Florida residents before U.S. annexation had begun to challenge Spanish rule, it nonetheless took the federal government to make the challenge real and to finalize annexation. In 1811, Congress secretly passed the No Transfer Resolution, which expressed America's resolve that Florida would not fall into the hands of any foreign power. Subsequently, General George Matthews bribed locals to foment discontent against Spanish rule and proceeded to use military force to seize East Florida in March 1812.[47] Although Matthews's efforts were later disavowed in public by President James Madison's administration, all of the Floridas were eventually taken under the auspices of the Adams-Onis Treaty in 1819. And this occurred only after the federal government's forceful hand had pounded the region. Andrew Jackson's army of close to three thousand men had invaded East Florida, conquered recalcitrant Seminoles, and occupied St. Marks and Pensacola.[48] Boundaries were thus born from bullets; frontiers were tamed by force.

The same is true for most of the other major territories acquired by the United States. Taking the Oregon Territory demanded displays of force to ward off Spanish, Russian, and English claims.[49] The conquest of the area that would eventually become Texas, California, and New Mexico entailed the deployment of federal troops, leading to the Mexican War in 1848. Nobel Laureate Octavio Paz called this war "one of the most unjust wars in the history of imperialism."[50] Later, it would take British commentators to remind prominent American statesmen of this conquest. In 1945, during postwar planning meetings, President Roosevelt remarked to the British Colonial Secretary Oliver Stanley, "I do not want to be unkind or rude to the British but in 1841, when you acquired Hong Kong, you did not acquire it by purchase." Stanley retorted: "Let me see, Mr. President, that was about the time of the Mexican War."[51]

The aftermath of such conquests demanded yet more state involvement. All of the new territories, once declared under U.S. sovereignty and organized into territorial governments (before statehood), were governed by military commanders. These commanders spent much of their time suppressing resistance and securing the conditions for peaceful settlement, exploration, and commercial development. The targets of suppression were Native Americans in most cases, but these were not the only groups visited by the coercive hand of the

economic development occurred at all. This also involved trade with Native Americans. See Robbins (1994), pp. 64–5; see also Limerick (1988), p. 82.

[47] Weeks (1996), pp. 35–6.
[48] Grupo de Investigadores Puertorriqueños (1984), p. 314; Weeks (1996), pp. 42–3.
[49] Brooks (1934);Ambler (1943).
[50] Paz quoted in Bender (2006b), p. 199. See especially Hietala (1985), pp. 153–5 and, for more on the war, Gómez (2007).
[51] Quoted in Sebrega (1986), p. 75.

TABLE 1.1. *U.S. Military Interventions and
Territorial Annexations by Region, 1810–1870*

Region	Number
Africa	4
Asia-Pacific	22
Caribbean, Central & South America	21
Europe & E. Europe	2
Middle East and N. Africa	3
N. American Continent & Mexico	19

Source: See Appendix: Note on Data.

American state. After Brig. General Stephen W. Kearny unilaterally annexed New Mexico to the United States in 1846, military occupation persisted until 1851. Kearny's Organic Act displaced the Hispano aristocracy and elevated the "American Party" of Anglos and some pro-American Hispanos into power. His successor, Colonel Sterling S. Price, then faced a series of uprisings from Hispano peasants and Pueblo Indians – led partly by Hispano aristocrats and clergy. In response, Price assaulted the town of Mora and led a force of 480 volunteers, regulars, and civilians from Sante Fe across to Taos Pueblo to suppress the remnants of resistance. In subsequent years, antigovernment assaults by *Nuevomexicanos* (1847) and the Navajo (1848) also met military force.[52]

The new U.S. state even deployed its power overseas (see Table 1.1). In the early nineteenth century, the U.S. Navy sent ships or troops as far as Tripoli, Tunis, and Algiers. It also intervened in the Caribbean to secure the promise of trade there and with Latin America.[53] As the United States later looked for profitable passageways to the Pacific through Nicaragua and Panama, it continued to deploy naval power, dispatching troops to Nicaragua on several occasions or meddling with Cuba and Santo Domingo.[54] The search for trade with Asia extended America's military hand even farther. Attempts to get Japan to open up to American goods in the 1850s led to various demonstrations of naval force, and troops were deployed on various occasions to Formosa, Korea, and China. Similarly, just as Walt Whitman's 1860 poem "The New Empire" suggested that the Pacific would become the "vast highway" to Asia, various instances of American force took place in the Pacific.[55] The American navy moved into Samoa, Fiji, and Drummond Island in the early 1840s, which in turn unleashed military attacks on native islanders.

All of this suggests that the U.S. state was no less militaristic or interventionist than the British state. Data on military spending are informative. Even

---

[52] Ball (2002), pp. 8–9.
[53] LaFeber (1989), p. 81; United States Congress Committee on Foreign Affairs (1970), pp. 50–3.
[54] By 1855, America's trade with Cuba had doubled from the previous decade (LaFeber 1989: 135).
[55] Ibid., p. 130.

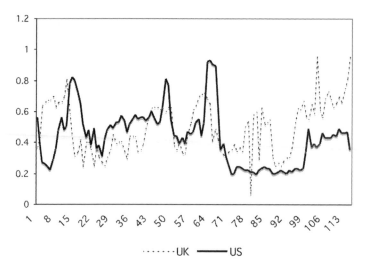

FIGURE 1.3. U.S. and U.K. Proportion of Expenditure Devoted to Military Spending. *Note:* The data cover the years 1700–1814 for the U.K., and 1800–1914 for the United States. *Sources:* Tabulated from data, for U.K., Mitchell (1988); for United States, U.S. Bureau of the Census (1976).

if we bracket local state militias, military expenditures far outweighed other expenditures of the national budget. It accounted for at least 72 percent of total spending and 94 percent each year (except for one year) between 1808 and 1848. This includes naval spending, which from 1798 to 1848 "either outpaced or approximately equaled all civilian federal spending combined."[56] When we compare U.S. and British expenditures directly (from 1700 to 1814 for Britain and from 1800 to 1914 for the United States), we see remarkable similarity in the structure of spending (see Figure 1.3).[57]

Both the U.S. and British states, therefore, were fiscal-military states. The British fiscal-military state financed itself partly by drawing on trade revenues. In turn, trade depended on expansion to cultivate more trade and protect existing trading networks.[58] Similarly for the American state, customs revenue constituted the greatest proportion of total federal revenues; customs revenue was continually enhanced by expanded trade in and with the western territories. Meanwhile, newly conquered land was fiscally lucrative for the state directly because tax on land was among the three top sources of revenue (besides customs and excise taxes), and indirectly because new settlement raised property

---

[56] Not surprisingly, as Katznelson shows, the periods of major increase in federal land sales over the nineteenth century (and hence the peaks of settlement) coincided with the more intense periods of Indian removal. Katznelson (2002), pp. 91–2.

[57] O'Brien (1988b).

[58] See Cain and Hopkins (1993), pp. 71–5; O'Brien (1998c), p. 68; Brewer (1989), pp. 202–4; Koehn (1994), pp. 20, 61–2.

values and contributed to income growth (that in turn facilitated increased customs and excise taxes).[59] Expansion was not an appurtenance. It was dependent
on American state power even as state power was dependent on expansion.

The interventionist U.S. state was more like the English state than American exceptionalist thought would have us believe. But was it also an *imperial*
state? The foregoing discussion discloses some similarities between Britain's
and America's territorial expansion. It remains to be seen whether this territorial expansion was also a process of empire formation.

The Forms of Enland's Imperial Ascendance

As seen, Britons in the long eighteenth century thought of Britain and its territories as an "empire." The called it the "British empire." They also referred to
overseas territories as "colonies." It seems, therefore, that Britain was a colonial
empire. But we have to be careful. The use of the term empire at the time does
not necessarily equate with the analytic concept used by scholars today to refer
to a system of unequal political power between a metropole and its territories.
It might have been used only to refer to the sovereign power of a monarch.[60]
Nor does the word colony as used by Britons at the time necessarily equate
with the notion of modern colonies (as administrative units subordinated to a
higher power). Beginning in the late 1600s, the word colonies was often used
synonymously with "dominions" and, in some instances, "plantations."[61] So
was this really a *colonial empire* in our analytic sense?

There are good reasons for staking the claim that Britain's overseas territories in the long eighteenth century constituted a colonial empire. On
the one hand, the earliest acquired territories were considered a part of the
monarch's direct domain (even chartered companies, although private bodies,
acted under the authority of the Crown). New territories were not unlike England's medieval territorial expanse by which all territories were equal (as in
equally subject to the authority of the Crown). These territories included the
Channel Islands of Guernsey and Jersey, Wales, and the Isle of Man.[62] On the
other hand, as more territories were later acquired, new distinctions emerged
that helped create a new colonial system, such as that between the monarch's
realm, which included England and Wales (and after 1707, Scotland), and the
monarch's "dominions" or "dependencies." The territories acquired during the

---

[59] Sylla (1996), p. 515. For a deeper analysis of expansion and revenue in the American context
and in comparison with the British state, see Heumann (2009) esp. pp. 115–55.

[60] Armitage (2000), p. 11.

[61] Finley (1976), pp. 170–1. Changes in England's own political institutions further complicated
matters for overseas territories. And the fact that England lacked a single-document written
constitution meant that there was never one authoritative text to guide policy toward overseas
territories Of course, the territories themselves had their own constitutions. But these were
largely customary, developed slowly, and often open to dispute. See Greene (1994b), pp. 25–
42.

[62] Steele (1998), p. 105; Marshall (1998), p. 10; Greene (1986), p. 7.

long eighteenth century occupied the latter category. Rather than being "Part of the Realm of England," they were considered as "Separate and Distinct Dominions."[63] In this sense, the new territories were incorporated as substates of a realm. But they were also *colonial states* in our analytic sense, for they were appendages of the metropolitan state and, most tellingly, subordinate to it. They were seen by Crown officials as "dependent dominions," where *dependence* signified "both weakness and subordination in relation to some person, body, or institution that was stronger or more competent and superior." The new territories were thus akin to the way in which "wives, children, servants were dependents."[64] As John Dickinson in Pennsylvania would remark in 1768, they were not only "*mixt*, but *dependent*" upon the Crown.[65] That is, they were juridically inferior and subordinate; they were rendered subordinate because they were deemed inferior.

The subordination of the territories was a layered historical development. Some of the earliest territories settled in the 1600s were proprietary governments whereby the Crown delegated appointments and political control almost fully to the proprietors. The monarch did not have representatives in the areas controlled by the Hudson's Bay Company or in the chartered governments of Rhode Island, Connecticut, or the Carolinas.[66] However, most of those early charters were eventually amended or revoked, leading to a form of "royal government" (also known sometimes as Crown Colonies or royal colonies) that involved direct royal control and hence an imperial hierarchy. This was the form that the vast majority of the territories in the Americas and the West Indies eventually took.[67] It found precedence in the early colonies of Jamaica and New York, both of which were classified as "conquered countries" akin to Ireland. As conquered countries, they were "subject to the King's Prerogative Royal"; the king would impose the identical laws of England at his whim, if at all.[68] Similarly, royal government meant that territories were subject to royal control in ways that domestic territories (or those that were "Part of the realm of England") were not. In this sense, they became "colonies" or, as many similar territories were later named, "British possessions."[69]

---

[63] "In this concept each colony was thus a separate corporate entity, a body politic authorized by the crown, with jurisdiction over a well-defined territory and its own distinctive institutions, laws, customs, and eventually, history and identity." From Greene (1986), p. 10.

[64] Ibid., p. 10.

[65] Quoted in Johnson (1998), p. 296.

[66] Steele (1998), p. 110.

[67] Greene (1898), pp. 2–22; Walker (1943), p. 17. Steele (1998), p. 110. Only two colonies were the exceptions; hence even the governor – the nominal representative of the Crown – was elected, together with the executive council. "Here the Crown had no authority at all." But this was the extreme of colonial autonomy. See Fieldhouse (1982), p. 61.

[68] Greene (1986), pp. 23–4.

[69] Later the distinction would be codified further by Parliament. The Interpretation Act of 1889 classified most overseas territories as "British possessions" and defined them as "any part of Her Majesty's dominions *exclusive of the United Kingdom*." Quoted in Finley (1976), p. 167; emphasis added.

Metropolitan control over the colonies was exercised in various ways. Perhaps the most important was royal appointment. Territories had their own elective assemblies (except for military outposts like Nova Scotia and Newfoundland). In Jamaica and Barbados, the rights and privileges of such assemblies had been established before 1689 and remained the strongest of the assemblies.[70] But the highest appointment, the colonial governor, was made by the Crown. In turn, the governor appointed members of the colonial council (that served as an advisory group, a colonial court of appeal, and a legislative upper house) and other bureaucratic posts. Furthermore, the governor exercised veto power over the assemblies and could call and even dissolve them. In these ways, therefore, the colonial governor represented "a monarchical power that was supposedly stronger in the colonies than in England."[71] In fact, whereas the monarchy at home was bound by the Triennial and later the Septennial, colonial governors could (and often did) dissolve the lower legislative assemblies without having to specify when they would be again summoned. And governors could establish courts of law and appoint and dismiss judges, even though the Crown at home had lost such powers with the Act of Settlement in 1701.[72]

As colonial governments became officially subject to the Crown's will, the organs of the Crown's will accordingly became more elaborate. Here we see the formation of an imperial hierarchy corresponding to an expanding imperial bureaucracy. In the 1670s, the Lords of Trade, a permanent committee of the king's Privy Council, was created to exert greater supervision over the colonies. It required reports from colonial governors and expanded "in scope and specificity the royal instructions given to governors to direct them in their conduct of government."[73] This body also enacted various measures to restrict the legislative assemblies' powers over the purse.[74] Such meddling was intensified during historical periods. During the 1740s and 1750s, for example, it used legislative review, royal instructions, and the royal veto over colonial laws to more closely supervise the colonies. Later, after being renamed the Board of Trade, it sometimes took on the responsibility of making appointments and issuing instructions to governors.[75]

The metropolitan Parliament also exercised control (not least as the Crown itself became subject to Parliament at home). In the late seventeenth and early eighteenth centuries, parliamentary legislation for the colonies was largely restricted to concerns of foreign affairs and trade (such as the Navigation Acts). But as the long eighteenth century progressed, so too did parliamentary power. From the Glorious Revolution through the first decades of the 1700s, Parliament passed laws that strengthened Crown control over colonies; these

---

[70] On West Indies legislatures see Watson (1995) and Greene (1994a).
[71] Steele (1998), p. 110.
[72] Bailyn (1965), pp. 66–72.
[73] Greene (1986), pp. 13–14, quote at 14.
[74] Ibid., pp. 14–15.
[75] Ibid., pp. 49–50; Marshall (2005), pp. 74–6.

included acts dealing with the Newfoundland trade (1699) and fixing the value of certain foreign coins in the colonies (1708).[76] Throughout the century, Parliament often acted in the interests of English business groups and other lobbies at home rather than in the interests of settlers and merchants in the territories. Those domestic lobbies had direct access and representation in Parliament, but the distance separating territorial subjects was too great to allow such access.[77] Finally, and most notoriously, Parliament increasingly meddled in the internal affairs of the colonies. By the time of the Stamp Act in 1765, Parliament had become "the ultimate arbiter of Imperial affairs."[78] Parliament exercised power, but colonists did not have representation.[79] The English state was an *imperial state* indeed.

America's Empire

Was the U.S. federal government also an imperial state? In one of the only explicitly comparative examinations of America's territorial expansion, the historian Robin Winks asks a similar question. Surveying the history of westward expansion to the mid-nineteenth century, he asks: "Was this first period of expansion imperialistic?" His answer: "Perhaps." Winks' reluctance rests on the fact that even though the U.S. federal government acquired new territory, it did not keep them as colonies. Instead, it turned them into equal states in the American Union. This makes U.S. expansion fundamentally different from European expansion. It "was not 'imperialism' per se but continentalism," says Winks.[80]

This is a standard part of the exceptionalist narrative. The western territories did not become colonial appendages or dependencies of the United States, but rather equal members of the body politic. Settlers were given equal rights and privileges under the law; they were equal citizens rather than subordinated colonial subjects. In this regard, the U.S. territorial system was not like Britain's empire.[81] The other part of this narrative is the supposed political genius of America's Founding Fathers. By making the U.S. government an expanding state that acquired territories and turned them into equal states, Thomas Jefferson and his peers inaugurated a novel republicanism that broke with their imperial English past. Rather than creating a hierarchy of power, they created a federated union of equal territories, "an expanding union of republics held together by ties of interest and affection."[82] Rather than an empire opposed to

---

[76] Steele (1998), p. 108.

[77] Greene (1994b), p. 66.

[78] Steele (1998), p. 109; Greene (1994b), pp. 39–40.

[79] See Pocock (1995), pp. 335–40.

[80] Winks (1997), p. 148.

[81] Because "each new US territory was settled or conquered it became, within a very short span of time, a new state within the Union... colonialism has never been an option for the United States." Pagden (2005), p. 54; see also Weeks (1996), p. x. See also especially ibid., p. x.

[82] Onuf (2000), p. 2.

liberty like England's empire had been, they created an "empire of liberty." The American founders thereby solved the age-old imperial problem of reconciling territorial expanse with liberty and law, security, and freedom.

In this light, American expansion appears as the antithesis of European empire – a notion registered at the time by David Humphreys, George Washington's officer:

> All former empires rose, the work of guilt,
> On conquest, blood, or usurpation built;
> But we, taught wisdom by their woes and crimes,
> Fraught with their lore, and born to better times;
> Our constitutions form'd on freedom's base,
> Which all the blessings of all lands embrace;
> Embrace humanity's extended cause,
> A world of our empire, for a world of our laws... [83]

Still, this exceptionalist narrative remains dangerously simplistic at worst and misleading at best. It is right to point out that the territories acquired on the continent (and later Alaska and Hawaii) eventually became fully fledged states in the Union. The story is wrong, however, as it covers up everything else that was involved.

Continental Colonialism

Consider how states were made. How did territories become states in the Union? It was not so simple as signing a document. Before settlers and subjects in the new territories could be granted statehood and citizenship, they had to undergo a period of "territorial government." This meant that the newly acquired territories were kept as subordinated dependencies, subject to the power of the U.S. president and Congress, without representation. The origins of this system lay in the Northwest Ordinance of 1787, which established a three-stage process before statehood. First, the federal government appointed a governor and three judges. The governor wielded legislative power; even settlers did not have a say. Second, when the free white male population had passed five thousand, an elective two-house legislature could be established; but the upper house remained appointees of the president. The federally appointed governor had absolute veto power and could "convene, prorogue, and dissolve the assembly at his pleasure."[84] Finally, the territory could write up a state constitution, only after which the territory could become a state. Even then, the U.S. Congress had the power to approve or reject statehood.[85]

The Louisiana Purchase of 1803 added yet more layers of control to the territorial system. President Jefferson started the important precedent of appointing a military governor to the territory before the territory could even get to the

---

[83] Quoted in Stephanson (1995), p. 19.

[84] Initially the upper house was to be chosen by the U.S. Congress. But after the Constitution went into effect in 1789, the president took on this role. Perkins (1962), p. 15.

[85] Sparrow (2005), pp. 232–3.

first stage of the process. The territory was then subjected to autocratic military rule – no governor, no judges. And during this stage of military government, inhabitants were not even given the protection of a bill of rights.[86] Territorial government would begin only when Congress decided it was ready.[87] This happened for many territories. California and New Mexico were run initially by military governors. Alaska was not organized as a territory for forty-five years, meaning that for those forty-five years inhabitants did not have representation in the metropole or even in a local legislature. Nor did they have a bill of rights. It was a military occupation.

In sum, the territorial system entailed a colonial structure very much akin to Britain's overseas empire. Just as the Crown, its bureaucratic agents, and Parliament ruled on high in the English system, so did the presidency, its branches (first the Department of State, the Treasury Department, and later, in 1873, the Department of Interior), and Congress rule at the apex of the U.S. territorial system.[88] Making territorial governors appointees of the U.S. president simply replaced the previous monarchical powers of appointment with presidential ones. Having symbolically cut off the king's head, the new American system replaced him with the U.S. president. Furthermore, the president's agencies charged with administering territorial affairs acted similarly to the Lords of Trade in the king's Privy Council. In the Department of State, "appointments and removals of governors and secretaries were studied and submitted for presidential action . . . leaves of absence were granted or refused in the name of the president . . . instructions, advice, and reprimands were sent out on a variety of subjects."[89] These appointment powers were used to meddle in territorial affairs, not unlike the practice of appointment by the Privy Council in the British empire. Not surprisingly, people in the western territories sometimes made unflattering comparisons between U.S. federal officials and the ministers of King George III.[90] A newspaper in the Dakota territory declared in 1877: "We are so heartily disgusted with our dependent condition, with being snubbed at every turn in life, with having all our interest subjected to the whims and corrupt acts of persons in power that we feel very much as thirteen colonies felt."[91] Later, in 1903, Albert Bushnell Hart (president of the American Political Science Association) noted that in "any other country such [territorial] governments would be called 'colonial.' . . . In truth, the territories are and ever have been colonies."[92]

---

[86] Perkins (1962), p. 17.

[87] Sparrow (2006), p. 22.

[88] For more on the administrative apparatus for the territories, see Pomeroy (1947). There was even an informal colonial service, as federal officials often moved from one territory to another. The clearest example of a "colonial service in operation" are the territorial judges. See Eblen (1968), p. 280.

[89] Pomeroy (1947), p. 5

[90] Limerick (1988), p. 23

[91] Lamar (1956), p. 205; see also Limerick (1988), p. 83.

[92] Hart (1919), pp. 368–9.

The imperial and colonial character to the territorial system was by design rather than in effect. The territorial governments were directly modeled after Britain's own colonies. James Monroe feared that the newly acquired territories would rebel against the federal government just as he and his peers had previously rebelled against the British empire. Consequently, he "considered a strong governor to be necessary from the beginning of representative government, both to get the people in harness and to prevent rebellions before statehood was attained."[93] The fact that the architects of the system had previously revolted against British imperialism did not temper the imperialism of their own system; it made them more willing to impose stronger controls over the territories than Britain had previously exercised.

In certain regards, settlers in American territories had less political autonomy than settlers in Britain's previous colonial empire. In the first stage of the U.S. territorial system, federal appointees monopolized legislative, executive, and judicial functions. But in Britain's empire, colonial assemblies were present from the beginning. Even in the second stage of the territorial system, when legislatures were established, the federal state had more powers over territorial subjects than did the British state (at least before 1763, when the British state tightened its controls over its territories). "In this light," notes Eblen, "the Ordinance of 1787 cannot be viewed as innovative or progressive in any basic sense, even in the provision for statehood; on the contrary, its system of colonial government was decidedly more authoritarian than that of the British."[94]

America's continental colonialism was more imperial and authoritarian than Britain's settler empire in theory, and it was even more so in practice. For instance, although the British state controlled top appointments and restricted the power of the colonial assemblies, the actual operations of the system gave colonial assemblies more power than official doctrine implied. One way in which assemblies influenced colonial governors was by their control over salary: Assemblies had the right to vote for the governors' pay from local taxes, which meant that governors often had to negotiate with powerful assemblymen and often grant them many concessions. Assemblies also wielded other informal powers, which made it easy for them to conceive of themselves as local variants of or parallels to the House of Commons at home.[95] By contrast, in the U.S. territorial system, governors' salaries and those of other officials were set by Congress, leaving the local legislative assemblies with little power.[96] Furthermore, most scholarship on the British system has shown that although there was an official imperial hierarchy, unofficially London was often forced to engage in a process of two-way "negotiation" with its colonies, whereby loyalty could only be secured by granting colonial privileges and

---

93 Eblen (1968), p. 42.
94 Ibid., p. 42.
95 Koenigsberger (1989), p. 147; Greene (1994b), p. 47.
96 Pomeroy (1947), pp. 38–50.

concessions.[97] In the U.S. system, Washington's control over all appointments and salaries made for a situation in which there was much less negotiation. The federal government often removed and replaced territorial governors at its whim. And the local courts were subject to direct federal control: Territorial judges were removed and replaced just as often as were territorial governors.[98]

The imperial character of America's territorial system is further disclosed in the federal officials' discourse about territorial populations, which took on a strong colonial tone. After the Louisiana Purchase, Federalists asserted that New Orleans was populated by "a Mixture of Americans, English, Spanish, and French and crouded [sic] every year... with two or three thousand boatmen from the backcountry remarkable for their dissipated habits, unruly tempers, and lawless conduct."[99] One official wrote that "Otters" were "more capable of self-government than Louisiana's *Gallo-Hispano-Indium omnimum gatherum* of savages and adventurers, whose pure morals are expected to sustain and glorify our republic."[100] Thomas Jefferson was no less condescending. He complained that the Creoles were "as yet incapable of self-government as children"; the "principles of popular Government are utterly beyond their comprehension."[101] Jefferson was not at all eager to see the territory pass into statehood and in fact suggested that statehood should be delayed for as long as possible.

Even relations with white settler populations took on an imperial tone. Secretary of the Treasury, Oliver Wolcott, referred to the Northwest Territory in 1795 as a "dependent colony."[102] The first ruler of the Northwest Territory, Arthur St. Clair, insisted that the inhabitants of the territories were not full American citizens but "subjects," and repeatedly referred to them as "infants." St. Clair used his autocratic powers to try to keep the territory in a subordinated position by, for example, splitting the territory into smaller divisions to divide the population and thereby preventing the population from reaching sixty thousand. In response, St. Clair's subjects often complained about his "colonial, oppressive and unequal government." One judge of Ohio complained to Jefferson in 1802 that the territorial government was a "true transcript of our old English Colonial Governments," adding that "our Governor is clothed with all the power of a British Nabob."[103] As late as the 1880s, territorial subjects deployed such discourse. In 1884, Martin Maginnis, a delegate to Congress from Montana Territory (who could speak but not vote), declared

---

[97] On this point, see Marshall (2005), p. 76; Olson (1992), p. 134; Greene (1994b), pp. 1–24 and Greene (2002).

[98] Pomeroy (1947), p. 52; on the British system, see Steele (1998).

[99] Quoted in Sparrow (2006), p. 21.

[100] Ibid., p. 21.

[101] Ibid., p. 22.

[102] Quoted in Onuf (1987), p. 71.

[103] Quoted in ibid., pp. 71–2; more on criticism of governors see Eblen (1968), pp. 143–5; on conflicts and events in the Northwest Territory, including St. Clair and Winthrop, see ibid., pp. 52–86.

that the "present Territorial system . . . is the most infamous system of colonial government that was ever seen on the face of the globe." He continued:

> Territories are the colonies of your Republic, situated three thousand miles away from Washington by land, as the thirteen colonies were situated three thousand miles away from London by water. And it is a strange thing that the fathers of our Republic . . . established a colonial government as much worse than that which they revolted against as one form of government can be worse than another.[104]

The standard exceptionalist narrative covers up such discourse and the imperial relations of which it bears witness. It likewise occludes how prevalent the territorial system has been in the history of American state formation. Exceptionalist thought tells us that "only very briefly has the mainland United States ever been considered an empire rather than a nation"; but this overlooks the fact that "three-quarters of the area of the fifty states was at one point under territorial government of some kind" (as the political scientist Bartholomew Sparrow notes).[105] The cumulative existence from 1784 to 1912 of the twenty-eight contiguous territories before they became states amounts to 544 years.[106] New Mexico suffered the longest period before statehood: sixty-two years.[107] This means that "children born when New Mexico was first brought under American control were to be in their sixties when New Mexico became a state."[108] It follows that the United States has never been "a nation of states" with equal standing.[109] For nearly all of its history, it has had territories alongside its states. The United States has been primarily an *empire-state* rather than a nation-state.[110]

Comparative Exceptionalisms

If exceptionalist narratives run the risk of downplaying the imperial dimensions of American territorial expansion, they likewise run the risk of *overstating* the imperial dimensions of the British empire. The second follows from the first. Treating the American empire of liberty as exceptionally novel and liberal, the exceptionalist narrative portrays the British empire as vulgarly authoritarian. But was it?

For a start, the discourse of empire among Britain's territorial subjects is telling. As seen, America's territorial subjects registered complaints about the territorial system. The views of British colonials, however, were much less oppositional. Surely the planters of Jamaica or other Britons abroad often criticized London's imperial meddling. And the concatenation of criticisms among New Englanders led to the American Revolution. But prior to the

---

104 Quoted in Pomeroy (1947), p. 104; see also Limerick (1988), p. 79.
105 First quote from Pagden (2005), pp. 54–5; Sparrow (2005), p. 232.
106 Eblen (1968), p. 13.
107 Sparrow (2005), p. 242.
108 Pomeroy (1947), p. 2.
109 Sparrow (2005), p. 232.
110 On "empire-state" see Cooper (2005), pp. 153–204.

revolution, British settlers had developed a view of the British empire that was remarkably positive. More importantly, they had developed a view of their empire as exceptional; as uniquely free, liberal, and democratic. This prefigured the Americans' later sense of imperial uniqueness. It also set the basis for the notion of an "empire of liberty."

The British sense of imperial uniqueness began to emerge as early as the Glorious Revolution. As Greene notes, "many contemporary observers, English and foreign, agreed that the English people's unique system of law and liberty was what principally distinguished them from all other people on the face of the globe. The proud boast of the English was that they, unlike most other Europeans, had retained their identity as a free people by safeguarding their liberty through their laws."[111] The identity was forged in direct opposition to other European states. Sir John Fortescue in the early seventeenth century set the tone. He contended that England, unlike France where "what pleased the prince...had the force of law," enjoyed a unique system whereby the monarchy was constrained by the law and the people "preserve[d] their rights through the law." Englishmen were the only ones who were "ruled by laws they themselves desire[d]." Their laws "favour[ed] liberty in every case."[112] Later, Whig theorist Henry Care similarly contended that nations like France and Spain were ruled by "Arbitrary" tyrants, whereas England's government was "the best in the World."[113] Other writers such as John Milton insisted that England was "the mansion house of liberty," and that this was the essence of "England's peculiarity."[114]

After the Glorious Revolution, this notion of English exceptionalism was deployed in regard to empire as well as nation. Settlers carried the ideology to the New World, conceiving themselves as geographically afar but politically subject to the same privileges of law and liberty as at home. Their sons in the colonies considered themselves "born to Liberty."[115] As Greene notes, "the English system of law and liberty was thus crucial to their [the settlers'] ability to maintain their identity as English people and to continue to think of themselves as to be thought of those by those who remained in England as English."[116] As with the Americans' self-conceived imperial identity, this image of a liberal empire did not include subject peoples like Native Americans. But it did include all white colonial subjects overseas, from Barbadians to North Americans, who increasingly came to conceive of themselves as part of a larger community of Britons. This was a community "in which Caledonians and Americans, as well as the English, could participate."[117] Arthur Young pointed out in 1772 that peoples in the colonies were conjoined with Britons at home, living under

---

[111] Greene (1998), pp. 208–9.
[112] Fortescue as quoted in ibid., pp. 209–10.
[113] Care quoted in Greene (1998), p. 210.
[114] John Milton quoted in Greene (1998), p. 210.
[115] Jonas Hanway quoted in Colley (2003a), p. 97.
[116] Wilson (1995), p. 277 see also Greene (1998), p. 222.
[117] Wilson (1988), p. 104.

"one nation, united under one sovereign, speaking the same language and enjoying the same liberty."[118]

Given the hierarchical structure of the empire, how were such ideas about liberty even possible? Part of it was an increasing sense of community covered under the term "British Empire." During the second quarter of the eighteenth century, as noted earlier, Anglophones in North America and the West Indies began "for the first time habitually to describe their community as the 'British Empire.'"[119] Enabled by transformations in communications around the British Atlantic, colonists saw themselves in union with the British Isles.[120] This imagined community, however, took on its meaning as a community based on shared liberties more specifically through the political structure of the empire itself. The very sorts of settler privileges and freedoms discussed earlier formed the basis for the ideological conception. For instance, although colonists did not enjoy representation in Parliament, their assemblies nonetheless gave them local representation. In Barbados, "the Council and Assembly were regarded by the white settlers as the equivalent of the House of Lords and House of Commons in England."[121] Like other whites in the British Atlantic, they likewise considered their territory as "extensions of England, rather than extended dependencies."[122] We have seen that the colonies were indeed dependencies in the sense that, officially, they were subordinated to the will of the Crown-in-Parliament. But the idea of metropolitan extension was not completely off the mark. In the northern colonies, the assemblies were elected by a wide franchise of white men and, as noted, they did exert certain checks against Crown-appointed governors. In Jamaica, the local assemblies had been especially powerful, obtaining a reputation for being particularly assertive.[123]

Besides using their assemblies, colonists also developed legal apparatuses granting them rights and privileges that were not dissimilar from those they would have enjoyed at home. The British state never established once and for all which laws from home applied abroad (the common law or the statue law only?), but this indeterminacy helped rather than hindered the colonists' cause. Lacking concrete decrees from London, local courts and legislatures "had wide latitude to determine for themselves which laws [of England] applied" and so used all kinds of English law – "the common law, presettlement statutes, and postsettlement statutes [etc.]."[124] The lieutenant governor of Virginia, holding position from 1727 to 1749, could thereby declare that the colonies enjoyed laws that were "exactly suited to the Circumstances of the Respective Governments, and as near as possible [as] it can be, conformable to the Laws

---

[118] Greene (1998), p. 222 quoting Young. For more on British identifications of liberty and empire, see the essays in Greene (2010).

[119] Armitage (2000), p. 171.

[120] Steele (1986).

[121] Sheridan (1998), p. 405.

[122] Watson (1995), p. 90.

[123] Ibid., p. 92.

[124] Greene (1986), p. 27.

and Customs of England." These included guaranteeing "traditional English legal guarantees of life, liberty, and property."[125]

The conception of the empire as based on law and liberty was not restricted to the colonists. It was also articulated in the metropole.[126] English public opinion at home did not find the privileges enjoyed by colonists inappropriate. Conceiving of overseas colonists as commercial vanguards who contributed to the kingdom through their commercial ventures, they took "pride in the commercial vigour that was thought to flow from the local liberties appropriate to communities of free British people living overseas."[127] Various prominent writers and philosopher-thinkers contributed to the ideology (especially in the 1740s with the War of Jenkins' Ear and anti-Walopean agitation), formulating Lockean connections between property and liberty. Such connections ultimately contributed to "a vision of the British Empire as Protestant, commercial, maritime and free founded on the sanctity of property as much at home as abroad, in the metropolis and in the colonies."[128]

In brief, the British empire was conceived by contemporaries as a fundamentally unique empire. It was a "free and virtuous empire, founded in consent and nurtured in liberty and trade."[129] It was "Protestant, commercial, maritime and free" in opposition to Catholic Spain and France.[130] In America, said Arthur Young, "Spain, Portugal and France have planted despotisms; only Britain liberty."[131] As David Armitage summarizes, the British empire was "everything that the aspirant universal monarchies of seventeenth-century were not, and could not be – an empire for liberty."[132] Of course, with the Stamp Act, this ideology of a benign British empire was shattered. But the discourse of British exceptionalism reveals that the Americans did not so much invent a novel conception of expansion and empire as they did appropriate and rearticulate the idioms and ideology of their former imperial master. After all, American revolutionaries did not at first revolt: Working from the ideology of the British empire as an identity of interests, right, and peoples, they hoped only that Parliament would more properly enact the ideology. The problem – from the Americans' standpoint – was that King George III was corrupt, deviating from the true tradition and ideals of the British empire. So when the Americans embarked on the revolutionary path, they did so with reluctance. And they did so only to try to enact the ideals already laid down for them by the very imperial masters they sought to cast off. They aimed for a more perfect union rather than an entirely different one.[133]

---

[125] As quoted in ibid., p. 27. See also Steele (1998), p. 112.
[126] Armitage (2000), pp. 181–95.
[127] Marshall (2005), p. 73.
[128] Armitage (2000), p. 188.
[129] Greene (1998), p. 122.
[130] Armitage (2000), pp. 173–82.
[131] Greene (1998), p. 223.
[132] Armitage (2000), p. 195.
[133] See Onuf (1987), Onuf (2000).

Empire of Liberty?

What remains, then, of the notion that American expansion in the nineteenth century was an "exception"? It is not that expansion was devoid of colonial rule: The territorial system was even more authoritarian than British colonialism. Nor is it that Americans articulated a liberal imperial identity in opposition to other empires; the British had already prefigured that move. It might even be said that *all* empires conceive of themselves as unique, special, and exceptional. The only thing that remains is the fact that the territories, although subjected to colonialism, were *eventually* admitted into the Union as equal states. This remains one of the key bases for exceptionalists who resist the claim that American expansion was "imperial" and who, therefore, see no warrant for comparing the United States with the British empire.[134]

Still, even this presumably exceptional dimension of American expansion is rightly subject to question. First, incorporating colonized lands and peoples as equal entities in a political formation is not unique to American expansion. The Russian, Ottoman, and Chinese empires all had imperial systems at one point or another whereby territories were incorporated as equal units. France's "assimilation" strategy was also incorporative in important respects. And England had incorporated Wales and Scotland as equally subject parts of the realm.[135]

Second, America's "empire for liberty" that incorporated territories as states did not apply to everyone. For nonwhites, it was as repressive as any stereotypical empire. To be sure, slavery was a vital part of America's imperial formation, yet it was not abolished until 1865. The British empire had abolished slavery much earlier, in 1833.[136] Furthermore, territorial expansion was a fundamentally racialized process. Whereas white settlers may have initially welcomed territorial annexation by the federal government, there were thousands upon thousands of inhabitants whose wishes were never consulted. Native Americans, freed blacks, Creoles, and various populations of varied Spanish and Mexican descent were essentially forced into accepting U.S. sovereignty.[137] In New Mexico, as we have seen, many of these groups violently resisted annexation from the outset. Furthermore, once subjected to U.S. sovereignty, these populations remained imperial subjects.[138] "The Empire of Liberty was to be made up of one people, dedicated to liberty under republican institutions,"

---

134 "American nationalism and American imperialism are unique in world history and cannot be understood by comparison to other nationalisms or imperialism." Weeks (1996), p. x.

135 On the Russian empire, see Lieven (1999), pp. 180–1, Lieven (2002), and Burbank and Hagen (2007). For a good comparison between Russian and U.S. expansion, see Cooper and Burbank (2010), pp. 251–86. On the Ottoman empire, see Barkey (2008). On France, see Betts (1961), Conklin (1998), and Deming Lewis (1962).

136 The other areas in the British empire that did not abolish slavery included the possessions of the East India Company, Ceylon, and St. Helena.

137 Sparrow (2006), p. 25

138 On Jefferson and African Americans, see Onuf (2000), pp. 147–88. On the genesis of American ethnoculturalism and identity, see Kaufmann (1999).

explain Tucker and Hendrickson. "There was to be no place here for subjects, only for citizens. This was why, in principle, Negroes could have no permanent position within the palladium of freedom and why, in practice, Indians as well had to be excluded from it."[139]

Indeed, the American state's dealings with Native Americans is exemplary of the racialized character of America's empire of liberty. As noted earlier, the military repeatedly waged war on Native Americans and seized their land. The federal government justified this process by the "right of discovery" doctrine inherited from the British imperial system. In the 1823 Supreme Court case, *Johnson v. M'Intosh*, the Native Americans' "right of occupancy" was subordinated to the United States' "right of discovery" (i.e. white man discovers brown men and women already living on land, but because the discoverer is white, he was there first).[140] Then came the Indian Removal Act under President Jackson in 1830, which was followed by a violent appropriation of Native Americans' land. By 1837, the Jackson administration had managed to remove 46,000 Native Americans from their land, thereby opening up yet more territory for white settlement.[141] To Jackson, the Native American population was not even worthy of treaty. They were "subjects" plain and simple, and for the federal government to negotiate treaties with subjects was an "absurdity."[142] The Supreme Court shared this view. In its 1823 decision, it declared that Indians were "an inferior race of people, without the privileges of citizens, and under the perpetual protection and pupilage of the government."[143]

From Continental Colonialism to Overseas Empire

America's treatment of Native Americans is informative, but even that does not tell everything about the American empire during its ascendancy. If we look beyond the North American continent, we find the limits of the exceptionalist narrative in their starkest form still. The American state conquered the continent, and it also extended its reach overseas. Part of this extension took the form of military rule over foreign lands, turning them into de facto protectorates. The story should be familiar: the Platt Amendment in Cuba's constitution in 1902 followed by bouts of occupation; military occupation of Nicaragua (1912–1925); invasion and occupation of the Dominican

[139] Tucker and Hendrickson (1990), p. 161. Schemes were proposed for governing these peoples in ways that *might* lead to eventual liberty. Jefferson believed, for example, that only if African Americans were transplanted back to Africa might they become able to attain liberty. But for the time, and even in the long run, the empire of liberty was aimed at whites only. Hence, three years after the 1787 Northwest Ordinance was enacted, the Naturalization Act of 1790 made citizenship a possibility only for "free whites."

[140] Tomlins (2001), pp. 335–6.

[141] See Wallace (1993).

[142] Prucha (1994), p. 153.

[143] See for an excellent discussion of this status, Wald (1992), p. 90.

Republic (1916–1924) and Haiti (1915–1934).[144] But the overseas empire did not just involve such temporary occupations. It also involved direct and prolonged colonial rule.

In 1898, the United States declared sovereignty over Hawaii and former Spanish colonies of Puerto Rico, Guam, the Philippines, and the "Moro" islands of the Philippine archipelago. It later took half of Samoa (1900); the entire Panama Canal Zone (1903), holding approximately 62,00 inhabitants; and the Virgin Islands (1917), with over 26,000 inhabitants (at least 19,000 of whom were classified as "Negro" by the Census).[145] The significance of these acquisitions for U.S. imperialism cannot be overstated. On the one hand, they can be seen as a continuation of westward expansion. Commenting on the Treaty of Paris in 1898 by which the United States acquired Spain's former colonies, the London *Times* observed:

The signing of the Treaty of Paris... marks the beginning of a policy of expansion that seems wholly at variance with the traditional aims of American statesmen.... But... the new foreign policy is not so alien to the national character or so much at variance with the previous history of the Republic as might at first sight appear. The Anglo-Americans have at bottom the imperial instincts of the great governing and conquering race from which they are sprung.... By swift steps they have carried the dominion of the Republic from the Atlantic to the Pacific, and have conquered, both politically and economically, a vast extent of territory.

On the other hand, the new acquisitions marked something comparably new. First, unlike previous territories on the western frontier, the new overseas territories were not accompanied by the arrival of white settlers. Except for Hawaii, white settlement was minimal. Instead, the U.S. military first occupied the territories and were later replaced by civilian administrators from the mainland. This was a form of administrative colonialism rather than settler colonialism: A handful of white officials ruled at least two and a half million colonized subjects.

Second, and more importantly, all of the new acquisitions except for Hawaii and Alaska were declared "unincorporated" through a series of Supreme Court cases known as "the insular cases." The status of unincorporated meant that the territories were "foreign in a domestic sense," subject to the plenary power of the U.S. Congress, but not afforded the full protection of the American Constitution. Colonial peoples enjoyed some "fundamental rights," but not all

---

[144] Perkins (1981).

[145] Population data on Panama from 1912 census figures and for Virgin Islands for 1917 in United States Bureau of the Census (1943). Although traditional scholarship has overlooked this colonial empire, a number of recent works have begun to explore its multiple dimensions. For a comparative overview on colonial governance, see Thompson (2010). The other literature is too large to list in full, but see the essays in McCoy and Scarano (2009). Earlier seminal work includes Perkins (1962) and Pratt (1950). See Kramer (2006) for an excellent discussion of some of the racial dynamics of U.S. rule in the Philippines.

rights, and statehood was not necessarily the end goal.[146] In fact, none of the legal documents that codified the conquests promised that the inhabitants of seized lands would become citizens or that the new colonies would become states. The U.S. Congress was given the right to decide. Given this, William Willoughby (who served as a colonial official in Puerto Rico) accurately stressed that the new acquisitions marked "the development of an entirely new phase in the expansion of the United States." Whereas previous acquisitions involved "the incorporation of the new territory into the Union upon full equality with the other States," the new acquisitions meant that the territory under U.S. sovereignty "would have to be divided into two classes having a different political status; the one constituting the United States proper and enjoying full political rights and privileges, and the other dependent territory in subordination to the former and having its form of government and the rights of its inhabitants determined for it." In short, the United States had "definitely entered the class of nations holding and governing over-sea colonial possessions."[147]

We see here the clear limits of Jefferson's "empire of liberty" and the exceptionalist narrative. U.S. expansion did not in fact entail the incorporation of all territories as equal states. Instead, the rule of colonial difference was firmly applied. Some territories were states with equal citizens; other territories and peoples were rendered dependent and subordinate.[148] The Supreme Court's distinction between "incorporated" and "unincorporated" territory encapsulated the difference exactly. Supreme Court Justice Henry Billings Brown clarified that the difference was about race. Whereas contiguous territory in the west had been "inhabited only by people of the same race [e.g. settlers], or by scattered bodies of native Indians," he said, the new overseas territories represented "differences of race, habits, laws and customs."[149] The idea was that Puerto Ricans, Filipinos, Chamorros (in Guam), Samoans, Panamanians, and Virgin Islanders were racially inferior and so not worthy of self-government. They did not deserve independence or statehood. What Jacob Schurman of the Philippine Commission said to President McKinley about the Philippines represents the views held of all the colonies: "There is no prospect of their assimilation in any period of time. They are distant from us by the diameter of the earth, the inhabitants are barbarous and they are populous, and ... we shall have to hold them as perpetual vassals."[150]

---

[146] Justice White justified the distinction between incorporated and unincorporated by "the precedents of the Louisiana and Florida territories that were, he said, dependencies initially and were later formally incorporated into the United States" [see Leibowitz (1989), p. 23]. For more on the insular cases and "unincorporation," see Burnett and Marshall (2001) and Sparrow (2006).

[147] Willoughby (1905), pp. 7–8.

[148] As Pratt noted, the United States "acquired not 'territories' but possessions or 'dependencies' and became, in that sense, an 'imperial' power." Pratt (1950), p. 68.

[149] Quoted in Weiner (2001), p. 71.

[150] Jacob Schurman to Wm. McKinley, Aug. 12, 1898 (MP ser. 1, reel 4).

Keeping the new colonial subjects as vassals is exactly what happened. Congress had to decide what to do with the territories. For Puerto Rico and the Philippines, it passed organic laws that created colonial governments with no end point in clear sight.[151] Colonial control was to be extended indefinitely. "There is a period in childhood," summarized Secretary of War Elihu Root, who was placed in charge of the territories, "during which the obligations of a guardian can not be performed without the power to control the child's actions."[152] Guam and Samoa met a similar fate and in some respects a worse one. In their case, Congress did not even enact legislation establishing a proper government. In the absence of congressional action, the two territories were at the mercy of the U.S. president, who could create whatever form of government he wished – including none at all. He ultimately made them (and the U.S. Virgin Islands later) subject to naval control, in effect establishing permanent military governments wherein the naval commander became the de facto colonial governor with autocratic powers.[153]

The notion of "American empire" in this context took on a new meaning. It was not an empire for liberty but rather an overseas colonial empire. Notably, the discourse of American empire heightened in this period to reflect the new meaning. In the *New York Times*, the number of articles using the phrase "our empire" or "American Empire" leaped during the years 1898 to 1901. Some of this empire talk was critical of America's new ventures. Anti-expansionists such as the Anti-Imperial League were quick to attack the new imperialism.[154] But much of the discourse was not so negative. Supreme Court Justice John Marshall used the term "American Empire" without negative connotation in his rulings on the insular cases.[155] A spate of popular books with titles like *Our Island Empire* also emerged. One unapologetically referred to the United States as an "Imperial State" ruling over a "Federal Empire."[156] Articles in popular magazines proliferated on the topic. As one writer observed, "'Colonial' and 'Imperial' are among the terms extensively used, in recent years, in referring to the relations newly assumed by the United States."[157] In 1906, the *New York Times* pondered not whether the United States was an "empire" (for its articles often spoke of it), but whether it would ever fall.[158] Decades later it had not: In 1930, the *Saturday Evening Post* carried a two-part article,

---

[151] For Puerto Rico, the Foraker Act of 1900; for the Philippines, the Philippine Bill of 1902 (aka the Organic Act of 1902). The Philippine Bill of 1902 was "an act to *temporarily* provide for the administration of the affairs of civil government in the Philippine Islands" (*US Statues at Large*, 1902, vol. 32, p. 691); while the Foraker act was also "an act to *temporarily* provide revenues and a civil government" (*US Statutes at Large*, 1900, vol. 31, p. 77).

[152] Root to Lowell, Feb. 11, 1904 (USNA, RG 350, entry 364–2).

[153] On Samoa, see Gray (1960); for Guam, see Thompson (1944).

[154] See Murphy (2009), Schirmer (1972), and Welch (1979).

[155] *New York Times*, Jan. 9, 1901, p. 7.

[156] Morris (1899); Snow (1902).

[157] Pierce (1903), p. 43.

[158] *New York Times*, Aug. 6, 1906, p. 9.

"The American Empire," offering a "concise compendium of the American empire."[159]

The fact that America's new empire was neither of nor for liberty had ramifications. In the Philippines, a group of landed elites based in Luzon, joining others around the archipelago, had already begun a war of independence from Spain by the time Admiral Dewey entered Manila Bay in 1898. Led by General Emilio Aguinaldo, they had declared an independent Philippine Republic with its own constitution and legislature at the town of Malolos. The sudden arrival of the Americans during the Spanish-American War was not a welcomed contingency. The revolutionaries had already been fighting Spain; they were not open to facing yet another imperial master. The result was a war of national liberation that became, from the Americans' side, a war of conquest. Ultimately the war claimed some 400,000 Filipino lives and the lives of 4,000 U.S. soldiers.[160]

During the war, atrocities abounded (unsurprisingly, because many of the U.S. military had prior experience against Native Americans in the west). In 1901, Brig. General Jacob Smith vowed to turn the island of Samar into a "howling wilderness." He ordered: "I want no prisoners. I wish you to kill and burn, and the more you kill and burn the better you will please me. I want all persons killed who are capable of bearing arms in actual hostilities against the United States." The age limit was ten. Civilians were killed along with those bearing arms. Villages were burned and work animals slaughtered. Samar's population subsequently dropped by at least 50,000 over the next five months.[161] In other parts of the archipelago, the U.S. military deployed torturing techniques that would later resurface in Vietnam and Iraq. The primary one was the "water cure," known today as "water boarding." A. F. Miller of the 32nd Volunteer Infantry Regiment explained it: "Now, this is the way we give them the water cure. Lay them on their backs, a man standing on each hand and each foot, then put a round stick in the mouth and pour a pail of water in the mouth and nose, and if they don't give up pour in another pail. They swell up like toads. I'll tell you it's a terrible torture."[162]

The war officially lasted for three years, but so-called insurgents fighting for independence continued to resist occupation over the next decades. But if the denial of independence summoned anti-imperial resistance among some revolutionaries, the denial of statehood summoned resignation and resentment among others. In the Philippines, a small group of wealthy men in Manila (leaders of the Philippine Federal Party) had made statehood their goal. These elites were distinct from the revolutionaries in the countryside: They had quickly collaborated with American occupation under the impression that statehood was

---

[159] Hard (1930), p. 12.
[160] On the war, see among others Linn (2000), May (1991), and Shaw and Francia (2002).
[161] Quote from Coats (2008), p. 196.
[162] Quote from Pettigrew (1920), p. 285.

a real possibility.[163] Yet U.S. officials, not to mention Congress, consistently brushed away their demands for incorporation. After many failed attempts, and after some of them experienced the racism of their colonial masters first-hand at the St. Louis Exposition of 1904, their calls for statehood quieted. They astutely recognized the limits of America's empire of liberty and the expanse of its racism at once.[164]

In Puerto Rico, demands for statehood had also been registered from the very outset of military occupation. Juan Nieves summarized the attitude of his educated peers in 1898: "Puerto Rico, annexed, living under the shelter of the model Republic, will be a prosperous, happy and respected people." Nieves added that the very reason why the Puerto Ricans had been so quick to accept American occupation and turn their backs on Spain was because the people expected "to be constituted as a State, free, within the American Union."[165] Many of the Puerto Rican elite had had some knowledge of American continental expansion and were hopeful that the "grand empire... which began in California, Texas, and Florida" (as one of their leaders put it) would incorporate Puerto Rico similarly.[166] The Puerto Rican elite saw continuity between America's continental past and its overseas present, and their political demands followed. They believed, as the exceptionalist narrative would have them believe, that the United States would offer them an equal stake in the empire of liberty as an incorporated territory. What they did not foresee was the racism of their new imperial masters, which contributed to repeated rejections of their calls for statehood status. Subsequently, many Puerto Ricans became disillusioned with U.S. rule. Although they had never done so before, some even began calling for national independence.[167]

As neither national independence nor statehood was given to Puerto Rico and the Philippines, the two colonies were instead subjected to control by Washington. Both initially faced military governments whereby military governors ruled according to their whims. The subsequent civilian administrations concentrated power too. The governor general of the territories was invariably a white U.S. citizen appointed by the U.S. president. Some local representation was offered through executive councils and legislative assemblies, but the governor general and his peers from the mainland wielded ultimate control. These were autocratic regimes akin to the territorial governments in the west, yet there was no hope of later transitioning to statehood. Likewise, Puerto Ricans and Filipinos were denied rights afforded U.S. citizens. The Supreme Court and Congress decided that they were not U.S. citizens even though they were subject to the control of the U.S. government. Later, in 1916, Congress indeed passed the Jones Act, granting Puerto Ricans citizenship, but this was an

---

163 Federal Party of the Philippine Islands (1905). See more in Paredes (1988).
164 On the Exposition, see Kramer (1999).
165 Nieves (1898), pp. 9–10.
166 Rivero Méndez (1922), p. 411.
167 I discuss these matters in detail in Go (2008a).

emergency measure designed to shore up Puerto Rican support for the pending war with Germany.[168] And this was a very limited citizenship that was decidedly different from the kind white mainlanders enjoyed. It did not give Puerto Ricans a trial by jury system. It did not grant them the right to vote for the U.S. president, even though the president could send them to war. It did not give them an equal voice in Congress. And if it so desired, Congress could take away even this limited form of citizenship with the stroke of a pen.[169] Democracy, liberty, and citizenship had no place in this new American empire.

But was this *really* an empire? The relations between metropole and colony followed the rule of colonial difference: The United States treated the colonized as inferior, both discursively and by law. Furthermore, it monopolized political control. This was direct political control from above, constituting a formal colonial empire by any stretch of the definition. Still, some might accept that the United States had an overseas colonial empire but dismiss its importance or insist that it was not properly a colonial empire.

Some commentators, for example, admit of America's overseas empire but then insist that it was too small to be significant or worthy of comparison with other empires: America's overseas colonies were "too few and too small to constitute an overseas empire."[170] But this is muddy thinking. A proper comparison should not compare the U.S. empire in the late nineteenth century with the contemporaneous British empire. It should look at the U.S. empire in the late nineteenth century with the British empire before 1815, that is, when the British empire too was only developing and when the British state was only ascending in power. Doing so reveals less difference than similarity. Before 1815, the British empire was small too. As David Fieldhouse notes in his comparative survey, Britain's overseas territories "could not compare in size, wealth, population or civilization with such Spanish possessions as New Spain or Peru. The British colonies were young... and in 1715 they did not cover the eastern seaboard of North America let alone their hinterlands."[171] Are we to say that, because it was small, this was not an "empire"?

Even as the eighteenth century wore on, the British empire only consisted of scattered holdings on the east coast of the United States, a few Caribbean islands, and trading ports dotting parts of Asia and Africa (see Figure 1.4). This was not substantially larger than America's colonial empire in the early twentieth century. That empire included Alaska, Hawaii, the Philippines, Puerto Rico, Guam, Samoa, the Virgin Islands, the Panama Canal Zone, and a host of other areas temporarily occupied, such as Cuba, the Dominican Republic,

---

[168] Carrión (1983), p. 199.

[169] On issues of empire and citizenship regarding Puerto Rico, see Cabranes (1979), Duffy Burnett (2008), and Erman (2008).

[170] See Pagden (2005), p. 54; Rauchway (2006), pp. 13–15. See also Subrahmanyam (2006), p. 227, Maier (2006), Leopold (1966), and Winks (1997), p. 150.

[171] Fieldhouse (1982), p. 57.

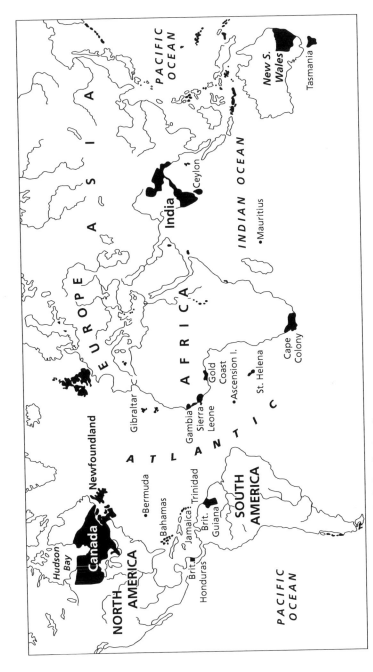

FIGURE 1.4. Map of the British Empire in 1815.

and Haiti. This list even excludes America's vast western territories. An astute article in the *New York Times* in 1925 was on the mark:

For the American Empire there is, indeed, no precedent.... Consider the unemotional geography of it. The area of the thirteen original States was 892,135 square miles. That was seven times the size of the United Kingdom.... The twentieth century is still young, yet already this formidable Bird of Prey has swooped upon the Philippines, Panama, Cuba, Haiti, and Porto Rico [sic]. And the territory of the United States has grown from 900,000 miles to four times that area. We may fairly ask: What conquests had Alexander the Great or Julius Caesar or Winston Churchill to match with these?[172]

Some have pointed to the lack of a colonial office to suggest that the U.S. empire was not really an empire proper.[173] It is true that the various overseas colonies were administered by different agencies in the aftermath of 1898. Alaska and Hawaii were run by the Interior Department, which had previously administered America's western territories. Puerto Rico and the Philippines were administered in the War Department by the Bureau of Insular Affairs. The Virgin Islands, Guam, and Samoa were run by the Navy Department. Meanwhile, the Bureau of Indian Affairs dealt with Native American issues. Nonetheless, there was some centralization. For example, the Bureau of Insular Affairs also had oversight over the Panama Canal Zone, the Dominican Republic occupation, and the Haitian occupation, just as it oversaw Puerto Rico and the Philippines. Furthermore, in 1934, President Roosevelt established the Division of Territories and Island Possessions in the Interior Department that finally centralized territorial administration. This became the colonial office proper.[174]

Even the British empire did not always have a strong centralized colonial office. The British Colonial Office was not established until the 1850s – that is, at the height of British supremacy and after centuries upon centuries of colonial expansion. Before that, no proper colonial office could be found. There was only a small office that had been part of the Secretary of State's office for War and Colonies. Even in the 1770s, after at least a century or more of overseas establishments, there was no centralized colonial apparatus: "[N]o central machinery for the government of the first British Empire existed."[175] Instead, there were different departments with no clear jurisdictions, and they did not even deal exclusively in colonial affairs.[176] Probably up until the 1850s at least, Parliament had much of the power (a fact that shows how American congressional involvement in dealing with America's empire is not unique).[177] So if we compare the two empires during their respective periods of hegemonic ascent (say, the United States in 1934 when the Division of Territories and Island Possessions was established, compared with the late 1700s when Britain

[172] Wilson (1925).
[173] See Leopold (1966) and Winks (1997) among others.
[174] Pomeroy (1944).
[175] Quoted in Marshall (2003), p. 173.
[176] Marshall (2005), p. 74; see also Davis and Huttenback (1988), pp. 12–15 and Manning (1965).
[177] Marshall (2003), pp. 178–9.

had no comparable office), it is the British empire that looks wanting, not the American empire.[178]

Still, it might be suggested that if this was indeed a proper American empire, it was nonetheless too short-lived to merit attention. Some have asserted that "the infatuation with empire subsided as quickly as it had arisen."[179] Supposedly, Americans no longer had the stomach for colonialism, even if they once did initially. "If for a brief period at the turn of the century things appeared differently," writes one political scientist, "the outlook quickly returned to normal."[180] If this were the case, exceptionalists would be right to brush American colonialism under the rug, sight unseen. It was just a deviation, the exception that proves the rule.

But what is evidence for the assertion? Part of it lies in the rise of "Wilsonianism" after 1912, when the Democratic Party took charge from the Republicans. The assumption is that President Woodrow Wilson represented anticolonialism. With his presidency, America's true anticolonial character finally triumphed. Did not Wilson's famous Fourteen Points speech in 1918 famously express America's exceptional character? Did it not affirm self-government for all peoples and portend a new American order in which the empires of old would pass away to be replaced by a world of equal nation-states?

Yet, Wilsonianism did not equal anticolonialism. When President Wilson spoke of "national self-determination," he did not mean it for all colonized peoples of the world. Strategically directed toward keeping the Allies in the war, his discourse of self-determination was meant only for southeast Europe. It was not directed at America's own dependencies.[181] Wilson's secretary of state, Robert Lansing, expressly stated that Wilson's principle of self-determination

---

[178] Even if we look at the British apparatus later, in 1892, the Colonial Office listed only 2,400 personnel as running the empire, whereas the total during the previous thirty years had been less than 1,000. This excludes the India office, which had in 1896 about 3,000 personnel, many of whom were Indian; hence Davis and Huttenback estimate that the empire was "managed by less than 6,000 souls!" Davis and Huttenback (1988), p. 14. It is also the case that there was an informal colonial service in the U.S. empire whereby officials circulated through and across the empire. Personnel from the Bureau of Insular Affairs had served in the colonies and vice-versa. Staff in the colonial states in Puerto Rico also served in the Philippines or Guam; colonial governors of the Virgin Islands also served in Samoa, and so on. In the imperial metropole, too, there was circulation and career making through America's imperial experience. Elihu Root, who oversaw colonial governments in Puerto Rico, the Philippines, Samoa, and Guam from his position as Secretary of War later became Secretary of State and won the Nobel Prize. William H. Taft was the first civil governor of the Philippine Islands and later became president. The man who would become President Harding had served as Chairman of the Senate Committee on Territories and Insular Possessions (ca. 1916). Felix Frankfurter, a law officer in the Bureau of Insular Affairs supervising America's colonial empire, later became a U.S. Supreme Court Justice. After serving as governor of the Philippines, Henry Stimson became the U.S. Secretary of State (1929–1933) and U.S. Secretary of War (1940–5) and oversaw the expansion of U.S. forces during the Second World War (and recommended the use of the atomic bomb on Japan).

[179] Ninkovich (1999), p. 25. See also Smith (1994), p. 149.

[180] Smith (1994), p. 149.

[181] Lynch (2002), Manela (2006), pp. 22–34.

did not apply to "races, peoples, or communities whose state of barbarism or ignorance deprive them of the capacity to choose intelligently their political affiliations."[182] Presumably this included America's overseas colonies, which is why Wilson did little to nothing to decolonize the U.S. empire. Wilson signed the Jones Act, giving citizenship to Puerto Ricans, but this was a practical exigency that had no impact on Puerto Ricans' existing colonial status. If anything, it perpetuated their subjection as an "unincorporated territory."[183] And two years earlier, in 1916, Wilson had initiated a military occupation of Haiti that lasted until 1935.

In fact, the Wilson administration *added* to America's colonial holdings. In 1917, the United States officially took possession of the Danish Virgin Islands. Under the threat of force, Lansing had persuaded Denmark to sell the islands to the United States for $25 million (the most it had ever spent on acquiring territory).[184] Subsequently, the U.S. government controlled the islands as a colonial dependency. The first bill introduced into the House to set up a colonial government vested all powers in the president. In House hearings over the bill, Congressman J. Willard Ragsdale noticed this and pointedly said to Secretary Lansing that the bill would essentially "create an absolute monarchy, without any supervision over the subject by either branch of Congress." To this, Lansing simply responded: "In the island of Guam we have that to-day, identically."[185] As a result, the 26,000 inhabitants of the Virgin Islands, the majority of whom were of African descent, were quickly subjected to the autocratic control of naval governors (some of whom had served in Samoa). When criticisms of U.S. rule surfaced from the so-called Negro press in the islands, governors responded by imprisoning editors or deporting them as "undesirable aliens."[186] All the while, they urged Washington to keep the existing system intact rather than grant territorial government or statehood. Governor Sumner Kittelle told President Warren in 1922 that "above all the white element [in the islands] must remain in the lead and in supreme control."[187] Such was the system that Wilson's presidency inaugurated, some twenty years after America's 1898 initial foray into colonial empire. Colonialism was hardly a passing phase; it was enduring rather than abjured.

Other evidence has been culled to suggest that America's colonialism was fleeting. For instance, the United States eventually granted independence to the Philippines. According to this story, the United States took the Philippines and other small colonies but did not really mean to stay long. So, after realizing it didn't have the stomach for formal European-style empire, it quickly gave its empire away.[188] Yet this is hardly special. Britain eventually gave independence

---

[182] Lansing quoted in Manela (2006), p. 24.
[183] Gatell (1960–1961); Fernandez (1996), pp. 62–77.
[184] Boyer (1983), pp. 83–4.
[185] United States House of Representatives Committee on Foreign Affairs (1917), p. 6.
[186] Lewis (1972), pp. 52–3.
[187] Gov. Kittelle to Harding, 27 Feb, 1922, quoted in Boyer (1983), pp. 115–16.
[188] See Ravenal (2009) and Schwabe (1986), p. 17, among others.

to colonies like India. Is this to say that colonialism for Britain was a passing phase too?[189] More to the point, the granting of independence to the Philippines was not preordained. American officials did not plan for its independence from the get-go; nor did they easily cut and run. When soon-to-be President Harding was chairman of the Senate Committee on Territories and Insular Possessions in 1916, he insisted that the United States could not withdraw from the Philippines: "I think it is impossible for us to honorably withdraw."[190] As late as 1922, Franklin Roosevelt wrote to his friend Leonard Wood in the Philippines: "The vast majority of people in this country, I have always been certain, understand that complete independence for all these peoples is not to be thought of for many years to come."[191] That same year, Secretary of War John W. Weeks spoke for himself and President Harding, saying to a New York newspaper, "I am not in favor of granting immediate independence to the Philippines, and the President is not."[192] In 1927, the Philippine legislature passed a bill asking for a plebiscite that would enable the Philippine people to express their views on whether they should get independence. The governor general at the time, Leonard Wood, vetoed the bill, and President Coolidge gave his wholehearted support of the veto.[193] Nor was this against the wishes of the American public. Gallup polls in 1938 showed that 76 percent were against granting independence to the Philippines.[194] All the while, members of the Philippine political class clamored for concrete moves toward independence, sending independence missions to Washington in 1919, 1922, 1923, 1924, and 1925. These were to no avail.[195] The U.S. government eventually did pass the Hawes-Cutting Act in 1933, which declared that the Philippines would receive independence in ten years' time.[196] This, however, was against the desires of President Hoover and his administration. And those who did support the bill did not act on behalf of America's anticolonial values or Wilsonian principles. Supporters of the bill were largely farm and labor lobbies who, faced with the Great Depression, wanted Philippine independence to halt economic competition from Philippine products and workers.[197]

This suggests that the United States has hardly been the reluctant imperialist. To be sure, the *only* colony of all America's unincorporated territories to receive independence in this period was the Philippines. The rest – including Puerto

---

[189] If we consider the actual amount of time India was subject to Crown control (as opposed to the control of the East India Company), the time is not that different from America's rule over the Philippines. India was directly ruled by the Crown from 1857 to 1946.

[190] Forbes (1945), p. 374.

[191] Roosevelt quoted in Dulles and Ridinger (1955), p. 3.

[192] Forbes (1945), p. 374.

[193] Ibid., p. 376.

[194] Gallup poll reported in Gallup and Robinson (1938) p. 389.

[195] Churchill (1983).

[196] Hoover vetoed the bill in 1932. The U.S. Senate overrode the veto in 1933. This bill did not pass the Philippine Senate, and so the actual bill that ensured Philippine independence was the 1934 Tydings-McDuffie Act that was nearly identical to the Hawes-Cutting Act.

[197] Friend (1963), pp. 511–14.

Rico, Guam, Samoa, and the U.S. Virgin Islands – continued to be tied to
the United States in various respects through World War II. If the empire
constructed after 1898 was merely a passing fancy, and if independence for the
Philippines is to be taken as proof, we would expect America's other colonies
to be decolonized as well. But they were not. And this was in spite of continued
protests from the islands' inhabitants. A petition to Congress from political
elites in Guam in 1917 requested citizenship and the end of arbitrary U.S. rule,
but it was ignored. Similar petitions were sent in 1925, 1929, 1933, 1947, and
1950. All were dismissed or ignored.[198] Similar requests emerged in Samoa,
one of which in the 1920s had led to a violent rebellion. But these were ignored
too.[199] Americans in Washington remained deaf to the voices of their imperial
subjects just as King George had been to those Americans' forefathers.

This is one among many facets of America's rise to global dominance that
has been too long obscured in traditional stories of American uniqueness and
exceptionalism. As seen in this chapter, there were many ways in which the
United States was imperial during its period of ascent. All of them reveal that
the U.S. empire was not a deviation from its British predecessor but a worthy
variant that often drew inspiration from it. It remains to be seen whether the
U.S. empire has been as special, unique, or different as exceptionalist thought
would have us believe.

[198] See Perez Hattori (1995) and Hofschneider (2001).
[199] Chappell (2000).

2

Colonial Rules

In no other Oriental country, whether ruled by Asiatics or by Europeans, is there anything approaching the amount of individual liberty or self-government which our rule has brought to the Philippines.

– U.S. President Theodore Roosevelt (1902)[1]

The truth is that the Americans are learning in the Philippines some of the things with which England has become familiar in India and in Egypt.

– Editorial in the *Times* of London (1910)[2]

The United States empire up to World War II does not easily fit the frame forged by traditional exceptionalist thought. Contrary to exceptionalism's portrayals, America's westward expansion entailed imperialism, and its overseas expansion resulted in a formal empire stretching from Puerto Rico and the Virgin Islands to the Philippines and Samoa. We have seen how, even in terms of size and bureaucracy, this empire was not fundamentally different from Britain's empire during the latter's comparable phase of development. The Council on Foreign Relations in the 1920s noted this similarity:

Like Great Britain, we have reached the point of rapid city growth and a relatively diminishing agricultural population. In colonial possessions, in the relations of an advanced country to countries less "civilized" or backward, in the export of capital for foreign investment and in the competition for raw materials and foreign markets, we have moved toward the English situation. While our problems may be different in detail, they involve us in the study and settlement of questions often similar to those of Great Britain. Panama has many resemblances to Suez, and our relation to Panama is in many respects analogous to that of Great Britain to Egypt. It was constantly on the tongues of the Englishmen at the Peace Conference that many of our new problems in the Philippines resembled their own in Egypt and the Far East. The wide geographical distribution of our territorial problems – . . . the Philippines, Alaska to Panama – puts us at last in

---

[1] London *Times* Nov. 21, 1902, p. 3
[2] London *Times* Nov. 8, 1910, p. 5.

the same general position that Great Britain has long occupied; that is, we impinge upon most of the major problems of the world.[3]

Yet is this to say that the U.S. empire was exactly the same as the British empire?

The United States had an empire, but it may be the case that it was special and unique nonetheless – perhaps even exceptional. Proponents and practitioners of America's overseas empire often made this very claim. While admitting that the United States was an empire, they insisted that the new overseas empire would be distinct for its benign and liberal treatment of colonized subjects. "In no other Oriental country, whether ruled by Asiatics or by Europeans," declared President Roosevelt in 1902, "is there anything approaching the amount of individual liberty or self-government which our rule has brought to the Philippines."[4] The United States, in other words, may have seized colonies, but it nonetheless treated its colonial peoples with a unique liberal approach. This view persists in exceptionalist thought today. Presumably, what makes the United States exceptional is not its lack of colonial empire but its particular *type* of colonial empire. Traditional exceptionalism represses the word empire, but this revised exceptionalism proclaims a distinctly American imperialism – a unique liberal empire or "liberal imperialism." Let us call it *liberal exceptionalism*.

There are three steps to this mode of thought. First, admit that the United States forged an overseas colonial empire at the turn of the twentieth century. The fact that the United States took the Philippines and other islands cannot be easily dismissed. Second, while admitting empire, demonstrate that this empire was uniquely liberal and benign. Americans took overseas colonies but ended up democratizing them, teaching other peoples the ways of self-government, and spreading American doctrines of freedom and liberty.[5] Finally, explain *why* the U.S. empire had this liberal character by reference to America's democratic traditions, values, and institutions. The U.S. empire has been distinctly democratizing, liberal, and tutelary rather than repressive because that is how America does things. It is a reflection of America's unique style and national character.[6]

The purpose of this chapter is to further interrogate this version of exceptionalism. Might liberal exceptionalist thought best capture the distinctiveness of American empire? The chapter begins by discussing liberal exceptionalism's model: the Philippines. Scholars and contemporaries alike have referred to U.S. colonialism in the Philippines as the example *par excellence* of liberal exceptionalism. As we will see, this is not without reason. But although we begin in

[3] Howland (1928), p. 19.
[4] London *Times* Nov. 21, 1902, p. 3.
[5] Boot (2003), p. 363.
[6] "The United States...having fought a revolutionary war to gain its independence of Britain...continued to hold to certain principles which...injected republican assumptions into colonial relationships." Winks (1997), p. 152.

the Philippines, the rest of the chapter looks elsewhere. A proper interrogation of liberal exceptionalism demands a wider comparative view. Accordingly, the chapter begins in the Philippines but later takes turns through Puerto Rico, Guam, and India – and other places in between. The tour will show us the limits of liberal exceptionalism. Where colonialism does appear so exceptional, this chapter will show us why. Ultimately we will arrive at a working theory of colonial regimes and an explanation of the diversity within empires that exceptionalist discourse covers up.

Liberal Exceptionalism and the Philippines

As seen in Chapter 1, when the United States acquired its overseas colonial empire at the turn of the twentieth century, many Americans at the time were ready to admit that the United States had a new empire. "Empire" was not necessarily a dirty word. But although many Americans admitted empire, they also crafted a distinctly American imperial identity. Scholars, statesmen, and officials proposed that the United States was better suited than Europeans for taking up the imperial mantle. Herein lie the origins of liberal exceptionalism. Notice the writings of Bernard Moses (an academic from California who later served in the Philippines) and Woodrow Wilson (then an academic whom colonial officials often cited). Moses reviewed the history of British colonialism in Asia and Africa and found that it had been "reckless and tyrannical." Because of England's monarchical tradition, it had failed to live up to the promise of developing the "lesser races." In contrast, the United States was special. Because of its unique democratic history, Americans were endowed with a liberal character unmatched by any other. Thus, only the United States would be able to construct a "wise and beneficient [sic] governmental authority over a rude people," and offer its imperial subjects an "impulse and guidance toward the attainment of a higher form of life and larger liberty."[7] The United States would be an empire, but unlike other empires it would use its power benevolently, taking up the task of transforming, uplifting, and democratizing foreign peoples. "If America has any mission outside of her continental limits, it is not to preserve among less developed peoples such institutions and customs as make for bondage and social stagnation, but to put in their place the ideas that have made for freedom, and the laws by which this nation has been enabled to preserve its freedom."[8]

Wilson similarly insisted that democracy was an essential part of America's being, a "thing of principle and custom and [our] nature" that is "admirably expressed" in "our institutions."[9] This American character derived from America's historical ties to Britain, according to Wilson, but because of America's lack of monarchy and feudalism it was more purely democratic. For this

---

[7] Moses (1905), p. 7.
[8] Ibid., p 18.
[9] Wilson (1901), p. 289.

reason, the United States was not only a more perfect union, but also a more perfect liberal empire. Only the United States could "moderate the process [of imperialism] in the interests of liberty; to impart to the peoples thus driven out upon the road of change... our principles of self-help; teach them order and self-control; impart to them... the drill and habit of law and obedience."[10]

The model of this liberal exceptionalism soon appeared: the Philippines. Of course, proponents of liberal exceptionalism could not point to the Philippine-American War as evidence for America's special liberal imperialism. The brutality of the war betrayed the self-proclaimed image. Rather, liberal exceptionalists pointed to colonial policies on the ground as the war waned. The idea, as President McKinley put it, was to "develop, to civilize, to educate, to train in the science of self-government."[11] This was a mission of so-called democratic tutelage. The United States would subdue the rebellion but then institute a colonial regime that would provide elections and political offices so that Filipinos would learn the ways of democratic self-government. In place of bullets would come ballots. President McKinley's instructions to the Philippine Commission (who were to help plan and run the new colonial government) thus insisted that the commission should institute policies that would aid in the Filipinos' political "development" according to the "traditions" and political ideas "from which we have benefited." This is what would distinguish American empire from the "tyrannical" empires of European powers.[12]

On the ground, the commission put the plan into action. They insisted that theirs would be a tutelary government whereby the colonized would receive an "education" in the ways of American-style political ideas, institutions, and values under America's "strong and guiding hand."[13] In part, this involved building a public school system that would offer civics classes for the "ignorant" and "credulous" masses.[14] Another part of the project was a so-called practical political education for the more powerful strata of society.[15] The presumption was that the Filipinos, as a result of centuries of Spanish rule, had not yet learned how to govern themselves in accordance with the principles of democracy. "They are as incapable of forming a just conception of civil liberty," said Senator William Dudley Foulke of Indiana, "as we are of understanding the institutions which prevail upon the planet Mars. How can they know it when they have never seen anything like it?"[16] The Filipino elite were capable of learning; they had just not yet learned. A policy of "practical political education" would fill the presumed gap, giving the elite the civilizing influences that, supposedly, Spanish rule had not provided.

---

[10] Ibid., pp. 289, 295–8.

[11] McKinley quoted in Wheeler-Bennett (1929), p. 506.

[12] McKinley quoted in Forbes (1928), p. 443.

[13] United States War Department (1899), p. 24.

[14] Taft (1908), p. 24.

[15] Ibid, p. 24.

[16] Hon. William Dudley Foulke of Indiana, "The Filipinos. Their Fitness for Self-Government Judged in Light of Much Testimony," pamphlet, n.d., WP.

The colonial state itself was to serve the educating process. In small towns across the islands, American authorities first permitted elective offices and other minor municipal posts to be filled by Filipinos. Bernard Moses wrote in his diary: "[W]e are trying to make the town governments schools of politics in which the people may acquire some knowledge of self-government, and make their first attempts in political self-control."[17] Governor Taft and other officials like Dean Worcester often referred to Tocqueville to claim that the municipal governments would "afford a school of politics for the education of the people in the duties of good citizenship."[18] American authorities also constructed a civil service to give native bureaucrats "a political education which will show them the possibility of the honest administration of government."[19] Later, in 1907, the commission established a national legislative assembly, the Philippine Assembly, manned by elected Filipino officials. This was to allow Filipino legislators to "receive instruction in the principles and methods of government . . . in the practical school of experience" and to learn such "lessons" as the "American method of a strong executive separate from the assembly."[20] Elections with an initially restricted suffrage were to aid the ostensible curriculum.

We must not be mistaken. This was still a colonial government. Filipinos could vote and participate, but American authorities, appointed by the U.S. president, retained ultimate control. The Philippine Assembly was more like a lower house, not a full Congress with two houses; American authorities retained veto power. But although this was a colonial government, it was nonetheless a distinct tutelary colonial government. U.S. authorities were in charge, but they were to offer "object lessons" in the ways of good government. The stated goal was that the colonized would participate and learn and would be ultimately transformed into American types – even if they were not to be transformed into "Americans" proper. By being granted some amount of governmental participation, Filipinos would get the proper training and experience in American styled-government so that they might one day rule themselves. Colonial policies and the very structure of the colonial state followed from this overarching principle. With elections, political offices, a legislature, and other semblances of democracy – this was a seemingly liberal and unique colonial state.

It is exactly because of these features of U.S. colonialism that liberal exceptionalists upheld the Philippines as their proof and model. William Washburn, chairman of the Philippine Civil Service Board, insisted that U.S. colonialism was better than British colonialism because of its unique liberal features: "[N]ever before has there been instituted a scheme of colonial government so beneficent and humanitarian. . . . There is no precedent in history."[21] William Cameron Forbes, a member of the Philippine Commission and later governor

[17] Moses, Diary, Part 3, May 30, 1901 (BM).
[18] Taft quoted in *Manila Times*, 31 Jan. 1901, p.1.
[19] Taft to Hoyt, Sept. 8, 1900 (CE, I, 1.16).
[20] United States Philippine Commission (1900), pp. 92–3.
[21] Washburn quoted in Kramer (2003), p. 76.

general, claimed that whereas European colonialisms were driven by "the profit motive," American rule in the Philippines was guided by "altruism" and was "designed solely for the welfare of the Philippine people." Forbes even claimed that when European rulers later engaged in civilizing missions, they simply "followed the example set by the United States."[22] In the 1930s, historian Julius Pratt added: "Probably no group of men in history ever took so seriously the task of administering colonies in the interest of their inhabitants as the best of the American officials... [who] worked to bring the Filipinos to a higher level of health, prosperity, education, and political capacity." "The Philippines," he concluded, "constitute Exhibit A among projects of benevolent imperialism."[23]

Liberal exceptionalist discourse today continues this long tradition. Some political scientists have claimed that America's special "mission" has been to "export democracy" to the world and point to the Philippines as one of their examples. "Compared to the Europeans," says Stanley Karnow in his Pulitzer Prize–winning book, "the Americans were far more liberal politically.... [They] encouraged elections soon after their arrival, so that the Filipinos had a national legislature, the first in Asia, as early as 1907.... This was a time when the British, despite their own democratic creed, were detaining Indian dissidents without trial and the French, for all their dedication to the principles of liberty, equality, and fraternity, were summarily executing Vietnamese nationalists."[24] President George W. Bush played the theme too. In October of 2003, he visited Manila and gave a speech to the Philippine Congress, referring to the Philippines as "America's oldest ally in Asia" and suggesting that America was responsible for making the Philippines into the "the first democratic nation in Asia." "America," he said, "is proud of its part in the great story of the Filipino people."[25]

Comparing Colonialisms

So how might we assess liberal exceptionalism? It would seem difficult to refute the fact that the U.S. regime in the Philippines had a tutelary character. The United States did set up local governments and elections and gave Filipinos some amount of participation in the government. Even when historians attack liberal exceptional discourse about the Philippines because it seems to promote U.S. imperialism, they do not refute the facts it enlists. For instance, the *Wall Street Journal* writer Max Boot refers to tutelage in the Philippines to claim that "compared with the grasping old imperialism of the past, America's 'liberal imperialism' pursues far different, and more ambitious, goals. It aims to instill

---

[22] Forbes (1928), II, pp. 391–2, 394–5.
[23] Pratt (1934), pp. 277–8.
[24] Karnow (1989), p. 13; see also Smith (1994), p. 45.
[25] Remarks by the President to the Philippine Congress, Manila, Philippines, Office of the Press Secretary, Oct. 18, 2003, http://www.whitehouse.gov/news/releases/2003/10/20031018-12.html. Accessed 1/03/2005.

democracy in lands that have known tyranny."[26] In response, critics charge Boot with promoting U.S. imperialism but not with getting the facts wrong. One such critic concedes: "As for the claims that Filipinos fared much better under U.S. imperialism than their counterparts elsewhere did under European colonialism, and that the Philippines was the first Asian state to establish a national legislature (1907), all are true."[27] Faced with the fact of American colonialism's tutelary elections, native offices, and promotion of eventual self-government in the Philippines, it would seem that even the most virulent critics of exceptionalist thought have few if any counterarguments to make.

Lacking amidst these debates, however, is a comparative understanding. A comparison would be telling. The underlying claim of liberal exceptionalism is that America's colonial regime in the Philippines was fundamentally different from other colonialisms. A colonial state replete with elective political offices and liberal native participation; a program of training and teaching colonized subjects the ways of democracy; the idea of civilizing and uplifting; and the rhetoric of eventual self-government – all such things, manifest in the Philippines, were supposedly unique to U.S. colonialism. But was this really so unique?

British observers were nonplussed. In 1902, a London *Times* article commented on a report regarding the Philippines by U.S. Secretary of War Elihu Root. Root's report had boasted that the U.S. colonial administration was "critically involved in creating a good government" in the islands. It pointed out that the United States had set up municipal offices with elections and native participation, that it was constructing a public education system, and that it had set up a civil service – all the usual things that presumably distinguish U.S. colonialism from other types of colonialism. But the *Times* article saw all of this as evidence of similarity to British colonialism rather than difference: "This outline and the extracts from the report [of Root] will show how completely the United States has departed from the old Spanish methods of colonial government and how closely it has assimilated to those employed in British colonies."[28] A 1910 piece in the *Times* made similar points. It claimed that America's experience in the Philippines was little else than a reproduction of Britain's own experience: "[T]he more the American lives in the Philippines and comes to understand the Orient the better he comprehends, and the more he is drawn to sympathize with, the work which Great Britain has done, and is doing, in the world."[29]

What was all this about? Coming from British observers, we may rightly wonder if the boasts about British benevolence had any substance. But at the very least, they suggest that we should take a closer look at British colonialism in order to assess the comparable uniqueness of U.S. colonialism in the

---

[26] Boot (2003), p. 261.
[27] Bankoff (2002), p. 180.
[28] London *Times*, Dec. 26, 1901, p. 8.
[29] London *Times*, Dec. 2, 1910, p. 5.

Philippines.[30] Contemporary proponents of America's liberal exceptionalism themselves looked to the British example, if only to craft a difference. As we have seen, Moses and Wilson were among the proponents who classified the United States as different from Britain. So too were policy advisors like the members of the Schurman Commission (named after Jacob Schurman, the head of the commission). In their report to President McKinley in 1899, the commission concluded that, in places like India, British rule had been too autocratic. "The British Government [in India] has entire control of legislation and the administration is carried on by officers under the control of that Government.... [A]s the government is imposed upon the people from without, it is inimical to the habit of self-government, and this... is its fatal defect. For this reason it must be rejected as a model for the Philippines."[31]

So who was right? Surely pro-exceptionalists like Moses, Wilson, or the Schurman Commission can be forgiven for highlighting Britain's tyrannical exercises of power over colonies like India. The violent response to the Indian Mutiny from 1857 to 1859, when India was still under the official control of the East India Company, is but one indication of the brutality and terror of British rule. On the other hand, although pro-exceptionalists may have been correct in pointing to British tyranny, they were not entirely right in denying British liberalism. There is enough in the history of British rule in India to suggest that British colonialism had not been as "inimical to the habit of self-government" as the Schurman Commission believed.

In fact, just as Americans violently repressed the Philippine revolution and followed it up with tutelary institutions for the defeated Filipinos, so too did the British follow up their repression of the Indian Mutiny with widened participation for Indians and the construction of an incipient tutelary state. In 1861, soon after the British government declared sovereignty over India upon taking control from the British East India Company, Parliament passed the Indian Councils Act. The act changed the nature of the Legislative Council that had been established earlier under Company rule. Although the council remained advisory, providing support and input to the governor general, its membership was enlarged to include Indians. The first session of the council under the new act included the Maharaja of Patiala, Dinkar Rao, and Deo Narain Singh. Not long afterward, British officials took steps to decentralize local government functions, giving Indian officials increasing fiscal responsibility and control over local services. The first result was the creation of municipal governments across India. Whereas British district commissioners previously – during Company rule – ran the show, the new municipal governments were run largely by native Indians who were put in charge of local taxation and services such as roads, education, and health.[32] Subsequent developments saw more

[30] For more on cross-imperial discussions and exceptionalism among Britons and Americans, see Kramer (2003).

[31] United States Philippine Commission (1900), I, p. 105.

[32] Tinker (1968), pp. 35–47.

devolution. In 1870, Lord Mayo, who had recently been appointed Viceroy of India by Disraeli, passed a Resolution on Provincial Finance that decentralized financial functions even more.[33] Lord Mayo even set up local elections in some districts, such as in the Central Provinces and the North-West Provinces. This was decades before Americans established elections in the Philippines.

Admittedly, these steps were cautious and limited. The Indians chosen to serve on the Legislative Council were picked for their "loyalty and their conservative sentiments."[34] And Lord Mayo's devolution policies were partly dictated by practical necessity. As the British Crown had just inherited a colonial regime from the East India Company in dire financial straits, devolving responsibility for local finances was fiscally expedient. Still, the effect was to give the colonized participation in governance, pushing the colonial state in India in a more liberal direction than American exceptionalist discourse allows.[35] In fact, officials often fashioned their policies in tutelary rhetoric, suggesting that they would serve an educating purpose leading to eventual self-government.[36] Lord Mayo said his policies would "afford opportunities for the development of self-government, for strengthening municipal institutions, and for the association of natives and Europeans, to a greater extent than before, in the administration of affairs."[37] He further explained in private correspondence:

> I have gradually to commence the establishment of native municipal institutions.... Were we to quit India tomorrow we should leave whole Provinces in which would not be found a man capable of administrating [sic] the affairs of a small district. It can only be a work of time; and, as in other countries, to the growth of municipal institutions has generally been traced the powers of self-government, so in India do I believe that we shall find the best assistance from natives in our administration ... by quietly entrusting as many as we can with local responsibility, and instructing them in the management of their own district affairs.[38]

In fact, this discourse of native capacity and tutelary self-government extended back to the 1850s, when some Parliament members had clamored for native participation in the Legislative Council.[39] In 1858, Gladstone held that "India is to be governed for India and as far as may be proved practicable by India."[40] In the 1860s, men like Henry Fawcett and John Bright in the House of Commons insisted that Indians should be given more control over the reins of the

---

[33] Richard Southwell Bourke, the sixth Earl of Mayo, was of the Conservative Party. For Mayo's resolution of 1870, see Venkatarangaiya and Pattabhiram (1969), pp. 96–103.

[34] Metcalf (1964), p. 267.

[35] Venkatarangaiya and Pattabhiram (1969), pp. 96–7. The participation of Indians on the Legislative Council was not that different from the Filipino participation on the Philippine Commission during U.S. rule. Filipinos were allowed to hold seats, but they were always outnumbered by Americans and the American governor general wielded final say.

[36] Haynes (1991), p. 105.

[37] Quoted in Venkatarangaiya and Pattabhiram (1969), p. 10.

[38] Mayo as quoted in Gopal (1965), p. 93.

[39] Metcalf (1964), p. 262.

[40] Hammond and Foot (1953), p. 77.

state. Bright held the view that British rule over India was only temporary and hoped that British policies would be aimed at preparing Indians for full self-government.[41]

Evident here is a strong liberal tradition that held that human nature was the same everywhere and that people could be transformed if need be. No doubt, this view could at once legitimate empire and repudiate it.[42] For their part, British liberals in the nineteenth century applied it to India to justify continued colonial control while also pointing to a more tutelary type of rule. Indians were to take part in governance so that they could learn to eventually govern themselves. Governor General John Lawrence was positive about the Indians' capacity for some amount of self-government. "The people of this country," he said, "are perfectly capable of administering their own local affairs."[43] Samuel Laing, who had helped initiate the decentralization process, was similarly positive. Outlining his fiscal plans for colonial governance in 1862, he said, "India is not altogether devoid of that spirit of self-government which characterizes the Anglo-Saxon."[44] The same view of Indian capacity had been expressed in James Mill's classic *History of British India*. Mill had argued that Indians were not interminably inferior; rather they could undergo "stages of progress," get "training" in self-government, and develop the "active self-helping character" necessary for self-rule.[45]

This liberal colonialism (which, like the American approach to the Philippines, treated Indians and India as potentially self-governing) was only one approach among others. An alternative was simply to maintain the status quo, ruling through local princes who commanded obedience from putatively docile Indian subjects. That approach implied a different view of Indians than the liberal one; it implied they were naturally and interminably inferior, hence incapable of self-government.[46] But the liberal view was dominant and persistent enough to be a serious contender. It was strong enough for journals like *The Economist* to declare, in 1857 at the height of the Indian Mutiny, that the British people had to choose "whether in future ... we are to rule our Asiatic subjects with strict and generous justice, wisely and beneficently, as their natural and indefensible superiors ... or whether we are to regard [them] ... as our equal fellow citizens, fit to be entrusted with the functions of self-government, ripe (or to be ripened) for British institutions, likely to appreciate the blessings of our rule, and, therefore, to be gradually prepared, as our own working classes are preparing, for a full participation in the privileges of representative assemblies, trial by jury, and all the other palladia of English liberty."[47]

---

[41] Cumpston (1961), p. 282.

[42] Metcalf (1994), p. 29. Pitts shows that this was part of a larger movement including in France on liberal imperial thought. Pitts (2005). On British liberalism and empire in India, see esp. Metcalf (1994), pp. 28–65 and Mehta (1999).

[43] Quoted in Tinker (1968), p. 36.

[44] Venkatarangaiya and Pattabhiram (1969), p. 96.

[45] Mill quoted in Metcalf (1994), p. 33.

[46] Haynes (1991), p. 104.

[47] Quoted in Metcalf (1994), p. 58.

British colonialism oscillated between these two approaches.[48] From 1876 to 1880, when the Conservative Party led by Disraeli appointed Lord Lytton to India, the conservative approach was remounted. Lytton was more intent on securing India's frontiers and enlisting the support of Indian notables (the "powerful aristocracy") than expanding opportunities for self-government.[49] Yet the liberal option remained potent in the late nineteenth century. Its clearest expression came with Lytton's successor, Lord Ripon.

Ripon had served in the House of Lords in the 1850s. Appointed to India by W. E. Gladstone, he immediately embarked on a series of liberal reforms. He repealed the Vernacular Press Act that Lord Lytton had previously imposed. The act had meant to restrict nationalist inflammations in the vernacular press; Ripon felt this was antithetical to the development of representative institutions.[50] He also appointed the very first Indian to serve as acting chief justice at High Court. In conjunction with the Ilbert Bill that had passed under Ripon's watch, this meant that British planters, settlers, or any citizens could find themselves in court to be tried by an Indian. As Ripon explained to Gladstone, this was all part of his policy "of governing India for herself and not for Englishmen."[51]

Ripon's other major advance was to more firmly institutionalize the elective principle for local governments. Lord Mayo had allowed for limited elections in certain districts, but Ripon now insisted that they be spread throughout India. Ripon had originally hoped to introduce elections for the Legislative Council, making it more akin to British Parliament and thereby advancing "the political education of the people...along the same road of extended self-government."[52] But as this idea was considered too radical in London, Ripon turned to local elections as an alternative step. He explained in a memo that introducing local elections across India was part of his plan to "extend the principle of popular representation and...make a larger use of it as an instrument of political education of the Indians."[53] His Resolution on Local Self-Government of May 18, 1882, was the result. It required that at least two-thirds of members on all local legislative bodies should be elected nonofficials (i.e. not from the civil service), thereby enabling more Indians to hold office and vote for their own members. It further legislated that chief executive officers should meddle as little as possible with the local legislative bodies, thereby giving them ample autonomy for "the purposes of training the natives to manage their own affairs." Ripon modeled this part of the resolution on municipal bodies in England.[54]

Ripon's reforms were received positively by educated Indian leaders like S. N. Banerjea, G. K. Gokhale, Pheroze Shah Mehta, and Raja Peari Mohan

---

[48] See Scott (1995) for an early theoretical statement on British colonial "governmentality."

[49] Martin (1967), p. 70.

[50] Ripon quoted in Gopal (1965), pp. 144–5.

[51] Ripon to Gladstone, March 24, 1883, RP as quoted in Moore (1966), p. 39.

[52] Ripon to W.E. Forster, May 26, 1881, RP in Seal (1968), p. 152.

[53] Ripon's note, April 27, 1882, RP as quoted in Rahman (1975), p. 56.

[54] Mathur (1972), p. 184.

Mukerji.[55] The Committee of the Bombay Branch of East India, led by Vishwanath N. Mandlik, further offered gratitude. In 1883, the committee addressed Ripon's ally Sir E. Baring in 1883, who had helped Ripon with the policy:

We gratefully acknowledge the action of the Government of India in carrying out the principle of entrusting Natives of India with a constantly increasing share in the administration of the country.... In the same spirit, we feel great pleasure in being able to testify to the value of the assistance you have rendered in the noble work of securing to the people the right of local self-government, a measure which needs only to be loyally persevered in on the broad and generous principles laid down in the famous resolution of the present Government of India, to render it the vehicle of immense good to the people, by the gradual development of their public spirit and the steady growth of their political education.[56]

This is not to say that Ripon's policies were entirely progressive.[57] His election policy put high restrictions on the suffrage. In some provinces, the municipal electorate was less than 2 percent of the urban population. In Bengal, it was closer to 5 percent.[58] Therefore, only the more privileged of the population held office.[59] But the point here is to offer a comparison with U.S. tutelary programs in the Philippines, not to laud or denigrate Ripon's politics. The comparison reveals more similarity than exceptionalist discourse admits. As Ripon's policy put high restrictions on suffrage, so did American officials in the Philippines also impose high restrictions. For Philippine municipal elections, the electorate was initially restricted to the point where only 2.4 percent of the population could vote.[60] In terms of office holding, American rule in the Philippines was hardly more open to native participation. Indians had a surprisingly large presence in the colonial government. From 1867 onward, the percentage of natives in the highest paid offices of public service slowly increased from 65 percent in 1867 to 67 in 1877 and to 71 percent in 1887.[61] In the Philippines, although exceptionalists boast of wide Filipino participation in government, the percentages are not radically different. In 1903, the percentage of non-Americans in the higher administrative posts of the government was close to 72 percent. Over the course of the subsequent decade, it fell to

---

[55] Tinker (1968), p. 58.

[56] Bombay Public Meeting (1883), p. 1.

[57] Nor should we uncritically praise British rule in India for being benevolent or generous. The so-called Cambridge School of Indian studies has been accused of this by Guha (1997), esp. pp. 84–95.

[58] Tinker (1968), p. 50. Even in England at the time the working classes had not yet the franchise.

[59] See ibid., pp. 50–1; Mathur (1972), pp. 189–95; Gould (1974).

[60] May (1980), p. 46.

[61] Seal (1968), Appendix 3, p. 361. These figures in fact underestimate Indian participation because they refer only to the total positions in the highest paid jobs (e.g. at Rs 75 per month or higher). "Natives" refer to Hindus, Muslims, and "Eurasians"; if "Eurasians" are not included as "natives" than the Hindu and Muslim share is about half of the total posts.

as low as 66 percent.[62] Perhaps the only major difference between American tutelary elections and offices in the Philippines and those institutionalized by the British in India is that the British enacted their policies decades *before* the United States took the Philippines. America's putatively liberal colonialism in the Philippines was not as unprecedented as exceptionalism's proponents insist.

The Diversity of Empire

Is it fair, however, to compare U.S. rule in the Philippines with British rule in India? It might be that British liberalism in India was unique rather than representative of Britan's colonial empire. To be sure, Britain enacted a very different type of colonial regime in other territories. Fiji is instructive. After he was appointed as the first governor in 1874, Arthur Hamilton Gordon instituted a colonial state in Fiji that looked nothing like liberal British India. There were no local governments modeled after British towns and no elections or councils meant to be imitations of British councils at home. Instead, Gordon's goal was to keep intact "customary" life in Fiji. Part of this meant constructing a colonial state that deployed the preexisting system of Fijian chieftanship. The chiefs would rule local populations according to so-called native tradition; British officials would simply dictate from above. The goal was preservation rather than education or transformation. Native institutions, customs, and structures were to be maintained rather than adjusted or transformed. As Gordon himself later put it, his goal was to "abstain from seeking hastily to replace native institutions by unreal imitations of European models," and was instead meant to "seize the spirit in which native institutions had been framed." The avowed goal was "to preserve the traditional laws and customs, to maintain in authority the local chiefs, and in all possible ways to utilize the existing native organization."[63] Thus, rather than try to force an "affectation of European ways and habits," British rule should "maintain existing native laws and customs."[64]

This was a regime of "indirect rule." It was closer to the conservative option in India and was akin to the strategy of ruling through Indian princes. The imperative: Do not transform native institutions but rather preserve and use them. Of course, exactly what was "native" or not often had to be invented on the spot by local chiefs or sometimes by British authorities themselves. But whether truly native or not, the point is that British officials made an effort to sustain what was perceived as "native" and "traditional" rather than replace them with Anglo-British culture. Nicholas Thomas describes this type of colonial governmentality: "[T]his was essentially a segregationist rather than an assimilationist vision: the emphasis was on the difference between European

---

[62] USPC 1913, p. 86; Cullinane (1971), p. 48. These figures refer to provincial government posts.
[63] Gordon (1883), p. 713.
[64] Gordon (1897), I, p. 199.

and essentialized African or Fijian cultures, which were not to be subsumed to a European model but sustained in their distinctiveness."[65]

Indirect rule was later popularized for British Africa by Lord Lugard. As Governor Donald Cameron in Tanganyika articulated Lugard's idea: "It is our duty to do everything in our power to develop the native on lines which will not westernize him and turn him into a bad imitation of a European."[66] The result was what Mamdani calls "decentralized despotism": a modality of rule that entailed fabrications of what was native and customary and also a complex hierarchy of rules and orders dictated by British officials to be carried out by chiefs on the spot. Chiefs, for example, had to supply forced labor for defense, public works, or other "needs of the colony" – as the 1891 Natal Native Code dictated.[67] The chiefs themselves had little choice in these matters: Their position depended on gaining continued acceptance from British authorities. The British even eventually abolished any sense of hereditary succession in such positions. All chiefs in administrative positions were appointed and subject to approval and dismissal by British authorities. In Rhodesia in the 1920s, it was expressly determined by the courts that the governor general had the "unqualified right to appoint who[m]soever he considered suitable to chiefship" such that hereditary rights of succession were effectively "abolished."[68]

Given this form of governance, it is obvious that liberal British rule in India was not representative of British colonial forms as a whole. Within the British empire, there was a continuum of possible modalities of rule – a multiplicity rather than a single type of colonialism: There was no single "rule" of British colonial rule. The Duke of Newcastle acknowledged this diversity in his testimony to the House of Commons in 1861. It would be an "entire folly," he noted, to think "that one rigid rule can be applied to the whole of the colonies of the empire." The theory that one policy suits all "will not bear examination, nor can it be carried into practice."[69]

But if it is folly to assume a singular "style" or policy across the British empire, so too is it folly to assume uniformity across the American empire. Put differently, if we cannot take the liberal reformists' policies in India as representative of a distinct or uniform British style of colonialism, neither should we take the Philippines as representative of a uniform U.S. style. The problem with liberal exceptionalist thought is that it fails to heed this warning. One of the underlying assumptions of liberal exceptionalism is that there is indeed such a thing as a single national style of colonial governance; a singular rule for all of America's colonial rules. To say that the U.S. empire is special or unique for its colonial governance is to assume that there is a uniformity to colonial practice and forms across the U.S. empire – a unique type. If there was

---

[65] Thomas (1994), p. 115. Thomas's analysis offers one of the more original of this sort of colonial governmentality; for a subsequent analysis that builds upon Thomas's insights in regard to German colonialism, see Steinmetz (2003).

[66] Thomas (1994), p. 115.

[67] Mamdani (1996), p. 52.

[68] Ibid., p. 55.

[69] Quoted in Morris (1900), p. 80.

not, then we could not pinpoint a type of American empire that was different from other empires, much less an exceptional type.

It follows that exceptionalism would be compelled to assume that the United States enacted liberal tutelary regimes in *all* of its colonies; not just in the Philippines. And this is true if we look at Puerto Rico. There, colonial policies were very similar to those in the Philippines. Although later citizenship laws would differ, and although the Philippines would later become independent whereas Puerto Rico remained tied to the United States, the early years of U.S. rule in Puerto Rico brought the same sort of tutelary colonial state: a large-scale public school system, elections, local offices, a national legislative assembly, and a rhetoric of "political education."[70] However, things look entirely different when we consider two other U.S. colonies acquired around the same time as Puerto Rico and the Philippines (and which, unlike Hawaii or Alaska, were also declared "unincorporated territories"): Guam and Samoa. In neither of these colonies did authorities endeavor to cast the colonized in metropolitan molds; talk of tutelage was markedly absent.

Something of this difference is seen when we look at the public school systems. As late as 1920 there was only one state-funded school in Samoa. Although Guam saw a few more, neither saw the kind of educational program carried out in the Philippines or Puerto Rico.[71] The criticism of one traveler was acute: "We have gone quite mad over education in the Philippines, and not quite mad enough over Guam."[72] More telling are the forms of colonial governance. Both Guam and Samoa were put into the hands of the Navy Department. In turn, commanders of the naval base assumed the role of colonial governor responsible for devising policies, programs, and all legislation. In Samoa, the result was a form of rule first laid down by Governor Tilley and kept in existence for several decades. Tilley divided the islands into administrative districts corresponding to what he took to be the "ancient" sociopolitical divisions, and he appointed hereditary native chiefs to administer them. The goal was not to uproot local forms of authority but keep them intact, preserving rather than transforming Samoan "customs." Governors in Guam structured their colonial regime similarly. Guam did not have hereditary chiefs, but under Spanish rule it had had native district officials known as *gobernadorcillos* (or "little governors"). American authorities did not then try to transform the system. Instead, they maintained it by reappointing the *gobernadorcillos* as "commissioners." Thus, in stark contrast to the Philippines or Puerto Rico, local leaders were not chosen through American-style elections. There was no talk of "practical political education"; the state was not fashioned as a "school of politics." As one historian notes, "political conditions hardly changed at all" from Spanish to American rule.[73] If anything, the movement was in reverse. During Spanish

---

[70] Go (2008a).
[71] United States Congress. Committee on Territories and Insular Possessions (1928), p. 7; Governor of Samoa (1927), p. 81.
[72] French (1905), p. 379.
[73] Rogers (1905), p. 128.

rule, the position of *gobernadorcillo* had been elective (albeit through a very restrictive suffrage), but American officials abolished these elections entirely.[74]

Successive colonial rulers in Guam and Samoa thus maintained control autocratically – a type of personal rule that concentrated legislative, executive, and judicial functions in the American governor.[75] No effort was made to instill the "principles" of American governance such as the separation of powers, much less the ideas of America's beloved democracy. The difference was not lost on astute contemporary observers. Pratt heralded American rule in the Philippines as "exhibit A" of "benevolent imperialism," but he also noted that "elsewhere there is less to be proud of and more to deplore." It is "true that naval governors [in Samoa and Guam] have permitted native life to go on with no great amount of interference," but this "is a negative kind of beneficence, not the strenuous bearing of the burden sung by Kipling."[76]

In short, contrary to Moses's claim that America's "mission" was not to "preserve social stagnation" but rather uplift and transform, American authorities in Guam and Samoa aimed for preservation. Calling this "indirect rule" is on the spot. In fact, Tilley's model for his government in Samoa, as he said himself, was British indirect rule in Fiji. American colonial governance in Samoa was decidedly not inspired by American traditions, territorial governments at home, or even Native American reservations but rather British colonialism.[77]

The American version of indirect rule was no less arbitrary or tyrannical than its British precedent, a fact not lost on the colonized peoples. In 1910, the naval commandant in Guam discovered an anonymous handbill that had been circulating among the Chamorros. It read in part:

> Salam! Salam!
> I'm the Governor of Guam,
> I'm glorious and great,
> I'm a pampered potentate,
> So I am.
> I run things as a I please
> Get down on your knees,
> I'm the ruler of the tightest little island in the seas,
> That's me.
> Those who do not like me,
> I shut up or send away,
> I'm a wonder and I know it, –
> Of the thirty-third degree.
> Behold! Behold!
> I'm fearless and I'm bold.
> I'm the government, the law;
> Kings refer to me with awe,
> So I'm told.[78]

[74] Cox (1917), p. 78.
[75] Keesing (1934), p. 132.
[76] Pratt (1934), p. 277.
[77] United States Navy Department (1901), pp. 85–6.
[78] Perez Hattori (1995), p. 4.

In Samoa during the 1920s, more direct resistance emerged. Samoan chiefs had been complaining about the copra tax and had been wondering where the money went. The people, reported one officer, were concerned "that the Government was stealing the money of the Samoan people."[79] Complaints about other policies, such as a ban on marriage between Samoans and whites, also aroused complaint. These grievances culminated in an anti-navy movement known as the Mau rebellion. The rebellion, which had parallels in neighboring German Samoa, ended up in a truce, but the causes of the rebellion remained. The Mau had not only called for an end to certain policies by the naval commanders, they had also asked that Congress establish a civil government and grant the islanders citizenship.[80]

If arbitrary rule was displeasing to some, however, little was done in response. Requests from Guam throughout the first half of the twentieth century to replace military rule with a civil government fell on deaf ears in Washington.[81] This meant that naval commanders in Guam and Samoa could continue to rule the islands autocratically. By not establishing a civil government to replace the military government, Congress essentially let the navy do as it pleased. This was not accidental neglect: The executive branch often pushed for such congressional inaction, thereby ensuring that the islands would remain under its direct control. "If left alone Congress will probably do nothing about providing a form of government for the Islands [of Guam]," wrote Secretary of State Elihu Root to the Secretary of the Navy in 1905. "[T]he inactivity of Congress must be deemed to be an approval of the continuance of the existing government. It is very desirable that this should be so."[82]

The Provinciality of American Empire

The treatment of Guam and Samoa starkly reveals the limits of liberal exceptionalist thought. Liberal exceptionalism contends that the U.S. colonial empire was uniquely liberal and benign, democratizing its colonial subjects and training them for self-government. Not only does this presume that other empires failed to enact tutelary regimes or policies, it also presumes a uniformity to colonial practice across the U.S. empire. The diversity of colonial regimes belies this notion. However, if there was such diversity within both the U.S. and British empires, what accounts for it? This is worth pursuing.

Liberal exceptionalism tries to account for colonial regimes with a metropolitan-centered explanation. In this explanation, colonial policies and practices abroad reflect metropolitan characteristics at home. To wit: America's presumably unique liberal colonialism in places like the Philippines reflects America's own liberal institutions and political culture. As Susan Carruthers observes of this reasoning: "If the U.S. was uniquely virtuous ... then it stood

---

79 Quoted in Chappell (2000), p. 233.
80 American Samoan Commission (1931), p. 28.
81 See Perez Hattori (1995) and Hofschneider (2001).
82 Jessup (1938), p. 349.

to reason that American modes of imperial governance must be reflective of that virtuosity, both in the uplifting ends to which U.S. interventions aspired, and the lightness of touch with which American agents pursued them."[83] We can now see the problem with this account. If national style, character, or values determine an empire's colonial forms, then we would expect similarity in colonial forms within each empire as well as marked differences between empires in colonial forms. As just seen, neither the U.S. nor the British empires conform to this expectation. The question remains: What explains variation in colonialism within empires? Why, for instance, did the United States enact in the Philippines and Puerto Rico a tutelary regime but did not in Guam or Samoa?

A better explanation would not focus on the metropole, national character, or national styles. It would rather provincialize empire and look at what happened at the point of power's application.[84] Note, for example, that when contemplating and crafting colonial policy, American rulers were less often dictated by metropolitan values or traditions than by the legitimacy of their rule to colonized groups. This is most evident among the early U.S. officials in the Philippines who faced armed resistance from Philippine insurgents. In order to win the insurgents over to the U.S. side and better establish U.S. control, the Schurman Commission suggested that they needed to demonstrate their benevolence. To quell resistance, the regime had "to create a situation where those in favor of peace can safely say so, and can argue with their brethren in the field not only that our intentions are good but, by pointing to accomplished facts, show the advantage of accepting our authority."[85] Even replacing the existing military government with civil government "would do more than any other single occurrence to reconcile the Filipinos to American sovereignty."[86] The commission not only claimed that winning hearts and minds would help quell resistance and establish American rule, they likewise insisted that it would help sustain it in the long run. "Americans and Filipinos will have to trust each other," Schurman wrote to Secretary of State John Hay in Washington. "[W]hile the Filipino stops at nothing nor thinks of death when influenced by hatred, resentment or revenge, he is much moved by sympathy and generosity of [a] powerful superior, whose power he has felt. Believe magnanimity our safest, cheapest, and best policy with Filipinos."[87]

Even in the territories where armed revolution was absent, U.S. officials were concerned about legitimating their occupation. In Samoa, the Assistant Secretary of the Navy, Charles Allen (who later governed Puerto Rico), instructed

---

[83] Carruthers (2003), p. 10. One historian's analysis of the U.S. colonial project in the Philippines insists that the tutelage project there was distinct in comparison with European colonialisms because of the American officials' unique "American past" in May (1980), p. 17.

[84] Chakrabarty (2000). I use the term "provincialize" in the spirit of Chakrabarty's analysis, but in a different manner. For more of an exposition, see Go (2007).

[85] Williams (1913), p. 60.

[86] United States Philippine Commission (1900), p. 90.

[87] Schurman to Hay, June 3, 1899 (MP).

the first commander in charge of local policy: "While your position as commandant will invest you with authority over the islands embraced within the limits of the state, you will at all times exercise care to conciliate and cultivate friendly relations with the natives. A simple, straightforward method of administration, *such as to win and hold the confidence of the people*, is expected of you." This clause was repeated in the orders to every subsequent governor of the islands.[88] Similarly, in Guam, President McKinley's instructions to the first appointed governor read: "[I]t will be the duty of the military commander to announce and proclaim in the most public manner that we come, not as invaders or conquerors, but as friends.... [I]t should be the earnest and paramount aim of the naval administration to win the confidence, respect and affection of the inhabitants of the Island of Guam."[89]

We see here a logic of legitimation at work rather than a set of national values or national character. The logic was twofold. First, the fledgling colonial regimes had to determine the needs, desires, and interests of the inhabitants. If authorities hoped to "persuade" the colonized, this necessitated understanding what exactly what would best persuade them. If authorities aimed to secure "cooperation," "confidence," and "trust," this demanded ascertaining what the colonized would cooperate with and what exactly they would trust. Second, perhaps most critically, authorities had to incorporate what they learned into their ruling practices. They had to signify their rule as meeting local demands and incorporate at least some of those demands into their policies and programs. To achieve a successful occupation without the use of force, colonial rulers had to construct accommodating states – ruling regimes that would partially shape themselves to perceived local molds.

In all of the colonies, the Americans' legitimating efforts followed this logic. The critical difference had to do with local conditions in the colonies as the American rulers perceived them, and these therefore dictated what local interests and demands they incorporated into their ruling forms. This explains the variation across the U.S. empire.

Let us turn to conditions in Samoa first. Samoa had not been previously ruled by European colonial powers. Missionaries, traders, and diplomats had been around, and treaties with European powers had been made, but Samoa had not been ruled directly by a foreign power in the same manner that Spain had ruled Guam, the Philippines, and Puerto Rico – that is, with elaborate colonial administrations.[90] In addition, Samoa was less dependent on the world economy than other territories. Although vast agricultural lands of Puerto Rico and the Philippines had been devoted to export production for centuries before U.S. rule, the copra trade in Samoa was comparably undeveloped and participation in the wage economy was not necessary for local survival.[91] These features

[88] Governor of Samoa (1913), p. 10.
[89] Beers (1944), pp. 18–19.
[90] Gray (1960), pp. 27–91.
[91] Ellison (1938), pp. 29–38.

of Samoa are important. Combined with preexisting Western discourses on oceanic peoples (such as those provided by the writer Robert Louis Stevenson), they contributed to a perception among American officials that the islands and their people were locked in an "undeveloped" state of existence in which Samoans were comparably content and happy – so much so that American officials often idealized and romanticized their existence.[92] In his early reports from Samoa, American consul Henry Ide suggested that the climate and lack of external influence had left Samoans in a near prelapsarian condition of existence in which Samoans lived in perfect harmony with their natural surroundings: "They have abundant fertile land to supply their wants and those of their posterity for all time." The Samoans likewise appeared peaceful and docile. Ide suggested that although intermittent conflicts among the people had previously erupted, Samoans were very much unlike "our Indian territory filled with murder and violence." "Absolute peace has prevailed for nearly three years." Ide's conclusion was that the inhabitants were "picturesque, kindly, polite, and hospitable."[93] Others repeated the theme. The Samoans, wrote Governor Schroeder, "are as a rule good natured and generous. . . . It is doubtless a natural law that there can be development without hardship, and nature here is so kind that the natives practically never have to face hardships. They move along through life, as did many generations of their forefathers, without the necessity of any great amount of work or of privation."[94] Therefore, the average Samoan "is happiest when in his natural state."[95]

In conjunction with the legitimating imperative, these constructions had important implications for colonial governance. For if the people were already happy and contented (or seen to be), if their "wants" were relatively few and simple, colonial rule would fare best to ensure and perpetuate this condition. This would make for an enduring occupation. Herein, then, lies the origins of the preservationist governmentality associated with indirect rule. On the one hand, a preservationist policy was partly a matter of expedience. When Governor B. F. Tilley in Samoa first tried to secure consent to U.S. sovereignty from Manua chiefs, he noted that the Tui Manua (ruling chief of Manua) "did not wish any interference with his 'kingdom' by any outside power." Tilley further learned that the chiefs "feared that I would take way their lands and other property." In response, Tilley declared: "There is no intention to disturb your quiet, peaceful living, or interfere with your property or affairs. We do not want your lands or anything that you have unless we buy them

---

[92] My claim is not that preexisting conditions in Samoa alone determined the American officials' views. They rather converged with already circulating ideas about Pacific islanders. I discuss the interplay of preexisting historical conditions, racialized meanings, and policy formation in Samoa and Guam in further detail elsewhere. Go (2004). Steinmetz (2007) offers a nuanced analysis of the convergence of such ideas with other factors to shape German colonial policy.

[93] Ide (1897), pp. 263, 169, 171–2.

[94] United States Navy Department (1904b), p. 7.

[95] United States Congress. Committee on Territories and Insular Possessions (1928), p. 52.

with your consent." After this declaration, the chiefs finally accepted the new arrangement.[96] Keeping things intact was a way of securing consent.

On the other hand, leaving local conditions intact was also a way of securing rule in the long term. Tilley's premise for his preservationist government was that the people were already "in a most happy and peaceful state.... No changes in the local government of the island will be necessary."[97] He later added:

The natives of Tutuila are a gentle, kindly, simple-minded race and are easily governed.... I considered that the best way to govern these people was to let them, as far as possible, govern themselves, by continuing their good and time-honored customs and gradually abolishing the bad ones.... My aim was to modify this system so as to adapt it to requirements of civilized government, without at the same time interfering with the deeply rooted customs of the people or wounding their susceptibilities in any way.[98]

Securing consent and maintaining rule meant keeping the natives happy, but as the natives were perceived to be happy already, successful rule meant maintaining rather than altering their way of life. "Native" ways had to be preserved to in turn preserve the integrity of rule. "No effort was made to make any radical changes in the long established customs," Tilley reported, because "the natives, naturally docile and easily ruled, are happy and contented."[99]

This explains the preservationist policy in Guam too. Local conditions in Guam were not entirely different from those in Samoa. Despite the fact that Guam had been ruled by Spain, it remained relatively unpenetrated by market forces. Besides a small amount of export agriculture, the island was largely self-sufficient; islanders lived off land and sea. Politically, colonial rule had relied on a handful of elite representatives from the landowning class known as the *mana'kilo*. This class had not previously made demands for major political reforms or independence. With only intermittent complaints about taxation, the island had seen decades of calm.[100] These conditions contributed to American perceptions homologous to those in Samoa – that is, the Chamorros were perfectly content in their existing state and surroundings, worthy of romanticization. "There was very little crime," noted one governor as he reflected on conditions as he found them "...[and] little violation of the law."[101] The Chamorros were a "peaceful, good-natured, law-abiding people"; the small class of local intermediaries "have never shown the slightest resistance or opposition."[102] Observers likewise saw the Chamorros as untainted by civilization's corruptions, free from modernizing desires or pressing needs.

---

96 United States Navy Department (1900), pp. 100, 105.

97 Ibid., p. 100.

98 United States Navy Department (1901), p. 86. Tilley's model of governance, borrowed from Fiji, remained the model for successive rulers in subsequent years. Darden (1951), p. xiii.

99 Tilley (1901), p. 601.

100 Carano and Sanchez (1964), pp. 125–58.

101 Schroeder (1922), p. 242.

102 United States Navy Department (1904a), pp. 131, 171.

"If wealth consists in the ability to gratify one's wants," wrote Governor William Safford, "the people of Guam may be called rich." Governor E. J. Born added: "[T]he islander lives his life in peace and contentment, and is, apparently, far happier than the average dweller in many a more advanced country."[103]

As in Samoa, preservationist policies followed. Because the "children" of Guam were deemed contented, a successful occupation necessitated that they should best be left to play on their own without rearing them into maturity. Indeed, authorities rejected public education because "it would be of doubtful advantage to attempt to educate them in subjects likely to induce feelings of restlessness and dissatisfaction with their simple lives."[104] Similarly, when devising the political system, policy makers concluded that a "political education" program would not be appropriate – for there was no apparent demand for it.[105] The implicit theory was that, because the natives did not feel that anything was broken, there was nothing to fix. Any attempts to alter or "develop" their world would do little else than disturb their putatively prelapsarian state, thereby posing disruptions to the regime's otherwise smoothly operating system. As one early official wrote in his memoirs: "When I first arrived, it seemed to me that I had discovered Arcadia, and when I received a letter from a friend asking whether I believed it would be possible to 'civilize the natives,' I felt like exclaiming, 'God forbid!'"[106]

The U.S. tutelage policy in Puerto Rico and the Philippines can be understood by the same logic. On the one hand, as in Guam and Samoa, American authorities in Puerto Rico and the Philippines insisted that they had to legitimate their rule and recognized that doing so first meant ascertaining local needs and wants.[107] On the other hand, preexisting conditions in Puerto Rico and the Philippines were very different from the other territories. Compared with Guam and Samoa, both Puerto Rico and the Philippines had been more deeply penetrated by export production for the world market long before American occupation.[108] This made for a distinct history of class formation: the construction of a powerful and wealthy class of landowners, merchants, and professionals who enjoyed the market's monetary fruits. These groups then used their wealth to cultivate local power and a cosmopolitan outlook. Elite families sent their sons to schools of higher learning in Manila and San Juan or to Europe for study and travel. Students returned filled with ideologies of the Spanish Enlightenment, political tracts from France, and various works of literature from the European world. In the Philippines, these elites were known as the *"ilustrados"* (literally, "enlightened ones"); in Puerto Rico they fashioned

---

[103] Safford (1903), p. 507.
[104] Governor of Guam (1901–1941), 1904, p. 10.
[105] Ibid., 1904, p. 8.
[106] Safford (1903), p. 508.
[107] United States Philippine Commission (1900), p. 90; Carroll (1899b), p. 7.
[108] Dietz (1986) provides a good overview of Puerto Rican socioeconomic history; for the Philippines, seminal work includes McCoy and Jesus (1982).

themselves as the "leading class." Participation in global and local institutions – from Masonic lodges to scientific associations to political movements – secured their Westernized intellectual orientation.[109]

This background is important for it had contributed to political movements that framed their demands in modern liberal discourses of self-rule, liberty, and individual rights. In Puerto Rico, one such movement came in the late 1870s, when wealthy landowning families led a rebellion in the district of Lares for independence from Spain. The rebellion was soon repressed, but in its wake came the "autonomist" or *autonomía* movement. This movement, led by professionals, landowners, intellectuals, and urban middle classes, demanded that Puerto Rico be incorporated into the Spanish federal system as an equal self-governing province. It likewise called for expanded educational systems, freedom of the press and speech, protection of individual rights, "personal liberty and security of the home," and universal suffrage – among many other related demands.[110] Parallel movements emerged in the Philippines. Resistance emerged in the 1880s when *ilustrados* demanded political reforms from Madrid and sought equal citizenship with Spaniards. In the 1890s, these demands continued, but some *ilustrados* joined a cross-class movement for national independence. The movement culminated in the 1896 revolution and the establishment of the Philippine Republic based in the town of Malolos. The Malolos constitution drew from the Cuban constitution, France's rights of man, and ideas of the Spanish Enlightenment. It declared a "free and independent Republic" whereby "sovereignty resides exclusively in the people"; separation of the legislative, executive, and judicial branches; the "freedom and equality of all religions"; and an extended list of individual rights.[111]

American authorities were not unaware of these preexisting demands. To be sure, the Schurman Commission in the Philippines, having announced that its first task was to discern the "wishes" and "ideals" of the people, devoted much of its time to learning about them. It held hearings and conducted interviews in Manila with "eminent Filipinos." Commissioners also collected information from their commanders in the field and dug into documents from the Philippine Republic, the revolution, and "pacific organizations of other Filipinos."[112] Even before this commission's work, the Hong Kong consulate general had met with exiled leaders of the Philippine revolution. Likewise, investigative commissions in Puerto Rico held hearings with prominent elites, while military commanders had previously engaged in discussions with Puerto Rico's "leading classes."[113] Thus, as American authorities began devising their colonial policy, they did what their counterparts did in Guam and Samoa: They tried to

---

[109] On the Puerto Rican elite and their background, see Quintero Rivera (1981). For the Philippines, see Cullinane (2003). See also Go (2008a).

[110] "Plan de Ponce para la Organizacion del Partido Liberal de la Provincia" (Nov. 14, 1886) in Bothwell Gonzalez (1979), pp. 166–71.

[111] For excellent discussions of the constitution and its influences, see Majul (1967).

[112] United States Philippine Commission (1900), p. 83.

[113] Carroll (1899b), p. 7.

incorporate perceived local demands and desires into their own discourse, policies, and ruling forms. The difference was that the Puerto Rican and Filipino elite had articulated very different demands and desires than did Chamorros and Samoans.

The traces of this process can be discerned in the first public proclamations issued by American authorities in the Philippines. One of them was McKinley's "Proclamation to the Philippine People," issued in late December 1898. This was McKinley's "benevolent assimilation" proclamation, the earliest public issuance articulating tutelary ideals. Existing scholarship has referred to the proclamation as evidence for America's uniquely benign goals, but the references elide an important fact: The proclamation came six months after Washington had already received reports on the Philippines from R. Wildman, the U.S. consulate general in Hong Kong. Wildman had met with exiled revolutionary leaders. His subsequent report – titled "The Policy and Hopes of the Insurgent Government of the Philippine Islands" – was telling. It first contended that the Filipinos "cannot be dealt with as though they were North American Indians." The Filipinos were far too Westernized; insurgent leaders like Emilio Aquinaldo or Teodoro Sandiko "are all men who would all be leaders in their separate departments in any country"; their supporters were wealthy and educated families who "would hold their own bankers and lawyers everywhere." Wildman then noted that the insurgents wanted "annexation to the United States first, and for independence secondly." And they were not driven by primitive instincts, but "are fighting for freedom from the Spanish rule and rely upon the well known sense of justice that controls all the actions of our Government as to their future."[114]

Given this background, it is no accident that McKinley's proclamation portrayed Spanish rule as tyrannical and American rule as benign; nor is it accidental that it conjured concepts like freedom and justice: "[W]e come, not as invaders or conquerors, but as friends . . . the earnest wish and paramount aim of the military administration [is] to win the confidence, respect, and affection of the inhabitants of the Philippines by assuring them in every possible way that full measure of individual rights and liberties which is the heritage of free peoples, and by proving to them that the mission of the United States is one of benevolent assimilation, substituting the mild sway of justice and right for arbitrary rule."[115] It is as if McKinley's discourse had been directly shaped by Wildman's report. Indeed, previous proclamations – before Wildman's report – did not contain tutelary rhetoric. They simply announced American sovereignty and demanded compliance from the population.[116]

---

[114] Wildman to U.S. State Department, July 18, 1898 (USCG #19).

[115] Quoted in Forbes (1928), II, p. 438.

[116] For example, the phrase "benevolent assimilation" was reproduced again in a proclamation by General Otis of January 4, 1899, but earlier proclamations by Otis (August 14, 1898) did not contain the tutelage rhetoric. It only declared the establishment of military rule [ibid., II, pp. 429–30, 437–8].

McKinley's proclamation aimed to incorporate the demands of the colonized into its fold to first establish sovereignty, but the incorporation of local demands also guided recommendations for colonial policy in the longer run. The Schurman Commission, whose recommendations on policy were widely influential, had spent much time trying to ascertain local interests; they met with prominent Filipinos in Manila and emissaries from the Malolos government and studied the constitution of the Philippine Republic, speeches of *ilustrado* leaders, and a host of other documents – all of which the commissioners deemed "of the most vital significance" for crafting colonial policy. From their investigations, the commissioners concluded that the majority of Filipinos wanted "the tutelage and protection of the United States" rather than independence.[117] Consulting Manila-based *ilustrados* like Pardo de Tavera (who indeed stated a desire for American rule), the commissioners argued that the people wanted a more liberal form of colonial government than Spain had provided. The commissioners also concluded that the Filipinos who had rebelled against American sovereignty wanted the same thing. Referring to documents from the revolution, they concluded: "What the people want above every other thing, is a guarantee of those fundamental human rights which Americans hold to be the natural and inalienable birthright of the individual but which under Spanish domination in the Philippines were shamefully invaded and ruthlessly trampled upon."[118]

The commissioner's recommendations for U.S. colonial government were guided by these revelations. "If these abuses [from Spanish rule] are remedied," they reported, "if a capable and honest government is instituted, if the Filipinos are permitted to the full extent of their ability to participate in it . . . if church is separated from state, if public revenues are used solely to defray the legitimate expense of government . . . if, in a word, government is administered in the Philippines in the spirit in which it is administered in the United States, the people of that archipelago will, as already a few of them foresee, enjoy more benefits than they dreamed of when they took up arms against the corrupt and oppressive domination of Spain."[119] The commissioners' final conclusion was that a liberal tutelage government was necessary. Such a government should give Filipinos a place in the colonial state, attend to public education, and point to the possibility of self-rule in the future (either in the form of statehood or national independence). More specifically, the commissioners recommended the very governmental form that colonial rule finally took – control by American authorities in the central branch but with native participation, an elective national legislative assembly, and elective local posts. Such a government would put the colonized on "a course of development under American training [and] eventually reach the goal of complete local self-government" as well as eventual "contentment, prosperity, education, and

---

[117] United States Philippine Commission (1900), I, p. 83.
[118] Ibid., I, p. 84.
[119] Ibid., I, p. 82.

political enlightenment."[120] Yet it would also be predicated on local demands and interests. "It has been a leading motive with the commission in devising a form of government for the Philippines," Schurman later reported, "to frame one which, to the utmost extent possible, shall satisfy the views and aspirations of the educated Filipinos."[121] Finally, by the same logic, a tutelage government would realize the Americans' own interests in sustaining a successful occupation. As the commissioners wrote when registering their recommendations, "The United States can succeed in governing the Philippines only by understanding the character and circumstances of the people and realizing sympathetically their aspirations and ideals. A government to stand must be firmly rooted in the needs, interests, judgment and devotion of the people, and this support is secured by the adaptation of government to the character and possibilities of the governed – what they are, what they have it in them to become, what they want, and, not least, what they think they are entitled to have and enjoy."[122]

The same process unfolded in Puerto Rico. One early investigative commission was led by Henry Carroll. The Carroll Commission conducted a range of investigations, including interviews with local leaders, and thereby unearthed various complaints about Spanish rule. Spanish rule had been too centralized, preventing Puerto Ricans from holding high positions; it had impeded Puerto Rican autonomy for far too long; funds for public education had been lacking; and the colonial state's economic policies had benefited Spanish bureaucrats and residents alone. The commission further learned about the autonomy movement that had long been registering these complaints. The dominant Puerto Rican political parties had demanded full incorporation into the Spanish regional system, which meant equal rights, an extended suffrage, and increased levels of participation in the colonial government.[123] Finally, the commission discovered that the local population welcomed American intervention but hoped that it would eventually lead to statehood in the American Union (as Puerto Rican leaders' own speeches from the time stated clearly).[124] Carroll's recommendation for colonial government followed directly from these discoveries. Carroll suggested that colonial policies should be devoted to building public schools and regenerating agricultural industries (which had been suffering as a result of an economic crisis). He further contended that the colonial government should give the Puerto Rican elite political participation

---

[120] Ibid., I, p. 109, 120; Philippine Commission to Elihu Root, Aug. 21, 1900 (MP 31–3). In proposing the specific form of tutelary government, the commissioners in part drew from models of territorial government, but this does not affirm the exceptionalism argument. In Guam and Samoa, territorial government at home was not the model, and as seen, the Schurman Commission turned to the territorial model only after concluding that the model would help meet local demands.

[121] Schurman (1902), p. 49.

[122] United States Philippine Commission (1901), I, p. 82.

[123] Carroll (1899a), p. 56.

[124] Ibid., p. 55.

and offer the opportunity for eventual statehood.[125] This kind of government would serve a dual purpose. For one, it would offer an education in self-government. "They will learn the art of governing the only possible way – by having its responsibilities laid upon them." For another, and by the same token, it would establish and maintain legitimacy by meeting the Puerto Rican elites' own desires. "We do not need to promise statehood to them, [but] we certainly ought not to forbid them to aspire to statehood. It is an honorable aspiration and would put them on their best behavior."[126] Other recommendations for colonial government in Puerto Rico were similar. Ultimately, Elihu Root incorporated all of these suggestions into his own recommendations, and the Foraker Act passed by Congress in 1900 put the plan into practice.[127]

In brief, the formation of America's colonial regimes resulted from the opposite of what existing exceptionalist thought predicts. U.S. officials in the Philippines and Puerto Rico did not work from their political values to produce colonial states reflecting those values. Instead, as they strove to cultivate consent and compliance, the process worked the other way around. They made regimes that ultimately went native, shaping themselves to local conditions and incorporating what they found there. In this sense, America's presumably exceptional empire was the product of historical and geographical accident. Take away the fact that the Puerto Rican and Filipino elite had already espoused discourses of self-determination, rights, and liberty, and American occupation there might have looked more like American rule in Samoa and Guam. The implication regarding exceptionalism is straightforward: Where seemingly exceptional colonial policies surfaced at all, they had less to do with America's unique values, virtues, and traditions than with the specific character of the colonies themselves.

Britain's "Native Policy"

The foregoing analysis should serve to unsettle if not upend exceptionalism's portrayal of American colonialism. However, an alternative interpretation of the same events could be marshaled to endorse it. It may be, for instance, that U.S. policy makers and authorities were uniquely benign in attempting to meet perceived local conditions and accommodate local demands. What made the U.S. colonial empire exceptional was that U.S. colonialists cared about legitimating their rule at all. According to this logic, other colonialists were not

[125] Ibid., p. 63.
[126] Ibid., p. 58.
[127] Berbusse (1966), p. 151. General George Davis's recommendation followed Carroll's and was in part borrowed from communications with political leaders like Muñoz Rivera who in fact suggested a similar type of government to that which U.S. officials finally enacted. See Davis (1900), p. 75 and L. Muñoz Rivera to E. Root, Aug. 14, 1899 (USNA, RG 350, 168–170). One exception was the recommendation of A.C. Sharpe, who concluded that only military rule could best serve both the Americans' needs and the Puerto Ricans'. United States Major-General Commanding the Army (1899), I, p. 342.

concerned about legitimation and instead followed the principle of "dominance without hegemony."[128] Is this the case? Again, a comparative look at the British empire is warranted.

Although it is impossible here to examine all of Britain's colonial regimes and explain their formation, it is appropriate to focus on two colonies: India and Fiji. After all, as just seen, in devising his paternalistic governmentality in Samoa, Commander Tilley had declared that British Fiji was his model. We might rightfully query how that Fijian policy came about in the first place. Further, in India, British officials constructed liberal colonial policies that prefigured America's tutelary regime in the Philippines. We should wonder about the origins of those liberal colonial policies too.

First, what accounts for the strategy of paternalistic preservation in Fiji? Although some elements of the strategy had precedents in the conservative approach to India (which supported and maintained Indian aristocrats and their privileges), it would not be a stretch to say that the origins of the policy lie with Sir Arthur Gordon. The youngest son of the fourth Earl of Aberdeen, Gordon had served in Trinidad, New Brunswick, and Mauritius before his appointment to Fiji. Gordon largely invented indirect rule for Fiji. So what guided his approach? At least two considerations were important to Gordon. The first had to do with state coffers. The home government was determined to make Fiji economically self-sufficient so that it would not become a financial burden. Gordon subsequently worried about the dearth of funds for his administration.[129] Second was the relationship between Fijians and foreigners. By the time Gordon came, Fiji had already seen its share of missionaries, settlers, merchants, and cotton planters. This had not made for a happy situation. British planters were scheming to obtain Fijians' land and deploy Fijian labor to meet global demand for cotton (which had been increasing since the Civil War in the United States). In turn, Fijians were cautious if not fearful altogether of British residents and government agents. After a measles epidemic killed 40,000 of the estimated 150,000 Fijians, rumors circulated that British diplomats had deliberately introduced the disease to kill them off.[130] Suspicion filled the air.

Both of these issues shaped Gordon's preservationist approach. The lack of funds might have been enough to compel Gordon to adopt it. If Gordon could not hire a sufficient number of British officials to administer the islands, using indigenous political structures would have been a good alternative. However, the tension between Fijians and foreigners was also an important factor. For Gordon, this was a major issue indeed. To him, it spoke to more fundamental ones, not least how to deal with "native" populations in general. The problem, according to Gordon, came down to the fact that the "white settlers in Fiji had not colonized an empty waste[land] . . . only roamed over by nomadic savages." They were instead "scattered here and there among a large and

[128] Guha (1997).
[129] Gordon to Gladstone, March 22, 1876 in Knaplund (1961), p. 65.
[130] Chapman (1964), p. 159.

industrious settled population," outnumbered "by more than fifty to one."[131] In this situation, the problem of how to rule native populations was pressing. Unlike settler colonies in North America – where whites outnumbered natives and where there were at most "nomadic savages" to fret about – the large number of natives posed a potential threat, and colonial control carried the possibility for arousing resistance. A distinct governmentality was required. As Gordon put it, conditions in Fiji raised the "question – one which has seldom been answered in any satisfactory manner – how a large native population should be governed by a handful of white aliens?"[132]

One option was to succumb to the settlers' and planters' demands and expropriate Fijian land and labor. In Gordon's view, however, this was impossible. Turning Fijians into instruments of British capital was not only morally objectionable, but also damaging to British legitimacy.[133] The natives had to be protected from settler abuses in order to ensure "the credit of England," as Gordon put it.[134] Such protection would also help sustain British rule in the long run. Here we see the similarity with policy formation in the American empire: Gordon was concerned about legitimacy and winning compliance from the colonized. As he explained to Gladstone, protecting "the native race from oppression and fraud" would create "a better feeling" between the British and the natives. Cultivating this "better feeling" would be essential for British rule; there would be "no longer any fear of anarchy or disorder."[135]

Many of Gordon's policies followed from this protectionist imperative, such as laws limiting the amount of land that passed to Europeans, for instance, or importing laborers from India so that Fijian laborers would not have to be enlisted.[136] If maintaining British rule was the goal, however, why not other measures rather than paternalistic protection and preservation? Gordon's regime could have protected the natives from settler exploitation and thereby prevent disorder while also "civilizing" and transforming them. Why not prevent settler abuses of natives while also developing the natives into British-like subjects? Why not an electoral political system with local governments and large legislatures like those at home or those being developed in British India, which aimed to teach the natives British-style self-government?[137] Yet Gordon rejected this approach with the same determination that he rejected the settlers'

---

[131] Gordon (1883), p. 713.

[132] Ibid. Gordon may have overstated the novelty of the problem. British rule in North America and in the Caribbean had also encountered its brand of "the native question," and Gordon had already served in Trinidad and Mauritius. Herman Merivale, who served in India, had prefaced the problem as early as 1839, contending that the native question posed the "greatest moral difficulty of colonization" [Merivale quoted in McNab (1977), p. 361]. Still, this does not negate that Gordon himself faced the problem of governance in Fiji.

[133] Chapman (1964), p. 182; org Gordon to Carnarvon, Aug. 9, 1877, Stanmore Papers, 49199.

[134] Gordon to Selborne, Aug. 3, 1877 in ibid., p. 182.

[135] Gordon to Gladstone, March 22, 1876 in Knaplund (1961), p. 65.

[136] Sohmer (1984), p. 148.

[137] This sort of strategy would amount to a "civilizing mission" that was supported by some British quarters (such as humanitarian groups like the Anti-Slavery Society and the Aborigines Protection Society).

approach. The reason had to with Gordon's perceptions of the Fijians' character and lifestyle. Like his American counterparts in Samoa and Guam, Gordon romanticized and idealized Fijians. Gordon repeatedly insisted to his friends at home that Fijians were "a good deal away from barbarism" and in fact were "civilized"; they had a "civilization of their own."[138] "I think the civilization of the natives," he wrote to Gladstone, "would excite surprise at home."[139] Gordon was especially taken by their "respect for agricultural labor" and the "high position of women" in Fijian society.[140] He likewise romanticized the natural environment of Fiji, which, combined with the presumed communal land system and the industriousness of the people, produced a near paradise wherein any single village "may be so rich and prosperous" as to provide all the necessities of life.[141] Gordon thus disdained comparisons that settlers made between Fijians and the Australian "savage." To Gordon, Fijians are "as superior to the savages of Australia as we are to Fijians – perhaps more so." They were "peaceable, orderly, educated and [in] their own fashion civilized."[142]

As Gordon saw idyllic Pacific islanders just like his American counterparts in Samoa and Guam, so too did he oppose transformative policies. He did not want to transform the natives because he saw little need to improve them. Given the presumably simple and idyllic existence of the natives' lives, attempts to "civilize" or radically transform Fijians would only stir trouble. Putting "pressure . . . upon the native to adopt European habits" would leave "the natives, bewildered and depressed, deprived of all interest and object in life, [and they would] sink into indolence, apathy, and vice and, exposed almost without any safeguard to snares and temptations innumerable, they lose position, property, self-respect and health." Rather than try to transform the natives, it was better to preserve their ways and deploy them. "It is manifest that the more the native policy is retained, native agency employed, and changes avoided until naturally and spontaneously called for the less likely are these results to follow."[143]

Gordon's policy of preserving and using native institutions was thus born. Based on a romantic construction of Fijian life, it was a strategic necessity aimed at keeping natives happy and thereby ensuring an enduring British rule. Or as Gordon himself put it, "policy and necessity pointed in the same direction as right and justice."[144] Rather than oppress or civilize, colonial rule should preserve and protect, if only in order to better maintain itself. Gordon was unequivocal here. Given that "whites" were "outnumbered" by Fijians, and given the fact that the Fijians already had a "complex social and political organization in vigorous activity," "*it is not safe*, even if it be practicable,

---

[138] Gordon to Gladstone Oct. 12, 1876, in Knaplund (1961), p. 70.
[139] Gordon to Gladstone, Oct. 12, 1876, in ibid., p. 75.
[140] Gordon to Gladstone March 22, 1876, in ibid., p. 67.
[141] Gordon (1883), p. 727.
[142] Gordon to Gladstone March 22, 1876, in Knaplund (1961), p. 66.
[143] Quoted in Chapman (1964), p. 192.
[144] Ibid., p. 182.

to deny to the natives a large measure of self-government" – that is, self-government according to perceived political "custom."[145]

In short, the logic of legitimation worked in Fiji to produce a preservationist colonial governmentality. What, then, about India? There, too, the logic of legitimation operated, but because India exhibited very different conditions than Fiji, the policy also differed. On the one hand, officials in India were concerned with the legitimacy just like their counterparts in Fiji or the Philippines, Puerto Rico, Samoa, and Guam. In part, financial considerations made this concern all the more pressing. The Crown had inherited a financially unstable regime from the East India Company, and during the latter decades of the nineteenth century it was almost continually at war defending India's borders from rival empires.[146] To pay for defense, British officials in India had to levy income taxes and extract resources from localities. Doing so demanded cooperation from local Indian elites and leaders. British officials had to win them over.[147] The so-called Indian Mutiny of 1857–1859 further pushed the legitimacy issue to the fore. In the shadow of this tumultuous event, the Crown faced the nagging threat of more rebellion. This was a context of concern and worry for British rulers not unlike that faced by American rulers in the Philippines during and after the Philippine rebellion against them. Coupled with the colonial regime's financial concerns, it meant that successive British rulers had to pay attention to local demands and wants, not least those of the elite, to maintain British rule. In the wake of the revolt, Charles Wood warned the House of Commons in 1859 that the British state needed to open up to Indian demands rather than repress them. "We have seen the consequences, and if we hope to retain India in peace and tranquility we must take care so to govern it not only to consult the interests, but the feelings of the Native population."[148]

On the other hand, although the imperative of legitimacy was prevalent in India just like everywhere else, what led to the liberal colonial policies there as opposed to Fiji was the conjunction of this imperative with particular local developments. India exhibited very different conditions than Fiji. India was not a seemingly idyllic island in the remote Pacific visited by scattered sailors, settlers, and missionaries. It was a series of expansive provinces that had been under East India Company rule for at least a century. Rather than putatively pristine natives living in remote villages, British rulers faced a politically active elite often educated in Western political ideas and ideals. Since 1835, when Lord Macaulay initiated important educational reforms, elite education had spread exponentially (Sir Charles Wood's grants-in-aid system beginning in 1854 spread education even more). From 1864 to 1885, a total of 48,251 Indian students entered university across the provinces.[149] Concentrated mostly in

---

[145] Gordon (1883), p. 713; emphasis added.
[146] Robinson (1971), pp. 318–4.
[147] Moore (1999), pp. 430–1.
[148] Quoted in Metcalf (1964), p. 93.
[149] Seal (1968), p. 18.

urban centers like Calcutta, Bombay, and Poona, these were "men of high status but frequently of low income"; many belonged to landowning families but were not necessarily aristocratic themselves.[150] Typically they entered public service or the professions. They also led new politically oriented associations that became a critical component of India's political life and eventually shaped colonial policy.[151]

Who were these associations and what did they want? The first important associations were formed in Bengal, Bombay, and Madras: the British Indian Association (founded in Calcutta in 1851), the Bombay Association (founded 1852), and the Landholders' Society (which came out of the Zemindars' Association, as it was first called in 1837).[152] Other groups subsequently emerged. The British Indian Association represented long-standing landed interests. Surendranath Banerjea's new Indian Association became a venue for the latest generation of educated middle classes (one of the founding members had a degree from Cambridge). The demands of these groups constituted a "moderate nationalism." As historian Sanjay Seth notes, this was "moderate" in the sense that few if any of the leaders actually demanded independence. They wanted more participation and representation. Leaders such as Banerjea stated that they "prided themselves on, and reiterated at every opportunity, the gradualist and constitutionalist nature of their political activity."[153] Yet despite this gradualism, their demands were consistent and framed in terms of liberal theory and the language of British politics. The British Indian Association initially demanded the appointment of at least one native member to the Legislative Council, arguing that "the natives of India . . . are deeply sensible of the value of political freedom."[154] In 1856, the Association argued for a "deliberative body which shall possess all the requisites of a constitutional legislature."[155] In 1860, it argued for the need to find an institutional place for "the voice of the people . . . their views, their wishes and their wants."[156] The Association also campaigned against the Calcutta municipal bill of 1854 and the salt monopoly in 1855; it pushed for court reform, petitioned for a Commission of Inquiry into the Indigo riots, and proposed a governor-in-council for Bengal.[157] As other groups joined these and other efforts, and as their numbers proliferated, so too did the demands. Many began petitioning not just for native participation in office, but also for elections.[158] At its first session in 1885, the Indian National Congress called for an expansion of the elective principle and advisory

---

[150] Ibid., p. 111.
[151] Ibid., pp. 114–30.
[152] Ibid., p. 198.
[153] Seth (1999), p. 101.
[154] Quoted in Seal (1968), p. 200.
[155] Quoted in ibid., pp. 200–1.
[156] Quoted in ibid., p. 201.
[157] Ibid., p. 203.
[158] Tinker (1968), p. 41.

councils. It later demanded that at least half of the members of the Imperial and Provincial Legislative Councils be elected.[159]

The emergence and proliferation of these groups was important. It meant that British officials faced a flurry of political activity and mobilization from educated professionals, urban elites, and powerful rural landowners who spoke their language, deployed their political concepts, and demanded the sorts of privileges and political institutions that rich Englishmen were afforded. "One hears a great deal at home about the immobility of the East," Lord Ripon wrote to Gladstone in 1881, "but I have, on the contrary, been much struck by the changes which are evidently being effected in India by ... the spread of English legal ideas and methods, and by the increasing knowledge on the part of the people of their legal rights."[160] Equally imposing was the fact that, beginning in the 1870s, Indian political leaders took inspiration from the Home Rule movement in Ireland and found allies in Parliament.[161] Lord Dufferin was especially worried about this. "[E]vents at home in regard to Ireland," he noted, "[have] produced a very considerable effect upon the minds of the intelligent and educated sections of our own native community."[162]

The post-Mutiny context, the states' fiscal considerations, and the rising educated classes and their "modern democratic agitation" eventually gave colonial governmentality in India its tutelary and transformative tone, making the regime in India look very different from Fiji and more like the Philippines. In fact, liberal concessions had begun almost immediately after the Mutiny, with the replacement of Company rule by Crown rule. Charles Canning, governor general of India (1856–1862), admitted natives onto the new Legislative Council in an effort to win over the princely classes. As one official explained, by this policy the natives "will no longer feel, as they have hitherto done, that they are excluded from the management of affairs in their own country."[163]

Whereas these early efforts at reconciliation by the Crown involved cultivating key elements of the aristocracy, the proliferation of middle-class political associations meant that successive British officials would have to call on them to collaborate too.[164] Lord Ripon was one of the officials who recognized their

---

[159] Seth (1999), p. 107.

[160] Ripon to Gladstone, 22 Oct. 1881 (RP).

[161] Brasted (1980).

[162] Dufferin to Lord Kimberley, March 21, 1886 (CC, BL, Mss Eur E243 #21).

[163] Quoted in Metcalf (1964), p. 267. Canning's policy followed the principles laid down in Sayyid Ahmad's famous essay on the causes of the rebellion (translated and published by the government). Ahmad had written that one of the causes of the revolt was widespread dissatisfaction among Indians about participation in government; he thus concluded that letting Indians into the Legislative Council would help ward off future trouble. Had there been Indians already on the council, he surmised, there would have been no uprising. See ibid., p. 90.

[164] The Queen's 1876 assumption of the title "Empress of India" was part of an attempt to win the "sympathy and cordial allegiance" of that aristocracy, the winning of which would be "no inconsiderable guarantee for the stability of the Indian Empire," as Lord Lytton declared. See Moore (1999), p. 431.

importance and the need to incorporate their Western-style demands. Touring the Punjab and Sindh in 1880, he noticed the demands in the Indian press for more self-government and later wrote to Gladstone: "[T]he problem is how to deal with this newborn spirit of progress...so as to direct it into a right course."[165] He further wrote: "[T]here are few Indian questions of greater importance in the present day than those which relate to the mode in which we are to deal with the growing body of Natives educated by ourselves in Western learning and Western ideas."[166] "Thirty years of education upon a European basis" in India, he insisted, "...must henceforth be recognized in our Indian policy."[167]

Ripon was determined to win over these "highly educated natives." Accordingly, as he explained to Lord Kimberley (undersecretary for India), he decided to "take steps to supply the legitimate outlets for those aspirations and to satisfy those ambitions consistent with the maintenance of authority."[168] His policies on local self-government and elections followed. The day after his Resolution on Local Self-Government, he explained to his friend W. E. Forster that his policies were driven by the "hourly increasing...necessity of making the educated natives the friends, instead of the enemies, of our rule."[169] In explaining his policies to Gladstone, he said that the developments in education and the spread of English political discourses among the Indian elite

lead me to attach much importance to measures which...are calculated to provide a legitimate outlet for the ambitions and aspirations which we have ourselves created by the education, civilization and material progress, which we have been the means of introducing into the country; such measures will not only have an immediate effect in promoting gradually and safely the political education of the people, which I hold to be a great object of public policy, but will also pave the way for further advances in the same direction as that education becomes fuller and more widespread.[170]

Before his departure from India, Ripon left a note to his successor, Lord Dufferin, explaining that the "most pressing problem before the Government was to provide a field for the legitimate aspirations and ambitions of English educated Indians, and thus to make them friends and supporters of the British Raj. They constituted a growing force and unless they were conciliated and befriended the Government would find soon to its dismay landed in a difficult and intricate situation."[171] Dufferin was not an avowed liberal, but he apparently took notice. Initially, Dufferin was less interested in the educated activists and more about princely support for military operations against Russia's advances in Central Asia. However, as the educated classes made their

---

[165] Ripon to Gladston, Oct. 6, 1882 (RP).
[166] Quoted in Martin (1967), p. 68.
[167] *Times*, Feb. 26, 1885, p. 10.
[168] Ripon to Kimberley, May 4, July 10, 1883, RP.
[169] Ripon to W.E. Forster, May 19, 1883, RP.
[170] Ripon to Gladstone, Oct. 6, 1882, RP.
[171] Yasin (1977), p. 255.

demands clearer and louder, he soon reconsidered his strategy. He was especially worried about the fact that "associations and sub-associations are being
formed all over the country." "Day after day," he said, "hundreds of sharp-
witted Babus pour forth their indignation against their English oppressors in
very pungent and effective diatribes."[172] He thus wondered to Kimberley: "I
cannot help asking myself how long an autocratic Government like that of
India . . . will be able to stand the strain implied by the importation *en bloc*
from England, or rather from Ireland, of the perfected machinery of modern
democratic agitation."[173]

   It is for this reason that Dufferin responded to local conditions in India
in ways that Ripon probably recognized clearly. Whereas Dufferin's taxation
policies conceded to the economic interests of the entrenched landed aristocracy, many of his governmental policies paid heed to the wishes of the rising middle classes and educated elites.[174] In December of 1886, the Indian
National Congress demanded that at least half of the provincial councils be
elected. Early the next year, Dufferin adopted the same proposal as his own. He
explained that his goal was to prevent a "Home Rule organization established
in India, on Irish lines, and under the patronage of Irish and Radical Members
of Parliament."[175] His reasoning was that a "concession now would stop a
good deal of agitation. . . . By extending this small and restricted political privilege to responsible Bodies constituted by law we should . . . take the wind out
of the sails of the Associations."[176] For Dufferin, these policies were politically
expedient. "Amongst the natives," he explained to Lord Kimberley in 1886,

there are a considerable number who are both able and sensible, and upon whose loyal
cooperation one could undoubtedly rely. The fact of their supporting the government
would popularize many of its acts . . . and if they in their turn had a native party behind
them, the government of India would cease to stand up, as it does now, an isolated rock
in the middle of a tempestuous sea, around whose base the breakers dash themselves
simultaneously from all the four quarters of the heavens. Now that we have educated
these people, their desire to take a larger part in the management of their own domestic
affairs seems to me a legitimate and reasonable aspiration, and I think there should be
enough statesmanship amongst us to contrive the means of permitting them to do so
without unduly comprising our Imperial supremacy.[177]

The fact that Dufferin's policies continued the liberal approach of his predecessors, despite his Whig leanings, attests to the larger point. Within India,
British officials' personalities or political affiliations did not determine British
policy. As they all faced similar local conditions, and as they were subject to the
logic of legitimation, they produced similar policies. We can now see that this

---

[172] Quoted in Gopal (1965), p. 161.
[173] Dufferin to Lord Kimberley, March 21, 1886 (CC, BL, Mss Eur E243 #21).
[174] On taxation see Gopal (1965), pp. 156–8.
[175] Quoted in Moore (1966), p. 55.
[176] Dufferin to Cross, Jan. 4, 1887, and March 20, 1887 (CC).
[177] Dufferin to Lord Kimberley, April 26, 1886 (CC).

principle applies across empires as well as within them. In the U.S. and British empire alike, colonial rulers had to worry about the appearance and legitimacy of their rule. What differed were the sociopolitical conditions that gave certain types of concessions more valence than others. As a result of varied local conditions and contingencies, officials in Samoa and Fiji perceived different wants and interests in local groups than those perceived by officials in India, the Philippines, or Puerto Rico. Subsequent policies and practices varied across these sites accordingly. In short, colonial policies were not shaped by national character, values, or styles but by the very spaces and scenes they aimed to manipulate and manage. To this, America's colonial empire was no exception.

3

Hegemonies and Empires

> Other nations in history have fought in foreign lands and remained to occupy and exploit. Americans, following a battle, want nothing more than to return home.
> – George W. Bush, Speech on the USS *Abraham Lincoln* (2003)

In 1940, Adolph Berle, the undersecretary in the U.S. Department State, penned a prescient passage in his diary. "I have been saying to myself and other people, that the only possible effect of this war would be that the United States would emerge with an imperial power greater than the world had ever seen."[1] It is unclear what Berle meant exactly by "imperial power." Most likely, he meant it as the founders of the American Revolution had meant it – that is, sovereign strength or greatness. If so, Berle's statement was on the spot. The United States did emerge from World War II as the world's leading economic and military power. In 1950, its GDP was higher than all of Europe's put together and near equal to Europe's and Russia's combined. The United States was the world's leading exporter and foreign investor. Its financial and industrial strength was matched by its agricultural exports. The United States was "the workshop, bakery, and banker of the world."[2]

On the other hand, Berle's characterization of America's postwar power as "greater than the world had ever seen" was arguably overstated. Portraying the United States as fundamentally different from other countries, it implied that America's standing had no modern parallel or precursor. Yet, the United States was not the world's first great power to emerge from a world war. A century earlier, the world had also seen a great war – the Napoleonic Wars – and Britain had emerged from the ashes of that war as the leading hegemon. As Metternich's advisor, Friedrich von Gentz, wrote after the Vienna Congress, "Britain appeared in Vienna [with] a solid basis of prosperity and power such as

---

[1] Quoted in McCormick (1995), p. 33.

[2] Ibid., p. 47.

no other country has acquired in our days."[3] For the next sixty years at least, Britain dominated the globe economically and militarily, just as the United States did from 1945 to the 1970s. "The United States," noted the British foreign secretary soon after World War II, "is in the position today that Britain was at the end of the Napoleonic Wars."[4]

Berle's characterization overlooks another similarity between the United States and Great Britain. Not only did both reach hegemonic maturity during their respective centuries, their paths to power had been paved by imperialism. As seen in previous chapters, Britain's pre-hegemonic career had involved settler colonialism in the Western hemisphere and then further expansion into India, the African coast, and parts of Asia. Similarly, by World War II, the United States had conquered the North American continent and then reached overseas to seize colonies in the Pacific and the Caribbean. In light of these similarities, new questions arise. Both the United States and Great Britain rose to global economic power during their respective centuries of ascendance, and both had constructed empires along the way. Yet questions remain: What happened during their respective periods of hegemonic maturity? As they stood at the pinnacle of economic global power, did they act imperiously as they had acted during their ascent?

The concept "hegemony," recall, refers to a relational economic position in the world system. It is therefore distinguishable from empire, which is a political relation. A state can be imperial without being a hegemon. And a state can enjoy a preponderance over the world economy – that is, be hegemonic – without being imperial. Our task in this chapter is as follows: We will examine whether hegemonic status corresponded to any imperialistic practices and how the two hegemons' practices compare. Addressing this issue will enable us to better pinpoint what, if anything at all, differed between America's exercises of global power in the mid-twentieth century and Britain's exercises in the mid-nineteenth. At stake in the comparison is another goal: to confront exceptionalism. We have seen how exceptionalist thought has been deployed to make sense of America's activities prior to World War II, when the United States ascended to global power. But what about exceptionalism vis-à-vis America's post–World War II activities? Might it be here that exceptionalism tells us something useful?

Let us begin by returning to the Philippines.

Exceptionalism Returns

On July 4, 1946, while Americans celebrated their independence from Britain, another celebration of national independence was occurring halfway around the world. In the Philippines, a crowd of some 400,000 gathered in Manila

[3] Quoted in Nicolson ([1946] 2001), p. 128.

[4] Quoted in Sandars (2000), p. 7. On British and American hegemonies in comparative perspective, see O'Brien (2002) and Wallerstein (2002b).

to watch the lowering of the American flag, thereby ending a half century of American colonialism. Presumably, the event was an expression of America's liberal essence. "Our Nation covets no territory," declared President Roosevelt in his message to Congress on Philippine Independence; "it desires to hold no people against their will." Senator Millard Tydings of Maryland colored the event monumental, calling it "one of the most unprecedented, most idealistic, and most far-reaching events in all recorded history." General Douglas MacArthur, who gave a speech at the ceremonies, claimed that it marked nothing less than an entirely new world order. MacArthur's own father, Arthur MacArthur, Jr., had led American forces in "pacifying" the islands at the turn of the century and briefly served as military governor in Manila. More than four decades later, his son Douglas declared: "Let history record this event as foretelling the end of mastery over peoples by force alone – the end of empire as the political chain which binds the unwilling weak to the unyielding strong."[5] When the ceremony ended, MacArthur exclaimed to Carlos Romulo, his former staff member and prominent member of the Philippine oligarchy, "Carlos, America buried imperialism here today!"[6]

This rhetoric about Philippine independence encapsulates the ways in which exceptionalist thought has portrayed America's post–World War II activities. In exceptionalism's conception, the United States has been a benign world power, intrinsically anticolonial, inaugurating a world free from imperialism. There are a number of elements to this picture. One has to do with America's colonial empire. As noted, that empire was not unlike European empires, but the exceptionalist narrative readily domesticates it into its very architecture. In the exceptionalist story, even if the United States briefly had an empire, it quickly gave it away and refrained from acquiring any new colonies. "The year 1945 brought the final American rejection of empire," asserts David Fieldhouse.[7] Supposedly, this distinguishes the United States from other empires. "Athenians, Romans, Ottomans, and the British wanted land, colonies, treasure, and grabbed all they could get when they could," notes one historian, but the United States "hasn't annexed anyone's soil since the Spanish-American War."[8] To Eric Hobsbawm, this means that "the differences between . . . US ambitions and those of Britain of a century and more ago are stark."[9]

Besides pointing to America's reluctance to colonize, traditional exceptionalism insists that the United States supported national self-determination around

---

5 Quoted in Friend (1965), p. 262.
6 Quoted in ibid., p. 263.
7 Fieldhouse (1982), p. 347.
8 Hanson (2003) p. 147. See also Ikenberry (2001b), p. 204. Supposedly America's previous colonial ventures were a temporary deviation from America's true character; an "experiment" in colonialism, a "Great Aberration" or "unhappy exception." Smith (1988), p. 299. See also Bender (2006b), p. 299 and Winks (1997), p. 146.
9 Hobsbawm (2003). According to one foreign relations historian: "Americans threw their weight around, but they did not build a functioning empire like their predecessors in Great Britain, France, and Spain did," Suri (2009), p. 525.

the globe. The American state pushed for the decolonization of the European empires and helped construct a world order consisting of nation-states rather than empires. When it did employ its military to occupy other countries or engage in war, it was never intent on long-term colonization, leaving behind independent states rather than colonies.[10] The exceptionalist story also sees America's overseas interventions as benign attempts to promote democracy. Presumably, whereas European colonial empires repressed independence, markets, private property, and political rights, the United States has long adopted a distinct "mission" of "exporting democracy."[11] It has promoted American civilization and spread the light of liberty. On these grounds some historians reject any comparison between the United States and European empires. "No other military force has displayed the same consistent commitment to creating functioning, if limited, democracies in societies under occupation. No other military force has taken control of distant territories with the same consistent commitment to an early departure."[12]

A related part of the story is that the United States took on the comparably unique task of opening the world to free commerce for the benefit of all. This was concomitant with its opposition to colonialism. In the ideal version of the free market according to Adam Smith, free markets are antithetical to colonialism and its mercantilist protections. Whereas empires seek colonies to obtain privileged access to raw materials and exclusive markets, anticolonialism means the support of free market ideals.[13] Historian Thomas Bender notes of this view:

Americans are always anxious to deny the relevance of empire to their history. They tend to rely on a contrast with Europe to justify this way of understanding their past. They point out that except for an aberration that resulted in the taking possession of Puerto Rico, Guam, the Philippines, and, indirectly, Cuba, Americans did not colonize or rule territories as European powers did. Instead, they used their economic, military, and diplomatic leverage to create a world of free trade available to all. America's activity in the world, according to this account, was primarily that of private actors in the marketplace, not government rule over distant peoples and territories.[14]

Bender adds that the "American way of empire [after World War II] was even presented as *anti*-imperialism because it guaranteed openness, in contrast to the exclusivity of the old empires."[15]

Exceptionalism returns. The claim is that, although the United States may have been imperialistic during its ascent to global hegemony, it has acted

---

[10] Schwabe (1986), pp. 28–9.

[11] Smith (1994). See also Hanson (2003), p. 153.

[12] Suri (2009), pp. 529–30.

[13] Bruce Cumings asserts that empire refers to "some form of direct or monopoly control of another nation or of regions of the world economy (such as sterling blocs and frank blocs)," but inasmuch as the United States does not possess "monopoly controls in the world economy," it cannot be classified as an empire [Cumings (2003)].

[14] Bender (2006b), p. 191.

[15] Ibid., p. 233.

fundamentally differently from other powers during its period of hegemonic maturity. It decolonized its empire, refused to take new colonies, pushed for free markets, and supported self-determination around the world.

Traditional exceptionalism, though, has not been the only approach. The revisionist school animated by W. A. Williams and the Wisconsin School offers a different one. The revisionist story does not dispute that the United States was reluctant to annex new territory or that it pursued free trade. It stresses, however, that the lack of colonies does not mean a lack of empire. "One need not send out ships, seize territories, and hoist flags to construct an empire," notes John Lewis Gaddis. Empire is a matter of influence and control, and these may occur with or without the crude hand of direct colonialism. It can happen "informally" or indirectly. Magdoff initially called this "imperialism without colonies."[16] More recently, others have relabeled it "empire by remote control" or "nonterritorial imperialism."[17] Revisionist narratives thus tell tales of an American empire based on "commerce and finance" or other subtle mechanisms of power rather than territorial control.[18] Through military interventions, temporary occupations, covert operations, "alliances, bases, investments, and bribes," the United States has cultivated a network of client states nominally independent but nonetheless subject to American power and influence.[19] This is a new type of empire transcending the territorialism of old-world imperialism. As opposed to traditional exceptionalist thought, revisionism insists that the American state was "imperial," but defines imperialism as involving more or something other than just colonization.

The difference between traditional exceptionalism and revisionism partly turns on definition. Does "empire" only mean formal colonialism? Or should it not accommodate other types of power? But, beyond this difference, both approaches share important ground. Both suggest that America after World War II was nonterritorialist in the sense that it did not seek new colonies. Both also see something novel in America's activities. Brushing away America's earlier colonial expansion as an "aberration," both approaches see America's global activities in the mid-twentieth century as special (either because they involved constructing an empire or because they involved constructing a new type of empire). Indeed, some revisionists assert that informal empire is exactly what differentiates the United States from Britain. Rather than colonizing, "the US operated instead with dependent and satellite states."[20] Others add that the very refusal of exceptionalists and the American public to call the United States an empire manifests America's distinctiveness. Attempts to deny empire are but predictable manifestations of a "denial and displacement" of America's

---

[16] Magdoff (1972).

[17] Ho (2004); Steinmetz (2005).

[18] Bender (2006b), p. 183; Bender (2006a).

[19] Steel (1995), p. 30. See also Wood (2003).

[20] Hobsbawm (2003), p. 1. Bender sees America's informal exercises of power after World War II as constituting a distinctly "American way of empire" involving methods that were "novel, even technically creative." See also Wood (2003) and Judt (2004), pp. 38–41.

indisputable imperial history.[21] Denying empire is simply what makes the U.S. empire unique. As the diametric opposite of exceptionalism, therefore, revisionism carries some of the assumptions of its predecessor. By insisting on imperial uniqueness, it inscribes exceptionalist logic at the point of its possible dissolution.

There is another similarity between traditional exceptionalism and revisionism: Both approaches depend on comparison even though they do not actually conduct the comparison themselves. It is one thing to say that United States was reluctant to take new territory, that it supported the independence of other states, or that it pursued global free trade. It is another thing altogether to say that this makes the United States different from other powers or renders the United States exceptional. Similarly, it is one thing to say that the United States disavowed colonialism to exercise informal imperialism; it is another to depict this as something unique, unprecedented, unusual, or novel. In order to validate the latter part of these claims and thereby assert American exceptionalism, we would have to make visible and interrogate the rule against which America's presumably unique reluctance and nonterritorial tactics are measured. The premise of exceptionalist thinking is that there *is* such a rule. The notion is that other empires were not so reluctant, were always eager and determined to seize new territory, and aggressively sought "land, colonies, and treasure," whereas the United States creatively employed more subtle means. The related depiction is that other powers preferred colonial empire over mechanisms of money, trade, alliances, and clientelism, and that they were never hesitant to proudly label themselves "empires." The question that then arises is whether this has in fact been the rule of other empires. If not, perhaps the presumed American way of empire has not been so distinctly American. At stake in reconsidering existing approaches to America's postwar empire is not just how we define empire: It is how America's postwar activities fare comparatively.

In particular, at least two issues regarding the British empire merit attention. First, both traditional exceptionalism and revisionism portray non-American empires as consistently and unqualifiedly expansionist in the territorial mode while never failing to proudly label themselves an empire. But is this how the British state behaved? Second, exceptionalism and revisionism tend to measure America's activities against British colonial expansion, thereby reducing British power to territorial rule. Yet is formal empire the only "rule" of the British empire against which we can measure America's informal imperialism?

Reluctance, "Free Trade," and Denial

In April of 1868, British troops led by Charles Napier took control of Magdala, the seat of power in Abyssinia. The British had come to Magdala to rescue Europeans and the British consul who had been captured, imprisoned, and reportedly tortured by King Theodore of Abyssinia. The king, a.k.a. "Emperor

---

[21] Kaplan and Pease (1993).

Theodore, King of Ethiopia, King of Kings and the Chosen of God," was a notorious tyrant. He had previously constructed his own mini-empire by attacking neighboring Moslem provinces.[22] The military campaign aimed to stop this perceived menace and also free European captives. With 13,000 British and Indian combat troops, 291 naval vessels, and the latest military technology, it was highly successful. The 265 prisoners were freed, King Theodore killed himself at the threat of capture, and only two British officers lost their lives in the entire expedition. On April 13, the British flag was raised. Charles Napier – and Britain – emerged as the undisputed victor.

Important for our purposes is not the campaign itself but what happened afterward – or more precisely, what did *not* happen. The capture of Magdala, with Napier as the lone victor, gave Britain a unique opportunity to take Abyssinia as a colony and thereby add to its empire. To be sure, Britain had had interests in the region that would have made it an attractive acquisition. British merchants had been trading in the area for decades; Abyssinia and Britain had entered a treaty allowing those merchants to continue; and reports boasted of the region's fertile soil, gold, and ivory. However, disorder in the outlying areas had thwarted trade. British colonial rule would have helped establish order and security. Furthermore, British officials had long feared French ambitions in the region; Abyssinia was seen as a possible route to India.[23] Fittingly, some British consuls had been urging the Foreign Office to consider turning Abyssinia into a British domain. "Were an English governor [here]...," wrote Consul Plowden urging annexation, "how soon would the impulse of British energy, industry, and commercial enterprise be felt throughout this noble plateau extending nearly to the Equator, comprising some of the finest countries in Africa, and some of its most docile and intelligent races!"[24] Yet Britain did not seize the opportunity. Napier, although the undisputed ruler of Magdala, a result of his overwhelming military victory, instead lowered the flag. Rather than leaving behind British troops, colonial governors, or administrators, he left the conquered King Theodore's former subjects in the hands of a northern prince who had aided the British. On June 18, a few months after first seizing Magdala, the very last British troops left African soil. The next day, Her Majesty's ships sailed for home. There had been no attempt to retain British control. Nor had London sent orders to establish a permanent British presence. The British won but then ran.[25]

The decision to exit rather than maintain a colonial presence is suggestive. First, it suggests a shift from the previous century. Whereas Britain had expanded its territorial holdings in the century prior to the Napoleonic Wars,

---

[22] Chandler (1967), p. 111.
[23] Rodgers (1984), pp. 130–1.
[24] Walter Plowden to Foreign Office, June, 20, 1852, FO 1/7, PRO.
[25] Marry's Memo on Interview with Napier, Aug. 4, 1868, FO 1/26, PRO. Suggestions to take Abyssinia had also been rejected previously (Clarendon to Plowden, Oct. 13, 1853, FO 1/7). See also Chandler (1967), p. 151 and Rodgers (1984), p. 132.

it now – during its period of hegemony – appeared more reluctant to take new territories. Second, the withdrawal offers a comparative caution. As noted, both conventional exceptionalism and its revisionist counterpoint depend on an implicit comparison. Presumably, whereas the United States disavowed formal empire, other powers, like the British in the nineteenth century, were unqualifiedly aggressive in the territorial mode. Yet the decision in 1868 to just leave suggests that the British state was not as imperialistic in the territorial mode as exceptionalist thought portrays. As T. O. Lloyd notes, the refusal to annex after the Abyssinian expedition shows that "if expansion in Africa was now possible, British politicians were not interested."[26] This may be overstated considering Britain's other activities in Africa (to which we will later turn). Yet it does raise the question: Might it be that Britain, as it achieved hegemonic maturity, turned away from territorial aggrandizement just as the United States ostensibly did in the mid-twentieth century?

Cautious Colonialism

The refusal to take Abyssinia was not an isolated incidence of indifference. In fact, the British rejected various other opportunities to expand its territorial empire. At the peace of Amiens, the British handed back twenty of their conquests.[27] In 1806 and 1807, amid the Napoleonic wars, British forces occupied Montevideo and Buenos Aires, but they did not stay for long. Rather than seizing them as colonies, the British swiftly exited.[28] During the Opium War of 1849–1852, British troops numbering 50,000 subdued Nanking and surrounding areas, but London gave no orders to establish territorial rule. Later, in 1860, British and French forces took Peking and burned the emperor's palace, but those forces too swiftly exited.[29] A year later, British troops similarly occupied Vera Cruz in Mexico. The instructions from London were unequivocal: British troops were not to be used to colonize but only to help settle outstanding British claims and protect British residents.[30] In 1857, Napoleon III made overtures to Lord Palmerston that northern Africa should be divided between them as territorial spoils. This would have given Britain precious Egypt. But Palmerston was not interested. "We do not want Egypt," he declared. "[L]et us abstain from a crusade of conquest."[31]

This is not to say that Britain disavowed territorial expansion altogether from 1816 to the 1860s. As many scholars have stressed, the British state *did* add to its colonial empire.[32] Still, there are important qualifications. First, although the British state expanded its holdings during its period of hegemony,

[26] Lloyd (1996), p. 183.
[27] Martel (1991), p. 680.
[28] Ferns (1960), p. 60.
[29] Lloyd (1996), p. 184.
[30] "Correspondence Relating to the Affairs of Mexico," PP 1862, LXIV, No. 1.
[31] Palmerston to Clarendon, March 1, 1857 (CP). See also Cromer (1908), p. 92.
[32] E.g., Kennedy (1987), p. 155; Kennedy (1984); Fieldhouse (1982); Abernathy (2000).

it acquired much less during this period than before. From 1763 (after defeating France in the Seven Years' War) to 1815, Britain had acquired thirty-nine new colonies, but from 1816 to 1873 it only acquired twenty-three.[33] Second, many of the new annexations were not really "new," nor did they necessarily imply unqualified territorial aggression. Some reflected an administrative reorganization of existing territories (the Gold Coast, the Straits Settlements, and Turks and Caicos). Others reflected commitments made much earlier (e.g. Queensland) or simply replaced the existing jurisdiction of British trading companies (e.g. British Columbia). Others still were claimed for Britain by enterprising individuals on the spot without the authorization of the home government. These, accordingly, were disavowed later (Queen Adelaide's Land; Labuan).[34] Others were indeed new, but many of the additions were contiguous with existing holdings, such that the British state fashioned them defensive rather than aggressive (e.g. various districts in Australia; the Punjab and Sind; Assam and other areas northeast of India; and British Kaffraria).[35]

There is a final and perhaps more important qualification: Although the British state indeed expanded its holdings, it also rejected as many opportunities to expand. This was the case even when British control was invited. Some sectors of the Cuban elite expressed interest in Britain taking Cuba as a colony, but London did not respond. At various times from 1838 to 1848, the Montevideo government (in Uruguay) "offered England concessions tantamount to creating a British protectorate," but all of the offers were refused.[36] Offers came in from approximately 1838 to 1856 to take parts of present-day California, but these were dismissed.[37] In the 1850s and 1860s, a series of offers from chiefs in Fiji to establish a British colony flooded the Foreign Office, but these too were rejected.[38] In the 1840s, the Dominican Republic made overtures to turn itself over to Britain, but the response was negative.[39] The British state also refused to annex various small territories, even though such additions would not be costly. When British merchants urged the Foreign Office take some guano-rich islands off the coast of Peru, Her Majesty's Government refused to act. From 1855 to 1861, the White Rajah of Sarawak repeatedly offered his titles to Britain, but successive governments in London politely refused (despite reports from the ground that taking Sarawak would halt an imposing Dutch threat, offer all kinds of mineral resources, and help

---

[33] Calculated from data discussed in Appendix.

[34] These cases and others are discussed in Darwin (1997) and Knox (1973). Administrative histories of the acquisitions are given succinctly in Stewart (1996).

[35] See Kennedy (1984); Platt (1968b); Knox (1973).

[36] Winn (1976), p. 107.

[37] Adams (1909).

[38] Minutes by Carnarvon and Bulwer-Lytton, January 21, 1859, on Denison to Bulwar-Lytton, October 12, 1858. Colonial Office manuscripts: New South Wales correspondence, C.O. 201/504.

[39] Doyle (1986), p. 254.

establish a route for telegraphic communication to China).[40] London likewise refused to take Katanga in 1874.[41]

Even when important trading interests were at stake, Britain did not always extend colonial control. Consider West Africa. By mid-century, Britain had been exporting textiles and metal goods to the Niger Delta in exchange for vegetable oils. It also had a man on the spot, the British consul John Beecroft, ready to be appointed colonial administrator. Again, Britain did not turn the region into a colony. In 1865, the Parliamentary Select Committee went so far as to recommend against colonialism entirely in most parts of Africa, even suggesting that London should dispose of its existing holdings in the region (with one or two exceptions).[42] In some cases too, Britain handed back territories. It returned Java in 1816 and Sumatra by 1824 to the Dutch after occupying them. In 1846, the home government disavowed D'Urban's attempt to annex Queen Adelaide's Land in South Africa.[43] Britain also ceded the Bay Islands to Honduras in 1859.[44] In 1864, Britain evacuated the Ionian Islands after having been there for some fifty years, giving them back to Greece.[45]

If these examples unsettle exceptionalism's assumptions that the United States has been a uniquely "reluctant" hegemon, so too should the many instances when the British state actively supported the sovereignty of other states. Rather than remain in Montevideo as an occupying force, the British state encouraged the creation of the independent state of Uruguay. After the Napoleonic Wars, the British state eventually landed on a policy of supporting the independence of Latin American republics. Rather than seize Turkey or its territories as the Ottoman empire weakened in the mid-nineteenth century, Britain lent resources to promote the integrity of the Turkish state. Britain also fought the Crimean War to protect Turkey against Russian aggression, even as it had helped secure the independence of Greece from Turkey. Britain similarly used influence of various sorts to support the independence of Tunis and Morocco and the domains of the Sultan of Zanzibar.[46] In 1847, Britain made an agreement with France to guarantee the independence of various islands in the Pacific and, in accordance with its decision to not occupy Mexico, continually supported Mexican independence.[47]

The notion that the British grabbed all they could while the United States uniquely promoted the independence of foreign states is misleading if not

---

[40] On proposals for taking Sarawak, see "Memo for Lord Clarendon," Feb. 4, 1858, FO 12/25; Brooke to Grey, Feb. 11, 1858, F.O. 12/35, PRO; for the negative decisions, see "Minutes and memo" attached to Brooke to Fitzgerald March 19, 1858 FO 12/35 and Foreign Office to Brooke, April 15, 1858, FO 12/35.

[41] Hyam (1999), p. 34.

[42] Chamberlain (1988), p. 125.

[43] Darwin (1997), p. 620.

[44] Knox (1973), p. 158; on the Bay Islands, see Waddell (1959).

[45] Knox (1984)

[46] Flournoy (1935), pp. 258–60.

[47] Fieldhouse (1982), p. 217.

false altogether. Alongside the actual annexations that took place were various refusals to expand colonial holdings and a series of policies supporting the independence of certain foreign states. This suggests that the actions of the British state during its period of economic hegemony hardly amount to a singular rule of territorial aggrandizement and aggression against which we can easily assess America's exceptionalism. To be sure, as historian John Darwin has shown, there was little "firmness of imperial purpose" in this period; no singular official policy, hence no official "mind" or uniform rule dictating that the British state take new colonies.[48]

If there was an official policy or overarching ideology at all, it was not about empire but economics: specifically, free trade. This is a feature of British foreign policy that exceptionalist thought has run the risk of occluding by treating free trade as somehow America's special provenance. However, Britain articulated the free trade ideal long before presumably anti-imperial Americans did. Originating in Adam Smith and David Ricardo, the ideal surfaced strongly in the political writings of Richard Cobden and the Manchester School. Cobden never held political office, but his views resonated in London circles. Many parliamentarians were tied to the rising world of finance, and so many of them embraced the free trade dogma.[49] "Cobdenites" also had prominent policy-making positions. The Board of Trade and its departments overseeing foreign policy were famously pro-laissez-faire.[50] Free trade beliefs thus contributed to liberal policies. Foreign Secretary George Canning declared in 1824 that Britain sought "no exclusive privileges of trade... but equal freedom and commerce for all."[51] Liberalization proceeded through the 1840s with a series of bilateral free trade treaties. In 1846, Britain unilaterally repealed the Corn Laws.[52] By the Cobden-Chevalier Treaty in 1860, Britain reduced tariffs with France and extended the same reductions to all other countries. As historian Patrick Karl O'Brien explains, this was "the most significant trade liberalization agreement of the nineteenth century," because it became a "cornerstone of a new international trading system and an example that other European countries emulated."[53] Here there was no contradiction between colonies and free trade. Britain simply opened up its colonies to foreign trade.[54]

These steps to liberalize world trade were part and parcel of larger ideologies that have been heralded as the unique provenance of the United States. One was that Britain would serve as a leading "civilizing" force in the world. This notion, as colonial historians are wont to show, later fed into British justifications for colonialism; but it also combined with the free trade ideal. Although free trade was obviously good for British business, proponents argued that it

---

[48] Darwin (1997).
[49] Porter (1999), p. 14.
[50] Platt (1968b).
[51] Quoted in Platt (1968a): 90), p. 90.
[52] Irwin (1993), p. 94.
[53] O'Brien and Pigman (1992), pp. 98, 101.
[54] Cain (1999), pp. 39–40.

was also good for the "uncivilized" world. Lord Palmerston saw British commerce with Africa as a civilizing force. In 1850 he declared: "[We, i.e. the cabinet] ... wishing most earnestly that civilization may be extended in Africa, being convinced that commerce is the best pioneer for civilization, and being satisfied that there is room enough in ... Africa for the commerce of all the civilized nations of the rest of the world, would see with pleasure every advance of commerce in Africa, provided that such commerce was not founded on monopoly and was not conducted upon an exclusive system."[55] Palmerston was also a vehement antislaver, and he used the British navy as well as treaties to curb the trade in Africa and Latin America. This too combined with the free trade ideology, not to mention the view of Britain as a "civilizing" and benign force in the world. According to Palmerston, the anti–slave trade campaign was not only "calculated to promote the interests of humanity," but also to make sure that "the greatest commercial benefit would accrue, not to England only, but to every civilized nation."[56] Lower-level officials in the heartlands agreed. "[I]t is to the commercial supremacy of the British Empire," said J. Snape, councilor in Manchester, "that we must look for the advancement of freedom and civilisation throughout the world, for the happiness and comfort of our families at home, and for the intellectual, material, and religious progress of the world." He added:

I am a thorough and real Free Trader. . . . [L]et the world see that England will be at the forefront of commercial progress, and maintain the country great, glorious, and free. We are willing to extend those blessings to foreign nations if they will accept them upon fair and equal terms. We ought to proclaim to foreign nations that if they will accept our terms we are not afraid of Free Trade, and we will allow them free markets in this country for whatever they choose to send, if they will allow us to do the same in their country.[57]

A related ideology was limited government abroad. The state should not set up mercantilist protections or meet particularistic interests, but rather only help expand trade. "It is the business of Government," Palmerston wrote in 1841, "to open and secure the roads for the merchant."[58] The ideology was often put into practice, much to the dismay of British ventures abroad. When British troops occupied Vera Cruz in 1862 and later departed to leave behind an independent Mexico, London instructed the British minister of Mexico to remember that "neither in Mexico nor in any part of the world do Her Majesty's Government seek any exclusive political influence, nor any commercial advantages which they are not ready to share with all the nations of the earth."[59] British claimants and creditors in Mexico were sorely disappointed.[60]

[55] Quoted in Robinson and Gallagher (1961), p. 35.
[56] Quoted in Hyam (2002), p. 43.
[57] Snape (1882), p. 2.
[58] Quoted in Platt (1968a), p. 85.
[59] "Correspondence Relating to the Affairs of Mexico," PP 1862, LXIV.
[60] Platt (1968a), p. 300.

Similarly, throughout the 1840s, British commercial interests asked the government to pressure the Peruvian government to help them in the invaluable guano trade. They hoped for London to use the navy to provide support to British merchants searching for alternative guano supplies along Peru's coast or force the Peruvian government to reduce prices, but London was not interested in helping them.[61] Further, as noted, the British government often refused to annex territories in Africa, China, or the Pacific – even though British consuls and traders often pressured for annexation to protect their particular economic interests.[62]

The ideology of laissez-faire, in fact, was intimately connected with Britain's refusals to expand its colonial holdings. After previous centuries of colonization in the Americas and attendant mercantilist policies, the turn toward free trade in the mid-nineteenth century implied that colonial economic barriers were no longer desired; hence colonies were less desirable.[63] When Palmerston refused to seize Abyssinia, he explained, "I do not see any advantage in our getting land in these quarters. All we want is trade and land is not necessary for trade; we can carry on commerce on ground belonging to other people."[64] Palmerston likewise explained his decision to turn away from a "crusade of conquest" in Egypt in 1857. "We want to trade with Egypt and to travel through Egypt but we do not want the burden of governing Egypt. Let us try to improve all those countries by the general influence of our commerce."[65] He famously put it later: "We do not want Egypt or wish it for ourselves, any more than any rational man with an estate in the north of England and a residence in the south [for which read India] would have wished to possess the inns on the north road. All he could want would have been that the inns should be well kept, always accessible, and furnishing him when he came with mutton chops and post-horses."[66] Britain's trade in the mid-nineteenth century would have supported Palmerston's view on the relative importance of economic liberalism over neo-mercantilism and colonial preferences. The average value of Britain's trade with its empire was 76 million pounds between 1855 and 1859. The value of trade with foreign countries in the same period, however, was more than double, reaching 209 million pounds.[67]

If the presumed imperial rule does not fit traditional exceptionalism's characterization, neither does British discourse match the revisionists' claim that the distinctiveness of American empire lies in self-denial. Britons of various social classes sometimes denied the existence of a British empire, or at least were barely cognizant of its existence.[68] When they were cognizant of it, they

---

[61] Mathew (1968).

[62] Platt (1968a).

[63] Fieldhouse (1982), p. 177.

[64] Quoted in Hyam (2002), p. 107.

[65] Palmerston to Clarendon, March 1, 1857, CP.

[66] Quoted in Cromer (1908), p. 92.

[67] Thornton (1959), p. 6.

[68] Porter (2004).

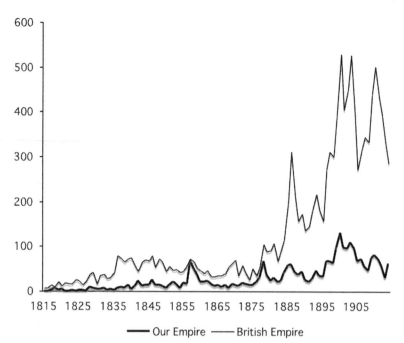

FIGURE 3.1. British "Empire" Discourse: Number of Times "British Empire" or "Our Empire" Appeared in the *Times* of London, 1815–1914. *Source:* Counted from the *Times* of London, digital archive online.

did not always think of it as an expansive overseas political system whereby subject races were tyrannized by British administrators. That would come later, with the "new imperialism" of the latter part of the century. Before then, the term British empire typically referred to the "United Kingdom of the British Isles and to England in particular." It was rarely if ever deployed to discuss foreign affairs.[69] Hence, one of the handful of books that purported to examine the "circumstances of the British Empire" in 1823 did not mention Britain's overseas possessions. It instead discussed issues of British trade, the Poor Laws, and its national debt.[70] Likewise, a comprehensive guidebook on British overseas possessions in the east did not speak of those possessions as part of the "British Empire in the East" but rather as the "British *World* in the East."[71] The relative frequency with which the phrase "British Empire" was used is suggestive. A word count of articles in The London *Times* shows that uses of the phrase "British empire" or "our empire" were much less common in the hegemonic period than in the period following the late 1870s (see Fig. 3.1). In this sense, denying empire is not as distinctively American as apple pie. It may

[69] Koebner and Schmidt (1964), pp. 45–6.
[70] An Officer of His Majesty's Navy (1823).
[71] Leitch Ritchie in Koebner and Schmidt (1964), p. 37.

well be that *all* hegemons, whether of the British or American variety, prefer not to inscribe the sign empire on their flags or foreheads.

In light of all of this, the trajectory of British imperial historiography makes perfect sense. In fact, ever since classic works like J. R. Seeley's *Expansion of England* (1883) and H. E. Egerton's *A Short History of British Colonial Policy* (1897), there has been a long scholarly tradition suggesting that Britain in the mid-nineteenth century, like the United States in the mid-twentieth century, was not exactly an empire or that, at the very least, it was not as "imperialist" as it had been in earlier years. The tradition was continued in classic economic theories of imperialism – beginning with Hobson (1902) and proceeding through Marxian variants (such as Lenin's theory of imperialism). These theories were predicated on the notion that Britain in mid-century was anti-imperial or indifferent to empire and that it was only imperialistic in the latter decades of the century. Later works, such as Bodelsen's *Studies in Mid-Victorian Imperialism* (1924) and R. L. Schuyler's *Fall of the Old Colonial System*, took up the mantle, repeating the notion that the mid-Victorian "empire" was not quite an empire. Even in the late 1960s, some prominent statesmen were still articulating this notion. "The myth of the British Empire," declared conservative parliamentarian John Enoch Powell, "is one of the most extraordinary paradoxes in political history. During the whole of the period in which Britain is imagined to have been creating her empire, she was not only unconscious of doing any such thing, but positively sure she was not. The Romans . . . they indeed had an *imperium* which embraced almost the whole civilized world, and they said so, and Virgil told them it was their mission to 'rule the peoples with their sway.' Not so the British."[72] Conventional British historiography itself thus prefigures traditional American exceptionalism. Both at times refused to name empire.

Persistent Territorialism

The foregoing suggests that the hegemonic British state was *less* imperialistic than exceptionalist thought presumes. However, a case can also be made that the United States after World War II was *more* imperialistic in the territorial mode than conventional and critical wisdom has allowed. It is no doubt the case that the United States granted independence to the Philippines. As noted in a previous chapter, however, this does not mean that the United States disavowed its empire. Out of all the territories annexed by the United States in the early twentieth century, only the Philippines was given official independence in this period.[73] Nonetheless, we might wonder: Did not the United States finally show its true anticolonial character after World War II?

To answer, exceptionalist thought might not only point to decolonization of the Philippines, but also to the fact that Puerto Rico was eventually given

---

[72] Powell (1969), p. 247.
[73] Even this granting of independence by the United States was not unprecedented. England, for example, gave up the Ionian Islands.

commonwealth status in this period.[74] Yet this is hardly evidence of an exceptional anticolonialism. First of all, Britain had given some of its settler colonies a similar status decades earlier. The very label "commonwealth" had been drawn from Britain's imperial framework. Why isn't Britain therefore classified as exceptionally anticolonial? Furthermore, and most important, commonwealth status for Puerto Rico did not mean independence or decolonization. It was even more stringent than it was for Britain's commonwealth dominions. Puerto Ricans still did not have the right to vote for the president, and the U.S. federal government retained the right to legislate significant aspects of Puerto Rico's affairs. The term commonwealth obscured persistent colonial ties.[75] Finally, to this day, the United States maintains imperial ties with these territories. Puerto Rico has some measure of self-government, but it does not vote for representatives to Congress or for the president of the United States. Officially, the president can order Puerto Ricans to war, the federal government appoints judges, and Congress can pass legislation for Puerto Rico. Something similar persists for Guam and the U.S. Virgin Islands. American Samoa votes for its own officials but is still administered by the Office of Insular Affairs in the Department of the Interior. Citizens of these territories do not enjoy the full protection of the U.S. Constitution. They each have internal autonomy, but Congress officially sanctions that autonomy and could revoke it overnight if it desired. These areas remain under the control of the U.S. federal government. In this sense, the United States is probably the *only* colonial empire that has *not* decolonized. By some estimates, these persistent ties make the U.S. empire the largest territorial empire in the world today.[76]

The continuation of these colonial ties was not due to indifference or inertia. The colonies remained of vital value to Washington. Before World War I, they had already shown their geostrategic value. They had been the only overseas locations for America's military installations. Then, as the Second World War ended, the colonies remained central to the American military's strategic planning. As planners were worried about sea approaches to the Western hemisphere, Puerto Rico, Cuba's Guantánamo Bay, and the Virgin Islands were ever more vital.[77] The war in the Pacific had reemphasized the importance of Guam and Samoa, and these remained central for the Pacific defense perimeter, not least because Roosevelt's strategies envisioned a postwar defense system based on sea and air. This was part and parcel of a reconceptualization of what America's basing system should be about. Rather than merely defensive posts, overseas bases would also serve as "springboards" for offensive action should the need arise. Pacific bases were critical for this new system.[78]

[74] Pagden (2005).
[75] On the legal aspects of Puerto Rico's status, see Burnett and Marshall (2001).
[76] Sparrow (2006), pp. 214–16.
[77] Campbell (1947), p. 42.
[78] Ibid., p. 41.

For these reasons and more, the sun had yet to set on America's colonial empire in the postwar period. Neil Smith – joining a larger chorus in the exceptionalist mode of thought – has recently intimated the irrelevance of America's colonies, calling them "geographical crumbs" of Spain's disintegrated empire.[79] Yet America's military establishment and postwar planners did not find them irrelevant. To the contrary, they made them pivotal for their plans. If America's colonies were crumbs, no one in Washington could imagine American global power without them.

If the oft-repeated claim that the United States had an empire but quickly "gave it away" is simply wrong, so too is the assertion that the United States failed to annex new territory after the supposed "temporary" phase of colonial expansion in the earlier part of the century.[80] In 1943, the Joint Chiefs of Staff and the Navy Department envisioned new acquisitions beyond those already acquired. Foreseeing America's victory in the war, they began plans for a new postwar network of bases and military installations that would span the globe. Although America's existing colonies were important for their strategy, their plan also called for additional colonies in the Pacific. Of immediate interest were Japan's former territories, later known as Micronesia (e.g., the Marshall Islands, the Carolines, and the Marianas). Strategists also marked the Bonins, the Ryukus, and Okinawa on their maps. These were all to be part of a new postwar expanded American empire of the old-school variety.[81]

These plans were not the only ones circulating in the minds and offices of Washington. Various memos and documents from a number of policy committees had similar expansionist designs. Some even went further than the early 1943 plan. They called for America to take all of Samoa rather than just America's existing half and to add the Japanese Kurile islands (with a permanent population of about 18,000 inhabitants). They even called for the seizure of the British and French colonies in the Pacific.[82] Although defense strategists were often the first to make such calls, even civilian officials in Roosevelt's administration produced similar schemes. The Bureau of the Budget's plan called for direct American control over Polynesia and Micronesia; for "adequate participation in Melanesia" (including "Fiji, New Hebrides, New Caledonia, and Soloman Islands, the Bismarck Archipleago, New Guinea, and adjacent islands"); and "a strong position in Indonesia." The only question was which agency should act as the colonial office. The War Department? The Bureau of Insular Affairs?[83] Such plans also noted that additional Pacific territories would not only be useful for the purposes of defense but also for commerce. They pinpointed Southeast Asia's raw materials and the economic

79 Smith (2003), p. 16. See also Motyl (2006).
80 "Americans presumed their imperial role would be a short one, as indeed it was." Winks (1997), pp. 146–7.
81 Louis (1978), pp. 264–6.
82 Ibid., p. 266.
83 "Memorandum on Organization for Civil Affairs in the Pacific Islands," Wayne Coy to Harry Hopkins, Jan. 10, 1944, (HP, Box 334).

promise of Asia in its entirety. Yet proper access to the markets and materials would demand a long string of air bases, each necessitating an operational radius of seven hundred miles. Japan and Manila would be the main points of access in this Pacific-Asian commercial circuit; Guam, Samoa, Hawaii, and the new annexations would complete the chain.[84] Gunboats and commercial boats alike would follow the flag.

These plans were widely known, so much so that the media began speaking affirmatively of a new "American colonial empire" in the Pacific.[85] Only Rupert Emerson, writing in *Pacific Affairs*, noted the irony: "It is a curious coincidence that the United States, just at the time when it is by its own voluntary act surrendering control over the Philippines, should be in the process of fathering to itself a new empire in the Pacific."[86] Still, the idea of an expanded colonial empire and additional colonial subjects was warmly welcomed by at least some sectors in the United States. An informal poll of American legislators revealed that congressmen and senators favored annexation of the Japanese islands by two to one.[87] "I want those islands," declared Tom Connally, chairman of the Senate Foreign Relations Committee.[88] None of it was lost on British observers. The Earl of Halifax, writing to the London Foreign Office from Washington, warned his superiors of "the straight jingoes in Congress and beyond who want annexation."[89] Sir Frederick Eggleston added: "The Americans are very keen on this... strategic area [in the Pacific], and it gives a lie to the lot of their absurd criticism of the [European] colonial system before the war."[90]

The culture of old-world imperialism and great-power politics persisted into the post–World War II days – to the victor go the spoils. In this case, however, the outcome was only slightly different. While the military establishment, the American public, and American legislators clamored for colonial annexation, the State Department pushed for a more moderate stance. Working most closely with the Allies amid the postwar negotiations, the State Department felt pressure from the British and French to turn the Japanese territories into international mandates rather than taking them outright. After much deliberation, the State Department recommended the mandate approach, fearing that America's recolonization would justify a new scramble for territory on the part of the European allies and Russia. Harold Ickes in the Department of the Interior agreed. Directly annexing Pacific territories would permit any one of the Allies to claim the same rights in the Middle East, thereby threatening "our great stake in Middle Eastern oil."[91] A fierce battle in Washington ensued,

---

[84] Louis (1978), p. 74.
[85] Trumbull (1946), p. 13.
[86] Emerson (1947), p. 263.
[87] *New York Times*, Jan. 31, 1946, p. 6.
[88] Quoted in Sebrega (1986), p. 70.
[89] Earl of Halifax to Foreign Office, Washington to Foreign Office, April 22, 1945, CO 968/161/2.
[90] Quoted in Louis (1978), p. 566.
[91] FRUS 1945, I, p. 141; see also Friedman (1995), p. 353, and Louis (1978), p. 85.

marking – as the British ambassador reported – "a rift in the American family on this issue."[92]

The final result was a strategic compromise. Rather than making the islands a proper United Nations Trust Territory, the Joint Chiefs of Staff successfully pushed to turn them into a "Strategic Trust Territory." This was an entirely new category of international mandates, created for this case only. It was an attempt to give the appearance of international supervision, but it left the United States with full direct control. The Navy Department was given the task of acting as a colonial administration, with power to legislate for the islands as it pleased. The Pentagon later boasted that the United Nations had a veneer of control. In effect, the United States "retained all the attributes of sovereignty."[93] The U.K. delegation to the negotiations correctly wrote home that the plan simply gave the United States "a free hand in these islands except for nominal control by the [UN] Security Council."[94] Rupert Emerson wrote in *Pacific Affairs* that the trusteeship policy is "virtually indistinguishable from annexation."[95] The American press was not mistaken either. A *Washington Post* editorial reported, "the United States is taking over a vast empire of four million square miles in the Pacific."[96] Decolonizing the Philippines, the American state simply recolonized the rest of the Pacific.

The Form of Informal Empire

The foregoing suggests that the American state was not as anticolonial as conventional narratives portray. Rather than transcending the territorialism of old-world imperialism, the American postwar state persisted in and depended on it. But there is a final sense in which the American state was more colonialist than exceptionalist or even revisionist stories would suggest. Those stories conjure how Roosevelt and his aides in the aftermath of World War II pushed for the decolonization of European empires, but they overlook the fact that the postwar American state actually *supported* the European empires. Leaders and policy makers may have talked a big game about a world of independent nation-states (talk that scholars today continue to see as exemplifying a unique American anticolonialism), but they did little in practice after World War II to match their rhetoric with reality. Until the 1960s or so, Washington lent the European empires critical funds so as to keep their colonial systems intact. Rather than pushing for their end, the United States came to rely on and purposively deploy the empires about which they spoke so negatively.

---

[92] Earl of Halifax, April 8, 1945 to Foreign Office, CO 968/161/1.
[93] Joint Chiefs of Staff quoted in Foltos (1989), p. 332.
[94] Telegram, U.K. Delegation, San Francisco (Jacob) to Secretary of State for Foreign Affairs, May 12, 1945, CO 968/161/2.
[95] Emerson (1947), p. 266.
[96] *Washington Post*, 1 Dec. 1946, B1.

We will learn more about this in a later chapter. For now, we should turn to other ways in which the United States was more imperial than conventional exceptionalism would allow. After all, the foregoing discussion about colonialism measures empire in a restrictive way. Looking for all the spots marked red on the map, it classifies empire as a matter of territorial acquisition and direct colonial rule. Are there are not other ways in which states can be "imperial" besides colonial annexation? We come here to critics of traditional exceptionalism who suggest that although the United States did not construct a colonial empire, it was imperial nonetheless – if only because it embarked on a different brand of imperialism, a particular "American way of empire." This type of imperialism is worth exploring further. It is also worthy of comparative investigation.

An "American Way of Empire"?

Already in 1951, an article in *The Nation's Business* noted something of this particular American way of empire. Reporting on America's new overseas basing system (still dependent on Europe's colonies), it contended: "Some nations achieve empire, while others have empire thrust upon them. It's hardly news to Americans that world-wide responsibility has been laid on their doorstep like an unwanted foundling.... This new American imperialism (and let's not boggle at the term until we've redefined it in terms of mid-century realities) is based firmly on a curving line of aerial outposts from Iceland to the Azores; from French Morocco on the eastern shore of the Atlantic to Libya on the southern shore of the Mediterranean."[97] In calling this basing system imperialistic, this writer for the *Nation's Business* was probably uniquely astute for his time. The British ambassador in Washington wrote home amidst the debate over the Japanese territories in 1945: "Bases do not seem to most Americans to be colonies in the unpopular sense of the word."[98] Still, the notion that America's global network of bases constituted a sort of "empire" has been raised in the revisionist histories first produced by William A. Williams and the Wisconsin School. In these histories, if the United States did not construct a new formal colonial empire, it did establish a string of overseas military installations that stand as new American versions of old-style colonies.

Beyond America's basing system, however, there were other means of exercising power. Something of this is seen in the case of Philippine independence. In theory, Philippine independence meant national freedom, but in practice it came with various strings. The Bell Trade Act, which specified the economic conditions for granting independence, pegged the Philippine peso to the U.S. dollar. It also required that the new Philippine constitution provide U.S. citizens and corporations access to Philippine raw materials and specified duty-free and quota-free trade between the United States and the Philippines.[99] Independence

---

[97] Alexander (1951), pp. 27–8.
[98] Earl of Halifax, April 8, 1945, From Washington to Foreign Office, CO 968/161/1.
[99] Shalom (1980), p. 500.

also came with military strings. Before the granting of independence, the Philip-pine president, Manuel Roxas, signed a preliminary statement with President Truman binding the archipelago to a future military agreement. In 1947, the Military Bases Agreement granted the United States the use of twenty-three bases in the archipelago for at least ninety-nine years. A few days later, another agreement was signed. The Military Assistance Agreement provided that the United States would arm and train the Philippine armed forces and offer other services (such as intelligence). It also set up a Joint U.S. Military Advisory group "to assist and advise the Republic of the Philippines on military and naval matters."[100]

These provisions are notable because they enabled the United States to use the Philippines as it always had when it exercised direct colonial rule – namely, for capital accumulation and as a nodal point in its network of national secu-rity. Congressman Jasper Bell fittingly remarked that the Bell Trade Act would "recreate our sixth best customer in world commerce."[101] The South could regain a market for its cotton; New England for its textiles; and dairy pro-ducers for their diary. Similarly, the prolonged presence of the U.S. military helped to round out America's Asia-Pacific defense system, connecting bases in Europe's colonies and America's own colonies.[102] In short, although the Philip-pines became nominally independent, the United States retained influence and control, enabling it to fulfill traditional imperial imperatives. The more things changed, the more they stayed the same.

Of course, the form of this influence and control was different than before. American colonial governors, backed by colonial armies and policing, no longer ran the show. Formal colonial control was over; the United States no longer claimed sovereignty; it could not influence the islands' political and economic system by direct command. Yet the United States nonetheless exercised power to fulfill its wider economic and strategic goals. First, it exploited unequal economic conditions. When the Bell Trade Act was offered to the Philippine legislature, it stipulated that if the legislature accepted it, not only would the country receive independence, but also $800 million in U.S. aid for recon-structing the country – funds that were vital for the war-ravaged archipelago. Second, the United States exploited internal divisions to cultivate clients. The Bell Trade Act provided Americans access to Philippine resources, but it like-wise helped the Philippine sugar elite who had come to depend on access to American markets.[103] Similarly, the new president, Manuel Roxas, had been

---

[100] Quoted in Pomeroy (1992), p. 164.
[101] Quoted in Friend (1965), pp. 259–60.
[102] The value of the Philippine bases in particular was later demonstrated over and over again. In 1950, in response to the outbreak of the Korean War, they served as the jumping point for patrolling the line between Communist China and Taiwan, presumably to defend the latter from a Red Army invasion. Later in the decade, Philippine bases were used for operations in Indonesia against President Sukarno, whose Communist orientation had struck fear into State Department officials.
[103] Shalom (1980), p. 504.

facing the threat of Communist revolution in the countryside. He needed American military support and aid to quell it if he was to retain power. He therefore accepted the new military agreements for U.S. bases, but only after American emissaries had threatened to withdraw U.S. troops if the base agreement was not accepted.[104] In short, rather than controlling the islands by the threat of direct force or an imposed foreign colonial governor, the United States offered Filipino leaders money and military support. Colonial subjects became free citizens of their own sovereign nation, but they also became allies and dependent clients, propped to help fulfill America's post–World War II imperatives. In some ways, this new relationship was even better than before. As Yale political scientist David Nelson Rowe told a meeting of foreign policy makers in October 1946, "the United States is actually in a stronger position in the Philippines although the islands are independent now."[105]

The end of U.S. rule in the Philippines has been taken by exceptionalist historiography and contemporaries alike as a model for an anticolonial postwar order based on American values, but it can also be taken as exemplifying a new way of empire. After noting that the conditions of Philippine independence put the United States in a stronger position than before, David Nelson Rowe added that the same type of "economic, cultural, and military relations through the consent of new governments might well be applied to other territories in the Far East."[106] This was exactly what happened, even beyond Asia, leading to the construction of a wider network of power constituting an informal empire. Unlike in the Philippines, the tactics here did not always involve constitution writing. Only in precious few areas could the United States actually control that process (Japan, for one). Instead, the tactics entailed flows of favors and exchanges alongside and around America's existing colonial empire – punctuated by covert and overt military operations to help establish and defend the network.

Latin America provides examples. The United States made it a near official policy to support military and dictatorial regimes there, turning powerful elements in the region into friendly clients akin to colonial collaborators. Beginning in 1946, American officials began selling military equipment to Latin America, guided by the notion that this was an effective way to influence local affairs. In a secret hearing to Congress on the policy, a representative from the War Department explained: "In those cases where the army or the navy does not actually run the government, they come so close to it that any influence on them has great national importance to those countries. Our military missions there are working with the most influential people in those governments."[107] In the first years of the 1960s, President Kennedy's ambassador to the Organization of American States established the Inter-American Defense College in

---

[104] Pomeroy (1992), p. 163.
[105] *New York Times*, Oct. 12, 1946, p. 5.
[106] Ibid.
[107] United States Congress Committee on International Relations (1976), VI, p. 479.

Washington to train Latin American military officials, insisting that the military would serve as a "force for stability" in the region.[108] In 1964, a joint report of the State and Defense Departments reiterated that the "potential for advancing US interests and objectives through effective US influence upon the Latin America military is great" and so attached "highest" priority to continued relations with Latin American military officers.[109]

The results of this approach should be familiar. To take just one example, the 1948 military junta in Venezuela resulted in a decade of military rule. Combined aid from the United States jumped from $.5 million per year (on average) before the junta to an average of $4 million per year afterward (plus about $54 million in U.S. loans).[110] Similarly, in Bolivia, an overthrow of the Villarroel regime in 1952 established the rule of Victor Paz Estenssoro, and U.S. economic aid subsequently heightened. When his regime became recalcitrant in the early 1960s, his military overthrew him with American support.[111] At issue in all of these relationships was the same issue guiding America's support of Europe's colonial empire: capital and containment. But in fact, until the Cuban Revolution, the issue was less Communist penetration than it was economic security. The 1948 overthrow in Venezuela was good for the United States because the overthrown Acción Democrática regime had threatened U.S.-owned oil companies. After the State Department recognized the new junta and stepped up aid, U.S. oil companies regained access and reinvigorated their profits. In Bolivia, the Paz regime was unabashedly Marxist in tone, but the United States supported it because the previous regime had threatened American tin interests.[112] Such activities helped create a boon for American companies. From 1951 to 1955, profits on all U.S. investment in Latin America were 13.9 percent, and from 1956 to 1958, they were 12.0 percent; corporate profits in the United States during the same eight-year period were only 7.8 percent.[113]

Beyond supporting already-existing regimes or capitalizing on coups, the United States also played a more direct hand in installing friendly client regimes, often through covert or overt operations. In Brazil in 1964, covert encouragement, previous American training of local military officers, and the presence of offshore U.S. naval units helped the military overthrow João Goulert's presidency. Goulert had threatened American interests with a land reform program, limitations on foreign capital, and friendly recognition of Cuba.[114] The new president, General Castelo Branco, swiftly became a close American ally.[115] Ten years earlier, one of the first overt U.S. military interventions after

---

[108] Morrison (1965), p. 225.
[109] Quoted in Kolko (1988), p. 148.
[110] Calculated from data in USAID, *Overseas Loans and Grants* (www.usaid.gov/policy/greenbook.html, accessed 1/06/2009).
[111] Kolko (1988), pp. 100–1.
[112] Ibid.
[113] Ibid., p. 95.
[114] See Weis (2001).
[115] Westad (2005), p. 150.

World War II had taken place in Guatemala, leading to the ousting of Arbenz, whose regime had threatened the United Fruit Company. The CIA began a campaign to overthrow him. A U.S. aircraft attack in 1954 authorized by President Eisenhower helped finish the job.[116] The result was the installation of Colonel Carlos Castillo Armas, who, along with other Guatemalans, had been trained by the CIA in nearby Honduras (another client state of the U.S. military).[117]

These sorts of tactics were generalized throughout the region. After the overthrow of Arbenz, John Foster Dulles said that the military dictators in Latin America "are the only people we can depend on."[118] But the creation and support of client states – sometimes by the hand of covert activity or overt military operations – were not restricted to the Western hemisphere. In the Middle East, and in Iran in particular, clientelism became an important mechanism of influence too. After World War II, Iran quickly became a centerpiece of strategy in the region. As the war showed signs of ending, the State Department warned of Soviet attempts to gain oil concessions there; it therefore suggested that the United States ensure Iranian independence. The stated goal was to "construct a strong and independent Iran, free from the internal dissensions and weaknesses which invite foreign intervention" (not unlike the goal of the British state in regard to the failing Ottoman empire in the nineteenth century).[119] However, when Prime Minister Mohammed Mussadiq threatened to nationalize the oil fields beginning in 1950, the situation became untenable. Nationalization threatened existing Anglo-American oil ventures and made Soviet access more likely. In response, the United States and its allies overthrew Mossadiq and replaced him with the Shah. Observers were not mistaken. "There is on our side," wrote Sir Roger Makins, the British ambassador in Washington, after the overthrow, "a very understandable suspicion that the Americans are out to take our place in the Middle East. Their influence has greatly expanded there.... Are the Americans consciously trying to substitute their influence for ours in the Middle East?"[120]

Makins's query was on the spot, except that it did not only apply to the Middle East. Around the globe, the American state maneuvered to fill the spaces left behind by the ailing European empires. As we will see in the next chapter, the United States had initially supported the European empires in the postwar period. As those empires nevertheless began to implode, however, the United States was forced to withdraw its support and instead find other means to exert influence. The American state used the tactics it had been using in Latin America and Iran. In the Congo, various types of U.S. intervention in the wake of

---

[116] Cullather (1999), p. 69.
[117] On Honduras, see Bowman (2001) esp. pp. 144–6.
[118] Quoted in Westad (2005), p. 148. On Guatemala, see Marks (1990). On Brazil, see Weis (2001).
[119] United States Department of State (1955), pp. 340–5.
[120] Quoted in Louis (1985), p. 396.

Belgium's decolonization led to the establishment of Joseph-Désiré Mobutu's brutal dictatorial regime.[121] Close to half of all of America's financial aid to Africa thus went to him.[122] American financial power replaced Belgian colonial power. In Vietnam, by 1954 the United States was subsidizing about 40 percent of the entire French effort to squash the Communist nationalist movement there.[123] When French forces were defeated at Dien Bien Phu in 1954, the United States was forced to disavow its support and step in directly. The result is well known: the creation of a client state and desperate continued military efforts to defend it, ending with the Vietnam War. In Indonesia, initial attempts by the Eisenhower administration to win over President Sukarno failed. Sukarno publicly told the United States: "Go to hell with your aid."[124] A CIA-backed coup attempt in 1958 failed miserably, as did attempts to fund the Indonesia military in the hopes that it would serve as an alternative center of power.[125] Success only came later, after the United States supported the coup by General Suharto and subsequently enlisted him as America's client.[126] Washington was happy. Walt W. Rostow, national security adviser and proponent of modernization theory, told President Johnson: "Suharto is making a hard try at making something of Indonesia which could be very good for us and the world."[127]

Informal Empire in Comparative Context

The fact that the United States did not initiate a new round of colonization after acquiring the Japanese territories does not mean a lack of empire. It simply meant a different type of empire. In this empire, clients took the place of colonies, and financial aid took the place of administrators. The revisionists' approach would be affirmed. America engaged in a new imperialism without colonies. Yet our story cannot end with a simple affirmation of the revisionist approach. There is a certain strand of revisionism that we must further interrogate. In this strand, the foregoing informal exercises of empire manifest a distinct "American way of empire." This is one way in which American exceptionalism has been reinscribed amidst the revisionist critique. Presumably, whereas the British empire was constituted by colonies and colonial administrators, durbars, and pith helmets, America's empire in the twentieth century stands distinct for employing "novel" and "creative" indirect means of influence.[128] If the United States has had "an informal empire," this just shows that "Americans, unlike the Romans, the British, and the French, are not colonizers of

---

[121] Westad (2005), pp. 140–3.
[122] Kolko (1988), p. 193.
[123] Fraser (1992), p. 114. McMahon (1999), p. 363. Rotter (1984), p. 333.
[124] Quoted in Brands (1989), p. 794.
[125] McMahon (1999), pp. 85–8.
[126] Brands (1989). On America's support, see Sieg (1997).
[127] Quoted in Brands (1989), p. 804.
[128] Bender (2006a), p. 233.

remote and exotic places."[129] America's informal imperialism, in other words, is itself exceptional.

British activities in West Africa in the mid-nineteenth century tell a different story. The British exerted formal control in some parts of the region. Britain established the Gold Coast Settlements in 1842 and seized Lagos in 1861.[130] However, in the late 1840s and early 1850s, before the seizure of Lagos, Palmerston tried to force King Kosoko in Lagos to accept a treaty that would have met Britain's goals without declaring sovereignty. He had instructed the admiralty to "induce [Kosoko] to conclude a Treaty for the abolition of that [slave] traffic." The treaty would have also opened up the area to commerce.[131] King Kosoko, however, proved intractable – he refused to sign it. In response, Captain John Beecroft, who had been appointed consul to the region, led a British naval force in 1851 to depose King Kosoko and replace him with the ex-king, Akiyote, whom the British saw as more "docile" and amenable to British interests.[132] Lagos remained formally sovereign and Akiyote, as Britain's client, was now in charge. Consul Beecroft hung around as Akiyote's unofficial supervisor (1852).[133] A decade later, when it was finally decided to annex Lagos, the Foreign Office astutely noted that annexation was but the tip of the iceberg because "the Consul [Beecroft] in fact for some years has been the *de facto* ruler of the place."[134]

The overthrow of Kosoko was but one instance among many informal imperial tactics in coastal Africa. Britain repeatedly tried to induce local rulers to accept treaties that would curb the slave trade, open up commerce, and prevent French expansion.[135] To compel local rulers to accept the treaties, Britain offered subsidies, stipends, promises of protection, or portions of trade revenue. By the 1860s, an estimated 107 such treaties had been signed throughout East Africa.[136] When local rulers did not sign treaties or violated their terms, overthrow was the norm. In 1852, Beecroft deposed King Aqua in the Cameroons and replaced him with "Prince Jim" on the grounds that Aqua was a "drunken imbecile, a liar, and a great rogue" who had been hampering British trade.[137] Beecroft similarly helped overthrow King Pepple of Bonny (later Nigeria), who had been "doing all in his power to obstruct and annoy us in our trade." Beecroft thus replaced Pepple with Prince Dappo, in whose honor British warships fired twenty-one guns.[138] In the 1840s, the British also cultivated the

---

[129] Schlesinger (2005), pp. 45–6.
[130] Lynn (1986), pp. 23–4; Hyam (2002), p. 105.
[131] Palmerston to Admiralty, quoted in Short (1977), p. 14; see also Lynn (1982), p. 160.
[132] Short (1977), p. 11–15; Lynn (1982), pp. 156–8.
[133] Lynn (1982), p. 161.
[134] Minute by Wylde, Jul. 11, 1861, on Acting Consul at Lagos to Russell, no. 2, June 7, 1861, FO 84/1141. See also Robinson and Gallagher (1961), p. 35.
[135] Lynn (1982); Lynn (1999), p. 24.
[136] Newbury (1965), pp. 15, 18–20, 25.
[137] Quoted in Dike (1956), p. 129.
[138] Ibid., pp. 131–47.

Imam of Zanzibar and Muscat, Seyyid Said, as a key collaborator along the coast to help curb slave trafficking, limit French designs, and increase Africa's trade with India. In exchange for Said's support, British agents helped him expand into neighboring terrain and suppress local resistance to his authority. British agents boasted that Said was being used "as a powerful political engine."[139]

It is not difficult to see how the use of African clients, through manipulation, bribes, and other forms of support, prefigured America's support of African dictators during the Cold War. Yet the British state employed informal tactics in other regions of the world too. Return to Latin America. As noted, the British state refused to colonize parts of Latin America and supported the independence of Latin American countries, but this was not because Britain had no interests there. To the contrary, the region remained a vital economic interest, necessary (as Lord Castlereagh had put it) for "the extension of our own commerce."[140] Rather than directly colonizing the region, however, the British state cultivated allies and clients.[141] Britain's relations with Uruguay are exemplary: In fact, the very establishment of Uruguay as a nation was made possible by Britain's hand. Known previously as the Banda Oriental, the area had been valued by Britain, Argentina (the United Provinces), Brazil, and the United States for its riverways, which offered important trading routes into the interior. However, in 1821 Brazil laid claim to the area, and four years later war erupted between Brazil and Argentina over the territory. The war threatened British commerce and aroused fears that the United States might extend its own influence in the region. The solution was to create an independent Banda, and accordingly Britain's minister to Buenos Aires aided local Banda leaders to form a nationalist separatist party. The subsequent independent nation of Uruguay served London as a crucial "buffer state" between Brazil and Argentina.[142] Although independent, Uruguay became a British client. As the U.S. consul general in Buenos Aires assessed, it was but "a [British] Colony in disguise."[143]

These tactics were not unusual elsewhere in the world where Britain had interests. In 1832, Britain supported the independence of Greece from the Ottoman empire only to turn it into yet another client state. After helping to install Bavaria's King Otto to the Greek throne, Britain gave loans and induced trade treaties aimed at facilitating British commerce. In similar fashion, the British state arranged for a treaty with the sultan in Morocco (1856) that effectively established Morocco as a quasi-protectorate and opened it up to British trade and investment.[144] To convince the sultan to accept the treaty, the Foreign Office instructed Drummond Hay, the British minister at Tangier, to tell the

---

[139] Quoted in Robinson and Gallagher (1961), p. 43.
[140] Quoted in Ferns (1953), p. 62. See also Memorandum of Dec. 31, 1841, FO 97/284, PRO; Mathew (1968) p. 565.
[141] The literature is large, but for a good overview see the essays in Brown (2008).
[142] Winn (1976), p. 103.
[143] Quoted in Pratt (1931), p. 328.
[144] Quoted in Flournoy (1935), p. 168.

sultan that if he accepted the treaty, Britain would "prove the value which [he] entertained for the friendship and goodwill of the British Government."[145] Hay also subtly threatened the sultan with the British navy; after the sultan finally agreed, Hay remained as British minister at Tangier.[146] Loans, military support, and training followed.[147]

Political support and financial incentives thus helped to sustain Britain's informal imperial network. However, the use of force played no less a role. As with the United States later, the British state sought to open up trade, but this sometimes involved the use of coercion to open up markets in the first place. "It may be true in one sense," wrote Palmerston in 1860, expressing the classic mid-Victorian dilemma, "that trade ought not to be enforced by cannon balls, but on the other hand trade cannot flourish without security, and that security may often be unattainable without the exhibition of physical force."[148] Accordingly, the overthrow of King Kosoko at Lagos had been prefaced by threats. Palmerston had sent instructions to Beecroft stating that, if Kosoko did not meet British interests, he should be reminded that "Britain's friendship is worth having and that her displeasure it is well to avoid," that "Lagos is near to the sea and . . . on the sea are the ships and the cannon of England."[149] Palmerston was not overstating British power. All along the coasts of Africa, the Royal Navy remained on call, ready to be summoned "to rescue traders, coerce African rulers, or compel the signature of commercial treaties."[150]

Latin America saw similar threats and uses of force. To establish Uruguay as a buffer state, Britain had to threaten Brazil with naval intervention. Later, in the 1840s, the navy was used to protect trading routes in Uruguay from incursions by Argentina.[151] A blockade was used in 1848 and 1849 to compel Brazil to adhere to antislaving policies and again in 1862 to retaliate against the seizure of a British trading ship. British forces were also used to punish the rulers of Algiers, Tunis, and Tripoli for attacking British ships and threatening trade (1816); to support Greek independence against Turkish forces (1827); to support the integrity of the Ottoman empire against Mehemet Ali's attempt to separate Egypt (1840); to occupy Veracruz in 1861 in response to Mexico's cancellation of its foreign debt; and to attack Japan in order to keep the Simo-noeski Straits open to foreign trade (1864). These and many other smaller deployments were common. Although systematic data is not obtainable, it is known that navy gunboats were called upon by consulars, traders, or governors around the globe at least 116 times from 1857 to 1861 alone.[152] When overt force was not used, Britain resorted to clandestine operations. In a campaign to

---

[145] Clarendon to Hay, no. 5, 17 June 1853, FO 99/57.
[146] Hay to Clarendon, July 21, 1853, FO 99/57.
[147] Flournoy (1935), pp. 202–15; on loan policy, see Platt (1968a), p. 44.
[148] Quoted in Porter (1999), pp. 10–11.
[149] Quoted in Lynn (1982), p. 160.
[150] Dike (1956), pp. 129, 145.
[151] McLean (1995).
[152] Data in Preston and Major (1967), Appendix C, pp. 239–50.

compel Brazil's rulers to end the slave trade, British operatives used Secret Service funds to "finance informants, bribe officials, and subsidize newspapers."[153] Clandestine activities were also used in 1839 to replace the intractable ruler of Afghanistan, Dost Mohammed, with a client ruler who would help thwart Russian intervention.

Britain also initiated more massive military campaigns than gunboat diplomacy or small covert operations. The Opium Wars against China stand out clearly (1840–1842; 1858–1860). After the wars, although Britain did not annex Chinese territory, it did leave behind a series of treaties that pried China open for foreign trade, imposed protections for British citizens and diplomats, and established the Tsungli-yamen in 1861 (which provided Western diplomats with an office for pressing demands on the government) as well as a new customs office.[154] A number of cities were also established as "treaty ports." Precursors to free trade zones, these provided various legal protections for foreign traders. They ranged in size "from 25 acres in the tea-exporting Yangtze port of Kiuiang (Jijuiang) to more than 1,000 acres in the North Ciense metropolis of Tientsin (Tianjin)."[155] The treaties, made possible by the hand of force, eventually had their desired economic effect. The total value of British exports to China increased from 640,000 pounds during the period 1844 to 1846 to about 1.1 million pounds ten years later.[156] Trade followed the gunboat.

So what was new about America's informal imperialism? Nothing at all. Yet this would not be unfamiliar to followers of Robinson and Gallagher. It was Robinson and Gallagher's analysis of mid-Victorian foreign policy that popularized the concept "informal imperialism" in the first place.[157] They contended with traditional imperial historiography that had long claimed that the mid-Victorian British state was anti-imperial. Robinson and Gallagher argued instead that although the British state was not as colonialist as it had been previously (or would be later), this did not mean that it was anti-imperial. To say so – as traditional or "orthodox" imperial histories did – would be to operate from a restricted territorial or colonial definition of empire, "which is rather like judging the size and character of icebergs solely from the parts above the waterline."[158] Robinson and Gallagher then disclosed all the ways the British state, although reluctant to take new colonies, simply exercised imperialism in the "informal" mode: "[P]ower was extended in subtler forms [than annexation] – prestige, cajolery, threat, the dangled loan reinforced occasionally with blockade, bombardment or expedition."[159] According to Robinson and Gallagher,

[153] Miller (1993), p. 54.
[154] Pelcovits (1948), pp. 19–20; Dean (1976), pp. 68–70. On the customs office, see Horowitz (1998).
[155] Osterhammel (1999a): p. 149.
[156] Kasaba (1992), p. 84.
[157] The term was first used by Fay (1940), p. 39.
[158] Robinson and Gallagher (1953), p. 1.
[159] Robinson and Gallagher (1961), p. 5.

these were the preferred methods of the British state until the late nineteenth century. "London resorted to one expedient after another to evade the need of formal expansion."[160] The British state, in short, "followed the principle of extending control informally if possible and formally [only] if necessary."[161] In this sense, America's informal empire was but a new variant of an older theme. As Wm. Roger Louis notes: "Robinson and Gallagher's Victorians would have recognized the methods of post World War II Americans."[162]

Yet the similarity does not stop here. Even the respective historiographies of British and American empires are similar. In American historiography, a certain sequence unfolded from traditional exceptionalism to revisionism. Traditional exceptionalism asserted that the United States was not an empire during the mid-twentieth century because it did not seize new colonies. Then Williams's revisionism and his Wisconsin School emerged to declare that the United States *was* an empire, but of an informal sort. Studies of the British empire follow the exact same trajectory. As noted, orthodox histories at first denied that Britain was imperial in the mid-nineteenth century. Then, beginning with Robinson and Gallagher's seminal work, historians reconsidered British activities to say that Britain was indeed an empire in the mid-nineteenth century, however of an informal sort. Even American historiography on empire is not so exceptional.[163]

---

[160] Robinson and Gallagher (1953), p. 12.
[161] Ibid., p. 13.
[162] See especially Howe (2003) for this extended point.
[163] Other parallels in historiography are astutely discussed in MacDonald (2009).

4

Imperial Forms, Global Fields

> Colonialism is successful where the subject people are unsophisticated and acqui-
> escent, as in the case of certain South Pacific islanders. Once the dependent
> people, even if a small minority of them, acquire a degree of worldly wisdom
> and personal ambition, complications set in. Discontent, resistance, and political
> psychoses develop.
>
> – U.S. National Security Council 51 (1949)[1]

> Colonialism is in its twilight hour.
>
> – Erasmus Kloman (1958)[2]

In what ways has the U.S. imperial formation differed from Britain's? It is
not the lack of overseas colonies. Nor is it that the U.S. colonial empire was
more benign or liberal, that the U.S. empire was uniquely informal, or that
its citizens refused to speak the empire's name. Rather, one important difference remains. Whereas both the U.S. and British imperial formations involved
colonies, and whereas both entailed informal modalities of power – cultivating
clients, cajoling enemies, and deploying military force – only the British empire
mixed informal and formal tactics during its period of hegemony. In the mid-
nineteenth century, the British crafted allies, invaded countries, and employed
various other informal tactics while also seizing overseas territory as colonial
dependencies. The British state did not seize as many colonies during its period
of hegemony as it did during its period of hegemonic ascent (a point to be
considered later). Yet it did seize some. Alternatively, during its comparable
phase of hegemony, the U.S. empire did not seize multiple new colonies. In
1947, it annexed the former Japanese mandates, but afterward the American
state relied exclusively on informal imperialism. Whereas the British empire

---

[1] NSC 51, US policy towards Southeast Asia, July 1, 1949, Declassified Documents Reference
Service at www.ddrs.psmedia.com (accessed August 3, 2009).
[2] Kloman (1958), p. 361.

was formal and informal at once after 1815, the United States empire *shifted* from formal to informal after 1947.

This is a significant difference indeed. Perhaps it is what gives credence to exceptionalist claims about American uniqueness. So what accounts for it? Why did the United States turn away from colonialism as a preferred mode of imperialism during its period of hegemony, whereas Britain mixed and mingled the modes? Existing works that have discussed America's informal *imperium* from the mid-twentieth century onward have not yet offered full explanations. The only ones on offer reinscribe exceptionalist themes. In these explanations, the United States resorted to more informal modes of exercising power because of its own national character and institutions. Firmly rooted in "democratic and anti-imperial features," as one historian of the postwar period puts it, the United States restrained from practicing colonialism and could only employ informal tactics that, although still imperialistic, nonetheless respected the integrity of national sovereignty. "The United States, in part because of its democratic structure, pursued policies of 'guns and butter.'" It "mobilized Americans for war but not for permanent foreign occupations."[3] Historian and former White House official Arthur Schlesinger, Jr. likewise suggests that the United States turned to informal imperialism rather than colonial rule because there has been "no sustained demand for empire" in the United States. The minor "spasm" of imperial enthusiasm at the turn of the twentieth century aside, the empire has faced "consistent indifference and resistance" from its democratically minded citizens. Accordingly, informal imperialism, which is "marginal to the subject of direct control," has been the preferred option.[4]

As an explanation, however, this account runs into trouble. Something of the trouble can be seen if we consider an event in the 1950s: Senator John Kennedy's speech on Algeria and the responses to it. This is fitting because Arthur Schlesinger, Jr., who offered an exceptionalist explanation for America's informal imperialism, later served under Kennedy. In 1957, Kennedy gave a speech supporting Algerian independence from France. He referred to "imperialism" as "the enemy of freedom" and decried America's "retreat from the principles of independence and anticolonialism" by not supporting the Algerian revolutionaries. According to exceptionalist thought, this should not be unusual: It is just another manifestation of America's anticolonial values. Yet Kennedy's speech was hardly without controversy. While colleagues and some sectors of the public supported him in his stance (African American civil rights leaders were among them), his speech also drew criticism. After it was publicized, his office received hundreds of letters from citizens across the country attacking him for his anticolonial stance, for "butting in with France's affairs,"

---

[3] Suri (2009), p. 531.
[4] Schlesinger (2005), p. 45.

and for "lacking a great deal of basic information" on French colonialism.[5] In fact, these latter views were much closer to America's official stance on Algeria: In 1956, the previous year, the United States refused to support a United Nations declaration in support of Algerian independence.

The different responses to Kennedy's speech manifest a complexity that belies the exceptionalist account for American imperial practices. Exceptionalism's explanation for America's turn away from colonialism after the Second World War posits a monolithic anticolonial political culture at home that directly dictated U.S. foreign policy. The divergent responses to Kennedy's stance on Algeria betray any such notion. Nor is this unique. In previous chapters, we have seen other examples of this ambiguity. Immediately after the Second World War, politicians scrambled to take the former Japanese territories, making no attempt to hide their designs, and sectors of the American public supported them. Gallup polls taken in 1944 showed that the majority of Americans wanted their government to take not only the former colonies of Japan but also those of Britain.[6] Seventy percent, in fact, responded affirmatively to a question asked by pollsters: "After the war should the United States keep all of the Japanese islands which we conquer between Hawaii and the Philippines?"[7] Of course, wartime enthusiasm may have pushed these procolonial sentiments beyond normalcy, but the point is that the exceptionalists' tacit assumption that the American public or politicians have been uniformly anticolonial, such that American foreign policy simply reflects these anticolonial values, simply does not hold.

The real issue, as we will see in this chapter, is not just that the exceptionalist explanation posits a uniform and static political culture that shapes policy. It is that the exceptionalist explanation focuses narrowly on domestic or national factors. It highlights events, processes, structures *within* the imperial metropole. This is a classic metropolitan-centered account. It explains imperial actions abroad by ideas, actors, beliefs, or institutions at home. A different approach would widen the lens. It would look beyond domestic political cultures, institutions, electorates, or "national character" and toward *global* structures. It would think harder about the wider international or global context in which the American state had to operate and compare it with the global context in which the British state operated in the nineteenth century. In brief, rather than pointing to metropolitan characteristics to explain imperial policies, it would take seriously the very global structures and relations or *global fields* in which empires had to maneuver.[8] This is the approach taken in this chapter.

[5] See Romahn (2009); quotes from p. 8.
[6] Gilchrist (1944), p. 642.
[7] Gallup poll #317, question 16, Field Date 4/25/1944 (http://brain.gallup.com; accessed October 26, 2009).
[8] I develop the notion "global fields," which is taken from the work of sociologist Pierre Bourdieu, in Go (2008b).

Outsourcing Empire

What was different about the global fields in which the United States and Britain operated during their respective periods of hegemonic maturity? One difference lies in political ecology. Scholarship on the expansion of the international system suggests that the political ecology of the nineteenth-century global system can be divided into three basic political units: (1) recognized sovereign nation-states, (2) colonial dependencies of sovereigns, and (3) unrecognized territories and polities that have not been incorporated into the Western-based state system. The first category was European-based and contained the seeds for the modern nation-state: It included those powerful states emerging from the Westphalia system to constitute members of "international society." They engage in formal treaties with each other and see each other as equal sovereigns.[9] The other two categories consisted of non-Western polities without sovereignty. Dependencies or colonies are "entities that sovereigns claim to possess or control."[10] Those polities known as "unrecognized" constitute the frontier of the sovereign system: They are neither formally subordinated to metropolitan states as dependences, but neither are they recognized as sovereign by the existing sovereign states. Of course, for the Africans, Pacific Islanders, or Asians who lived in these societies, their polities were perfectly recognizable and legitimate. But "unrecognized" here refers to the perception of the Western sovereign states. Polities known as "unrecognized" were "considered by Western states to be outside Western state society."[11]

Following this scheme, there were important differences between the British and U.S. periods of hegemony (see Table 4.1). One key difference is that in the first half of the nineteenth century most of the world (65 percent of the earth's land surface) consisted of unrecognized territories. Sovereign states, centered in Europe, took up only about 24 percent of the earth's land surface, and their colonial dependencies took up 11 percent. Even in 1878, just before the great imperial scramble, 32 percent of the world's land surface was unrecognized, mostly in Africa. Imperialism at the turn of the century then turned all of Africa into dependent territory. Therefore, by the time the United States reached hegemony in the mid-twentieth century, the field was radically different from when the British ruled. In 1946, only 16 percent of the world's land surface was unrecognized; the rest was occupied by European empires. The United States entered a global field wherein most of the world had already been colonized.

This is a simple but important difference. As studies of imperialism show, sovereign states tend to seize only unrecognized territories.[12] They are less likely to colonize either other sovereign states or even colonial dependencies of other sovereigns (except as "spoils of war"). This makes sense: Colonizing

[9] Bull and Watson (1984), Krasner (1988), Watson (1992): 202–13.
[10] Strang (1991): 149.
[11] Ibid., 151; Watson (1992), pp. 214–27.
[12] Strang (1991).

TABLE 4.1. *Comparative Political Ecology: Proportion of World's Land Surface Occupied by Recognized Polities and Unrecognized*

Hegemonic Cycle	Year	Percent World's Land Surface Occupied by:			
		Recognized Sovereign States	Recognized Colonies	Total Recognized (Sovereign States & Colonies)	Unrecognized Areas
UK	1816	24	11	35	65
	1878	54	14	68	32
	1914	53	31	84	16
US	1946	71	18	89	11
	1960	92	8	100	0
	1973	97	3	100	0

Sources: Data calculated from information in Goertz and Diehl's (1992) territorial changes dataset; the Correlates of War Project (2005) on state system membership; for colonial holdings and areas, Clark (1936); Henige (1970); *Statesman's Yearbook* (1864–); Banks (1976).

the territory of another sovereign state is an arduous task, a zero-sum game that would have to be resolved through outright purchase or war between sovereigns. However, unrecognized territories do not involve these complications. They appear as frontier areas ready for the taking, with comparably little worry about rival claims. It follows that the more unrecognized territory there is in the world, the more opportunities there are for colonization. This is why, as the historian Dominic Lieven points out, European empires could more easily expand outside Europe than within it. Whereas annexing recognized territories in Europe brought all kinds of jealousies, rivalries, and tensions, territorial aggrandizement outside of Europe – into "unrecognized" territory – was far easier.[13]

We might already see how these different field configurations impacted British and American imperial forms. Most obviously, the fact that there was less unrecognized territory in the mid-twentieth century served as a constraint on American colonization, whereas the fact that there was so much more in the previous century means that there were *more* opportunities for the British state to colonize. To be sure, the vast majority of the colonies Britain acquired from 1816 to the early 1870s had neither been sovereign states nor dependencies of another sovereign. They were unrecognized territories. Yet because the United States entered a field dominated by sovereign states (e.g. in Latin America) and vast territorial empires that took up most of the globe, it had fewer opportunities to colonize than Britain had. There was much less land to grab and fewer foreign peoples available to rule. For this reason alone – regardless of whatever anticolonial "values" or "national character" the United States might

[13] Lieven (2002), p. 46.

have had – the American state was simply less likely to institute a new round of colonialism in the mid-twentieth century.

This is only one part of the story, however. The United States emerged victorious from World War II, which proved its superior military strength, and European powers were becoming weak and dependent upon U.S. economic aid. In this situation, the United States might have taken European colonies by showing its new muscles. It might have taken colonies without too much fear of reprisal from its weak counterparts. So why not? Here arises the other critical difference between the global fields of the nineteenth and twentieth centuries. Given that so much of the world in the twentieth century was already subjected to the direct control of European imperial powers, the United States did not *need* to seize new colonies. It could just enlist preexisting European imperial networks to realize its goals, outsourcing territorial control to its European allies rather than seizing its own colonial territory.

Consider first the American state's imperial imperatives in the postwar period. One was expanded trade. Exceptionalist narratives and revisionist historians alike point out that the United States inaugurated a global free trade regime. For exceptionalists, this reveals how the American state was not imperial. For revisionists it shows that it invented new imperial tactics. Yet both sides run the risk of simplifying the complex activities of the United States in the immediate aftermath of World War II and through the early 1960s. On the one hand, in this period some politicians, sectors of the business community, and policy makers spoke valiantly of free trade. Worried about the 1930s exclusivism that had purportedly contributed to war, and concerned that wartime levels of growth would not be sustained in peace, they looked abroad for new markets and raw materials.[14] On the other hand, this was not intrinsically an anticolonial or anti-imperial stance. To the contrary, as the business sector and policy makers repeatedly stressed, the best way for the United States to get new markets and materials was not by dismantling the existing imperial systems, but rather by sustaining them and tapping into them directly. The colonial world was critical for supplying the ever-increasing demand for various raw materials.[15] Analysts noted in 1941 that the "United States is the greatest ultimate consumer of colonial products."[16] In 1950, the State Department produced memos stressing how important Africa was for providing raw materials and, in general, as a site for American "trade, investment, and transportation interests."[17] Various investigative commissions under the Truman administration demonstrated how important minerals, metals, tin, rubber, and other strategic materials were coming from colonies.[18] In 1952, another

[14] Darby (1987), pp. 194–207.
[15] Kolko (1988), pp. 54–55.
[16] Holcombe (1941), p. 76.
[17] FRUS 1950, p. 1527.
[18] Darby (1987), p. 205.

analysis stressed, "existing and potential production in colonial territories are vital to meeting these needs of Western industrial countries."[19]

The conclusion of these and other reports was that, to keep the supply incoming and in hopes of finding markets for American products, the United States should support European colonial structures rather than dismantle them. European rule, stressed a State Department report in 1950, offered "political and economic stability." As long as American capital was afforded "equal treatment," America's "economic goals...should be achieved through coordination and cooperation with the colonial powers."[20] The scholar Rupert Emerson observed in 1947 that "American interest and interests, narrowly interpreted, would be served more adequately by the maintenance of the old-time colonial set-up than by ventures into the uncharted waters of autonomy and independence," not least because the "old-time colonial set up" rather than a world of independent nation-states could better serve to meet America's need for raw materials and markets.[21] The State Department's policy on French rule in Africa followed: "Our primary objective in French West and Equatorial Africa is to keep those territories under friendly and effective administration. To this end we recognize the legitimacy and desirability of French political control."[22] In 1953, Undersecretary of State Byroade publicly announced that U.S. policy had been and would continue to be oriented toward maintaining European empires. He added how support of the European empires was tied to America's strategic interest in keeping Europe strong: "[T]he granting of complete freedom to those who were not yet ready for it would serve the best interests neither of the US nor the free world as a whole.... Let us be frank in recognizing our stake in the strength and stability of certain European nations which exercise influence in the dependent areas. They are our allies. A sudden break in economic relations might seriously injure the European economy upon which our Atlantic defence system depends, and at the same time prove equally injurious to the dependent territories themselves."[23]

These were not idle words. By the time Byroade had made his speech, the American state had already put its strategy of supporting the European empires into action. It pushed the European empires to open their doors to North American interests and in exchange offered financial aid and support that would help keep those empires intact. Such aid was sorely needed due to the devastation of the war. Without funds, Europe's empires would collapse. The American state decided to provide them.[24] The Marshall Plan was a part of this strategy. It was the economic aid package aimed at helping Europe recover from the

---

[19] Bell (1952), p. 97.
[20] FRUS 1950, V, p. 1527.
[21] Emerson (1947), p. 270.
[22] FRUS 1950, V, 1528.
[23] *Times*, 18 November 1953, p. 6.
[24] FRUS 1950, V, p. 1527, 1535; Louis and Robinson (1994).

devastation of the war, but it was not only aimed at Europe. Administered through the Economic Cooperation Administration (ECA), it was also directed at Europe's colonial empires. In fact, a large chunk of the ECA's work went to supporting Europe's colonies. Estimates by officials within the ECA reveal that approximately $7.5 billion were targeted for Europe's colonial empires in the early 1950s, with the French and British colonial empires receiving approximately $6.5 billion, and the Portuguese, Belgian, and Dutch empires receiving the rest.[25] In this way, Europe's economies could be restored not in spite of colonialism but through it. John Orchard, chairman of the ECA Advisory Committee on Underdeveloped Areas, explained that the program would help to reduce the "dollar gap" while also providing Europe with "increased supplies of essential commodities" and "wider markets for European factories." At the same time, the United States would benefit. The United States would gain access to the colonies, which would "supply additional raw materials for our factories and foodstuffs to supplement our agricultural production" and provide markets in the colonial world. It would further increase Europe's own purchasing power, enabling an economic recovery that would be open to new products from across the Atlantic.[26] For these reasons and others, the State Department conceded in 1950: "[T]he colonial relationship [between Europe and its dependencies] . . . is still in many places useful and necessary."[27]

Postwar economics was only one dimension of the outsourced American empire. The other was security and defense, a matter that was increasingly foregrounded after 1947 as the Cold War intensified. One goal was to use allied European empires as defensive bulwarks against Russia. As a State Department memo in 1952 explained, the United States must "rely upon the colonial powers of Western Europe to make an addition to American strength sufficient to deter and to hold in check the tremendous military power of the Soviet armies."[28] The United States therefore gave aid to the French military in Indochina and the Dutch in Indonesia.[29] Supporting the French military effort in Indochina (through aid that amounted to 80 percent of the French military costs by the 1950s) was aimed at stopping Vietnamese Communists from taking over the country and strengthening Britain's position in Malaysia against the spread of Communism.[30] Likewise, to the mid-1950s, the United States relied on the long-established British presence in key areas such as the Middle East as a bulwark against Soviet expansion.[31] To stop dominos from falling, the American state simply propped the European empires up against them. George Kennan of

[25] Orchard (1951), pp. 71–2.
[26] Ibid., p. 67.
[27] FRUS 1950, V, p. 1527.
[28] FRUS 1952–4, III, p. 1105.
[29] In 1950, the Truman administration allocated $10 million in military aid for the French-sponsored governments of Indochina and approved a program of assistance to them. See Rotter (1984), p. 333.
[30] Ibid.
[31] FRUS 1947, V, pp. 495, 524. Kolko (1988), p. 20.

the State Department's Policy-Planning Staff later declared: "The dissolution of the [British] empire was not in our interest as there were many things the Commonwealth could do which we could not do and which we wished them to continue doing."[32] Senator Henry Cabot Lodge, Jr. told fellow Senators, "we need...these countries to be strong, and they cannot be strong without their colonies."[33]

Supporting Europe's empires was also important for America's own military-base system. Prior to World War II, the United States had only a small network of military bases, with bases only in its own colonies (e.g., the Philippines, Hawaii, Puerto Rico).[34] By the end of the war, however, military strategists had planned for an extensive worldwide network of security. The war had already brought American forces to the far ends of the earth; how to keep them there? Military advisors and policy planners in the executive branch landed on an easy answer: Use the territorial domains already established by European colonialism.

The strategy partly originated in 1941 when the United States lent Britain war supplies in exchange for ninety-nine-year leases establishing military bases in the Britain's Caribbean colonies. After the war, the process continued, especially as the containment strategy emerged in the late 1940s. The United States gave loans to Britain so that Britain could reestablish its overseas empire after the war; in exchange, the United States was granted the use of any and all of Britain's overseas colonies for military bases or transport.[35] The United States made similar arrangements with the French in North Africa. French colonial control provided "stability, even though such stability is obtained largely through repression" (in the words of the Bureau of Near Eastern, South Asian, and African Affairs in the State Department).[36] This stability was deemed important for halting future Soviet aggression and for allowing the American state to maintain a military presence in the region. An agreement with France in 1950, for instance, enabled the United States to construct five new air bases in Morocco for Strategic Air Command.[37] Even though "imperial of the old school is practiced" in North Africa, concluded the State Department, "there is one favorable factor, that of US strategic interests, since we are in a position to use this area in time of war."[38] Similarly, the United States was allowed to set up an air base in the Azores by Portugal, but only if it supported Portugal's bid to reassert itself over Timor (that airbase, at Lajes, would later stand as the vital ground for U.S. airlift missions to Israel during the Yom Kippur War of 1973).

In the end, the United States was able to create its vast network of global military power by relying on rather than dismantling European colonialism.

---

[32] Louis and Robinson (1994), p. 499, fn. 42.
[33] Quoted in ibid., p. 468.
[34] Harkavy (1982): 66–7, 100.
[35] Louis and Robinson (1994); Harkavy (1982), pp. 127–53; Sandars (2000), pp. 42–61.
[36] FRUS 1950, V, p. 1528.
[37] Harkavy (1982), p. 50. See also Kolko 1988: 19; FRUS 1950: V, p. 1573.
[38] FRUS 1950, V, p. 1573.

Out of the top thirty-nine territories in Central America, the Caribbean, Africa, Asia, and the Pacific wherein the United States maintained troops from 1950 to 1960 (measured in terms of number of troops), eight were U.S. colonies (excluding Japan, which the United States temporarily ruled after World War II), and twenty were colonies or protectorates of European countries (Table 4.2). Therefore, close to 70 percent of America's troop outposts in the peripheral world were in colonies.[39] A secret memo in the State Department in 1950 stated: "[T]he security interests of the US at the present time will best be served by a policy of support for the Western Colonial Powers."[40]

We now have one part of an answer for why the United States did not take new territories in the mid-twentieth century: It did not *need* to. Because it entered a global field that was already populated by empires with which it could ally, all the American state had to do in order to meet its postwar economic and security goals was support those empires and outsource imperial functions to them. This was a not a privilege afforded the British empire a century earlier. For one thing, the British empire could not easily outsource imperial tasks to other empires. It did enlist the support of other empires when and where it was possible. It supported the Ottoman empire to block Russian expansion, maintain control over Mediterranean trade, and prevent an overland route to India from falling into enemy hands.[41] However, this approach could only go so far. Whereas the United States faced a situation wherein its allies controlled most of the world's colonies, the British state faced a world in which most of the major colonial empires were foes rather than friends. Russia or France could sometimes be enlisted for support; but they were just as often enemies.

It is also important that so much more of the world was uncolonized in the nineteenth century. This meant that the British state could not meet its economic goals without imperial expansion in the colonial mode. Like Americans in the mid-twentieth century, British statesmen and capitalists in the nineteenth century consistently looked for access to new raw materials and markets. Whereas the Americans could meet this goal by relying on the sociopolitical and economic structures created and sustained by European colonialism, the British could not. Because so much of the world was uncolonized, there were no such preexisting structures upon which to depend. To extract materials and find new markets, the British state had to create those sociopolitical and economic structures by itself, which meant the direct seizure and colonial control of territory. Sir Charles Dilke reflected on British expansion in the mid-nineteenth

---

[39] This counts countries that later received independence but were colonies when the United States first established troop bases.

[40] FRUS 1950–3, III, pp. 1078–9; see also FRUS 1952–4, III, p. 1081; Fraser (1992), p. 115.

[41] Lynn (1999), p. 111. The Convention of Balta Lima in 1838 was directed at this goal. See Owen (1992), pp. 10–11 and Kasaba (1992), pp. 73–4. Later, in 1855, Britain backed a private loan to help the Ottomans fight Russia during the Crimean War and sent a consulate, military advisors, and missions to facilitate the improvement of Turkey's administrative structure and military. See Rodkey (1930), pp. 222–4.

TABLE 4.2. *U.S. Troop Stations, 1950–1960: Top Thirty-Nine Non-Western Countries*

Country	Total No. of Troops	Dependency Status of Country[a]
Japan	1,687,509	Independent
Republic of Korea	1,573,585	Independent
Hawaiian Islands	456,264	US
Alaska	442,863	US
Philippines	153,324	US
Guam	152,246	US
Puerto Rico	142,486	US
Morocco	110,811	France
Taiwan	52,144	China
Libya	47,168	UK-France
Turkey	40,700	Independent
Bermuda	36,393	UK
Marshall Islands	25,963	US
Lebanon	18,105	Independent
Saudi Arabia	12,848	Independent
Midway	12,408	US
Hong Kong	11,343	UK
Vietnam	9,311	France
Eritrea	8,724	UK
Algeria	7,043	France
West Indies Federation	6,432	UK
Bahamas	5,404	UK
Malta	5,122	UK
Iran	4,271	Independent
Haiti	4,031	Independent
Johnston Island	3,749	US
Volcano Islands	3,562	US
Thailand	2,720	Independent
Bahrain	2,341	UK
Pakistan	2,276	UK
Trinidad	1,396	UK
Australia	1,374	UK
New Zealand	1,082	UK
Jamaica	1,016	UK
Malaysia	953	UK
Egypt	828	UK
Antigua	638	UK
Ecuador	525	Independent
India	499	Independent (1950)

[a] Refers to status at time of U.S. basing agreement or initial station; includes colonies, protectorates, or (for US) "outlying territories."

Sources: Dependency status, *Statesman's Yearbook*; Troops, U.S. Department of Defense, Statistical Information Analysis Division, "Military Personnel Historical Reports" (http://www.dior.whs.mil/mmid/military/history/309hist.htm. Accessed January 2006).

century by saying that "large markets" and raw materials had to be found in "almost all those territories in the globe *which did not belong to the European race*."[42] In other words, the British state tried to meet its imperial imperatives by entering previously untapped regions – areas untouched and uncontrolled by European empires. Exploiting these untapped regions of the world meant annexing and then controlling them directly to make them manageable.

To be sure, for the British state, the conditions for economic extraction, production, and trade would have been more difficult to secure without colonial control. Colonialism was necessary for seizing land, protecting settlers and planters, and articulating local labor systems to export production. It was also necessary for maintaining security and order when these prerequisites could not be secured by other means.[43] Thus many annexations began as enterprising merchants, landowners, and vanguard settlers pressed the home government to annex the territory in order to create stable conditions and provide protection in the frontier. Accordingly, much of the territorial expansion from the mid-century onward occurred on the frontiers of already existing colonies, such as around India, in Canada, or in Australia.[44] In other cases, annexation was necessary to consolidate trade networks and expand them. Contiguous areas around Bombay, in and near Australia, and in Malaya became increasingly important to British trade by the late century, and fittingly Britain then swallowed them up (e.g., outlying parts of India in 1815 and 1818; Western Australia in 1832; New Zealand in 1841; and the Malaya/Straits Settlements in 1867).[45] The scramble for Africa later in the century followed the same logic: Colonial control was necessary to secure the conditions for effective access and trade.[46] As Joseph Chamberlain remarked in 1896, "We, in our colonial policy, as fast as we acquire new territory and develop it, develop it . . . for the commerce of the world."[47] Relatedly, Hong Kong and Singapore were taken because they could serve as trading ports and naval posts necessary for Britain's attempt to open up China to trade. Similarly, the Falkland Islands were seized to consolidate Britain's trade with Latin America.

These seizures were also related to the other imperial imperative: security and defense. For much of the period after 1815, the British state pursued a "blue water policy," focusing much of its energy on home defense and keeping on eye out on continental powers. At the same time, however, Britain's military was moving around the globe, both to help its expanding trade and to keep rival European empires in check. In 1820, there were six overseas commands: the Mediterranean, the southeast coast of America, North America and the West Indies, the Cape of Good Hope, the west coast of Africa, and the East Indies. As the decades proceeded, increasingly more command stations were set up, not least in Australia and the Pacific, proportionate to the increase in duties

[42] Dilke (1890), p. 462.
[43] Platt (1968a), p. 153.
[44] Darwin (1997), p. 630.
[45] Cain (1999), p. 34; Tomlinson (1999), pp. 60–1.
[46] Hynes (1976).
[47] Platt (1968a): 365.

and activities that the navy faced.[48] Unlike the United States, Britain could not rely on other empires for military access to these sites. The British state had to take the territory itself to maintain safe basing stations. A handful of exceptions aside, the British basing system was set up within Britain's empire, not outside it or in other empires.[49] Is it any wonder that whereas "the British Empire took some two hundred years to reach its peak, the global security system of the US [took] a mere ten years"?[50] The British had to annex frontier territory around the world to establish its military bases, making for a slow and piecemeal process of expansion.[51] The United States, by contrast, could rely on the colonial domains already constructed by its predecessors to realize its military dominance, thereby taking a much shorter span of time. If America's aversion to colonization after World War II was at all a virtue, it was a virtue afforded by a luxury: the luxury of being a relative latecomer to empire.

The Subaltern Speaks Back

Understanding the political ecologies of the nineteenth and twentieth centuries helps us understand why the United States was reluctant to be imperialistic in the territorial mode, whereas the British state was more willing. But this raises more questions. Most important, why didn't the United States colonize after the 1960s? After all, while the United States relied on European empires to realize its imperial goals from 1945 to the 1960s, some colonies had already obtained independence by that time. Latin America had been independent for a long time. Furthermore, by the mid-1960s, the European empires finally crumbled. This meant that the United States could no longer rely on them, and a host of new countries became independent. The United States could have initiated an entirely new round of territorial imperialism. But it did not. Instead it deployed informal tactics, thus surmounting the territorial constraints of nineteenth-century imperialism.

Why? When the European empires finally broke down, why didn't the American state step in directly to replace them? Addressing this question brings us to the other dimension of the global field that we must consider: not political ecology, but political culture; and not the political culture of the imperial metropoles, but that of the colonized and postcolonized – the very people imperialism sought to direct and manage.

"The Age of Imperialism is Ended"

On Memorial Day, 1942, Sumner Welles gave a renowned address at the Arlington National Amphitheater. Welles was the U.S. Undersecretary of State and one of President Roosevelt's main foreign policy advisors. A year earlier, he had appeared on the cover of *Time* magazine. Given his position, and given

[48] Beeler (1997), p. 26.
[49] See the informative list of overseas stations in ibid., pp. 28–9.
[50] Sandars (2000), p. 6.
[51] Harkavy (1982): 46–50, Hyam (1999): 31.

America's entry into the war, British diplomats and others around the world took notice of his address – as it turns out, rightfully so. His speech did nothing short of calling for the end of empires. "If this war is in fact a war for the liberation of peoples," Welles declared, "it must assure the sovereign equality of peoples throughout the world, as well as in the world of the Americas. Our victory must bring in its train the liberation of all peoples. Discrimination between peoples because of their race, creed or color must be abolished. The age of imperialism is ended."[52]

Welles's address is notable because it appears to express a classic exceptionalist theme. Presumably, Welles, President Roosevelt, Cordell Hull, and the rest of U.S. officialdom planned to see a new world order emerge from the ashes of World War II. Operating from America's long-standing anticolonial and democratic tradition, they hoped to inaugurate a more liberal world that transcended the tyrannical tendencies of Old World imperialism. This was to be a world of independent nation-states rather than empires. Had not Welles played an important part in establishing the United Nations? In this light, Welles's speech would appear both reflective and prescient: the former because the speech manifested America's traditions of liberty and freedom and anticolonial values; the latter because, in the post–World War II period, the old empires were eventually abolished, with the United Nations – and the benevolent American hegemon – rising from their ashes.

We might already see the problems. For one, interpreting Welles's speech as prescient would occlude America's own imperialism. It would blind us to the fact that the United States took Japanese territories after the war as colonial possessions; or that the United States, as just seen, restored and propped up the European empires after World War II rather than dismantling them. For another, interpreting Welles's speech as reflective of American values would overlook the fact that, although Welles himself made grand anti-imperial pronouncements, he often reiterated age-old colonial maxims about colonized peoples' lack of capacity and their need for continued imperial control. A year after his Memorial Day address, he conjured that discourse to justify continued imperial intervention: "We all of us recognize that it will take many generations for some backward peoples to be prepared for autonomy and self-government."[53] In fact, Welles's grandiose speech – declaring that the "age of imperialism is ended" and asserting that the war should be fought for the "liberation" of all peoples – was pragmatically motivated. Penned in 1942, Welles had specific things in mind. Along with America's allies, he hoped to enlist colonized peoples in the fight against Germany. He pretended to be the champion of the anti-imperial cause in order to win nationalists in the colonial world over to the Allied side.[54]

---

[52] Louis (1978), pp. 154–5.
[53] *New York Times*, Oct. 17, 1943, p. 32.
[54] See Louis (1978), pp. 154–5.

Welles's speech should not be taken as reflective of anti-imperial American values; nor should it be read as heralding a new world order inaugurated by America's valiant agency. A different reading would see it rather as reflective of a *global* shift, a wider international wave of change that Welles and other officials chased and rode, rather than one they engendered by their own agency. In a later speech, Welles alluded to that global tide more precisely. "New and powerful nationalistic forces are breaking into life throughout the earth, and in particular in the vast regions of Africa, of the Near East, and of the Far East. Must not these forces, unless they are to be permitted to start new and devastating inundations, be canalized through the channels of liberty into the great stream of constructive and cooperative human endeavour?"[55] In other words, Welles's statement, "the age of imperialism is ended," does not so much reflect deep American values as it reflects transformations occurring in the wider global field. Those transformations made for a very different global field than that faced by Britain in the nineteenth century. I speak of the emergence, proliferation, and ultimate dominance of anticolonial nationalism in the colonized and later postcolonial world.

Nationalism Redounded

It is by now well known that anticolonial nationalism spread around the globe during the twentieth century. Revolts in the Americas in previous centuries – including the American revolt against Britain, the Haitian rebellion against France, and the Latin American republics against Spain – had established the precedent. However, what was new in the twentieth century was the emergence of anticolonial nationalism across the globe rather than in just one region, and among predominantly nonwhite colonized populations rather than white-settler or Creole populations in the Americas. Traditional histories locate its origins in the espousals of self-determination by President Woodrow Wilson and his Fourteen Points during World War I. Yet in fact, as other scholarship emphasizes, anticolonial nationalism and espousals of self-determination had emerged long before Wilson's speech (which is exactly why his discourse resonated among colonized peoples beyond Wilson's intentions).[56] The fact that European colonialism had taken over nearly all of the peripheral world by this time was itself a factor that helped to propel anticolonial nationalism. European colonialism had offered education and political experience to colonized elites while also generating discontent and redefining local identities into nationalized spatial boundaries.[57]

The earliest stirrings of anticolonial nationalism in the nonwhite world were already seen in the Indian National Congress (1885), the Islamic revival movements in the Middle East (beginning in the late nineteenth century), the Philippine Revolution against Spain (1896), and the Pan-African Congress in 1900.

---

[55] Welles (1943).
[56] Manela (2006).
[57] Grimal (1978), pp. 36–47; Goswami (1998).

The Japanese victory over Russia (1905) and the Xinhai Revolution in China (1911) added fuel to the fire, signifying to the colonial world that nonwhite peoples could determine their own destinies.[58] Seizing on this global development, V. I. Lenin joined the chorus, articulating anti-imperial rhetoric and calling for self-determination of all peoples.[59] It was Lenin's discourse that compelled Woodrow Wilson to add pronouncements on self-determination in his Fourteen Points. Rather than being the originator of anticolonial nationalism, Wilson was just trying to keep up.[60]

The period between the world wars was a turning point. President Wilson had received pleas for help from anticolonial nationalists around the world but, as he did nothing to help, disappointment spread. Imperial boundaries existing before World War I were reinscribed at the postwar Treaty of Paris, much to the further disappointment of anticolonial nationalists who held out hope that they would be dismantled. During the 1920s, as Ghandi's populism spread through India, his anticolonial stance received widespread attention from the newly educated colonial elites around the imperial world.[61] At the Fifth Pan-American Conference at Santiago, Chile, in 1923, Latin Americans joined the chorus, charging the United States with imperialism for intervening in the Dominican Republic and Haiti.[62] The 1930s Depression then laid the socioeconomic conditions for protests across Asia, Africa, and the Caribbean. World War II helped hasten the trend. It weakened colonial structures, armed colonized peoples, and raised questions about the strength of European empires and their future viability.[63] After the war, anticolonial nationalism continued to spread. In 1951, the General Assembly of the United Nations voted for a review of the UN system of territorial administration of mandates and for a statement to be inserted into Covenants that "all peoples shall have the right of self-determination" (the U.S. delegate voted against this).[64] The Bandung Conference in 1955 solidified these anticolonial sentiments while offering a powerful rallying point for an seemingly unstoppable nationalism around the world.[65]

The emergence and proliferation of anticolonialism significantly altered the global landscape, making for a new terrain of action. Foremost, it became a powerful mobilizing device, making possible new coalitions and political formations. As a symbol, anticolonial nationalism and its principle of universal self-determination mobilized disparate groups within and across imperial space. Tribes or religious sectarians could unite on national grounds whereas they

---

[58] Furedi (1994), pp. 27–8; Grimal (1978), pp. 4–36.

[59] Koebner and Schmidt (1964), pp. 282–4.

[60] Manela (2006), pp. 40–1.

[61] Easton (1964).

[62] Koebner and Schmidt (1964), p. 299.

[63] On the development of anti-colonial nationalism in the early twentieth century through World War II, see Holland (1985), pp. 1–12 and Furedi (1994), pp. 10–27.

[64] Pratt (1958), pp. 141–2.

[65] See for example Parker (2006).

may not have before, and colonized peoples from different countries could find common cause. After Italy attacked Ethiopia in October of 1935, for instance, protests erupted as far away as British Guiana, and activists in Harlem, NY, held mass meetings to enlist soldier volunteers. W. E. B. DuBois declared it to be a "cost in debt and death" for "the whole colored world – India, China and Japan, Africa in Africa and in America, and all the South Seas and Indian South America."[66] This reaction manifests the larger trend. Empires were increasingly seen as illegitimate, nation-states were becoming the ideal, and anticolonial nationalism could now become a tool for mobilization. As the historian Koebner observed in 1964: "The political word [imperialism]... had by 1940 become the rallying cry of an opposition outside the English-speaking part of the world."[67] In 1952, the Foreign Office prepared a memorandum on "The Problem of Nationalism" that circulated in Winston Churchill's cabinet. The memo warned of the "dangers inherent in the present upsurge of nationalism" around the imperial world and cautioned against the "intersections" of "Asian nationalism" and nationalism in "the Near East and Africa."[68] Anticolonial nationalism became a global force to reckon.

As anticolonial nationalism diffused across the global field, and as the principle of national self-determination became a potent tool by which to accrue political support, the terrain of geopolitical competition likewise shifted. The USSR, for instance, tried to use it as symbolic capital. This had begun during the First World War with Lenin's anti-imperial rhetoric, prompting Wilson, as mentioned earlier, to declare support for self-determination. But as anticolonialists mobilized further during and after World War II, and as the Cold War heightened between 1947 and 1951, officials in Washington became increasingly worried that the Soviet Union would penetrate anticolonial nationalist movements and use the new powerful discourse for their own ends. A 1950 policy paper from the Bureau of Near Eastern, South Asian, and African Affairs assessed the situation in Africa:

While Communism has made very little headway in most of Africa, European nations and the United States have become alert to the danger of militant Communism penetrating the area. The USSR has sought within the United Nations and outside to play the role of the champion of the colonial peoples of the world. While the greater portion of the areas of Africa have as yet no firm nationalist aspirations, there are certain areas such as French North Africa and British West Africa where the spirit of nationalism is increasing. The USSR has sought to gain the sympathy of nationalist elements.[69]

The diffusion of anticolonial nationalism is also significant because it redounded back to Europe and the United States to impact imperial thought. As colonized groups mobilized against empire, so too did anti-imperialist thought galvanize in Britain. The overwhelming tide of anticolonial nationalism likely

---

[66] DuBois (1935), p. 87. See also Furedi (1994), p. 23.
[67] Koebner and Schmidt (1964), p. 300.
[68] "The Problem of Nationalism," June 21, 1952, FO 936–217.
[69] FRUS 1950, V, p. 1525.

contributed to the Labor Party's anti-imperial stance and also to various colonial reforms in British territories designed to appease anticolonial sentiment.[70] In 1942, an editorial in *The Times* of London referred to the fall of Singapore to Japan to suggest that Britain should reconsider its imperial order and seek "new policies and a new outlook." In the future, "there is no place for the Britain of the past." An American executive policy committee on Africa commented on this editorial to conclude: "[W]hite people as represented in Great Britain should give up any thought of trying to control the world in the way often characteristic in the past."[71] In 1946, the former director of the Department of the Interior's Division of Territories and Island Possessions noted simply that the "time has passed when the peoples of the Indies, Indo-China, Burma and India would permit white men to dictate the tenor of their lives."[72]

The force of anticolonial nationalism ultimately prompted a search for new tactics to maintain some kind of imperial control in the face of the rising tide. The idea of international mandates or "trusteeships" was one such tactic. Originally proposed to President Wilson by Jan Smuts of South Africa, and later to President Franklin Roosevelt by Chiang Kai Shek, the trusteeship idea was a strategic response to anticolonial sentiment. The State Department noted that "the use of trusteeship... frequently avoids the controversial issue of the extension of sovereignty over the area by any State."[73] Accordingly, officials in Washington and London saw international mandates or trusteeships as one way to appear nonimperial while nonetheless exerting territorial control.[74] President Franklin Roosevelt had warmed to the idea of trusteeships after reckoning the power of anticolonial mobilization. In his discussions with advisors and representatives from Russia in 1942 about the postwar order, President Roosevelt argued that trusteeships would be preferable because there had been "a palpable surge toward independence" in Southeast Asian colonies, "and the white nations thus could not hope to hold these areas as colonies in the long run."[75] The 1952 Foreign Office memo on the problem of nationalism put it simply: "Progress towards sovereign independence is both inevitable and desirable. We are bound to swim with the stream but we can hope to exert influence on the speed at which the current runs."[76]

In this sense, when Sumner Welles, Franklin Roosevelt, and other American statesmen or officials portended the end of the age of imperialism in the 1940s,

---

[70] Louis (1978), pp. 99–103; Howe (1993). Rather than upset Middle Eastern nationalists by taking Iraq directly as a colony in 1922, for example, Britain created a kingdom for the benefit of Faisal, son of Hussein. This gave Britain the appearance of being liberal while nonetheless maintaining some amount of control over Iraq.

[71] As discussed and quoted in Committee on Africa (1942), p. 2.

[72] *New York Times*, Oct. 12, 1946, p. 5.

[73] FRUS 1952–4, III, pp. 1086.

[74] As one historian puts it, it was a strategic effort on the part of imperial states to "reconcile imperialism with the liberal notion of national self-determination" [Duus (1996), p. 56].

[75] Sherwood (1950), p. 573.

[76] "The Problem of Nationalism," June 21, 1952, FO 936–217.

they were simply observing the transformations around them, responding to the agency of colonized peoples rather than authoring or initiating it. The change in views of William Phillips, America's advisor to India, is one case in point. He was at first a supporter of empires but later urged President Franklin Roosevelt to support the Indian National Congress and its demands for a timeline toward independence. What changed his mind was his experience in India. After he witnessed Gandhi's fast in 1943 and the overwhelming support it received, he warned President Roosevelt: "Color consciousness is also appearing [in India] and more and more under present conditions is bound to develop. We have, therefore, a vast bloc of Oriental peoples who have many things in common, including a dislike and distrust of the Occidental."[77] Wallace Murray in the State Department suggested likewise that the United States should consider supporting Indian independence because if it did not, "we can expect a harvest of hate and contempt the like of which our imperialistically minded ally has never known."[78] As for President Roosevelt himself, he worried about the continuation of empires not just because of his political values, but also because he was a pragmatist. Given the strength of anticolonial nationalism around the world, anyone who supported empires would only make enemies. Roosevelt's support for the international mandate or trustee system followed. So too did his general support of the idea that, one day, colonized peoples would have to be freed. Charles Taussig, Roosevelt's confidant and advisor, noted about his conversations with Roosevelt about colonies that the president "was concerned about the brown people in the East. He [Roosevelt] said that there are 1,100,000,000 brown people. In many Eastern countries, they are ruled by a handful of whites and they resent it.... 1,100,000,000 potential enemies are dangerous."[79]

Shifting Strategies

The proliferation of anticolonial nationalism is vital for our story: It helps us understand why the American state shifted its tactics away from formal imperialism. As a response to the power of anticolonial sentiment and the new geopolitical terrain, the American state first reconsidered its initial strategy of imperial outsourcing. The United States supported European empires to help realize its imperial goals, but the unmistakable power of anticolonial nationalism complicated the strategy. For example, when and where American policy makers perceived anticolonial nationalism to be relatively weak or nascent, the United States was more willing to continue to prop up European colonialism.[80] In most of Africa in the early 1950s, the United States continued to support the European empires because nationalism was perceived to be weaker there, and

---

77 Philips to Roosevelt, April 19, 1943, FRUS, 1943, IV, pp. 217–20. See also Clymer (1984), p. 30.
78 Quoted in ibid. p. 29.
79 Quoted in Louis (1978), p. 486. For more on Roosevelt's complicated views, see Sebrega (1986).
80 FRUS 1952–4, III, p. 1105.

the efforts of the USSR to "win" over nationalists had been "unsuccessful."[81] The United States only stopped its support as nationalism and the threat of Communism developed more strongly in the late 1950s and early 1960s. Secretary of State John Foster Dulles insisted that the United States should aid nationalist forces in Africa rather than suppress them because America's "prestige" was at stake.[82] The State Department had summarized this policy in its policy paper on dependent areas: "In most dependent areas of the world the security interests of the US at the present time will best be served by a policy of support for the Western Colonial Powers. [But where nationalist movements] have so effectively challenged European administration . . . it is in the interest of the US to accept the situation as it is and to encourage the progressive and peaceful transfer of administration from the imperial power to the local inhabitants."[83]

This was part of the larger pattern: When and where Washington perceived nationalism to be comparably developed, it lightened its support of European colonialism. This approach was most clearly articulated in a series of policy papers circulating in the State Department. The shared assessment was that continued support of European powers would be fruitless in the end, for anticolonial nationalist movements would effectively destabilize colonialism.[84] The related assessment was that continued support would damage America's "reputation" and push nationalist forces to the USSR. Of particular concern was Soviet "propaganda" in the colonial world that portrayed the United States as imperialist. Such propaganda, playing on anticolonial sentiment, would turn anticolonial nationalists into anti-American allies of the Soviet Union. Strategists in Washington therefore insisted that the United States would have to disavow its alliance with the European empires if it was to win hearts and minds and prevent a global turn toward Communism.[85]

These fears are clear in the Eisenhower administration's response to the Suez crisis in 1956. The administration condemned the Anglo-French invasion against General Nasser in Egypt exactly because it feared that the invasion would summon a nationalist and Communist blowback throughout the region and across the colonial world.[86] The fears are also evident in relation to areas like India and Malaysia, where anticolonialism had developed relatively early. In such areas, the United States encouraged European powers to make concrete and well-publicized steps toward self-government to try to stem the tide against would-be Communists. Similarly, the Kennedy administration pressured Portugal to decolonize its African colonies in the hopes that this would take some of the fire away from the Communist movement (even though the United States

---

[81] FRUS 1950, V, p. 1528, 1525.
[82] FRUS 1955–57, XVIII, pp. 18–19.
[83] FRUS 1950–3, III, pp. 1078–9.
[84] On the reconsideration of policy see Kent (2000), pp. 171–4.
[85] Darby (1987), p. 175; FRUS 1950–53, III, pp. 1078–9.
[86] See especially Lucas (2000), pp. 147–154 and Louis (1985), pp. 413–17.

would reverse its position as the American base in the Azores became more and more important to U.S. interests).[87] The United States also stopped supporting French suppression of colonial nationalists in Vietnam and Dutch rule in Indonesia, but only when anticolonial forces had proven far too resistant to repression and when anticolonial movement waved anti-Soviet banners.[88] One State Department official summarized the strategy for Vietnam simply enough. Suggesting that the United States stop its support of French rule given the outpouring of anticolonial sentiment, he asked rhetorically: "Whether the French like it or not, independence is coming to Indochina. Why, therefore, do we tie ourselves to the tail of their battered kite?"[89]

Whereas the proliferation and power of anticolonial nationalism compelled the United States to diminish its support of the European empires, it likewise compelled the United States to turn away from colonialism altogether. If the United States worried about how its support of European empires would be perceived, it followed that the United States would not initiate a new round of territorial rule over postcolonial areas. After all, a new round of colonization would arouse nationalist resistance and significantly raise the costs of occupation. As Secretary of State John Foster Dulles noted in 1953, the peoples of the Near East and South Asia are "suspicious of the colonial powers," and so "the day is past when [nationalist] aspirations can be ignored." President Eisenhower told Winston Churchill in 1954 that "should we try to dam up [nationalism in the Middle East] completely, it would, like a mighty river, burst through the barriers and could create havoc."[90] A National Security Council report stated it boldly. Noting the staggering development of nationalist consciousness in Southeast Asia, the Council concluded simply: "19th century imperialism is no longer a practicable system in SEA [Southeast Asia]."[91]

Recolonization would also have other serious consequences: Foremost, it would arouse the indignation of postcolonial countries and nationalist movements around the world, pushing all of them toward the USSR. The United States would lose the Cold War even if it gained new colonies. As the National Security Council stated in a secret memo, "The peoples of the colonial states would never agree to fight Communism unless they were assured of their freedom."[92] In other words, to win hearts and minds and thereby win the Cold War, the United States had to support national independence around the world rather than squash it by recolonization. This strategy was clearly stated in a famous 1952 State Department paper identifying the "General Objectives of US Policy Toward Colonial Areas." It stated that America's main objective

---

[87] Fraser (1992), p. 119.

[88] Fraser (1992), pp. 116–17. McMahon (1989), p. 351

[89] Quoted in Gardner (2000), p. 133.

[90] Lucas (2000), p. 147.

[91] Quoted in Westad 2005: 113; orig. from NSC 51, US policy towards Southeast Asia, July 1, 1949, Declassified Documents Reference Service, on www.ddrs.psmedia.com).

[92] FRUS 1952–54, XIII, Part 1, 1259.

was to "favour the progressive development of all dependent peoples toward the goal of self-government." The reason was described as follows:

[S]ubstantial advocates toward self-government have been made in a number of territories and more than 500 million people have achieved independence. Nationalist movements are gaining strength in non-self-governing territories throughout the world. US policy must be based on the general assumption that nationalism in colonial areas is a force which cannot be stopped but may, with wisdom, be guided.... It is clearly in the interest of the US to give appropriate encouragement to those movements which are non-communist and democratic in character. [This would] contribute toward the building of colonial areas into bulwarks against the spread of communism. The very fact of a demonstrated US interest in democratic nationalist movements will strengthen the hand of these groups against their communist counterparts.[93]

U.S. policy, therefore, should "seek the alignment with the democratic world of dependent peoples and those achieving self-government or independence; in particular to maintain and strengthen their friendship and respect for the US. The importance of this objective is clear in view of the Soviet Union's obvious bid for the sympathies of colonial peoples."[94] The paper enhanced its views by quoting the Philippine Representative to the United Nations: "[T]he true goal of all dependent peoples is freedom *and not enslavement by a new master.*"[95]

In short, given the changed field, supporting the independence of weaker nations rather than colonizing them was a way to win political support from anticolonial nationalists and contain rival imperial power, in this case, the Soviet Union. This was feasible given the fact that global opinion had turned away from empire as a legitimate form of political power. The scholar Rupert Emerson's observations in 1947 were prescient here. He pointed to the new global "climate of opinion" against colonialism and pondered:

Should the US turn its policy in the direction of support for these [colonial] peoples? The answer should be clearly and unequivocally in the affirmative. The major reason for such an answer is that it ... will tend to align the US with the forces of the future rather than of the past.... There are new worlds in the making.... The Near East, China, and India are all moving forward in new directions, and the hold which the US has had on the imaginations of the hundreds of millions of peoples of these areas can be maintained only if the US makes it unmistakably clear that it is with them and not against them.[96]

In 1955, John Foster Dulles's statement on U.S. policy in Africa echoed Emerson's point. Dulles noted a rise in "African consciousness" and a "young nationalism" similar to the "nationalism of the Middle East and South Asia." As a result, the USSR had been trying to identify itself in the region "with 'the oppressed colonial peoples of the world.'" Accordingly, U.S. policy should aim to "consolidate its cultural and moral position with respect to the Africans."[97]

93 FRUS 1952–4, III, pp. 1084–5.
94 Ibid., p. 1087.
95 Ibid., p. 1085; emphasis added.
96 Emerson (1947), p. 271.
97 FRUS 1955–7, XVIII, pp. 17–18, 19.

A subsequent memo by the consul general at Leopoldville added some clarity on what this should involve: "Now that the issue of 'colonialism' is being moved front and center by the Soviets the essential thing it seems to me *is that we free ourselves from the vice....* The US should stand for freedom from all forms of oppression, for self-government, and for independence based upon self-determination." He concluded that financial aid should be given to the continent directly, rather than through the European colonial powers, and thereby "maneuver... by abolishing the vestiges of the 'older' imperialism."[98] Subsequent memos and policy statements reiterated the very same views.[99]

Finally, the new global climate of anticolonial nationalism and its use as symbolic capital by geopolitical rivals did not only compel the American state to turn away from colonialism. It also prompted the American state to shift from colonialism to informal imperialism by the same token. Informal imperialism enabled the American state to exert controls without declaring sovereignty over foreign territory. As such, it was useful for exercising power without as much risk of provoking anticolonial nationalists. Informal imperialism enabled the United States to appear respectful of postcolonial sovereignty while nonetheless permitting it to "pull the strings whenever necessary" (as one State Department official put it in talks with the British on strategy in Asia).[100] But how exactly did this shift occur?

To see it more clearly, we can briefly consider a case when the American state might have reestablished some form of direct colonial control over post-colonial countries but did not: Iran in the late 1940s and early 1950s. This is an especially informative case because Iran was an area of vital strategic interest to the Western powers. By the end of the Second World War, both the United States and the United Kingdom had become increasingly dependent on oil from the region and from Iran itself. Exactly because of this, Washington often worried about Soviet activities. In 1946, the United States had persuaded Soviet troops to leave the northern provinces, but the Soviet threat did not go away so easily. In 1947, the precursor agency to the Central Intelligence Agency warned that the USSR would not give up until it took all of Iran.[101] Given its importance, American policy makers declared that whatever policy they enacted in regard to Iran might serve as a "model" and "test case" for dealing with strategically important territories in the new postwar order.[102]

But how to maintain influence and thwart Soviet incursion? The possibility of establishing a new type of direct territorial control was in fact entertained early on. President Roosevelt and military strategists considered establishing

98 Ibid., p. 27; see also 1951, VI, pt. 1, pp. 8–9.
99 See, for instance, Vice-President Nixon's report to President Eisenhower on Africa in Pratt (1958), p. 147.
100 FRUS 1949, VII, part 2, p. 1199; see also Louis and Robinson (1994), p. 472.
101 "Developments in the Azerbaijan Situation," Central Intelligence Group, Office of Reports and Estimates (ORE 19), *secret*, June 4, 1947 (online www.gwu.edu/7Ensarchiv/NSAEBB/NSAEBB21/index.html, accessed 11/13/09).
102 United States Department of State (1955), p. 341.

an international trusteeship over Iranian railways and the Iranian port on the Persian Gulf. This would give the United States and its allies more direct control over critical functions relating to oil concessions in Iran while also serving economic and geopolitical goals. Not only would it "assist Iran economically," as the State Department report on the issue announced, it would also entice Russia to take part in the trusteeship as a partner. By providing the Soviets with a direct hand in territorial management, it would discourage "more forceful methods by Russia to gain an outlet to the Gulf" and thereby "develop international cooperation rather than rivalry in Iran."[103] Despite these potential rewards, however, the American state ultimately disavowed the strategy. The reason was simple: the threat of a nationalist uprising.

This threat had already been posed earlier. When Britain tried to establish Iran as a protectorate after World War I (by imposing the Anglo-Persian Agreement of 1919), it faced strong nationalist resistance. The Iranian Prime Minister Seyyid Zia-ud-din, in a declaration in 1921, loudly denounced it. The same threat faced the American state as it considered establishing a trusteeship to be operated by joint nations. "No matter how drawn up or proposed," read the State Department's summary for why a trusteeship was not feasible, "the plan would appear to Iran, and doubtless to the world, as a thinly disguised cover for power politics and old-world imperialism. Iranians are highly suspicious of foreign influence in the country and would unquestionably resent any extension of foreign control there.... The Department's judgment is that the trusteeship could only be imposed on Iran, a sovereign, allied nation, by force of arms."[104] The potency of anticolonial nationalism substantially raised the costs of an international trusteeship. The cost of direct colonial rule would have been even higher.

The problem remained: How would the United States maintain stability in the region, protect oil concessions, and ward off rival incursion if not by establishing territorial control? The answer was to use informal mechanisms. The United States would send financial aid, technicians, and advisors for helping to manage the port and the railways connected to the oil concessions. Presumably, this would exert U.S. influence in a manner more palatable to nationalists. Iran would retain official sovereignty, but the United States would be able to influence the control of its vital assets. As the "Iranians prefer to employ Americans or the nationals of small European countries (Sweden or Switzerland)," there was little threat of Soviets wielding undue influence. Therefore, by these informal mechanisms, the "laudable ends" in the proposal for international trusteeship could still be "accomplished in some measure."[105]

Even this type of indirect influence was not enough, though. More problems arose later, in 1951, when the Iranian premier Mohammed Musaddiq nationalized Iranian oil fields. Faced with this problem, the United States again

[103] Ibid., pp. 344–5.
[104] Ibid., p. 345.
[105] Ibid., p. 345.

considered direct intervention – this time beginning with a military invasion. However, that option had already been disavowed on the grounds that it would "provoke a communist rising with Soviet backing in northern Iran" and turn Iran into "another Korea."[106] The American state needed, as President Eisenhower told his advisors and the British foreign secretary in a secret meeting on the issue, "to find some new and imaginative approach to the Persian oil problem which kept Persia in the Western orbit." The preferred solution was to act covertly so as to hide American influence. Accordingly, the recently formed CIA (1947) orchestrated the overthrow of Mussadiq and the restoration of the Shah with the army of General Fazlollah Zahedi.[107] "Prompt and substantial economic aid," as CIA classified reports called it, was to be used to maintain the Shah's loyalty.[108] American companies thereafter got their hands on more oil concessions. For the American state, the subsequent stability and anti-Communist stance of the Shah's regime were a related boon. Winston Churchill conveyed to Washington that the new situation promised to "change the whole picture in the Middle East."[109]

The overthrow of Mussadiq was the first postwar instance of America's use of covert force to topple a foreign regime, besides perhaps in Latin America. It was surely not the last. We come to another telling instance when the United States might have directly colonized foreign territory but did not: the Philippines in the 1950s. The United States had granted the islands independence in 1946, but the postcolonial regime faced serious problems by the 1950s. The peasant-based guerilla Communist movement, known as the Huks, had been gaining ground. Philippine President Quirino's regime, in the eyes of the intelligence establishment in Washington, was unwittingly fanning their flames by its blatant corruption. This was a serious problem for America's geopolitical strategy. The Philippines remained an important nodal point in America's network of defense, and large U.S. military bases were maintained there. The fear was that, unless Quirino's regime cleaned up or was cast out, the Communists would continue to gain ground and ultimately push the archipelago to the USSR.

To deal with this issue, there was the possibility of a U.S. military occupation to suppress the Communist movement. As a policy information officer explained to Assistant Secretary of State for Far Eastern Affairs Dean Rusk, this would mean that "the American army will be fighting a Philippine guerilla army, which ... will have the support of the Nationalists," and thus "the process of recolonializing [sic] the Philippines will then be well advanced."[110] Yet given the power of anticolonial nationalism, no such "recolonializing" was

---

106 FRUS 1950, V, pp. 593–635.
107 Quoted in Moraes Ruehsen (1993), p. 474.
108 Memorandum from the Department of State, *top secret, circa* August 1953 (online www.gwu .edu/Ensarchiv/NSAEBB/NSAEBB21/index.html, accessed 11/13/09).
109 Quoted in Louis and Robinson (1994), p. 475.
110 FRUS 1951, VI, pt. 1, p. 8.

to occur. The problem would be that such direct intervention would invoke the ire of nationalists and push the Philippines even further to Communism. The Communists would then "have the support of the Nationalists just as Ho's regime [in Indochina] has had."[111] The policy information office for the Bureau of Far Eastern Affairs put it simply: Although the "process of recolonializing" would be "well advanced," given anticolonial nationalism and the threat of Soviet manipulation of it, "we shall not get away with it."[112] The State Department's Livingston Merchant had earlier worried about this very situation, offering the same conclusion. In 1950, in the wake of the loss of China to Communists, he wrote a memo to Assistant Secretary of State Dean Rusk in which he warned that "the dilemma the United States Government now faces is how to force an ineffectual local government to do internally what it must do, without reoccupying the country." Why not reoccupy the country? Because it would "cause violent repercussions throughout Asia and Western Europe as well."[113] It would, in other words, evoke an outcry from anticolonial nationalists who would rightfully turn instead to the USSR. As with Iran, then, the preferred solution to colonial occupation was to use covert tactics and informal mechanisms. Rather than initiating a new round of colonization that would diminish America's symbolic capital and push the Philippines toward Communism, CIA operators manipulated the Philippine elections to ensure the victory of Ramon Magsaysay over Quirino. The United States then established Magsaysay as America's preferred client in exchange for an influx of aid.[114]

From the Japanese Mandates to Fiji: A Comparison
As direct colonial rule was no longer an option given the proliferation of anticolonial nationalism, the American state was limited to employing informal means to exert influence and needed to construct a new network of clients and collaborators rather than just colonies. If this were true, it would follow the American state would have employed formal imperialism when or where anticolonial nationalism had not taken root and where, therefore, the threat of resistance based on anticolonial principles was minimal. It is difficult to test this proposition properly because, as seen, anticolonial nationalism had become a global phenomenon in the mid-twentieth century. There were few if any areas where nationalist consciousness had not developed to levels perceived as dangerous by would-be American imperialists. However, a look at the Japanese-mandated territories in the Pacific after World War II is telling.

As seen in an earlier chapter, the United States took control over the former Japanese territories in 1947, under the guise of the mandate system. As strategic "Trust Territories," these islands became the one area where the United States

---

[111] Ibid., p. 8.
[112] Ibid., p. 9.
[113] Quoted in Macdonald (1992), p. 50.
[114] Kolko (1988), pp. 63–4.

did not in fact employ informal imperialism and instead resorted to old-fashioned colonialism. This stands as an exception to our story: the only case where the United States established direct control over foreign territory after World War II. So why was the American state willing to do this for the Japanese territories but not for other parts of the peripheral world? Was it not concerned about anticolonial resistance to direct territorial control or Soviet manipulation of it? There was some concern in Washington about the public image of the United States if it were to take the islands as colonies. President Roosevelt's 1943 investigative commission into the question of taking the Pacific territories worried that taking them as colonies would put the United States at risk for being "charged with imperialism" and "aggrandizement."[115] Still, despite these worries, the United States proceeded to take the islands as Trust Territories.

There were two reasons. The first is that the Cold War had not yet taken off, so there was little threat of Soviet anticolonial propaganda. Indeed, the United States established control in consultation with the Soviets. The second reason is that the threat of nationalist resistance was minimal. As officials in the military establishment and the Committee on Dependent Areas saw things, the islands were small and distant and the population apparently too sparse to pose trouble. Henry L. Stimson, the U.S. secretary of war who had previously served in the Philippines, was among those who pushed Washington to seize the Japanese territories. He explained to Roosevelt that acquiring the islands was feasible because the situation was different from the time of World War I. There was "no population to be imperialized."[116] There was a population of 103,000 persons, excluding Japanese residents, but as one admiral put it, that was "pretty small potatoes."[117] In other words, a new round of colonization was only feasible where anticolonial resistance did not exist. A National Security Council report was clear on this point. On discussing policy toward Southeast Asia, it clarified that "19th century imperialism" is only "a practicable system... where the subject people are unsophisticated and acquiescent, as in the case of certain South Pacific islanders."[118] This was written in 1949, just as the American state was establishing its power over the "small potatoes" in the Japanese territories, where evidently the people were "acquiescent."

It should follow that the relative weakness of anticolonial nationalism in the nineteenth century explains why direct colonialism as opposed to informal imperialism was sometimes initiated by the British state. Let us consider this more deeply by going back to 1860, close to a century before the National Security Council issued its report on the feasibility of imperialism in the world. In 1860, Her Majesty's secretary of foreign affairs and other men in Lord Derby's

---

[115] Quoted in Louis (1978), p. 271.
[116] Ibid., p. 483.
[117] Ibid., p. 478.
[118] Westad (2005), p. 113.

government contemplated the possibility of extending British sovereignty over the islands of Fiji. British settlers and merchants had already been operating in the islands; a local chief Thakombau of Bau had made an offer of cession to the British Crown; and the British consul William Thomas Pritchard was pressing London to accept. Investigations were conducted, documents and reports passed hands, and memos were exchanged. Ultimately, however, the offer was refused. Britsh sovereignty over Fiji was not to be. Why not?

The reasons given by contemporaries for the refusal to take Fiji were numerous. However, among them was the threat of native resistance. Months earlier, war had erupted in New Zealand. Maoris resisted the usurpation of their land by white settlers and the British Army had responded with gunfire. Such was the context in which British officials considered Fiji. Indeed, the violence directly impacted the recommendation by the governor of New South Wales, who warned the Colonial Office that the "inevitable result" of taking Fiji and the subsequent arrival of whites "will be a war of races." The "cost of an attempt to maintain the supremacy of the white population," he predicted, "will be comparatively great and the loss of life enormous."[119] The Colonial Office, the Foreign Office, and the undersecretary of state agreed. Sir Frederic Rodgers, the new permanent undersecretary in the Colonial Office, summed it up: "The present juncture certainly is not one in which it would be convenient to become responsible for the Government of more warlike savages than we already have on our hands."[120]

The decision not to colonize Fiji due to this fear of resistance would seem similar to the American state's reluctance to colonize new territory in the mid- to late twentieth century.[121] But similarities stop here. Although London surely worried about a possible "war of races," this was not the only reason for turning Fiji down. There were other reasons, not least Fiji's lack of value at the time. Lord Carnarvon put it simply: "[W]e gain nothing by the acquisition."[122] The other difference is that, unlike the American state later, the British state eventually came around. In 1874, when the next opportunity to annex Fiji arose, British officials decided to take it. The reasons for the turn are multiple. We will explore them in a later chapter. For now we take note that the reason cited previously for not seizing Fiji – native resistance – was irrelevant this time around. Lord Carnarvon, who had previously stood against annexation, now declared that annexation was imperative rather than a burden. "England has

[119] Governor of New South Wales (Denison) April 10, 1860 to Lord Duke of Newcastle, CO 83/1. For more see Drus (1950), pp. 88–90.

[120] Quoted in Eldridge (1967), p. 177.

[121] To be sure, there is a parallel. Just as the American state was willing to colonize Japanese territories because local resistance would be "small potatoes" given the small number of inhabitants, so too did the Colonial Office, in considering Fiji, decide that the only Pacific territory that might be annexed was the island of Oparo (Rapa) on the grounds that it had "few inhabitants" [quoted in Drus (1950), p. 90].

[122] Minutes by Carnarvon and Bulwer-Lytton, January 21, 1859, CO 201/504, vol 3.

a mission," he asserted to Parliament, "to extend her policy of annexation in this part of the world."[123]

The fact that British officials worried about native resistance in 1860 but found it less worrisome in 1874 is indicative. In the nineteenth century, resistance to colonial rule was indeed threatening, but it was sporadic and inconsistent. This is exactly because anticolonial nationalism had not yet proliferated around the globe to mobilize populations against empires. In fact, prior to the time when the Crown took Fiji, in 1874, resistance to colonialism had been irregular. Available data reveals that, from 1816 to 1868 (after which Britain finally annexed Fiji), local populations had posed armed resistance to European conquests in about 24 percent of all cases (twenty-one conquests out of eighty-nine total). Compare this with what happened later, when nationalist consciousness began to spread. From 1868 to 1918, local populations posed resistance in 73 percent of all cases of conquest (fifty-eight out of eighty total conquests), a far greater percentage than the mere 24 percent earlier in the century.[124] The wars of resistance that would unsettle the halls of imperial power occurred mostly at that time. Cuba and the Philippines erupted against Spain in the 1890s. The Boer War posed unforeseen trouble for the Crown in 1899. The Sierra Leone Hut Tax War probably reflected, in the words of Governor Frederic Cardew, "the growing political consciousness of the African," but that was in 1898.[125] All of these events and others marked a shift toward a new global field in which anticolonial nationalism dominated. Before then, resistance to colonialism had neither the form, fire, nor fever that anticolonial nationalism would later inject.

Given this, it is unsurprising that British officials did not let threats of resistance undermine their decision to take Fiji in the 1870s. They may have worried about bouts of native recalcitrance here and there, but the relative weakness of nationalist consciousness in Fiji meant that they did not fret about sustained or infectious resistance threatening to overthrow colonial rule. In Fiji as in many other places coveted by the British imperial state, native resistance was most often localized along ethnic, tribal, or other lines. It did not have the mobilizing capacity of nationalism. As Johnson puts it, resistance was considered to be "tribal and sporadic." When there were the stirrings of nationalist movements, British officials saw them as "small, unrepresentative minorities."[126] Lord Carnarvon's views on Fiji in the 1870s express this wider perception exactly. "The Natives are scattered over 200 Islands," he explained, "they are divided in local jealousies; and with the exception of the 20,000 mountaineers, they are a milder and gentler class of Natives than those in New Zealand."[127] Although Carnarvon mentions resistance from the Maori in New Zealand, even

---

[123] Quoted in McIntyre (1967), p. 332.
[124] Calculated from data in Goertz and Diehl (1992).
[125] Cardew quoted in Boahen (1990), p. 69.
[126] Johnson (2003), p. 86.
[127] PP, vol 221, July 15–Aug. 7, 1874, p. 183.

that was not disabling. In response to an outbreak of violence in 1860 there, an editorial in the London *Times* concluded that there was little to worry over. The Maori resistance would be suppressed soon enough, it declared; "before much mischief has ensued." The editorial then referred to rumors that some among the Maori were showing nascent signs of a "nationality" and were considering "coalescing under a native sovereign to arrest the progress of the Europeans." Yet again there was nothing to worry about. The movement was "by no means universal." Most of the population had "discernment enough to...come at once within the pale of civilization and share the advantages of British rule." The minor resistances "are but the necessary incidents of the process by which a superior race displaces an inferior one – incidents, in fact, of colonization itself, and need suggest no reproach if we do but conduct ourselves with humanity and good faith."[128]

Informal Imperialism in South America

We can now understand the critical difference between the global contexts in which the British and U.S. empires operated. In the nineteenth century, for the former empire, anticolonial nationalism had not yet dominated the global field, and so it was much more feasible – hence more likely – for the British state (and other European states for that matter) to employ direct colonial rule as a means of exerting power over other societies. There was but one exception to this pattern during the nineteenth century: South America. Notably, it is here where the British state did what the United States did in the latter part of the twentieth century: trade colonialism for informal imperialism.

Already by early to mid-century, South America had undergone centuries of European rule. Already too South Americans had overthrown it. Independence movements had erupted across the region, partly facilitated by Napoleon's occupation in 1808. By the 1820s, the Spanish and Portuguese empires in the Americas were almost completely dismantled. In their wake emerged new nations wedded to the nation-state ideal and principles of national sovereignty. Britain recognized their sovereignty in 1822 at the Congress of Verona (the following year the Monroe Doctrine essentially accomplished the same for the United States). Even before the 1822 Congress of Verona, however, British officials had seen something of the region's nationalism. There was an invasion. Lessons were learned.

The invasion originated in military leaders like naval commander Sir Home Popham. During the Napoleonic Wars, Popham drew up plans to take Spanish America from Spain.[129] Some in London were skeptical of the grand scheme, but others shared the dream. Therefore, in June of 1806, Popham and his colonel, William Carr Beresford, descended on Buenos Aires with 1,600 troops. Upon his arrival to the outskirts of the city, Popham had learned that

---

[128] London *Times*, June 15, 1860, p. 8.
[129] Gallo (2001), p. 28.

the Spanish viceroy had fled to Montevideo, and the city of up to 70,000 inhabitants appeared open for the taking. Buenos Aires, as the capital of the Río de la Plata (encompassing present-day Argentina, Uruguay, Paraguay, and parts of Bolivia), was a prize. But the power of nationalist forces was soon felt. At least two independence movements had already been active in the area before the British occupation, and Creoles in the region "showed no enthusiasm for exchanging the rule of a senile Bourbon for that of a mad Hanoverian" (as one historian has aptly put it), and so they mobilized their forces.[130] Martin de Alzaga and Juan Martín de Pueyrredón, local merchants who commanded local influence, summoned civilian opposition within the city. Meanwhile, the independence leader and naval captain Rafael D. del Villar Santiago de Liniers mobilized more than 10,000 local gauchos and farmers, along with Spanish soldiers, to advance on the city from the countryside. By August, they managed to oust the British threat and recapture the city.[131] A second assault on Buenos Aires, this time led by Lt. General John Whitelocke, and another on Montevideo, fared no better: Whitelocke and his troops were forced to surrender and flee back to England and Capetown.

The failed invasions imparted lasting lessons. One officer, Colonel Browne, warned colleagues at home about nationalist resistance to foreign intervention: "You have not a friend among the inhabitants of South America."[132] After his failed venture, Colonel Beresford wrote to Viscount Castlereagh, the foreign secretary, to warn similarly about "the political sentiments of the great body of the people." Any attempt to conquer, occupy, and directly rule South American would face utter failure, Beresford insisted: "for they are decidedly inclined to throw off the yoke of Spain, they are still more hostile to receiving that of any other nation, and we conquering it for ourselves would be carrying a millstone about our necks, as they would be continually watching and plotting to get rid of us."[133] Castlereagh's own advisors in London hit the same cautious notes. Sir Arthur Wellesley counseled: "From what has lately passed at Buenos Ayres [sic], and from all that I have read of these countries, I am convinced that any attempt to conquer them, with a view to their future subjection to the British Crown, would certainly fail."[134]

These warnings, undoubtedly animated by the hard experience of confronting anticolonial nationalism head on in South America, directly influenced Castlereagh. In turn they helped set the course for British policy toward the region for much of the century. After the invasion of Buenos Aires, Castlereagh wrote to the cabinet summarizing his thoughts on Britain's relations with South America. Castlereagh insisted that, in any dealings with South America, "it seems indispensable that we should not present ourselves in any other light

[130] Winn (1976), p. 102.
[131] For the failed intervention, see Fletcher (2006).
[132] Colonel Browne to General Walpole, April 25, 1807 as quoted in Lynch (1969), p. 2.
[133] Quoted in Gallo (2001), p. 72.
[134] Wellesley Memorandum of Feb. 8, 1808 in Lynch (1969), p. 22.

than as auxiliaries and protectors" rather than as conquerors or invaders. This was much like the way in which U.S. officials during the Cold War would later try to win over the hearts and minds of third-world nationalists: Faced with nationalist consciousness in South America, Castlereagh hoped that his government would display sympathy for nationalist causes. Castlereagh then searched for ways of exerting influence over South America without colonizing it directly. The "question for the Cabinet to decide," he wrote, "is ... whether some principle of acting more consonant to the sentiments and interests of the people of South America cannot be taken up, which ... may relieve us from the hopeless task of conquering this extensive country, against the temper of its population."[135] The power of anticolonial nationalism in South America, manifest clearly in the failed occupations of 1806 and 1807, compelled Castlereagh to restrategize just as nationalist forces around the globe in the twentieth century compelled the American state to reconsider its policies.

The British state's approach to South America in subsequent decades followed in part from the early lessons. Castlereagh himself did not write nor promulgate a master blueprint for policy. But after the South American revolutions of 1810–1825, a repertoire of tactics surfaced and were eventually deployed. Direct colonization was out. "Dreams of imperialist expansion in the Americas," notes the historian Alan Knight, "were temporarily laid to rest."[136] Instead, the British state did what the American state later did when it came face-to-face with anticolonial nationalism around the globe: It turned to informal mechanisms of power. Bouts of blockades, political meddling, unequal treaties, and financial discipline replaced territorial rule. By 1841, James Murray's influential memo in the Foreign Office turned the unstated approach the British state had been taking into near official policy. Political instability and "civil discord" in the region, opined Murray, had been threatening British trade. This was all the more a threat given Britain's increasing economic interests in the region. Therefore, Murray stressed, "tranquility and good Government in South America would be favourable to British interests." However, imposing "tranquility" through direct colonial control was not an option; Murray did not even entertain it. Instead, he listed a range of tactics, all of which fell short of annexation: "offensive and defensive alliance" with key Latin American collaborators, trade treaties and financial meddling, vigorous protection of British merchants and residents, and a stronger naval presence threatening to deploy force should occasion demand.[137] This was informal imperialism sketched on paper.

As the historian John Darwin puts it, informal imperialism in South America was a "pragmatic acceptance of limited power" on the part of the British state.[138] We can now see that British power was indeed limited, if only because

---

[135] "Memorandum ... " May, 1, 1807 in Vane (1851), 2nd series, VII, pp. 319–21.
[136] Knight (1999), p. 126. See also Lynch (1969).
[137] James Murray, "Memorandum on British Trade," Dec. 31, 1841: FO 97/284.
[138] Darwin (1997), p. 619.

of the diametrically opposed power of anticolonial nationalism. Anticolonial nationalism in the region made colonization too costly. South America in the nineteenth century thus manifested regionally what the United States would later face globally: a powerful anticolonial nationalist consciousness emanating from the periphery to shape what the metropole would do. The lesson, in the end, is the opposite of what exceptionalist thought teaches. The forms of imperialism followed not from the character of the imperial nation, but from the character of the fields of their application.

5

Weary Titans

Declining Powers, New Imperialisms

> Rome... broke up, not from conquering too much, but from conquering too little.
>
> – Alexander Dirom, *Sketches of the State of the British Empire*, 1828 (p. 72)[1]

By 2009, at least sixty-two men and women who died in Iraq while serving in the U.S. armed forces did not come from within the United States. They came from the overseas territories of the United States: thirty-six from Puerto Rico; six from the Virgin Islands; seven from Guam; five from the Northern Marianas; and eight from American Samoa. An additional forty fatalities were American Indians or Native Alaskans, and forty-eight were Native Hawaiians or Pacific Islanders.[2] We should now know the significance of this. These numbers remind us of the tragedies of war, but they also evoke imperial continuities. They tell of connections between America's history of imperial intervention and its current imperial forays into the Middle East; of America's long-standing status as an imperial power; of resonances from the past to the present returns of empire. President George W. Bush alluded to similar continuities and imperial resonances when, in 2003, he gave a speech mentioning that "coalition forces, including Filipino peacekeepers and medical workers, are working for the rise of freedom and self-government in Iraq." He gave that speech in Manila, on the floor of the Philippine Congress that President William H. Taft had helped establish in 1907.

Referring to these imperial continuities, however, also raises questions about discontinuities. After all, when the United States seized the Philippine Islands and other overseas territories, it was only an ascending global power; merely a "New Empire," as Brooks Adams declared famously in 1903, positioning

---

[1] Dirom (1828), p. 72.

[2] From Fischer (2009), p. 3 and http://icasualties.org/Iraq/ByState.aspx (accessed May, 14, 2010). Sparrow (2006) notes the presence of colonial soldiers in Iraq.

itself to take over the world. The more recent imperial forays into Iraq have occurred in a very different climate, a very different geopolitical context. The United States has not been a hegemon ascending but a hegemon falling. Rather than a promising new player on the world scene whose imperial expansion once matched its youthful exuberance, the United States has been an aging empire watching dreadfully as rivals threaten to take their slice of the pie. In this very different context, what does imperial expansion mean?

One goal of this chapter is to address this question by casting a comparative eye on the British empire in the late nineteenth century. Britain too had faced economic decline. Beginning in the 1870s, rival powers like Germany, Russia, and the United States among others grasped increasing shares of world economic output. As a result, Britain's economic dominance was unsettled. Britain's economic decline thus prefigured America's decline in the late twentieth century. So what did this mean for their empires? As Britain and the United States began to face new competition from rivals, did their previous imperial modalities or intensities change too? Great powers can fall indeed; the purpose of this chapter to wonder whether such falls from economic dominance correspond with changes in imperial activity.

Features of Decline

Clarification is in order. We have said that Britain and the United States experienced decline, but the meaning of *decline* here should be foregrounded. Although there are a variety of ways to define the term, we refer to it in the narrow sense of *hegemonic decline*; that is, a fall in the hegemonic nations' relative economic standing in the world system. Decline does not mean a decrease in prestige or military power, although these things may accompany decline. It rather means a relative decrease in economic standing. What proportion of the world economy do the nations command? What is the nations' share of world GDP? This also means that decline is relative; relative to the nations' prior standing and to the economic standing of other nations in the system. Hegemonic nations enjoy a monopoly or preponderance over the world economy. When that share over world economic output decreases because rival powers are taking up more and more shares of their own, then the hegemon is in decline according to this definition.

Decline does not mean that the nation suddenly descends into the ranks of the world's poorest countries. In fact, during their periods of decline, both the United States and Britain remained among the world's most economically powerful countries. The point is that, relative to their previous economic monopoly of the world's productive powers and to the capacities of other nations, they descended. Furthermore, decline by this definition means that the global economic field as a whole is undergoing transformation. As the hegemon declines because rival nations take up a greater share of the world economy, the entire system passes from a condition of unipolarity – with one nation the economic winner – to a multipolar economic condition. A near-monopoly structure in the global economic field passes into a more competitive structure.

Using this definition, many scholars have traced Britain's decline. Most agree it began in 1868 and was exacerbated with the 1873 crash on the Vienna money market. After 1873 came the "long depression" that lasted at least until 1896.[3] This depression was part of the decline. It was marked by a worldwide overproduction of agricultural and industrial goods, especially in iron and steel, and decreasing profits.[4] It was also accompanied by rising unemployment and slower economic growth. The depression came in fits and starts. There was a period during the 1870s, for example, when some in the British business sector and the policy elite were comparably optimistic about the economic situation. Yet the overarching trends throughout the period remained consistent. From 1820 to 1840, industrial production had grown at an annual rate of about 4 percent and, from 1840 to 1870, about 3 percent. But between 1875 and 1894 it grew only at 1.5 percent annually.[5] By 1879, British economists and policy makers were already worrying, culminating in the establishment of a Royal Commission to investigate the "Depression of Trade and Industry." The commission concluded that there was a "serious depression, affecting most trades and industries, characterized by surplus production, low prices, poor investment opportunities and unemployment."[6]

The depression was just one dimension of the larger issue; that is, competition from rising economic rivals, especially Germany and the United States. This means that even though the British economy was not disastrous in absolute terms, it was significantly challenged in relative terms. Although some British industries such as coal or textiles increased their output, for example, their relative share of world production diminished. In other industries like steel, chemicals, and electrical goods, Britain lost its earlier advantage.[7] British agriculture likewise faced competition, as grain imports from the United States and South America posed new trouble. And generally, imports in multiple sectors rose.[8] "We import half our food," complained Dilke in his 1890, *Problems of Greater Britain*; "we import the immense masses of raw material which are essential to our industry."[9]

Britain's declining competitiveness can be seen by comparing relative shares of world manufacturing output. During the height of British hegemony, Britain's manufacturing output constituted 19.9 percent of the world's total, creeping up to 22.9 percent in 1880. Its share only slightly declined to 18.5 percent in 1900, but it fell to 13.6 in 1913. Most important, the United States and Germany increasingly took greater shares. By 1900, the United States had

[3] Chamberlain (1984), p. 148.
[4] Ibid., p. 149.
[5] Kennedy (1987), p. 228.
[6] Chamberlain (1984), p. 149.
[7] Kennedy (1987), p. 228.
[8] Chamberlain (1984), p. 148.
[9] Dilke (1890), p. 4.

already surpassed Britain. By 1913, Germany had too. Relative decline is also evident in Thompson's index of "leading sector share," which affirms the figures on world manufacturing output. This includes not just manufacturing, but a range of sectors that show a continual decline in Britain's leading sector share: from .546 in 1850 to .430 in 1880 to .333 in 1890 and to .146 by 1910.[10] In this context, it is not surprising that writers and analysts continually spoke of doom. The "dream" of Britain as the workshop of the world, wrote one in 1870, had become "a dream of the past.... Other nations have entered the race, and although we are still the great traders of the world, the singularity of our position has gone."[11] Another writer warned, "there seems to be reasonable grounds for fearing that England's commercial supremacy may already be in danger."[12] These worries about rivals became all the more common as the years continued.

The United States experienced a similar decline, beginning in the 1970s in the wake of the 1973 oil crisis.[13] As with Britain's decline, there was an initial recession marked by decreasing profits and productivity. The average annual increase in labor productivity in the United States from 1948 to 1973 was 2.8 percent, but from 1981 to 1986 it was only 1.2 percent. The rate of profit in America's traditional sectors like manufacturing fell similarly.[14] There was a brief stint of optimism through the 1990s, reflected in scholarship and pundits who declared that America was not in fact declining, and that it was just taking the lead in other areas beyond its traditional manufacturing base: that is, in service or technology and finance.[15] This too was similar to Britain's decline: There had been in Britain a brief period of optimism after the initial recession. And as with the British case, the optimism about the United States proved far too hopeful. Britain had also gained ground during its decline in finance and service; some have claimed that the turn to such industries is not a transcendence of decline but its dominant sign.[16] In any case, the apparent boom of the 1990s was but a bubble that already began to burst before the end of the decade.[17]

These domestic economic issues aside, America's economic standing in relative terms fell from the mid-1970s while competitors rose and continued to rise. Initially, beginning in the late 1960s even, the key competition came from Japan and Germany. Beginning in the late 1980s came the European Union as a whole, the rise of Russia as a potential economic monster, and then China.

---

[10] Thompson (2001), p. 287.

[11] Grant (1870), p. 184.

[12] Bodelson (1968), p. 82.

[13] For a recent study showing an earlier starting point than 1973 but affirming decline, see Chase-Dunn, Giem, Jorgenson, Reifer, Rogers, and Lio (2002).

[14] Corden (1990).

[15] Strange (1987).

[16] Arrighi (1994). On finance and the service sector in the British case, see Cain and Hopkins (1993), Cain (1985).

[17] Brenner (2002).

Various measures show this. One useful measure has to do with the largest multinational corporations. In 1956, forty-two of the biggest fifty multinationals in the world were American. The rest of the world only had eight. By 1980, only twenty-three were American. The number of European firms was about equal. Throughout, the Japanese increased their number of firms in the top fifty.[18] Other data show a continuation of the trend through the 1990s and into the 2000s. Non-American firms constituted nine of the ten largest electronics and electrical equipment manufacturers in the world; eight of the ten largest auto makers and utility companies (gas and electric); seven of the ten largest petroleum refiners; and six of the ten largest telecommunication companies. Half of the ten largest pharmaceutical firms were non-American too. Of the top one hundred corporations in the world in 2000, as ranked by foreign-held assets, only twenty-three were American. "Together, Germany, France, the United Kingdom, and the Netherlands, with a combined gross domestic product (GDP) seven-tenths that of the US, had forty; Japan had sixteen. During the 1990s, the share of US multinationals in the foreign sales of the world's one hundred largest multinationals decreased from 30 to 25 percent; the share of EU-based companies increased from 41 to 46 percent."[19]

Measures regarding shares of the world economy are similarly informative. In 1950, the United States supplied half of the world's gross product; in 2002 it only supplied 21 percent. Sixty percent of manufacturing production in the world in 1950 came from the United States, but that fell to only 25 percent by 1999. Studies using somewhat different measures arrive at the same conclusion. In 1999, the United States contributed only 28 percent to world GDP, whereas the European Union had 30 percent of the total. Japan was only 12 percent and China's only 4 percent, but East Asia (excluding Japan) was the world's fastest-growing economy since the late 1990s.[20] In 2007, *The Economist* magazine scoffed "Come on number one, your time is up."[21] In 2004, the Institute for International Economics (which included on its board prominent economists and policy makers like Paul Volcker and Larry Summers) had determined that "the United States is no longer the world's dominant economic entity."[22]

Both the United States and Britain experienced decline, but was decline accompanied by a shift or change in imperialism too?

Britain's New Imperialism, 1870s–1914

It is by now well established that something about British imperialism changed in the latter part of the nineteenth century. The English economist J. A. Hobson in 1902 characterized it as a "new aggressive Imperialism" and an "expansion

[18] Bergesen and Sahoo (1985).
[19] Du Boff (2003).
[20] Boswell (2004).
[21] *The Economist*, April 14, 2007, p. 12.
[22] Bergsten and Institute for International Economics (2005), p. 20.

of British political despotism."[23] Countless other analysts since have spoken of Britain's "new imperialism." The idea was not questioned until Robinson and Gallagher's seminal article on the "imperialism of free trade." On the one hand, Robinson and Gallagher were suspicious of the notion that there was a new imperialism at the end of the nineteenth century. In their view, Britain had been continuously imperialistic throughout the century. On the other hand, Robinson and Gallagher's overarching point was not to deny that a change occurred at all. Their claim was that British imperialism was continuous at one level but discontinuous on another. Specifically, Britain was continuously imperialistic, but it changed the *mode* or *form* of imperialism. Britain in the mid-century preferred informal imperialism, but during the late nineteenth century – concomitant with its relative decline – the British state tended to replace informal with *formal* modes.[24]

Following from this characterization, we can indeed detect a new imperialism in the late nineteenth century coinciding with Britain's economic decline. It involved a shift from informal to formal modes of imperialism. To be sure, many of the areas that Britain had previously declined to colonize during its period of hegemony were put under direct British control in this decline period. Whereas the British state had rejected ideas of taking Fiji in the 1860s, it changed its mind in 1874 and seized it. Whereas Palmerston had long rejected the idea of taking Egypt as a colony, in 1882 British forces entered the territory, defeated Egyptian forces in the Battle of Tel-el-Kebir, and subsequently remained. Whereas the 1865 Parliamentary Select Committee had warned against extensions of British sovereignty over West African territories, in the 1880s Britain announced various protectorates along the Bights of Biafra and Benin, over Niger Delta states, and eventually over the entire coast of what the British called the Oil River States (later Nigeria). In East Africa, where clientelism had previously been the rule, the British declared protectorates over Somaliland (1887) and, with the help of Frederick Lugard's East Africa Company, over Buganda (1894). Britain also took greater responsibility over Sarawak, whereas it had denied it before (the Foreign Office in 1888 took charge of Sarawak's external affairs). The policy of hands-off became one of hands-on.

The British state also went further by intensifying or extending its control over other areas too. In South Africa, Britain took the Traansvaal as a colony in 1877 and in 1879 took Zululand. From 1877 through the early 1890s, it declared protectorates over Somaliland, Matabeleland (and the areas later forming Rhodesia), and Nyasaland. In what would become Malaysia in Southeast Asia, Britain established the Residency system (1874), slowly extended its influence through the region, and eventually constructed the Federated Malay States (1896). It further established a protectorate over Brunei (1888), seized

---

[23] Hobson (1965 [1902]), p. 131.
[24] For a good assessment of Robinson and Gallagher's thesis and some of the key debates around it, see Kennedy (1984) and Louis (1976).

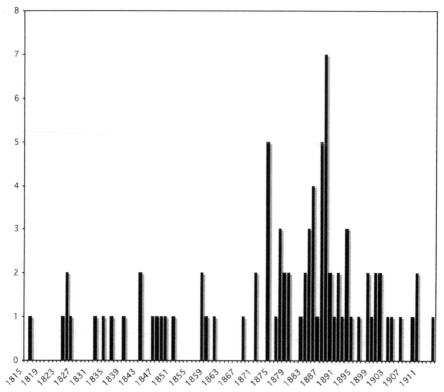

FIGURE 5.1. Number of British Colonial Annexations by Year, 1815–1914. *Source:* See Appendix: Notes on Data.

Burma as a colony in 1886, and sent British advisors to Thailand to help direct its financial and economic policies.[25] In the Pacific, besides seizing Fiji, Britain extended its rule over New Guinea (1884) and the Cook Islands (1881) while establishing the High Commission of the Western Pacific in 1877 to extend its control over the small islands of Gilbert, Ellice, the Soloman Islands, and the Pitcairn group; it further sent advisors to the monarchs of Tonga and Samoa. In short, there was both a shift away from informal strategies toward formal rule as well as an extension and intensification of political influence. The number of new colonies shows the trend. As Figure 5.1 reveals, the number of new territories directly annexed by Britain increased markedly in the last decades of the nineteenth century.

There is another sense in which Britain's imperialism shifted. Attendant with the extension or intensification of political control over peripheral areas was increased militaristic aggression. Of course, the British state had never been shy about using its military during its period of hegemony. However, the late century brought with it new military ventures. A look at the number of

[25] Brown (1978).

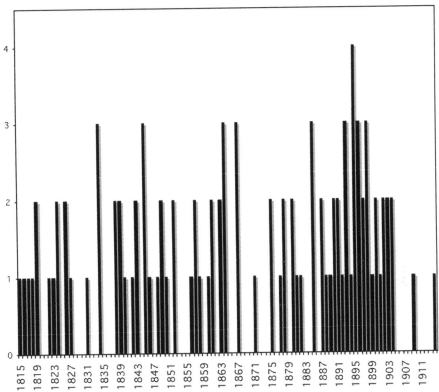

FIGURE 5.2. Number of British Military Interventions: Deployment of Troops or Ships outside Imperial Borders, 1815–1914. *Source:* See Appendix: Notes on Data.

military interventions initiated over the course of the century shows a higher amplitude and a greater frequency during Britain's period of decline compared with the previous period (see Figure 5.2). These included small wars with Arab slave traders in Nyasaland (1885–1889), attacks in West Africa on the Yonni (1887–1889), war with the Zulus (1887), the 1885 attack on Khartoum, the 1877–1878 Kaffir War, the 1878–1880 Anglo-Afghan war, and the Boer War, among others. In some cases, this use of force was related to the new territorial drive. Annexing Burma, for example, involved a war of conquest employing a military force 25,000 strong.

In short, Britain's new imperialism was not exactly a shift away from anti-imperialism. It was not about an absence of imperial power giving way to its presence. It was rather a change in the modalities and intensity of imperial power. It was a shift from indirect control to colonial rule as well as a new aggression – a greater willingness to blatantly use military power or otherwise establish formal political control. Rather than relying on clientelist networks, Britain became more and more determined to replace with them with colonial rule. And rather than sit idly by, the British state was more willing to use military power over others. British imperialism became more *direct* – more bold and aggressive.

There is yet a final feature to Britain's new imperialism: a shift in discourse. We have seen already that mid-Victorian Britons did not utter "empire" consistently or frequently. When they did utter it, they did not typically associate it with a formal overseas empire consisting of foreign lands and peoples around the globe. This changed in the latter part of the century. It became more common to associate "empire" with all of Britain's overseas domains.[26] What was once a term exclusively for the United Kingdom became a term encompassing Britain's colonial spaces as well. When, for example, Councillor of Salford J. Snape gave a lecture on "The Trade of the British Empire" to the Conservative Club in 1882, he included under the rubric "empire" Britain's overseas possessions in the Americas and Asia.[27] An 1876 atlas on the "Geography of the British Empire" likewise defined the "British Empire" to include "the United Kingdom of Great Britain and Ireland, with the numerous foreign possessions, situated in nearly every part of the world, called Colonies and Dependencies."[28] A new coherence was thus given to Britain's overseas activity and modalities of colonial governance. Furthermore, there was a shift in emotional investment. During the middle part of the century, most of the English population was either ignorant of or ambivalent about the phrase British empire. However, as the historian Kitson Clark observes, beginning in the 1870s or so, "more and more people in Britain seem to have become aware of the Empire as an entity, possibly as a source of problems, possibly a source of pride." The term empire acquired a "deeper moral significance and a greater emotive force" than before.[29] Finally, there was a change in the *extent* of discourse about empire too. The number of articles using the phrase the "British Empire" in the London *Times* increased in the late nineteenth century, with only one comparable peak around 1855 (see Figure 3.1, previous chapter). This suggests that not only did the British empire become more militaristic and imperialistic in the territorial mode, it also became more vocal and self-conscious – a renewed cultural assertion to match its new global aggression.

American Aggression Resurgent

Has the United States undergone a similar shift in its imperial activities during its decline? If there was an American counterpart to Britain's new imperialism, we might expect to find the United States doing exactly what Britain did: that is, becoming more aggressive militarily and territorially. Just as Britain showed a tendency away from informal imperialism and toward formal imperialism,

---

[26] Koebner and Schmidt (1964), pp. 81–106.
[27] Snape (1882), p. 5.
[28] Johnson (1876), p. 7.
[29] Kitson Clark (1967), p. 65.

we would expect the United States to have done the same during its period of decline. Yet there is good reason to think that an American counterpart to Britain's new imperialism – if there was a counterpart at all – would not take the form of colonization. As seen in a previous chapter, the global context changed significantly in the twentieth century. Especially after the 1960s, it no longer became possible to annex new territories as formal colonies. Even if the American state did become more imperialistic during its period of decline, we would not expect it to come in colonial form.

What, then, would be a reasonable American counterpart to Britain's new imperialism, given the changed global context of the late twentieth and early twenty-first century? Rather than a shift from informal imperialism to formal imperialism, we might expect an expansion or intensification of informal imperialism marking a new boldness and aggression. That is, rather than covert operations or financial aid to realize its goals, we would expect the United States to show a greater willingness to use military force or deploy other direct mechanisms of power such as temporary military occupations. We would also expect the sheer frequency and amplitude of such exercises in imperial power to have heightened during the period of decline compared with America's period of hegemony. This would mark a new aggression, a new assertion of power, akin to Britain's in the late nineteenth century.

Some scholars have taken America's invasion and occupation of Iraq in 2003 as a sign of such a new imperialism. To be sure, it represented a relatively novel use of imperial power. The so-called Coalition Provisional Authority that ruled Iraq from 2003 to 2004 was a colonial government of sorts, reporting to the Department of Defense. This was not just a military invasion. The occupation of Afghanistan is similar: Unlike the military interventions that occurred after World War II through the 1970s, it involved not only a military campaign but also a period of military rule and political control. America's dealings with Iraq and Afghanistan therefore suggest that the United States had become more willing to act as an imperial power, with a new determination and verve to overtly manage the affairs of other countries.

If Iraq and Afghanistan are the only examples of a new imperialism, however, America's new imperialism pales in comparison with Britain's. With only two instances compared with Britain's more general and expanded imperialism, America's new imperialism would hardly seem to be indicative of anything at all. At most it simply would be attributable to a single event: September 11, 2001. Without the tragedy of September 11, there might not have been the invasion of either Iraq or Afghanistan. There would be no new imperialism over which to ponder. Even if they were not solely due to September 11, they could be readily dismissed as a blip; two exceptions reflecting the particular desires of Bush the Younger's administration. If that were the case, again there would be little similarity to Britain's new imperialism. Britain's new imperialism was extensive and consistent, and it occurred by the hand of different political parties in power.

Yet the invasions of Iraq and Afghanistan can be seen as part of a bigger trend. Rather than only a response to September 11 or a reflection of Bush the Younger's administration alone, they are the culmination of a resurgent imperialism that had already begun to unfold years earlier. First, America's dealings with Iraq had occurred long before September 11. The first assault on Iraq was initiated by Bush the Elder in 1991. The Clinton administration extended the 1991 invasion with a barrage of air strikes through the rest of the decade. The war on Iraq did not begin in 2003. It began in 1991. It continued through Clinton's presidency and was merely picked up by the George W. Bush administration.

Second, and perhaps more important, the United States during its period of economic decline had been adopting a more aggressive and imperialistic approach to other areas in the world besides Iraq. The first instances of this new imperialism surfaced in the early 1980s, a time when America's economic decline in the previous decade had become painfully palpable.[30] In this period, in 1983, President Ronald Reagan authorized a force that ultimately totaled 7,000 troops to invade the island of Grenada. The force defeated the local People's Revolutionary Army and Militia and, within days, established control over Grenada's 100,000 inhabitants. Comparably speaking this was a "little war." But it is significant because it was the first use of American combat troops in the Caribbean in almost twenty years and the first major use of military force abroad since the Vietnam War.[31] The United States had gotten over its "Vietnam syndrome." To be sure, in 1988, President George H. Bush authorized yet another military invasion, this time of Panama, deploying some 24,000 U.S. troops. Grenada was the first major military deployment since Vietnam; the Panama invasion was the largest.[32]

Grenada and Panama were only small parts in a bigger play of renewed U.S. militarism in the Southern Hemisphere. In 1993, President Clinton ordered U.S. ships to embargo Haiti; in 1994 he decided to use 20,000 U.S. troops to occupy the country. The last U.S. troops did not leave Haiti for another six years. And later, in 2004, U.S. troops returned to Haiti for yet another occupation. There were also troop deployments to Colombia, Bolivia, and Peru as part of the war on drugs. Of course, covert tactics, typical of America's hegemonic period, persisted throughout. Reagan's support of the *contras* in Nicaragua is probably the only well-known example of them. However, the overt military deployments together suggest a greater willingness on the part of the American state to directly and openly intervene in the hemisphere than in previous decades. In fact, during the entire period from 1946 to 1982, there had been only *one* overt major U.S. operation in the Latin America, Central American, and Caribbean region. That was the deployment of troops to the Dominican Republic in 1965.

[30] Arrighi (2002), p. 21
[31] Nardin and Pritchard (1990), p. 1
[32] Haas (1999), p. 31.

These military operations occurred in Latin, Central, and South America: areas firmly within the United States' traditional sphere of influence. Other regions of the world, however, were also visited by the hand of American militarism. The 1980s saw interventions not only in Panama, Grenada, and Haiti, but also small troop deployments to Chad, Sinai, Egypt, Libya, the Persian Gulf, and Lebanon. The 1990s did not stop the trend. Besides the attack on Iraq in 1991 and continued strikes thereafter, the United States sent troops to Somalia, Kuwait, Zaire, Bosnia, Croatia, Haiti, Sudan, and Nigeria. The United States used military power twice in the Balkans and sent troops for an occupation mission, leading some scholars to call Clinton's presidency an "imperial presidency."[33] In light of this information, the claims of world-systems specialists like Giovanni Arrighi and Immanuel Wallerstein, who claim that the early 1980s mark a "drastic change in U.S. [foreign] policies," ring true.[34]

Some systematic data can help. The basic question is: Did the United States resort to military power to a greater extent during its period of decline than during its period of hegemony? One source for addressing this question is the 1999 report of the U.S. Commission on National Security, a blue-ribbon commission appointed by the U.S. government to consider America's national security policies. The report shows that during the decade of the 1990s alone, the United States had embarked on four times as many military operations as it had since the late 1940s.[35] This in itself is telling, but more in-depth data culled from other government documents and reports help round out the picture. If we count all of the overt military operations by the United States (including air raids and naval operations) from 1946 to 2004 (which was the first year after the invasion of Iraq), we see a trend. There is a higher frequency and amplitude in U.S. military interventions during the period attendant with America's economic decline (beginning in the 1980s) than during America's period of hegemonic maturity (1946 to the 1970s) (Figure 5.3). Military power was meted out in disproportion to America's relative economic power.

A few points demand elaboration here. First, the figures represent the number of interventions initiated. It does not refer to the duration of interventions. Still, duration might have more to do with other logics or factors besides historical phases. It might, for example, reflect the amount of domestic or local resistance to the intervention, the relative amount of military resources available, or various other events. What matters is the *decision* to employ force; the decision on the part of the government to reach and act beyond its borders – either by the deployment of troops, the use of air strikes, sending military support, or temporary military occupation. Second, the figures do not show the actual number of troops deployed. If the United States used less and less troops in the decline period, despite the raw number of actual discrete interventions,

---

[33] Banks and Straussman (1999).
[34] Arrighi (2002), p. 21; [Wallerstein, 2002 #1328], p. 64.
[35] United States Commission on National Security (1999), p. 127.

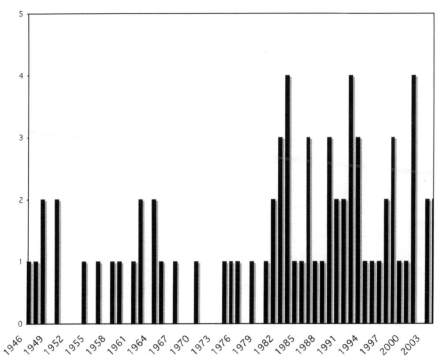

FIGURE 5.3. Number of Military Interventions by the United States, 1946–2004. *Source:* See Appendix: Notes on Data.

it might not represent a significant change or greater willingness to resort to military power. However, there are good reasons why troop numbers are not necessarily as informative as raw numbers of discrete interventions. One is that greater troop numbers might reflect the amount of local resistance to the intervention, the relative amount of military resources available, or various other events. If the U.S. military first intervenes and later escalates troops or resources, does this just reflect a contingent military strategy for winning the war or unexpected local resistance? Furthermore, comparing troop numbers over time would not necessarily be informative, due to the historical development of military technology. The use of one thousand ground troops in the 1953 might not be comparable to the use of one thousand troops in 1983, because the advances in military infrastructure mean that less troops might be necessary in the latter intervention, even if the troops were sent for the same kind of mission (and even if the proportion of troops to local population was the same). Yet even if we *do* count troops deployed, we still find that the United States employed greater military force during its decline period than during its period of hegemonic maturity. From 1946 to 1980, a span of thirty-four years, American troops used in military interventions totaled about 882,000. This includes Vietnam. Alternatively, during the smaller time span of twenty-five years, from 1981 to 2004, the total number of American troops deployed

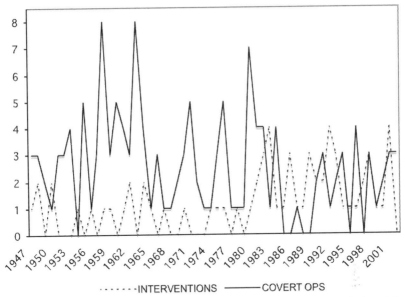

······INTERVENTIONS ———COVERT OPS

FIGURE 5.4. U.S. Military Deployments versus Covert Operations (Including Subverted Elections Aimed at Regime Change), 1947–2002. *Source:* See Appendix: Notes on Data.

in military interventions – by even the most conservative estimate – reached 1,425,809.

Further data helps affirm these findings and extend them. What if we compare covert operations to overt military activity? As discussed in a previous chapter, the United States during its period of hegemonic maturity constructed an informal empire partially based on a network of clients. This involved outflows of foreign aid to keep the clients in check. But it also, at times, involved electoral engineering and other types of covert activity to secure the victories of clients or keep them in power. Figure 5.4 suggests that, during America's period of hegemonic maturity, the American state preferred to use such tactics to direct military intervention. The data also show that those methods *decreased* as America's new imperialism was unleashed. Covert operations and electoral engineering were an alternative mechanism to direct military intervention. And during America's period of hegemonic decline, the American state preferred to use the latter than the former; marking a clear willingness to be overtly aggressive.

Just as Britain embarked on a new imperialism marked by increasing aggression during its period of decline, so too did the United States during its comparable phase of decline. Yet there is another similarity. Attendant with Britain's new imperialism, we have seen that there was a rise in *talk* about the British empire. American discourse of empire also appears to have proliferated during its period of decline (see Figure 5.5). The number of articles containing the phrase "American Empire" in the *New York Times* is small during America's

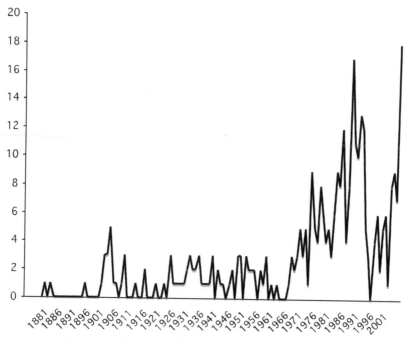

FIGURE 5.5. American "Empire" Discourse: Number of Times "American Empire" Appears in the *New York Times*, 1877–2003.* *Source:* Counted from the *New York Times*, Proquest Historical Newspapers. *Note:* References to "American Empire" that refer to a business or non-U.S. entity (e.g., South America) are not included.

period of hegemony, peaking at only three articles per year. However, a jump in the number of articles occurs in the late 1960s and carries through the 1980s. There was a slight dip in the early 1990s, but the number of articles picks up again in the mid-1990s and builds up to 2003. Clearly, talk of American empire proliferated after key events like Vietnam and September 11, 2001, and much can be attributed to those events alone. Yet the rise in discourse in the other years shows that the new imperial consciousness – just like the new militarism – was not restricted exclusively to those events. America's new imperialism has been more pervasive than a single event can disclose.

In short, both Britain and the United States embarked on new imperialisms during their respective periods of decline. The forms differed slightly. Britain's new imperialism was marked by a shift from informal modes of control to direct colonial annexation and increased militarism, whereas America's new imperialism primarily involved a shift from overt modalities of influence to more direct militaristic aggression and temporary military occupations. But both states intensified their direct imperialism while adopting more bold modalities of power. Both became more aggressive. And both did so during their respective periods of decline. This raises the question of whether decline was systematically associated with the new imperialisms and, if so, exactly how. We cannot assume a direct connection. The coincidence between decline and the new imperialisms could very well be just that: a coincidence. A closer examination is warranted.

Explaining Britain's New Imperialism

Ever since the founding works of Herbert Spencer and J. A. Hobson, scholars have long examined and debated the forces or causes behind Britain's new imperialism.[36] Yet despite the vast literature, there has been little consensus on which factor best explains British imperialism. This is partially because historians adjudicating the different explanations have looked at particular instances of the new imperialism to find some but not all factors at work.[37] A different approach would be to first consider the wider historical context in which the new imperialism unfolded. Rather than look for a single causal force, this approach would have us locate a conjuncture of possible factors that created a wider climate and a set of enabling conditions for increased imperial aggression. By this approach, we will see three forces in particular: economic crisis, geopolitical threats, and peripheral instability. We will then examine some specific instances of the new imperialism – from the invasion of Abyssinia to the annexation of Fiji, among others – to see the forces at work in particular contexts.

The New Context

One important novel feature of the late nineteenth century had to do with the economy: As seen, after enjoying decades of dominance in the world economy, Britain faced increasing competition from rivals and began its decline. But it is important to specify how this broader economic process played out in particular sites. First, at home, economic decline meant bouts of economic depression marked by unemployment and falling rates of profit. This in turn led to sociopolitical unrest. Public demonstrations after the 1866 crash, for instance, raised fears among the upper classes and the political elite that the "flood-gates to anarchy" were being opened and that revolutionary mobs would take power (as had happened in Paris in 1848).[38] John Godfrey, president of the Patriotic Association of Marylebone, worried in 1882 that "our power, our greatness, our character abroad, are being ruined; our trade destroyed; and at home, our country disgraced by a state of lawlessness, anarchy, assassination, and crime, causing in the wide civilized world an expression of contempt and loud

---

[36] Spencer (1902). Spencer's themes were picked up in Schumpeter's *Imperialism and Social Classes*. Hobson's theory set the conditions for Lenin's explanation of imperialism as the "highest stage of capitalism" and a variety of subsequent Marxist and neo-Marxist theories. See for overviews Brewer (1990), Etherington (1982), and Mommsen (1982) among others. Robinson and Gallagher's "excentric" theory later emerged, as have more recent variations on the economic theme by Cain and Hopkins. See Robinson (1972) and Cain and Hopkins (1993).

[37] Eldridge (1978), p. 133. For reviews of some of the vast literature, see Sturgis (1984).

[38] Harcourt (1980), p. 91.

reproach for the loss of that energy, power, and practical action of the old
English character."[39]

Economic decline, secondly, meant that economic interests abroad were put
at new risk. Part of the reason why Britain faced domestic economic troubles
in the first place was that Germany and the United States, and even France
and Russia to some extent, were increasing their market shares and productive
capacities; and this competition added another layer of threat to the economic
and political elite. Investigations by the Royal Commission on Trade and Industry in the mid-1880s concluded that surplus production, low prices, and weak
investment opportunities were the culprits for Britain's new economic woes.
Most representatives from industry blamed foreign competition rather than rising workers' wages. The view was that rival countries' agricultural and rising
manufacturing production was keeping prices and profits low. Other observers
repeatedly worried that those countries' growth in production, coupled with
Britain's free trade orientation, had made Britain increasingly dependent on
imports. Ostensibly, this economic competition was worsened by rivals' protectionist tariffs.[40] The United States had been maintaining high tariffs since
the Civil War. There were substantial tariff hikes across Europe, with increases
occurring in Russia, Spain, Italy, Germany, and France between 1877 and
1882 and continuing through the 1890s.[41] In this context, it is not surprising
that British capitalists and merchants became increasingly fearful. As one historian notes, at the end of the 1870s, the commercial confidence of previous
decades "were replaced by feelings of uncertainty, even of insecurity, and many
merchants began to fear that Britain's commercial supremacy was no longer
something they could take for granted."[42]

Another important factor to the new context was geopolitical. The rise of
rival economic powers came not only with economic threats, but also new
political and security threats.[43] One such threat had to do with the European Continent. During the mid-nineteenth century, Britain had been able to
avoid massive military commitments on the Continent by building a balance of
military and political power between the European states. However, with the
Franco-Prussian War and the subsequent unification of Prussia and Italy, this
balance of power was unsettled. Disraeli, in his 1871 response to the Franco-
Prussian War, feared that the balance of power was "entirely destroyed."
Britain faced "a new world, new influences at work, new and unknown objects
and dangers."[44] The European threat coincided with other dangers too. America's economic ascendance in the wake of the Civil War and the unification of
Prussia and Italy portended a world in which size was increasingly important

[39] Godfrey (1882), p. 4.
[40] Chamberlain (1984), p. 149.
[41] O'Brien and Pigman (1992), p. 104.
[42] Hynes (1976), p. 972.
[43] Kennedy (1981), p. 29.
[44] Quoted in Buckle (1920), pp. 1–134.

for power. An "era of big states" loomed on the horizon and many worried if "little England" would survive the new landscape. Might Britain, one writer worried, "sink as Holland had sunk into a community of harmless traders?"[45] Furthermore, rival states were not only unifying but also expanding overseas. France was taking on increasing involvement in Tahiti (1880), Tunis (1881), Tonkin (1882), and Madagascar (1884), among others; Germany was capturing its own colonies just as it was expanding its overseas commercial activity; the United States in the wake of the Civil War was making its presence felt more and more in the Caribbean and Latin America; Russia was advancing toward Afghanistan and building railways in Central Asia; and Japan was casting its eye ever more outward.[46] The growing military power of these rivals made matters worse still. Although Britain maintained its naval dominance in these years, other states were slowly building up their naval capacities.[47] "Great Britain," Francis and Tebbitt warned in 1880, "must be prepared for hostile combinations in the future, far exceeding in potency those whose fate our history recounts."[48] Meanwhile, General Charles George Gordon's humiliating defeat at Khartoum in 1885 put into question the capacity of the British army.[49]

The final relevant development in the late nineteenth century had to do with the periphery of Britain's imperial system. As noted in a previous chapter, British imperialism in the mid-Victorian period partly involved the creation of client states and collaborative regimes abroad that helped Britain extend trade and maintain a network of security for it. This was informal empire layered on top of Britain's formal empire. But informal empire itself created the possibility for new troubles and tensions. As it brought British consuls, merchants, missionaries, and explorers to new lands, and as it brought foreign aid, capital, and commodities, so too did it increase the possibility of conflict. The political logic of informal rule itself carried the possibility for such conflict. British proconsuls, advisors, or enterprises established collaborative relations with local rulers, but local rulers or chiefs could become recalcitrant to British aims over time. "The danger of new friendly overtures with Natives," recognized the parliamentary undersecretary in 1868, when confronted with suggestions to extend British informal influence over the Malaya states, "is that they always take them to mean more than they do."[50] Additionally, collaborative relations with one ruler or another could provoke resentment or aggression from neighboring rivals with their own agendas. In the Gold Coast, British settlements, Beecroft's attempts to curb the slave trading, and commercial trade with the Fanti all invoked the ire of the Fanti's enemies (the Ashanti Confederation), which in turn precipitated clashes with British forces.

---

[45] Quoted in Tyler (1938), p. 14.
[46] Kennedy (1975), p. 144; Beeler (1997), pp. 16–17; Kennedy (1981), p. 29.
[47] Lambert (1995), pp. 73–5.
[48] Lloyd and Tebbitt (1880), p. 58.
[49] Beeler (1997), pp. 16–17.
[50] Quoted in McIntyre (1967), p. 161.

Informal empire also entailed the influx of financial aid or capital investment to new areas, which could disrupt local economies and foment social
unrest or political disorder. Resentment from below could be unleashed, local
rulers or princes might find themselves financially indebted, and the local rulers'
capacities to maintain legitimate power (and therefore serve as effective clients
to British overlords) could be undermined. In Burma, Britain's trade treaties
in 1862 and 1867 with Prince Mindon compelled Mindon to impose "politically troublesome levels of direct taxation on his subjects," which, among
other events, put the country into socioeconomic crisis by 1878.[51] Similarly,
in Egypt, the establishment of free trade in 1841, financial aid and lending,
and the overthrow by Britain and France of the Khedivate led to economic
crises as well as indignation among local landlords, the military, and Muslim
religious leaders, leading to a wave of antiforeign sentiment and protonation-
alist revolt.[52] The potential for these scenarios around other parts of the world
probably increased in the late nineteenth century not only because of Britain's
informal political influence, but also because of the increased export of British
capital to peripheral regions. British capital exports rose significantly during
the 1850s to the 1870s and dramatically increased after the 1870s in response
to the perceived lack of investment opportunities at home.[53]

In short, three new forces marked Britain's period of economic decline: economic crisis, geopolitical threats, and peripheral instability. Admittedly, not all
of these forces were new. Britain had faced the threat of military rivals before.
It had always been concerned about maintaining security while simultaneously striving to maintain and expand its trade. It had also faced the potential
for disorder in its informal (and colonial) empire. However, as Paul Kennedy
points out: "What was different now was that the relative power of the various
challenger states was much greater, while the threats seemed to be developing
almost simultaneously."[54] In this sense, the world faced by Britain in the late
nineteenth century was indeed different from that of the mid-century, not least
because of hegemonic decline. This was the structure of the conjuncture that
propelled the new imperialism.

Context to Causation

To see the forces at work, consider some notable cases of Britain's new imperialism. The invasion of Abyssinia in 1867 is one such notable case, not least
because it has been taken by some scholars as a critical turning point. On
the one hand, the invasion was not exactly indicative of the new imperialism. British forces did not remain there and instead left behind an officially
independent client rather than a colony. On the other hand, it was indeed a
turning point. Previously, Britain had maintained a relatively cautious approach

[51] Webster (2000), p. 1006.
[52] Robinson and Gallagher (1961), ch. 4. See also Owen (1972).
[53] Davis and Huttenback (1988), p. 43; Edelstein (1982).
[54] Kennedy (1987), p. 227.

to Africa, preferring informal rule to colonization. However, the invasion of Abyssinia reversed this previous hesitation to intervene. It was followed by various other new interventions into the region. In these ways, the Abyssinian invasion marked a radical turn, a "decisive break with the past."[55]

So what induced this break with the past? Part of the answer lies in peripheral instability brought on by informal empire. The pretext for the invasion was King Theodore's seizure of Europeans, including some diplomats and missionaries. The British consul to the area, Walter Plowden, who had been attempting to expand trade, was killed in 1860 amidst disorder and unrest that had been sporadically erupting in the region. This was not the only factor, however. In fact, British interests in the region were comparably minor, which is why the British state had been relatively indifferent to Plowden and his post. The Foreign Office had even felt that the British presence in the region should just be withdrawn entirely, for a continued presence might "involve us in complications... most desirable for the future to avoid."[56] In other words, there was peripheral instability, but the British state did not have to intervene: It could have just let things go. Hence, what tipped the balance toward intervention was the fact of British economic decline. In May 1866, a wave of bankruptcies swept financial circles, and the repercussions of "Black Friday" were felt all over the nation. The sudden decline of profits put the middle classes into an unforeseen precarious position; food prices rose; the London shipbuilding industry fell apart; and unemployment and poverty proliferated. The depression was seen as "one of the most painful and severe of the century." It was accompanied by public protests against the administration of Lord Derby.[57]

This situation contributed to the invasion of Abyssinia. According to historian Freda Harcourt, the Disraeli government resorted to imperialism as a way to manage the economic crisis. Disraeli decided to invade Abyssinia as a unifying tactic to restore the government's popularity. Diverse social classes could rally around the flag. The invasion would demonstrate to the populace that Britain still had muscle despite the economic crisis and despite rivals' economic advances. It would confirm "Britain's position as a great power in a rapidly changing world... serve as a focus for the energies of the whole nation and provide a foundation for national unity."[58] Fittingly, after the battle, Northcote told Napier, "Where we were considered the weakest of military nations we have shown ourselves the strongest.... This expedition... will have effected as great an alteration in our position in the eyes of Europe as the battle of Sadowa effected in the position of Prussia."[59] The popular press likewise basked in the glory of victory, constructing it as Britain's "rehabilitation in the esteem

[55] Harcourt (1980), pp. 88–9.
[56] Marry's memo, on his interview with Napier, Aug. 4, 1868, FO 1/26.
[57] Harcourt (1980), pp. 89–90; quote on p. 89.
[58] Ibid., p. 89.
[59] Northcore to Napier, quoted in ibid., p. 103.

of the world" and as a restoration of "our old reputation."[60] In short, what determined the new imperialism in the case of Abyssinia was the convergence of peripheral crisis and the changed socioeconomic situation. The socioeconomic situation made jingoism and imperialism more attractive; political elites could gain electoral advantage by playing "the empire card."[61]

This was the process propelling many of Britain's other militaristic ventures too. Various military campaigns after the Abyssinian invasion carried with them bouts of popular enthusiasm and jingoism (e.g., the Ashanti campaign of 1874 and the Boer War in 1899).[62] In some cases, political elites made straightforward calculations about how interventions abroad might serve as an electoral tactic. In 1885, for example, the new secretary of state for India, Lord Randolph Churchill, suggested that a strong response to French advances in Burma might prove popular with the electorate and thus help Salisbury's minority Conservative administration.[63] The new discourse of empire that proliferated at this time therefore makes sense. The "British Empire" and "Our Empire" became signs under which various social classes (hence voters) could proudly gather.[64] A pamphlet published in 1886, "The Strength and Weakness of the British Empire: Dedicated to the Working Men of England," tells something of this. Written by an anonymous "Working Man," it beseeched the working class to become more familiar with and support the empire. It also urged them to disavow social protest:

Working men of England. In the future you must be your own protectors; that is, you must protect yourselves from falling into disgrace by the action of the mob at any time. The recent riot at the west-end of London, February 8, 1886, gave you a slight proof of what has already been told you; behind the mob comes ruin and desolation. Genuine English working men would never behave in that manner.... Do your duty; work quietly and effectively for a united Empire and a united people; and those that come after you will bless and esteem your memory.[65]

This suggests that domestic socioeconomic crises, along with the cynical manipulations of opinion inspired by the socioeconomic context, help account for the militaristic aspects of Britain's new imperialism. Yet the domestic economic situation can hardly account for all of Britain's new imperialism. There were other annexations that were not popularized. In these cases other factors were at work.

[60] *Lloyd's*, May 31, 1868, p. 6 quoted in ibid., p. 104.
[61] Chamberlain (1988), p. 132. For similar arguments on social imperialism and jingoism, see Cunningham (1971).
[62] See MacKenzie (1986), pp. 2–3; Cunningham (1971); Cunningham (1981). This is not distinct from the trend noted by Spencer. For Spencer, Britain's new imperialism marked a "re-barbarisation" whereby Britain's ruling classes, enamored with the ancient militarism of Rome, directed the press and Parliament toward a new jingoism celebrating aggression. Spencer (1902).
[63] Webster (2000), p. 1019.
[64] See also Kennedy (1984), p. 29.
[65] Anonymous (1886), pp. 152–4.

The invasion of Egypt in 1882 is telling. As with the case of Abyssinia, Egypt has been seen by historians as a critical turning point toward Britain's new imperialism and likewise as a sort of "test case" for assessing different theories of imperialism.[66] The subsequent literature on the occupation by historians reveals multiple factors at work. One was financial. British capital had been injected into Egypt during previous years. Prime Minister Gladstone himself had some financial stakes. Another was peripheral crisis. Although financial interests were at stake, what made intervention even more likely than before was the crisis brought on by social and political upheaval in the wake of stringent financial controls on the Khedive.[67] The final factor had to do with geopolitical threats that in turn posed economic threats. To the British state, Egypt's Suez Canal was vital: In the hands of a rival, it could undercut British power in the region and even cut off links to Britain's trade with India. "For India," noted Gladstone, "the Suez Canal is the connecting link between herself and the centre of power – the centre of the moral, social and political power of the world."[68] Gladstone and other Whitehall officials were especially worried about French control. The French had long had eyes on Egypt and had financial investments there too.[69] They also worried about Russia and its slow advance into the region. As Porter explains, "with Britain in Egypt not only would British gain advantage over France and greater security for the Suez Canal route to India but above all an important lever in negotiation with the Ottoman government to contain Russian expansion into Turkey and the eastern Mediterranean."[70]

Unlike the invasion of Abyssinia, the invasion of Egypt was a matter of global and not just domestic concern. Like Abyssinia, however, it was driven by the new climate of economic threat. The same could be said of other instances of the new imperialism. In West Africa, for example, British expansion was partly driven by geopolitical concerns, but economic competition also played a part. The need for new markets in West Africa had been a common call among merchants and manufacturers during the depression. These groups put continued pressure on the British government to take action in Africa. They were quick to argue that the need for new markets was especially important given the threat of rival economic blocs forged by new tariffs. The Council of the Birmingham Chamber of Commerce informed the Foreign Office, upon experiencing the effects of the McKinley tariff on their exports to the United States: "[I]n view of the successive limitation of our export trade, caused by hostile foreign tariffs and the need for developing fresh markets, Her Majesty's Government [is] urged to maintain the sphere of British influence in Africa."[71] These fears were

[66] Hyam (1999), p. 39.
[67] Cain and Hopkins (1993), p. 369.
[68] Gladstone quoted in Hyam (1999), p. 40.
[69] Dilke quoted in Galbraith and al-Sayyid-Marsot (1978), p. 484.
[70] Porter (1999), p. 12.
[71] Quoted in Hynes (1976), p. 977; for more on this, see ibid., pp. 973–7 and Hopkins (1968).

not unfounded. At the Berlin West Africa Conference of 1884–1885, countries like France and Portugal attacked the idea of keeping African holdings open to free trade. There had been mutual tariff discrimination between the British Royal Niger Company and French and German possessions.[72] The Liverpool Chamber of Commerce concluded:

In West Africa the British governments of the last decade have been outstripped by Germany and France; the Gambia has dwindled; the Cameroons has been lost; two foreign powers have intervened between Lagos and Gold Coast Colonies... the French have spread themselves over Senegambia and the British governments have yielded the districts of the Northern Rivers of Sierra Leone... the Chamber is of the opinion that wherever in the unappropriated territories of Africa preponderance of British trade existed, there British interests should have been secured, by proclaiming such territories spheres of British influence.[73]

These concerns led the British state to act decisively. Whereas it had been previously content with informal control, direct British rule was now the only alternative. "What moved a reluctant British government to act," notes the historian Muriel Chamberlain, "was the recognition that British trade was in danger and that, in the last resort, the government had a duty to protect that trade."[74]

What about Britain's imperialism elsewhere in the world, such as Southeast Asia or the Pacific? One factor driving British annexation of Burma in 1886 was, as in Egypt, peripheral instability brought on by informal imperialism. Trade treaties with Prince Mindon in 1862 and 1867 opened up Burma to British commerce and put Mindon on a path toward modernizing his country, but it also created a myriad of local troubles. Mindon was compelled to set high taxes on his subjects to pay for his reforms, and this coupled with other economic contingencies left Burma in crisis in 1878. When Prince Thibaw took power that year, after Mindon's death, he began a campaign of anti-British sentiment and refused to comply with prior trade treaties. He also tried to impose state monopolies over the trade in key articles like cotton; and he sent a delegation to France looking to obtain a new commercial treaty and replace British influence with French influence. Britain faced a recalcitrant client.

An additional factor in Burma was economic interest. Thibaw's attempts to meddle in the cotton industry threatened the interests of the British firm, the Bombay Burmah Trading Corporation (BBTC). In 1885, Thibaw accused the BBTC of underpaying royalties and wages to local workers and demanded repayment along with a fine in excess of 100,000 pounds. As this news and the news of Thibaw's deal with the French hit home, domestic opinion rallied. British chambers of commerce sent petitions to the India Office demanding British annexation. After Thibaw continued to refuse to resolve the BBTC

[72] Hynes (1976), p. 976.
[73] Robinson and Gallagher (1961), p. 382.
[74] Chamberlain (1999), p. 55.

dispute, the British launched an invasion. At work, then, was not only a recalcitrant Thibaw, but the economic and geopolitical effects of his resistance. Pressure on the British government from financial interests was critical, as was the thought of losing privileged access to cotton.[75] The fear of French control was also important. Not only would French control threaten to close off Britain's economic access, it would also threaten British India, whose economic importance for the British economy at the time could not be ignored.[76]

Finally we can turn to Fiji. The establishment of colonialism in Fiji is especially informative because, as seen, the British state had previously been reluctant to add it to its empire. So what had changed? First, the cotton trade with Fiji had become especially important after the American Civil War. The value of the cotton trade had increased from 6,000 pounds in 1865 to 92,700 pounds by 1870.[77] Second, the trade had brought numerous white settlers, missionaries, and foreign planters. The presence of these groups created tensions with local Fijian chiefs and the local populace. Soon enough, settlers and planters pleaded for help from the British state. When a British bishop was murdered, settlers and planters became more insistent on British control. In 1872, after the murder, the interest of the colonial secretary, Lord Kimberley, was finally peaked.[78] These two factors, though, needed a third. In fact, when Lord Kimberley corresponded with Gladstone about possible Fijian annexation, Gladstone was initially cautious.[79] It was not until fears about America's activities surfaced that the home government turned around. In 1872, news of America's treaty for Pago Pago harbor in Samoa reached London, and this caused alarm. One of Britain's main economic rivals was reaching into the Pacific, dangerously close to Britain's Australasian holdings. The fear was heightened when rumors of a U.S. naval base at Pearl Harbor circulated. And, in 1874, the American chargé d'affaires in London, Benjamin Moran, inquired at the Foreign Office about Britain's intentions toward Fiji, signaling that the United States might very well have its eyes on the islands. These concerns made the issue of peripheral instability all the more unbearable, and ultimately Britain decided to shift from informal imperialism in Fiji to direct control.[80]

In sum, although the cases discussed previously do not exhaust all of Britain's new imperialism, they show how the timing of Britain's new imperialism was not mere accident. The new imperialism occurred during Britain's period of

---

[75] See Webster (2000) for this story.

[76] In 1906, Winston Churchill, whose father had been Secretary for India and supported the seizure of upper Burma, wrote that fear of French control was a key motivation. The connections between Thibaw and the French "left no room to doubt the imminence of a dominant foreign influence ... involving the most serious and far-reaching consequences to the Indian Empire" (Churchill 1906, I, p. 521).

[77] McIntyre (1960), p. 366.

[78] Routledge (1974), p. 279.

[79] McIntyre (1962), p. 271.

[80] McIntyre (1960), pp. 360–1.

decline, because decline (and hence, by definition, enhanced economic competition abroad) created the conditions for it in the first place. It is true that some of the forces driving new militaristic ventures or annexations were not directly connected to decline. Political crises at home, disorder in the periphery, and geopolitical threats – these were not the direct result of Britain's decreasing economic standing. But decline mattered critically in at least two respects. First, decline was part of the cause of these other factors. As seen, political crises were also economic crises: When the Disraeli government used the invasion of Abyssinia as a performance of British power, the government was responding to a broader climate of economic depression and political malaise brought on by enhanced competition abroad. If the Disraeli government used jingoistic imperialism to enhance British prestige, such a tactic was only necessary given the threats to British prestige brought on by decline. Second, decline mattered by making otherwise benign forces into serious threats. Surely it made peripheral instability especially dangerous. Unless managed, peripheral disorder would invite annexation by foreign powers. Given Britain's already ailing economic situation, this was unacceptable. Rival powers' enhanced military capabilities and/or new territorial annexations threatened not just British security but also future economic opportunities – opportunities that Britain could not afford to miss given its economic dilemmas. In other words, hegemonic decline cultivated a wider sense of fear and threat that was different from the relative complacency of Britain's economic heyday. Increased aggressive imperialism was the British state's way of trying to manage this context – a way of trying to deal with the proliferating threats brought on by decline and competition. The new imperialism marked a new aggression, but the new aggression was a sign of weakness rather than of strength, a desperate act of defense against a new climate of competition and pending doom. Was America's new imperialism the same?

Understanding America's Turn

We should not jump to the conclusion that decline sparked America's new militarism abroad. The new threat of terrorism was surely behind some of America's new militarism. It was the pretext for the invasion and occupation of Afghanistan and various missile strikes and air bombardments in North Africa (e.g., Libya, the Sudan). And terrorist acts against the United States do not seem directly connected to American decline. Still, there are good reasons to think that more was going on. First, the various acts of terror that invited militaristic responses were not entirely contingent. The multiple terrorist incidents since the 1970s (beginning with the Iranian hostage crisis) can be understood within a larger historical context. As some have argued, they can be seen as "blowback": reactions and resistances to America's global power. They manifest peripheral disorder brought about by the logics of America's own informal empire. One recent study, for example, shows that transnational terrorism rose during the 1970s and continued to rise through the 1980s and 1990s – exactly in the wake of America's informal imperial interventions.[81] Second, and more important, America's new imperialism was not only about responding to terrorism. Many of America's militaristic ventures – from Panama in 1989 to Iraq in 1991, or Bosnia and Haiti in the 1990s – were not responses to terrorist threats. This suggests that understanding America's new imperialism demands an examination of more than terrorism.

Nutmeg and Prestige

Examine first America's counterpart to Britain's invasion of Abyssinia in 1867: the invasion of Grenada in 1983. This was the beginning of America's new imperialism, just as Abyssinia was for Britain. In the case of Grenada, clearly terrorism was not the driving force of this invasion. The official line of the Reagan administration was that the invasion was necessary for protecting the lives of American students and citizens in the country amidst internal disorder. The other reason was to stamp out Communism: The Marxist-Leninist New Jewel Movement, or NJM, had seized power. Other factors, however, were at work besides these. One has to do with economic decline, more specifically as it was felt in the form of rising unemployment and a falling profit rate in key sectors of the American economy since the mid-1970s. To deal with this situation, the Reagan administration sought ways to increase profitability. One was military build-up. By the end of the decade, about $300 billion had gone to the military; the profit rate on defense contracts outran profitability in durable goods manufacturing.[82] The other tactic was deregulation. This had begun already under President Jimmy Carter, but Reagan took it to new heights. The final tactic was to look abroad and increase foreign investment. The Reagan administration hoped to find new outlets abroad for American capital, and one part of the strategy was aimed at the Caribbean. In 1982, the year before the Grenada invasion, the Reagan administration announced the Caribbean Basin Initiative (CBI), which was aimed at providing aid and liberalizing the region.

The invasion of Grenada must be situated within this larger economic scene. Reagan's strategy of military build-up needed justification. Dov S. Zakheim, an official in the Department of Defense, explained the invasion as important for that reason exactly. It helped signal "a major step toward recovery from the Vietnam syndrome" and thereby served as a counterpart to Congress's insistence on reducing the military budget.[83] Furthermore, the threat of Communism (with Cuba nearby and the Sandinistas in Nicaragua) was not only a geopolitical matter but also an economic one. It posed a potential challenge to Reagan's regional liberalization strategy. If Communist regimes like NJM spread, fields for America investment would contract. Fittingly, soon after the invasion, the U.S. Agency for International Development reported that Grenada was "ripe for investors." U.S. aid to the country resumed and foreign capital

---

[81] Enders and Sandler (2000).
[82] Bernstein (1994), p. 23.
[83] Zakheim (1986), p. 179.

flooded the country.[84] Reagan visited Grenada in 1986, using it as a platform to announce a policy of enlarging the CBI and increasing investment by American firms in apparel industries across the region.[85]

Beyond economics, there was another issue. In 1983, Reagan publicly stated that "it isn't nutmeg that's at stake in the Caribbean and Central America; it is the United States' national security."[86] Presumably this meant that the Communist threat was the fundamental cause of the invasion, but in reality there was more to it. For the USSR, Grenada was but a "raindrop in the swimming pool."[87] The real issue was not the USSR specifically, but American strength in the world more generally. Vietnam had been lost seven years earlier. The Iranian hostage crisis still haunted Washington, DC. And just two days before Reagan made the decision to send troops to Grenada, he had received news of the Lebanon truck bombing that killed hundreds of U.S. Marines and additional French servicemen. The United States appeared to be weakening in strength. Combined with the economic problems and America's larger decline relative to other industrialized countries, the United States as a world power and leader was put into question.

The assault on Grenada followed from these combined economic and geopolitical pressures. Not only did the invasion and ouster of the NJM facilitate the Reagan administration's broader regional strategy for reinvigorating American capital (and justifying the military budget), it was also a strategy for restoring America's prestige amidst its putative decline. Officials in the Reagan administration were reported as stating that "the Reagan Administration's overriding reason for invading Grenada was to keep the US from being perceived as a 'paper tiger' in the eyes of both friendly and hostile Latin American nations." One senior official said, "if we said no [to the invasion], not only might there have been another Iran with the American students... but no one would have taken us seriously any more down there."[88] Vice President George Bush bragged at the Republican national convention in 1984: "Because President Reagan stood firm in defense of freedom [in Grenada], America has regained respect throughout the world."[89] Later commentaries and stories confirm these claims. Richard Haas, who would later serve under then Vice President George H. W. Bush, admitted that the invasion was not just about stopping Communism, but also "to show that the United States could still act effectively in the world in the aftermath of the Beirut debacle."[90] The invasion was also popular domestically: All polls showed that Reagan's popularity increased after the invasion.[91] In these ways, the invasion of Grenada

[84] Quoted in Shorrock (1984).
[85] Library of Congress Federal Research Division (2005), Appendix B.
[86] Quoted in Williams (2002), p. 661.
[87] Maynes (1986), p. 187.
[88] Gwertzman (1983), p. 1.
[89] *New York Times*, Aug. 22, 1984.
[90] Haas (1999), p. 25; Nardin and Pritchard (1990), p. 1.
[91] Zakheim (1986), p. 180.

was similar to Britain's invasion of Abyssinia not just because it marked the beginning of a resurgent imperialism, but also because the forces animating the invasion were systematically connected to economic decline.

Decline, the New Geopolitics, and Peripheral Instability

What about the other instances of America's new imperialism? It helps to begin by elaborating on the situation the United States faced amidst its economic decline. As noted, one aspect of the new context was global economic competition. The United States saw rising competition from emerging economic rivals: first Germany and Japan; by the 1990s the EU; and China by the very end of the century. But beyond this – and related to it – were other developments constituting a climate not unlike the one faced by Britain a century earlier. One development was new geopolitical competition. First, in the face of decline, America's relations with Western Europe took on a new tone. America's economic competitiveness was challenged by Europe's economic growth, but the end of the Cold War made the issue more challenging. The Cold War had provided the United States with significant political leverage over Europe. It had given justification for America's military power and economic hegemony, and served as the basis for a "social compact" between the United States and the European capitalist states. The United States delivered peace and security in exchange for European deference.[92] The end of the Cold War upended that justification and hence America's "crucial lever for hegemony."[93] In addition, the Maastricht Treaty of 1992, which turned the European Economic Community (EEC) into the European Union, not only mounted a further economic challenge (by creating a common market and currency), but also a political challenge. It created new institutions like the Council of Ministers and the European Commission that could advance common security and foreign policy frameworks across Europe, potentially against America's interests. At the same time, Germany and France announced a plan to form an all-European military corps.

That these events posed a potential threat to America's interest is seen clearly in the thinking of American defense planners and policy advisors. As early as 1991, National Security Advisor Brent Scowcroft complained about the meetings among Western European countries prefiguring the EU. He was concerned that they were discussing security issues without American participation.[94] Similarly, in response to the Franco-German Eurocorps, Bush administration officials feared that it "undercut the whole American *raison d'être* in Europe."[95]

---

92 Hence "continental Europe generally followed wherever America led. And it did so because America's nuclear shield and America's promotion of global economic expansion enabled it to deliver on its promissory notes of peace and prosperity to a continent that had known neither for four decades." McCormick (2004), p. 77. See also Lundestad (1986) and Layne (2006), pp. 107–9.
93 McCormick (2004), p. 81.
94 Carpenter (1999).
95 Clarke (1992), p. 4.

A secret Pentagon report in 1992 stated that the United States "must account sufficiently for the interests of the advanced industrial nations to discourage them from seeking to overturn the established political and economic order," and thus should "maintain the mechanism for deterring potential competitors from even aspiring to a larger regional or global role." It identified "Western Europe" as one such competitor, stressing that it has "resources . . . sufficient to generate global power." Therefore, the report concluded, it "is of fundamental importance to preserve NATO as the primary instrument of Western defense and security" and "prevent the emergence of European-only security arrangements which would undermine NATO."[96] The fear was echoed throughout Washington. The creation of the EU and its integration of national powers threatened the United States just as, more than one hundred years earlier, America's own post–Civil War union and German and Italian reunification had posed a threat to Britain.[97]

The question of Western Europe was also tied to the rising threat of Russia and the place of both within the larger question of "Eurasia." As the Cold War ended, the American foreign policy establishment conjured frightful images of a new imperial Russia. Fretting over scenarios painted by Mackinder's traditional "heartland" theory, they worried about Russia's geographic position next to vast natural energy reserves and its thousands of nuclear warheads. Strategists at the Naval War College thus stressed that the main geopolitical imperative in the post–Cold War world was to prevent "the rise of a hegemon capable of dominating the Eurasian continental realm and of challenging the United States in the maritime realm."[98] The 1992 Department of Defense plan warned that Russia retains "the most military potential in all of Eurasia." Russia will "remain the strongest military power in Eurasia and the only power in the world with the capability of destroying the United States."[99] Zbigniew Brzezinski in 1997 added that "America's global primacy is directly dependent on how long and how effectively its preponderance on the Eurasian continent is sustained"; but that preponderance on the Eurasian continent was also dependent on American power in Europe.[100] "The United States' ability to project influence and power in Eurasia relies on close transatlantic ties."[101]

The other development lay in the periphery. The 1970s and 1980s not only marked the beginnings of American decline. These were also years when America's preceding informal empire and the attendant geopolitical structure began to show signs of fissure. The issue extended beyond barbarians at the gate. It was about the breakdown of America's client regimes. Popular protests

---

[96] Gellman (1992), p. A1.
[97] Kupchan (2003), pp. 3–17.
[98] Mackubin Thomas Owens quoted in Foster (2006).
[99] Tyler (1992), p. 14.
[100] Brzezinski (1998), p. 30.
[101] Brzezinski (1997), p. 53.

and mass movements threatened to unseat American-supported dictators, from Duvalier in Haiti to Marcos in the Philippines. This was partially concomitant with the "third wave" of democratization beginning in the 1970s and carrying through the 1980s. Democratization in part implied a potential breakdown in American-supported authoritarian regimes.[102] The overall slowdown of the global economy in the 1970s and the subsequent debt crisis in the 1980s did not make things any easier. Around the globe, the ideology of postcolonial "developmentalism" fell apart, as so-called developing countries saw internal disorder and declining standards of living. The relative stability created by America's informal empire "gave way to disintegrating order, simmering discontents, and unchanneled radical temperaments."[103] The Middle East was one such site where unruly forces were unleashed. The late 1970s and 1980s saw the Iranian revolution and the seizure of American hostages in Iran, PLO terrorism and the Lebanon War, and the Iraq-Iran War.

America's economic activities abroad laid down the conditions for further peripheral problems. In the midst of falling profit rates at home, American businesses and the political elite increasingly looked abroad. The American state sought to facilitate investment through new trade agreements in the region – often as defensive moves against European and Asian trading blocs – such as the Caribbean Basin Initiative (which was expanded into the U.S.-Caribbean Basin Trade Partnership Act) and the Canada-U.S. Free Trade Agreement in 1988 (a prelude to NAFTA in 1994).[104] It also pushed countries in the Global South to liberalize their economies, encouraging structural adjustment programs that would open up fresh fields for investment.[105] Fittingly, the amount of American foreign direct investment abroad since the 1980s grew dramatically and continued through the 1990s (see Table 5.1). This growth in U.S. foreign investment was similar to Britain's increasing turn to foreign investment in the late nineteenth century when Britain also underwent economic decline.

The end of the Cold War raised even more possibilities for peripheral instability. When combined with the breakdown of developmentalism and the debt crises of the 1980s, the discipline over peripheral regimes became undone, and former clients were invited to be more recalcitrant to superpower dictates than before. The break-up of the Soviet Union itself posed trouble, unleashing nationalist sentiments, secessionism, and "long pent-up centrifugal forces."[106] By 1997, the Central Intelligence Agency's National Intelligence Council was worrying about the potential for nationalist revolutionary forces in the new Russia that might take power and work against U.S. interests. Its report also noted instability all around the world. It warned that "most conflicts today are internal, not between states" and that "this tendency will continue." The report

---

[102] On the "third wave," see Huntington (1991).
[103] [Wallerstein, 2002 #1328], p. 64.
[104] Hill (2003).
[105] Babb (2009).
[106] Bacevich (2002), p. 61.

TABLE 5.1. *U.S. Direct Investment Abroad 1990–1998, in billions dollars**

Destination	1990	1993	1996	1998
Europe	214,739	285,735	389,378	489,539
Asia & Pacific	254,889	92,671	139,548	161,797
Latin America	43,348	59,302	155,925	196,655
Africa	3,690	5,469	8,162	13,491
Middle East	3,959	6,571	8,294	10,599

* "Direct Investment Abroad" defined as ownership or control by one U.S. person of 10 percent or more of the voting securities of an incorporated foreign business enterprise or an equivalent interest in a unincorporated foreign business enterprise.
Source: Orig. United States Bureau of the Census 1999, *Statistical Abstract* 119th ed., p. 797.

astutely worried that with such conflict and breakdown comes the "potential for outside intervention."[107]

The context of American decline was thus very similar to that in which Britain began its descent. Economic decline carried periods of downturn at home, but it also meant global economic competition and the added threat of alternative economic and political regional centers. And as America's economic hegemony began to wither, so too did the geopolitical order that American informal empire had helped to create and tried to contain. It is in this context that the United States stepped up its imperialistic activity, not only in Grenada, but elsewhere.

From Panama to the Balkans

To see this more clearly, consider the 1989 Panama invasion. The invasion, or "Operation Just Cause," was ostensibly precipitated by Gen. Manuel Noriega's illicit activities and his harassment of American soldiers. But Noriega had long been a close ally of American agencies. He had worked with the Drug Enforcement Administration (DEA), had allies in the Department of Defense (DOD), and had been on the CIA payroll.[108] When he had abused his power, Washington had typically turned a blind eye.[109] But things got out of control. Beginning in the mid-1980s, Noriega heightened his repression of dissidents, thereby inciting popular protests across the country and a massive demonstration of 100,000 people in Panama City. He was also indicted for racketeering, drug trafficking, and money laundering – activities that did not have the Reagan administration's consent.

---

[107] National Intelligence Council (1997).
[108] Gilboa (1995–1996), p. 541.
[109] Ibid., pp. 541–2.

As Noriega continued to prove intransigent to American designs, he posed international trouble.[110] With the Soviet Union crumbling, the question of America's future status as a sole superpower capable of imposing a new discipline on the international system was being raised. As one expert put it, "If the United States could not handle a low-level dictator in a country where it maintained bases and large forces, how would it be able to deal with far more serious international challenges?"[111] The invasion of Panama, with its overwhelming use of force, was thus like the invasion of Grenada, however in a post–Cold War context. The power of the American military was summoned not only to deal with a resistant client, but also to help demonstrate America's power in a perilously changing world.

Even the use of American military force to reinstall Aristide in Haiti in 1994 can be understood within the context of hegemonic decline. On the one hand, the reinstallation was predicated on a breakdown of clientelism. The clientelistic relationship had plagued successive American administrations ever since the second Duvalierian regime (of Jean-Claude Duvalier, or "Baby Doc") began to crumble under the weight of domestic instability and popular protest. Aristide rode that wave of populism, but his fiery leftist and anti-U.S. rhetoric did not win him friends in Washington. The American-supported elections in 1990 were a pragmatic compromise: The Bush administration hoped that elections would subdue social disorder and elevate former World Bank official Marc Bazin into office, thereby replacing one client (Duvalier) with another (Bazin). However, Aristide's victory took Washington by surprise. The CIA waged a covert campaign to discredit him, while the Bush administration gave de facto support to the bloody coup led by General Raoul Cédras.[112] What followed was yet more popular protest, violent repression of pro-Aristide forces, and widespread international attention, as well as a refugee problem produced by the crisis. The Clinton administration was finally pressed to adopt a strategy of reinstalling Aristide while nonetheless aiming to discipline him and make him a more amenable client.

Although peripheral instability played a part in the installation of Aristide, America's economic interests played a role as well. One of the reasons why the United States took such an interest in the internal affairs of Haiti in the first place was that Haiti had been a critical site for the post-1970s strategy of exporting capital to manage falling profitability at home. The Caribbean Basin Initiative touted Haiti as one of its models.[113] Clinton's decision to send troops to Haiti was made in the same year that it announced plans to build on the CBI by extending NAFTA to the whole hemisphere (through the Free Trade of the Americas initiative). These plans, deemed by strategists as critical for managing hegemonic decline, were threatened by unrest and political disorder

---

[110] Bill McAllister, "Bush Vows to Press Noriega," *Washington Post*, Dec. 23, 1988.
[111] Gilboa (1995–1996), p. 559. See also Cramer (2006), p. 195.
[112] Morley and McGillion (1997), pp. 364–7.
[113] Robinson (1996), p. 270.

in Haiti. "If the international and hemispheric community allows thugs such as Raul Cedras, Michel Francois, and Phillipe Biamby to continue to rob and terrorize the people of Haiti," stated Deputy Secretary of State Strobe Talbott, "that country is likely to become a haven and a breeding ground for the forces of instability and criminality in the region."[114]

Aristide had to return to power lest America's economic plans were unraveled. Upon announcing his plan to end the embargo against Haiti, Clinton declared: "I want to do more than lift the embargo; I want to help rebuild the economy of Haiti. That would be good for America."[115] The president of International Industrial Exporters, Inc., a major transnational corporation dealing in contracting in Haiti, explained his support of Clinton's plan to restore Aristide to power as follows: "Mr. Aristide isn't any more the answer to Haiti's problems than is the military. But his return to power is worth the cost of the U.S. military incursion if it fosters a resumption of free trade and the sale of U.S. goods and services."[116] It followed that the reinstallation of Aristide by the hand of the American military came with a host of stringent conditions, including a new structural adjustment program.[117] Financial aid would help secure Aristide as a client. U.S. Deputy Secretary of State Strobe Talbott was unabashed: "Even after our exit in February 1996 we will remain in charge by means of the USAID and the private sector."[118] In turn, Aristide would restore stability and help the American state try to realize its regional strategy for managing its economic woes.

Whereas Haiti and Panama were within America's traditional sphere of influence, the Balkans were not. What explains America's successive interventions there in the 1990s? Peripheral instability was the spark. The integrity of Yugoslavia had been maintained by both the United States and the USSR, but the end of the Cold War unleashed intra-Yugoslavian conflict. This in itself solicited interest from the big powers. But if local disorder was the spark, geopolitical concerns in the context of decline fanned the flames. The reason why intervention in Yugoslavia was so important to the United States, and why it took the form of U.S.-led NATO operations, had to do with America's relationship with the European Union.

As noted, the Cold War had provided the United States with its primary justification for its military presence in Europe in the form of NATO, and hence for Europe's dependence on the United States, but the end of the Cold War threatened to unsettle this dependent relationship. Why should Europe depend on the United States if the Communist threat had been effectively tamed? Why should Europe continue with the NATO alliance? Why not form

---

[114] Strobe Talbott, "Pursuing the Restoration of Democracy in Haiti," speech, U.S. Department of State Dispatch, May 23, 1994.
[115] Quoted in Dow (1995), p. 15.
[116] Quoted in Robinson (1996), pp. 306–7.
[117] Hallward (2004), pp. 29–30; Manegold (1994).
[118] Quoted in Robinson (1996), p. 311.

a new European-based security apparatus outside the control of the American state? These questions plagued planners and policy makers in Washington in the early 1990s. Rightfully so. An end to American-controlled NATO would spell the end of American political hegemony in the region and enable new political-economic rivals to consolidate, grow, and expand. This was all the more terrifying given the increasing economic weight of the European Union, Russia, and China (which might ally with Russia).[119] Accordingly, a Pentagon paper in 1992 had declared that "Our strategy [after the fall of the Soviet Union] must refocus on precluding the emergence of any potential future global competitor."[120] As Western Europe was deemed by many in Washington as one such possible competitor from the Eurasia region, the continuance of NATO was critical. "A new Europe is still taking shape," Brzezinski stressed, "and if that Europe is to remain part of the 'Euro-Atlantic' space, the expansion of NATO is essential."[121] The real trick was to keep NATO intact while also ensuring U.S. control over it.[122]

The decision to intervene in Bosnia and the subsequent campaigns in the latter part of the decade followed from these considerations. Before the first campaign, Air Force Chief of Staff General Michael J. Dugan wrote in the *New York Times* that a "win in the Balkans would establish U.S. leadership in the post-Cold War world in a way that Operation Desert Storm never could."[123] In 1997, after the first 1995 campaign (but before the 1999 Kosovo operation), a document circulating in the CIA stated that the first intervention had created the exact outcome pinpointed by Dugan: "European publics will continue to support the US military presence in Europe, partly as a hedge against Russia and renationalization of defenses, and as a result of NATO's entry into the Bosnia imbroglio – a step that reaffirmed the effectiveness of the Alliance in managing post-Cold war crises. Europeans will not find anything sacrosanct about the number of US forces stationed in their countries – their views of American leadership will be determined less by the size of the American presence than by the use of these forces for combined operations."[124] As former Colonel Andrew Bacevich eloquently concludes, it is clear that Operation Allied Force "was neither planned nor conducted to alleviate the plight of the Kosovars.... The intent ... was to provide an object lesson to any European state fancying that it was exempt from the rules of the post–Cold War era. It was not Kosovo that counted, but affirming the dominant position of the United States" in Europe.[125]

Hitched to these concerns were direct economic interests. Europe had been a vital site for American exports. As Secretary of State Warren Christopher

[119] Brzezinski (1998), pp. 10, 198. See also Gowan (1999); Bacevich (2002); Layne (2006).
[120] Quoted in Bellamy Foster (2006), p. 3.
[121] Brzezinski (1997), p. 55.
[122] Bacevich (2002), pp. 103–7.
[123] "Operation Balkan Storm: Here's a Plan," *New York Times*, Nov. 29, 1992, p. E11.
[124] National Intelligence Council (1997).
[125] Bacevich (2002), pp. 104–5.

stressed in 1995, "all told, Europe accounts for almost half of the foreign revenues of American firms. Our investment in Europe alone roughly equals that
in the rest of the world put together."[126] A loss of standing in Europe, continued instability in the region, or the formation of a rival trading bloc would
be disastrous for the American economy. Former director of the NSA William
Odum warned in 1992 that "failure to act effectively in Yugoslavia will not only
affect US security interests but also US economic interests. Our economic inter-
dependency with Western Europe creates large numbers of American jobs."[127]
Stability in Europe was necessary for maintaining the profitability of American capital amidst the threat of economic decline; ending the Bosnia crisis was
necessary for that stability.[128] Just before the bombing campaign in Kosovo
in 1999, President Clinton said so. He told an audience of local government
employees of the AFL-CIO: "[I]f we're going to have a strong economic relationship that includes our ability to sell around the world, Europe has got to
be a key.... That's what this Kosovo thing is all about."[129] Senator Richard
Lugar (R-Indiana) hit the nail on the head. He said he supported intervention
in Bosnia because "there will be devastating economic effects in Europe of a
spread of war and, thus, the loss of jobs in this country *as we try to base a
recovery upon our export potential.*"[130]

America's approach to the African continent offers an informative contrast.
As Andrew Bacevich points out, Africa saw instability and disorder throughout this period, just like the Balkans, Central America, and the Caribbean. Yet
U.S. intervention there involved small deployments (Somalia) or missile strikes
(against the Al Shifa pharmaceutical factory in Khartoum in response to the terrorist bombing of U.S. diplomatic missions in Tanzania and Kenya).[131] These
deployments did not involve the same amount of military power deployed in
Panama, Haiti, or the Balkans. Nor did they necessitate continued visits. The
crisis in Haiti conjured American deployments not only in 1994 but also in
2004. The Balkans called for two major interventions in the 1990s. America's
hand in Africa, however, was minimal. Why? The answer is that Africa was not
important in the context of American decline. Although certain raw materials
had been seen as essential for America's economic base in the mid-twentieth
century, many of those raw materials had lost their vitality as alternative tech-
nologies and new industries emerged. Unlike Europe or the south of the Western hemisphere, therefore, it was not part of the American state's plan for
economic recovery amidst America's economic fall. The Clinton administration had hoped that, one day, the African continent and its "700 million

---

[126] Christopher (1995), p. 468.
[127] Quoted in Layne (1997), p. 100.
[128] U.S. investment in Europe "increased sevenfold between 1994 and 1998" and "trade between
the United States and the European Union also rose handsomely, to $450 billion per year."
Bacevich (2002), p. 105.
[129] Quoted in ibid., p. 105.
[130] Quoted in Layne (1997), p. 100.
[131] Bacevich (2002), p. 108.

consumers" might serve as a fruitful field for American products, but the fact remained that the entire continent only made for 1 percent of total U.S. trade in the 1990s. Whereas U.S. direct investment in Europe reached $389,378 million and in Latin America $155,925 million in 1996, it was a mere $8,162 million in Africa.[132] Given these figures, it should not be surprising that instability in Africa warranted minimal concern.

Iraq in Context

We can now put Iraq into a new light. Like the foregoing cases, American intervention in Iraq was the result of a conjunction of factors particular to the context of decline. The first factor was peripheral instability brought on by the logics of informal imperialism. Before Saddam Hussein invaded Kuwait, he had been a client of the United States. After Iraq and Iran had begun their war in 1980, the Reagan administration decided to enlist Hussein as an ally. The United States sent financial aid, agricultural exports, and military intelligence. Reagan also sent a presidential envoy (Donald Rumsfeld, then head of a major multinational pharmaceutical firm) to consult with Hussein and his regime.[133] Iran conceded defeat in 1988 and American support continued. Until at least 1990, U.S. firms sold aircraft to the regime; the U.S. government approved licenses for American firms to sell biological products and electronics equipment to Iraqi missile-producing plants; and under George H. W. Bush agricultural credits to Iraq were doubled to $1 billion a year.[134] Yet Hussein overstepped his bounds by invading Kuwait. In part, the logics of clientelism help explain the action: Hussein had previously sent "feelers" to the Bush administration to get a sense of how the United States would respond to an invasion. The responses were ambiguous. Although Secretary of Defense Dick Cheney responded that the United States would not take kindly to an invasion of Kuwait, the U.S. State Department and the U.S. ambassador implied that the United States would not take an opposed stance.[135] In any case, Hussein did invade Kuwait, and this created a scenario that called for some kind of U.S. action.

The reasons why the action took the form of a massive military strike are twofold. The first has to do with oil. This might be obvious, but it was not so simple as U.S. oil interests hoping to tap Kuwait. Rather, the threat was that Iraq might monopolize oil reserves in the Gulf. Washington feared that Iraq, by taking Kuwait, would not only have its own oil and Kuwaiti oil but also Saudi Arabia's oil. In such an event, Iraq would control a majority of the region's oil reserves. This was the frightful scenario of a single "oil hegemon"; to the power establishment in Washington, it was simply impermissible.[136] The possibility

[132] United States Bureau of the Census (1999), p. 797.
[133] Mearsheimer and Walt (2003), p. 56; Battle (2003).
[134] Simons (1996), pp. 317–19. See also Selfa (1999).
[135] Mearsheimer and Walt (2003), p. 54.
[136] Layne (2006), p. 178–9.

seemed real to U.S. officials. It is now known that the United States had made contingency plans to invade the Middle East as a result of the oil embargo of 1973.[137] The invasion of Kuwait appeared to be a similar contingency. Richard Haas, who received a Presidential Medal for his role in developing the invasion plan (he was the Special Assistant to Bush the Elder and National Security Council Senior Director for Near East and South Asian Affairs), thought so for sure. He said that the invasion of Kuwait raised fears in the administration that "Iraq was preparing to invade Saudi Arabia. Even if not, it was thought that an Iraq that controlled Kuwait could intimidate Saudi Arabia and the other Gulf states – and as a result dominate the world's energy markets." Therefore, an overriding objective of the invasion was to maintain "the security and stability of Saudi Arabia and the entire Gulf region." Among the more "immediate concerns" guiding the invasion, he said, were "energy interests and the well-being of America's traditional friends in the Middle East."[138]

There is, however, a final factor. This helps explain not only the decision to use force but also the fact that the use of force was so overwhelming – the largest deployment in the Middle East perhaps since World War II: that is, a symbolic display to maintain America's global position amidst potential charges of decline. In part, the display was a signal to Europe that it still needed American patronage. According to the historian Thomas McCormick, the 1991 invasion was not just an attack on Iraq but simultaneously a de facto policy toward Europe. It was a "'resource war' to remind Europe that it still needed America to maintain access to global raw materials in a post–Cold War world." The subsequent air strikes under Clinton served a similar function, acting "as a continuing reminder to EU nations (and Japan) that they still needed American protection to maintain the stability of the Persian Gulf region and its oil production, on which they depended."[139] At the same time, the war was a signal to American publics and the world more generally that the United States was not in fact in decline, that its military power could effectively maintain America's dominance, and that countries like Germany and Japan would not be able to overtake America. Casting out Saddam Hussein's army from Kuwait would "showcase the capabilities and competence of the US military"; it would not only justify the military build-up of the preceding decade, but also "demonstrate the utility of American military power, now outside the context of the Cold War." According to Colonel Bacevich, who was posted in the Gulf, "this would validate America's continuing capacity to exercise global leadership – thereby giving lie to the forecasts, then much in fashion, that the United States faced imminent decline, its standing soon to be eclipsed by economic powerhouses like Japan or a just-reunified Germany."[140] In the aftermath of the wildly successful operation, President George H. W.

---

[137] "Britain Says U.S. Planned to Seize Oil in '73 Crisis'" *New York Times*, Jan. 4, 2004, A6.
[138] Haas (1999), pp. 32–3.
[139] McCormick (2004), pp. 83–4.
[140] Bacevich (2002), pp. 58–9.

Bush began speaking of a "new world order": a world order that was to depend on America's leadership and patronage. If the United States could not dominate economically, at least it could dominate militarily.

The subsequent invasion of Iraq in 2003 in the wake of September 11 revealed the fissures of that new world order. It is already clear that terrorism and the threat of weapons of mass destruction were pretexts at best. At issue was control over oil. Oil had been at issue in 1991 too, but now the threat of a rival oil hegemon was even more frightening. For one thing, given that the September 11 terrorists were from Saudi Arabia, the United States faced the threat of having to eventually terminate its relations with its long-standing oil client. For another, the rapid rise of China had finally put it on Washington's list of potential alternative power centers. Already in 2000, the chairman of the National Intelligence Council declared: "[T]he real question, then, is not whether China will be a major regional power, but rather how big a power it will be and, more importantly, how China will use its power."[141] Later, in 2003, the year the U.S. invasion of Iraq was unleashed, the Council on Foreign Relations tried to downplay China's capabilities, asserting that it was decades behind the United States in terms of military power. But by then China's economic growth had already fanned fears among officials in Bush the Younger's administration of the rise of a Eurasian superpower capable of overtaking the United States once and for all.[142] And the Institute for International Economics, which had on its board prominent economic strategists like Paul Volcker and Larry Summers, warned of an "East Asian economic bloc that could create a tripolar world economy, with significant geopolitical as well as economic implications for the United States."[143]

These economic and strategic concerns regarding China were only further fueled by Russia's "strategic relationship" – as the National Intelligence Council called it – with China, which included the sale of Russian technology and weapons. Attendant with this fear was Russia's own bid for regional power, manifested in part by its continual attempts to gain oil and natural gas from the Caspian region.[144] Even the *Economist* magazine took note, warning in 1999 that China and Russia would work together to gain preferential control over the energy-rich Caspian Sea basin. The following year, in 2000, a National Intelligence Council report forecasted possible global scenarios that could unfold by 2015. One of them was that "China, India, and Russia form a defacto geo-strategic alliance in an attempt to counterbalance U.S. and Western influence."[145]

Many scholars across the political spectrum have argued that the Iraq invasion was motivated in light of these Eurasian economic and political threats.

[141] Gannon (2000).
[142] Donnelly, Kagan, and Schmitt (2000).
[143] Bergsten and Institute for International Economics (2005), esp. p. xviii.
[144] National Intelligence Council (2001).
[145] National Intelligence Council (2000), p. 81.

David Harvey (2003) notes that a permanent U.S. presence in Iraq would provide a new site for controlling oil that, in turn, would provide the United States with "a powerful U.S. military bridgehead on the Eurasian land mass." This would give the United States a "powerful geostrategic position in Eurasia with at least the potentiality to disrupt any consolidation of a Eurasian power."[146] The Chinese economy, after all, depends on foreign oil. Any future Chinese military force would also depend on foreign oil. In *The American Conservative*, Anthony Layne thus argues:

> The real reason the administration went to war had nothing to do with terrorism. . . . The administration went to war in Iraq to consolidate America's global hegemony and to extend U.S. dominance to the Middle East by establishing a permanent military stronghold in Iraq for the purposes of controlling the Middle Eastern oil spigot (thereby giving Washington enormous leverage in its relations with Western Europe and China); allowing Washington to distance itself from an increasingly unreliable and unstable Saudi Arabia; and using the shadow of U.S. military power to bring about additional regime changes in Iran and Syria.

Without access to administration documents, it is difficult to conclusively assess these arguments. Yet the facts already available speak volumes. The first is that, before the 2003 invasion, policy makers with experience in the Gulf were already forecasting the need for future American intervention. Richard Haas wrote in 1999 that the use of American military force was imminent because "vital U.S. interests would suffer sharply were the Persian Gulf to fall under the sway of a hostile Iran or Iraq."[147] The second is that Iraq's oil reserves, thought to be the second largest in the world, amount to five times the total in the United States and remain the least explored of the world's oil-rich areas. Only two thousand wells have been drilled in Iraq, whereas a million have been drilled in Texas alone.[148] The third is that, despite all talk of a temporary occupation, after the invasion the United States initiated the construction of massive military bases in Iraq that the Pentagon referred to as "enduring bases." By 2007, at least five self-sufficient bases were under way. One of them, reported in the *Washington Post*, is the Balad Air Base, which has a miniature golf course, a cinema, a football field, and a neighborhood called "KBR-land," named after a Halliburton subsidiary. All of the bases have been built far away from major urban centers but close enough to have "power projection capacity," that is, potentially capable of hitting regional targets outside Iraq.[149] Fourth, the Bush administration pushed the Iraqi government to pass a new law for dealing with the distribution of oil revenues. The U.S. version of such a law ceded nearly all the oil to Western companies, making it the most open to foreign control

---

[146] Harvey (2003), p. 85.
[147] Haas (1999), p. 127.
[148] Holt (2007), p. 3.
[149] Ricks (2006).

compared with the nationalized controls exercised by Saudi Arabia, Kuwait, and Iran.[150]

There are thus parallels and precursors. In more than one sense, America's military deployments in the Middle East at the turn of the twenty-first century replayed the scramble for Africa one hundred years earlier. They were part of a wider struggle to control raw materials vital for the world economy. The only difference is that whereas Africa had been the site of much of Britain's new imperialism in the late nineteenth century, one hundred years later the strategic site of concern had shifted to other regions – in this case the Middle East. But beyond this difference the overarching similarity remains. Both Britain's and America's new imperialisms were unleashed during the two states' period of decline and heightened global competition because, in several respects, they were responses to decline and heightened competition. They do not represent the work of powerful empires flexing their muscles, but rather ailing hegemons tactically trying to ward off impending doom. Rather than feats of strength, they are acts of desperation amidst the threat of final demise.

[150] Juhasz (2007).

6

The Dynamics of Imperialism

> The Eastern nations sink, their glory ends, And empire rises where the sun descends.
>
> – Inscription on rock in Monument Bay, Plymouth MA

In 1879, the British sociologist Herbert Spencer wrote to liberal parliamentarian and free trader John Bright. Urging him to support a new Anti-Aggression League, Spencer bemoaned the "aggressive tendencies displayed by us all over the world – picking quarrels with native races and taking possession of their land."[1] Decades later V. I. Lenin referred to a similar process. He spoke of the "tremendous 'boom' in colonial conquests" by the British state that had begun in the late nineteenth century.[2] Of course, Spencer and Lenin were speaking of Britain's "new imperialism," about which we already know. Occurring in the context of Britain's economic decline, it marked a new aggression on the part of the British state. We also know about the American counterpart to this. In the 1980s, in the context of its own economic decline, the American state too embarked on a new path of direct imperialism. Both states shifted their imperial modalities and intensity; they become more bold, direct, and aggressive.

However, the fact that both the British and American states embarked on new imperialisms should not be the end of our story. It merely invites us to consider larger historical dynamics. The fact that both states initiated new imperialisms intimates the possibility of older imperialisms. It suggests the possibility of imperial shifts or transformations over longer periods of time. It intimates a story about imperial states sometimes becoming more violent and bold and sometimes more restrained and less direct. The new imperialisms might just be fragments of a larger pattern of imperial expansion and contraction, relative stability and renewed assertion, and imperial stagnation and growth.

[1] Spencer to Bright quoted in Wiltshire (1978), p. 91.
[2] Lenin (1964), p. 256.

TABLE 6.1. *Patterns of Imperial Aggression by Historical Phase, U.K. and U.S. Empires*

Phase	Imperial Modality
Ascent UK: 1730–1815 US: 1803–1945	Expansion: Direct Imperialism/Heightened Aggression
Hegemonic Victory/Maturity UK: 1816–1873 US: 1945–1973	Abatement: Relative decrease in Direct Imperialism/Aggression
Competition/Decline UK: 1874–1939 US: 1973–present	Reassertion: Direct Imperialism/Heightened Aggression

This chapter explores such imperial shifts over time. Whereas previous chapters have looked at specific phases or moments in the two empires' histories, this chapter looks at the bigger picture. It illuminates overarching patterns, processes, and dynamics over the course of the two states' modern imperial histories. It locates a historical structure to imperialism. Since the fall of the Rome, it has become a cliché to speak roundly about the rise, decline, and fall of empires. This chapter does something different: It speaks about the ups and downs of imperialistic aggression.

The Phases of Empire

In previous chapters, we have seen the British and American empires' respective ascendancies to global power, their colonial policies and regimes, their preferred modalities of imperialism during their respective hegemonic phases, and their new imperialisms during their periods of decline. If we put these discrete stories together into a larger whole, however, we can induce a larger historical pattern. The pattern consists of three phases: imperial expansion, abatement, and reassertion. These phases roughly correspond with the two states' phases of ascendancy, hegemonic maturity, and decline (see Table 6.1).

To elaborate: The first phase occurred as the British and American states ascended toward global economic dominance. As seen in Chapter 1, during this period the two states' respective paths to global preeminence were paved by youthful imperial aggression. This aggression took the form of bold territorial conquests and military power to secure the conquests, expand trading networks, and protect borders. Britain expanded in the Americas and then into parts of Africa and Asia. Similarly, the United States reached westward in the Americas and took possessions in the Caribbean and the Asia-Pacific. The next phase of the sequence occurred during the two states' periods of hegemonic maturity. As seen in Chapter 3, in this phase, the two states' territorial expansion slowed if not stagnated entirely, and they resorted to informal imperialism. Rather than continuing to conquer colonies, both states preferred to cultivate clients. For instance, just as the British state preferred to establish allied sovereign dependencies in Latin America rather than ruling them as colonies, so did the United States cultivate its covert machinery to silently topple regimes rather than invade them. In short, as the two hegemons reaped the fruits of economic dominance in the world, both states opted for indirect means of exercising influence.

The final phase occurred during the two states' respective periods of hegemonic decline. In this phase, both states reasserted themselves in the world with new vigor. Facing increasing competition from rivals and new economic troubles, the British and American states became more and more aggressive in their imperial tactics. As we learned in previous chapters, the form of this aggression differed: The British empire became more aggressive through formal imperialism as well as militarism, whereas the U.S. empire's reassertion took the form of military invasion, air strikes, or temporary military occupations. But whatever the particular form, both states became more overtly and directly imperialistic in this period.

We can detect this overarching pattern of expansion, abatement, and reassertion by looking at quantitative data. Even if they do not tell us everything, numbers sometimes speak. The numbers here affirm the historical narrative of preceding chapters. Consider the number of colonies seized by the British state per year (i.e., the rate of British colonization). This offers a good indicator of Britain's imperial aggression: Land grabbing and direct rule are quintessentially imperialistic. When we look at these numbers, the historical structure surfaces. During the late eighteenth century (during Britain's ascent phase), we see bouts of expansion followed by a relative abatement in the mid-nineteenth century. Then, in the late nineteenth century, during Britain's decline, we see an upswing (Figure 6.1). Admittedly, the first phase of imperialism should be broken up into two peak periods: an upsurge in the 1760s and then a new and longer wave in the 1780s.[3] Yet when taken together, they can be seen as part of a larger single wave of imperialism; larger, that is, relative to the mid-nineteenth century.

We may also visualize the historical dynamics of U.S. imperialism by a similar approach, although we should be sensitive to historical context. Because colonialism had become illegitimate for any world power in the latter half of the twentieth century, we would not expect American imperialism to be measured

---

[3] These two waves are separated temporally and geographically: The first wave in the 1760s occurred largely in the Americas and the Caribbean (including the annexation of Quebec, Cape Breton, Grenada, St. Vincent, and Tobago), whereas the second wave beginning in the 1780s included not only territories in the Americas, but also new additions farther off in Asia and Africa (e.g., parts of India, New South Wales, Penang, Seychelles, Sierra Leone, and the Cape Colony).

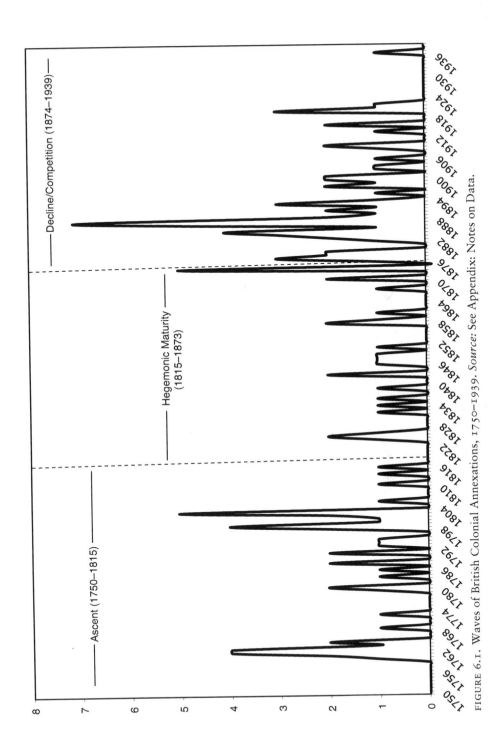

FIGURE 6.1. Waves of British Colonial Annexations, 1750–1939. *Source:* See Appendix: Notes on Data.

solely by direct colonization. Accordingly, if we wish to examine patterns of imperialism over the longer *durée* of the nineteenth century through the early twenty-first century, we should look at colonization and direct military interventions together. Although direct military intervention is not the same as colonization, it is nonetheless more costly and overt than diplomacy, financial aid, or other (perhaps more subtle) mechanisms of influence. Looking at both colonization and military interventions thereby provides a window into the historical ups and downs of U.S. imperial aggression that is more comparable to Britain's ups and downs. Doing so yields a complicated picture, but from it emerges the same sequence of expansion, abatement, and reassertion (Figure 6.2). There are four peak periods or waves of heightened imperialistic aggression (marked by letters A, B, C, D). The highest point is the period around 1898 (wave C). The next major wave occurs in the late twentieth century, beginning circa the 1980s (wave D). In between there is a low trough. The first three waves taken together correspond with America's period of hegemonic ascent. The fourth and most recent wave (wave D) corresponds to America's period of decline. The historical pattern of British imperialism is thus reiterated in American imperialism.

We should be more precise. We have been treating the entire historical period up until hegemonic maturity as part of a single ascent phase, but this is problematic. Surely we cannot consider the entire history of Britain up until 1815 as part of its ascent phase. So when does ascent begin? To address this, we can draw on world-systems theorists and their demarcation of global cycles. In this approach, the period of ascent officially begins when the prior hegemon declines and the global system becomes more competitive. For instance, the proper period of America's ascent would begin in 1874 when the prior hegemon (in this case, Britain) began its fall and the global field became more competitive. For Britain's ascent, the issue is more complicated, but we can take the year 1763 as a starting point. This is the year when Britain proved itself to be a real contender for global power by defeating France in the Seven Years' War.[4] Demarcating the ascent periods in this way does not alter our story: We still see more imperialistic activity in the ascent phase than during the maturity phase. We also see higher average annual rates of activity in these periods of ascent and decline than during the hegemonic maturity phase (see Tables 6.2 and 6.3).

In short, just as all empires surely rise and surely fall, so too have the two hegemonic empires in the modern era – the American and British empires – followed a pattern of extension, stability, and reextension. In the two states' imperial careers there have been moments or periods when they became more directly imperialistic, employing more direct and costly means to exert influence in the world than in other moments or periods. Furthermore, these fluctuations

---

[4] This periodization comes from Wallerstein, who asserts that in 1763 Britain proves to be a viable global hegemon, but does not consolidate its position until 1815. See Wallerstein (1980), p. 245; Wallerstein (1989), p. 57.

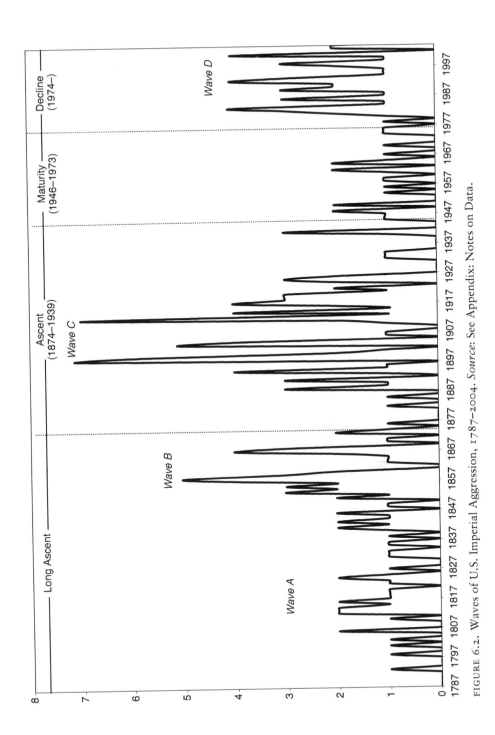

FIGURE 6.2. Waves of U.S. Imperial Aggression, 1787–2004. *Source*: See Appendix: Notes on Data.

TABLE 6.2. *Rate of British Colonial Annexations by Historical Phase*

Number of Years	Phase	Years	Colonies Acquired	Annual Rate
52	Ascent/Competition	1763–1815	39	0.75
57	Maturity	1816–1873	23	0.40
65	Decline/Competition	1874–1939	69	1.06

correlate with the phases of the two states' hegemonic careers. The two states were less aggressive during their respective periods of hegemonic maturity than during their periods of ascent or decline.[5]

Drawing on lessons from earlier chapters, we can see that there are other correlates to these phases. We have seen, for instance, that the phases of imperialism came with certain discursive patterns. During their respective periods of hegemony, talk of "empire" was suppressed or at least lessened in both countries. The banner of empire was lowered only to then be raised again during the decline phase. In fact, in the United States, talk of American empire proliferated during *both* the ascent and decline phases. As the United States constructed its overseas empire in the Caribbean and Pacific, talk of the United States as an empire came to the fore, just as it did during the late twentieth and into the present century as America's "new imperialism" was unleashed amidst America's decline. The structure of imperial discourse over time followed the fluctuations of imperial aggression.

U.S. and British trade policies roughly correspond with the phases of hegemony and imperialism too. During their respective phases of hegemonic maturity, both the U.S. and British imperial states pursued similar economic policies and espoused similar trade rhetoric at the same time that they lessened their direct imperialism. In particular, as seen in Chapter 3, both liberalized their trade policies and made gestures toward global free trade. For the British state, this was reflected in the repeal of the Corn Laws and various tariff reductions through the 1860s. For the American state, it was reflected in the General Agreement on Tariffs and Trade (1947).[6] This is not to say that both states acted as benevolent economic hegemons or that they uniformly pursued so-called free trade in full. Many economic sectors remained under tariff protection, and the free trade rhetoric was often performative, sometimes contradicted by hypocritical policies. It is the case nonetheless that the trade policies of both states were more liberal than during the ascent phase. As hegemons, both states not only

[5] Quantitative studies of the world system have suggested similar dynamics to imperialism, although they examine the dynamics at the level of global system (rates of colonization by all states). See Bergesen and Schoenberg (1980) and Boswell (1989).
[6] These economic parallels, as well as main differences, are covered in O'Brien (2002). On U.S. trade policy, see especially Chorev (2007).

TABLE 6.3. *Rate of U.S. Annexations and Military Interventions by Historical Phase*

Number of Years	Phase	Years	Annexations & Interventions	Annual Rate
65	Ascent/Competition	1874–1939	88	1.35
27	Maturity	1946–1973	18	0.67
30	Decline/Competition	1974–2004	53	1.77

preferred informal empire; they also preferred the open door to mercantilist gates – in rhetoric at least if not in practice.

The pattern thus holds: Both the British and American states extended their direct imperial aggression, retracted or at least stabilized it, and then reextended it during their respective periods of decline. This invites us to wonder whether there is some kind of deeper logic to it all. Is the pattern of imperialism explicable or just accident – a miraculous coincidence? The previous chapter has explained why the British and American states embarked on new imperialisms during their respective phases of hegemonic decline. Yet this only accounts for why the two states reasserted themselves during their decline phases. It does not explain why they both became more aggressive during their ascent phases or why their direct imperialism receded during their periods of hegemony. It is a historically specific explanation of one moment in a larger cycle; it does not illuminate the cycle in its entirety. The question remains: Might there be some kind of logic governing the foregoing fluctuations of imperial aggression?

Explaining the Pattern

Surely any explanation for the American and British cycles of imperialism would have to include a multitude of factors. Reaching across seas and over historical eras, the pattern of imperialism might not reduce to a single explanatory force. If the story were to turn on any single force at all, however, it should have to do with the structure of the global field; or more precisely, *global economic competition*. We would expect this to be important because it is exactly what differentiates the different phases of hegemonic cycles in the first place. The concept of hegemony refers to global economic structures. The idea is that the world system oscillates between phases of hegemonic maturity and competition. The hegemonic maturity phase (or "unicentric" or "unipolar" phase) is when one state enjoys a preponderance over the world economy. The other phase is one of competition (or "multicentricity" or "multipolarity"); this is a time of intense economic rivalry between states.[7] The former is a period when there is a single hegemon; the latter is when that hegemon declines as competition arises. Facing unprecedented rivals that are capturing increasing shares of

---

[7] Wallerstein (1984), Wallerstein (2002b).

world output, the hegemon no longer enjoys a preponderance over the world economy. The global field shifts from a unipolar or unicentric structure to a multipolar or multicentric structure.

We have just seen that the British and American cycles of imperialism correspond with these phases in the hegemony cycle. The two states turned to more direct modalities of imperialism and heightened their aggression when they faced decline; that is, when the global economic field became more competitive and entered a multicentric phase. The same goes for their periods of ascent. As each state rose to power, the prior hegemon was in decline and the global field became more competitive. In that phase, each imperial state was more prone to step up its imperial aggression. It was only during their respective phases of hegemonic maturity when the states' respective aggression and boldness gave way to indirect modalities of imperial power. Put differently, it was only when the field was less competitive and the system entered an unipolar phase that direct imperialism waned.

The pattern can now be understood in more precise relation to competitive structures of the global field. In brief, when economically dominant in the world economy relative to other states – that is, when the global field was *unicentric* and so competition was low – the British and American states preferred to cultivate clients through subtle mechanisms of power rather than deploying either colonization or overt military force. But when either state was struggling economically against other states in a more competitive global field – that is, when the field was *multicentric* – they were more willing to colonize or use overt military force. In short, competitive structures of the global field appear to breed direct imperial aggression. The question is why.

Competition and Multicentricity

To answer, let us turn first to Britain's waves of imperial aggression. In Chapter 5, we saw something of how competition in the global field during the late nineteenth century pushed the British state to become bolder and more aggressive. Beginning in the 1870s, Britain's economic supremacy was challenged by upstarts and older powers. British firms were threatened by foreign firms while competing states like Germany, the United States, France, Italy, and Russia introduced or reasserted new tariff systems that threatened to cut Britain out. Some of the rivals (not least Germany and the United States) began using their new economic muscles to build their military power. In this highly competitive context, British firms pushed the British state to annex new territory in order to secure routes, markets, and raw materials. The British state often responded affirmatively, operating out of its own concerns. Fearing rivals' military power and the loss of economic access, the British state annexed new territory and initiated military interventions in hopes of regaining some advantage, ensuring economic inputs, and keeping rivals at their heels. In short, although there were other factors involved in Britain's new imperialism – such as the breakdown of clientelism abroad and domestic economic crises – global competition played an important part by making the British state feel more threatened and insecure.

Imperial aggression was a defensive move against an increasingly competitive – that is, multicentric – global environment.

If this is true, then we should expect a similar logic to have produced Britain's earlier wave of direct imperialism in the eighteenth century (from the 1740s to 1815), when Britain was not in decline but struggling to ascend. This period was not different in structure from the later decline period from 1874 to World War I. Like that period, it was a highly competitive phase in the global system. In 1750, the United Kingdom's percentage share of world manufacturing output was 1.9. France's was 4.0, Russia's was 5.0, and Austria-Hungary's was 2.9.[8] The European system, as Paul Kennedy notes, was "one of five Great Powers – France, the Habsburg Empire, Prussia, Britain and Russia – as well as lesser countries like Savoy and declining states like Spain."[9] This economic and attendant political competition was thus expressed overseas. By the mid-1700s, for instance, Britain had already established a string of satellite colonies along the North American coast and in parts of the Caribbean (which were vital to Britain's growing economy); however, Spain and France were poised to halt Britain's advance.[10] France dominated the slave trade, the sugar sector, and the entrepôt trade in Caribbean produce; and both France and Spain were positioned to take over Britain's activities in other sectors.[11] In the Ottoman empire and the Mediterranean, British merchants also faced competition. Anglo-French rivalry in textiles was intense. Finally, Britain's trade with the European Continent faced repeated challenges. The Continent was the dominant destination of British exports until the early 1770s. In 1750, Europe accounted for 71 percent of British exports.[12] But Britain had to jostle against rivals, especially France, to maintain position in the European market.[13]

As with the late nineteenth century, this overarching climate of competition at the close of the eighteenth century created consistent worry and concern among British merchants, producers, and policy makers who fretted about being pushed out completely. Men on the spot, as well as intellectuals in London, watched Spain's activities in the Americas and predicted that Spain was making a comeback from its previous imperial heyday.[14] France was even more of a threat. A common fear was that France would "master the whole continent" in North America; that the French were "artfully working for universal Empire in America."[15] London also worried about French expansion in Europe, which would cut off Britain from a key market.[16] Meanwhile, in Asia, the British envoys in Constantinople repeatedly worried about French

---

[8] Bairoch (1982), pp. 280–1; Wallerstein (1989), p. 70.
[9] Kennedy (1987), p. 73–4.
[10] Cain and Hopkins (1993), p. 85; Price (1998), p. 89.
[11] Harris (1996), p. 135.
[12] Conway (2005), p. 358; Price (1998) pp. 87, 101.
[13] Black (1986), p. 135.
[14] Paquette (2004).
[15] Harris (1996), pp. 133–4.
[16] Conway (2005), pp. 358–9.

"encroachments on our trade" and that the French would "ruin us" in the East Indies.[17] British political economists framed the competition as a zero-sum game: Britain's rivals had to be out-competed rather than just allowed to coexist. Britain, they declared, must "control a general kind of *lead in commerce* distinct from any of the governments of Europe." Only by gaining a lead would Britain enjoy a vast "commercial dominion" without fear of rivalry.[18]

Given this context, the same processes that led to imperial aggression in the late nineteenth century unfolded during this phase too. First British capitalists and merchants pressured the British state to annex new territories for protection and advantage. Merchants pressed London for colonies so that they could have "safe and unimpeded access to the consumers and sources of supply" all around the world (much in the same way that merchants in the late nineteenth century pressed for African colonies to ward off rival tariff blocs).[19] Various other interest and lobbying groups – ranging from overseas planters to middle-class merchants to financiers – also pushed for expansion on the same ground.[20] The pressure intensified during the formative decades of Britain's industrial transformation (the 1760s and 1770s). As rivals threatened to undo Britain's progress, financial interests and manufacturing groups pressed more firmly for access to inexpensive raw materials and colonial markets.[21]

Second, the British state became increasingly concerned about geopolitical threats: The imperative of securing capital was conjoined with the imperative of containing geopolitical rivals. Economic competition did not only mean that capitalists' interests were impacted; it also had implications for security. In the Indies and the Americas, French merchants could undercut British trade while French colonial holdings could serve as springboards for invading Britain's wealthy settlements or blockading vital trade routes during wartime.[22] Furthermore, Britain's "fiscal-military state" of the time demanded that large portions of public funds go to the military, and public funds – when not borrowed – depended on healthy foreign trade. Taxes from customs revenues were especially important, not only as a new means to acquire money, but as a domestic political strategy to keep a lower tax burden on Britain's landed class (who remained important political actors despite the onset of industrialization).[23] Thus were trade and security intertwined. As one British writer in 1735 summed, "[O]ur trade is the Mother and Nurse of our Seamen; Our Seaman the Life of our Fleet; And our Fleet the Security and Protection of our Trade: And that both together are the WEALTH, STRENGTH, AND

---

[17] Quoted in Black (1986), pp. 134, 153.
[18] Pownall (1766), pp. 4, 6; see also Koehn (1994), p. 16.
[19] O'Brien (1998), p. 71.
[20] Olson (1992), Wilson (1995).
[21] Koehn (1994), pp. 18–19.
[22] Duffy (1987), p. 19.
[23] Brewer (1989), pp. 202–4; O'Gorman (1997), p. 177; Koehn (1994), p. 20.

GLORY OF GREAT BRITAIN."[24] Another writer asserted in 1765: "A *Nation* cannot be safe without *Power; Power* cannot be obtained without *Riches;* nor *Riches* without Trade."[25]

As with the late nineteenth century, British imperialism in this multicentric phase was a response to heightened competition. Imperial aggression became a way for the British state to fend off both economic and geopolitical threats from rivals amidst its own bid for dominance in the field. It followed that the targets of most of Britain's territorial aggression were in the Americas and the Caribbean; those very sites where Britain had growing economic interests and where rivals were well positioned.[26] Taking territories in these areas was aimed, first, at maintaining the security of Britain's preexisting colonies and trade routes against those rivals. William Pitt explained in 1761 that the key objective in acquiring territory in the New World was the "entire safety" of Britain's North American possessions and especially "the secure possession of that most valuable conquest of Canada."[27] Taking territory was likewise aimed at expanding trade into new areas, which in turn involved ousting or at least containing rival empires. "The growing advantages [of taking additional territory in Canada]," said William Shirley, former governor of Massachusetts, were

...the State of Security, which the Settlers in North America would be put into, by the Removal of the French; The extensive Trade with the Indians, the Increase of the Fishery, the Rich vacant Country for new Settlements, and the quick Growth of their Estates would make the Inhabitants increase if not in a Duplicate proportion to what they have hitherto done, yet in a much greater degree.[28]

The annexation of Florida was motivated similarly. It would remove the threat of Spanish invasion of British North America from the south while also, as Lord Shelburne explained, opening "a new field of commerce" and providing "great additional resources for the increase of our naval power."[29]

Territorial expansion was also aimed at undercutting rivals' trade and economic power, thereby removing the economic and security threat at once. In the 1740s, William Pitt had already laid out the essence of this idea, in regard to Cape Breton: "The possession of this valuable island," he said, "puts it in our power absolutely to ruin the great trade carried on by the French to North America."[30] Later in the century, British statesmen like Secretary of State Henry Dundas argued that taking complete control of the West Indies would be beneficial "both in the view of humbling the power of France, and with the view

---

[24] Quoted in Baugh (1994), p. 195.
[25] Quoted in Koehn (1994), p. 62.
[26] Ward (1998), p. 415.
[27] Quoted in Hyam and Martin (1975), p. 30. See also Peters (1993), pp. 50–1.
[28] Quoted in Koehn (1994), p. 171.
[29] Quoted in Hyam and Martin (1975), p. 31.
[30] Peters (1993), p. 37.

of enlarging our wealth and security."[31] Proponents of expansion in London in the 1790s asserted:

France is the only power whose maritime force has hitherto been a balance to that of Great Britain and whose commerce has rivaled ours in the two worlds; whose intrigues have fomented and kept alive the ruinous wars in India. Could England succeed in destroying the naval strength of her rival; could she turn the tide of that rich commerce, which has so often excited her jealousy, in favor of her own country... the degree of commercial prosperity... would exceed all calculation. It would not be the work of a few years only, but it would require ages for France to recover.[32]

France's Caribbean colonies had accounted for two-fifths of its total trade and two-thirds of its ocean-going shipping tonnage by the late eighteenth century. Taking former French colonies would disrupt this French circuit of economic and naval power while expanding Britain's own.[33] Fittingly, the British state took the French colonies Tobago and St. Lucia because of their strategic position within France's network and the prospect of consolidating Britain's network in turn.[34]

The similarities between Britain's period of ascent (1750s–1815) and its decline (1873–1914) should now be clear, as should the reason for why both were marked by imperial boldness and assertion. Both were periods of multicentrism, which in turn meant a competitive global field. Aggressive imperialism served as a way for the British state to gain or maintain position in that competitive field. During its period of ascent in the late eighteenth century, the British state was a rising contender, and direct imperialism accompanied its bid to hegemony. Territorial expansion and related military might were ways of cultivating strength while beating down rival bidders. By the same token but from the other historical end, the British state employed direct imperialism during its period of decline in the late nineteenth century to meet rising challengers. The very aggression that Britain had previously employed amidst its bid was exhibited by challengers in the late nineteenth century, and the British state responded in kind.

The fact that America's waves of imperial aggression corresponded to multipolar phases in the global field can be explained similarly. As noted, there were three waves of heightened imperialist aggression by the American state during America's long ascendancy from the late eighteenth century to World War II. These are worth elaborating. The earlier two waves followed regional and hemispheric dynamics (waves A and B, Figure 6.2). They were aimed at ousting rival European powers, securing territory and control over the frontier, and ultimately attaining hemispheric dominance. The earliest wave, beginning circa 1810, marked the American state's drive to regional dominance. It involved annexations and interventions to gain control over contiguous territory and to

---

[31] Duffy (1987), p. 25.
[32] *Times*, Feb. 8, 1793, p. 3. See also ibid., p. 24.
[33] Duffy (1998), p. 187.
[34] Fieldhouse (1982), p. 76.

TABLE 6.4. *U.S. Waves of Military Intervention or Annexation by Region, 1810–1870*

Region	1810–1825	1840–1870
Africa	1	3
Asia-Pacific	0	22
Caribbean, Central & South America	7	14
Europe & E. Europe	1	1
Middle East and N. Africa	1	2
N. American Continent & Mexico	9	10

Source: See Appendix: Notes on Data.

fend off threats from rival European powers. The War of 1812 with Britain was part of this wave. Other interventions included the occupation of the Oregon territory and engagements in Spanish Florida. Fittingly, near the end of this wave, President Monroe gave his 1823 annual message later known as the Monroe Doctrine. Monroe bragged that over the previous decades the United States had acquired vast new territories and had ended interference by Britain, France, Russia, and Spain. He concluded: "[T]he American continents...are henceforth not to be considered as subjects for future colonization by any European powers."[35] This wave was likewise aimed at securing mercantile power against rivals. Merchants had seen threats to their activities beginning in 1808, and trade with Latin America and Caribbean countries offered some hope, as long as the Spanish and British could be kept out and "freebooters" contained.[36] Accordingly, although some deployments in this period took place as far away as Tripoli, Tunis, and Algiers, most took place in the Caribbean (Cuba, Puerto Rico, and Santo Domingo) and involved troop landings to chase down or suppress freebooters, pirates, or "marauders."[37]

The second wave of aggression occurred in the years from 1840 to 1870. Whereas the previous wave marks America's rise to regional dominance, this wave represents America's consolidation of hemispheric dominance. Fewer instances of military force or territorial annexation involved activities in or around contiguous territory on the continent (Table 6.4). The other instances occurred outside the continent but within the hemisphere. For example, interventions in the Caribbean and Latin America doubled in number from the first wave. This suggests that the United States, having secured mercantile control, sought to expand it westward, looking for profitable passageways to the Pacific through Nicaragua and Panama. The Gadsen Purchase from Mexico was part of this endeavor, and American forces were deployed in Nicaragua at least twice. Merchants also intensified their interest in places like Cuba and Santo

---

[35] Crapol (1979), p. 414.
[36] LaFeber (1989), p. 81.
[37] United States Congress Committee on Foreign Affairs (1970), pp. 50–3.

Domingo, leading to various instances of force in those areas.[38] The United States also looked to the Asia-Pacific area as never before. The majority of instances in this second wave took place there, whereas none had taken place during the first wave (see Table 6.4).[39]

As opposed to the first two waves, the third wave from the 1880s to 1914 (wave C, Figure 6.2) was much higher in frequency and intensity. It propelled the American state onto the global stage. This was the period of America's ascent that coincided with heightened *global* competition. At the system level, it was a multicentric phase, occurring at the same time as Britain's decline from hegemonic status. For Britain, multicentricity meant the appearance of formidable rivals like Germany and the United States, poised as pretenders to power. But for rivals like the United States, it meant facing a declining hegemon threatening to reassert itself. It also involved potential confrontations with a range of other pretenders to power. The famous American thinker Brooks Adams, in his prescient book *America's Economic Supremacy* (1900), captured the scene. There was a "new struggle for life among nations," he wrote. It involved the relative decline of Britain (and older powers like Spain) and the emergence of Russia, Japan, France, and the United States as rising powers. Adams rightfully concluded that this period of heightened competition was "one of those memorable revolutions wherein civilizations pass from an old to a new condition of equilibrium." He also noted that the period was strikingly similar to the previous period of multicentricity in the late eighteenth century when Britain was on the rise (1760 to 1815). The "last such revolution ended with Waterloo," Adams wrote, and "the one now at hand promises to be equally momentous."[40]

Just as competition in the global field had fueled Britain's bout of imperial aggression in the late eighteenth century, so did it fuel the American states' imperial aggression in this period. As revisionist historians have long shown, American imperialism at this time was driven by multiple pressures felt in the metropole: new racial ideologies and Social Darwinian discourses, the economic crisis of 1893 and the related search for new markets and materials, and an increasingly capable American state poised for global greatness after emerging from the Civil War as a unified, powerful nation.[41] No doubt, these factors are critical for understanding this wave of imperialism. Domestic economic concerns associated with the 1893 depression would stand as particularly noteworthy. In fact, the Hobson-Lenin thesis that imperialism results from capitalists' fear of overproduction at home and the need for new markets

---

[38] By 1855, in fact, "America's commerce with Cuba had doubled during the previous decade, becoming seven times greater than Great Britain's and even four times larger than Spain's – which owned Cuba" (LaFeber 1989: 135).

[39] Graebner (1983).

[40] Adams (1947 [1900]), p. 63.

[41] This literature is large, but on shifts in the American states' capabilities, see Zakaria (1998); on racial ideology, see the classic work by Hunt (1987) and the recent work by Kramer (2006); on economic factors, see LaFeber (1963).

originated in American business and policy-making circles. Before Hobson and Lenin drafted their theories, American producers, led by the National Association of Manufacturers, and economists like Charles Conant argued that America's productive forces were overflowing and the domestic market could not keep up.[42] They urged the American state to help secure global markets to resolve the problem. The famed "China market" was one of the promised outlets.[43]

Still, the global climate of competition was also an important factor in driving America's imperialism. After all, domestic concerns may have made capitalists in the National Association of Manufacturers or other business groups pressure the American state to become interventionist overseas, but this in itself would not guarantee an agreeable response on the part of the American state. For imperialism to happen, the American state had to have interests in it too. It did. This is because the new economic competition also meant geopolitical competition.

For example, American policy makers and statesmen feared that upstarts like Germany would thwart America's hemispheric domination by making moves on Latin America or the Caribbean. President Roosevelt spoke of how the kaiser might "seize some Venezuelan harbor and turn it into a strongly fortified place of arms . . . with a view to exercising some measure of control over the future of the Isthmian Canal, and over South American affairs generally."[44] He and other statesmen at the time also worried about British or French encroachment. During the 1895 Venezuelan boundary dispute with Britain, Senator Henry Cabot Lodge of Massachusetts connected the issue to a wider context of threat. He argued that if the British were allowed to gain more territory in the Americas, France and Germany would do the same, and so the United States should take action lest "South America pass gradually into the hands of Great Britain and other European powers."[45]

America's subsequent involvement with Cuba and Puerto Rico in this period partly followed from these concerns about the European threat. Control over the Caribbean islands was seen as vital for controlling entry to the region and for securing the route to the Panama Canal, which was also seized by the United States at this time. The American state's numerous troop deployments and military occupations of Nicaragua, the Dominican Republic, and Haiti were similarly preemptive. Military power was meant to deal with internal disorder – this was important for American investment – but it was also meant to prevent rival European powers from stepping in. Unchecked domestic instability would

---

[42] Conant (1898).
[43] The classic work on this thesis is McCormick (1967). A more recent view of American expansion that sees Asia-Pacific more broadly as vital for U.S. interests is Cumings (2009). The argument that the United States expanded abroad to meet domestic economic demands is a common one among the revisionist historians: See, for instance, Williams (1972), LaFeber (1963), and Williams (1969), pp. 408–53 especially.
[44] As Quoted in Fry (1996a), p. 4.
[45] Lodge quoted in Healy (1970), p. 26.

give rival powers an excuse to bring their own military power and hence gain a foothold at the expense of U.S. interests.[46]

America's aggression in the Pacific was due to the same competitive structure. The United States seized islands in the Pacific as stepping stones toward the famed China market; that expansion was necessary to preempt control over China and Asia-Pacific trade by other powers. In part, this necessitated building up America's naval capacities in the region. Alfred Mahan, the naval strategist whose writings were widely influential on statesmen, was clear on this point. He pinned the need for territory in the Pacific on the need for a powerful navy, which was in turn necessary due to heightened international competition:

> The general strenuous impulse of the great civilized states of the world to find and to establish markets and commercial relations outside their own borders and their own people, has led to multifold annexations, and to commercial and naval aggressions. In these the United States has had no part, but they have constituted a political situation that immensely increases her political and commercial anxieties and consequently her naval responsibilities.

Mahan especially worried that other nations were expanding economically to seek privileged markets and control: "[T]here is ... the effort to extend and sustain commercial advantage by the extension of political power, either by controlling influence or by actual annexation, under cover of either of which the commercial system of the particular country obtains favored conditions, injurious to others, from special privilege all the way up to a practically exclusive market."[47] The only way to stop this was to expand militarily. That, in turn, entailed imperial expansion.

Mahan's views were representative and influential. In 1898, Charles Denby, U.S. minister to China, conveyed the same fear of competition. His worrisome observations are worth quoting at length, for they are indicative of the tenor of the times:

> The eyes of Europe are turned toward China and the European powers are arranging far-reaching plans dictated by territorial ambition.... France is annexing territory on her Tonquin frontier, and is building railroads into Yunnan. Russia has laid her hand on Manchuria, and six hundred miles of Russian railroad in Chinese territory will shortly connect the trans-Siberian system with the port of Viadivostock on the Pacific. Germany is obtaining concessions.... Japan ... is daily adding to her military and naval strength, preparing to take her part in the coming struggle for supremacy on the mainland. England has opened new territories for her commerce by asserting the right of British merchants to navigate the West River, the key to the southwest of China. British trade was never so flourishing in China as to-day and the supremacy of England's naval power in Asiatic waters sears testimony to her intention to defend it. All these powers recognize the fact that trade follows the flag. Where their ships go and where they make their national influence felt, there trade springs up to meet them. They recognize

---

[46] On this as a motivating factor, see Fry (1996a). For more on these interventions in the Caribbean and others in Central America, see Healy (1988), Perkins (1981), and Schoonover (1991).

[47] Mahan (1902), pp. 49–50.

that the present is a critical period in the history of China; that when the breaking up and the inevitable partition come, those who have established themselves will obtain recognition of their interests, those who have failed to do so must see their trade go to the masters of the soil.... The people of the United States must not be content to see their neighbors to the West, with their boundless potentialities of trade, handed over, an uncontested prize, to the ambitions of Europe.[48]

These concerns over European competition in the Asia-Pacific region had already led to America's interest in Hawaii and Samoa. "Hawaii holds in the western sea much the same position as Cuba in the Atlantic," wrote Secretary of State James Blaine in 1881. "It is the key to the maritime dominion of the Pacific States ... under no circumstances can the United States permit any change in the territorial control of either which would cut it adrift from the American system, whereto they both belong."[49] Most in Washington agreed, which is why both areas were seized. "We need Hawaii just as much and a good deal more than we did California," asserted President McKinley in early 1898.[50] Henry C. Ide pressed for the acquisition of Samoa and Hawaii in 1897 on the grounds that "European nations have been swift to seize upon the vantage points" in the region, and so the United States must swiftly do the same.[51]

America's wave of imperial aggression was thus directed toward the "Open Door": The door not only had to be thrust open through force, but kept open as rivals tried to close it.[52] The wider competitive environment made the threat of closure all the more frightful. The interest of the McKinley administration in the Philippines was partially dictated by this fear. McKinley worried that "our commercial rivals in the Orient," such as France and Germany, might annex the Philippine archipelago if the United States did not.[53] These fears were not allayed by the appearance of a German squadron in Manila Bay in early 1898; nor by rumors circulating in the State Department that Germany was hoping to annex the Philippines for itself. Taking the Philippines, Roosevelt argued, would preempt any such attempts.[54]

Other factors propelling America's imperial expansion in the late nineteenth century have been discussed in the scholarly literature. Here the point is to highlight the similarities between U.S. direct imperialism in the late nineteenth century with the late twentieth century and also the similarities between Britain's two phases of imperial expansion. On the one hand, each of these phases

---

[48] Denby (1898).

[49] Snow (1894), p. 372; also discussed in Zakaria (1998), pp. 141–2.

[50] Quoted in Zimmerman (2002), p. 291. For more on the motive behind the acquisition of Hawaii, see Pratt (1936). See also Healy (1970), p. 25.

[51] Ide (1897), p. 161.

[52] On the historiography relating to the Open Door, see Fry (1996b).

[53] Quoted in Fry (1996a), p. 8.

[54] Bailey (1939); see also Healy (1970), pp. 65–6. For a review of other factors shaping McKinley's decision, see Smith (1993). A similar concern over rivals guided the deployment of American troops in China during the Boxer Rebellion. See Fry (1996a), pp. 9–11.

of imperial aggression involved distinct casual factors: In the late nineteenth century, for instance, ideologies of racial inferiority likely helped propel colonization by the United States, whereas in the late twentieth century, U.S. imperial aggression was partly due to the breakdown in clientelist networks (as seen in the previous chapter). On the other hand, what all of these different bouts of imperial aggression share is that they occurred in the systemic state of multicentricity, those periods when one hegemon is in decline and rivals are ascending. From our foregoing examination, we can now see that this multicentric structure of the global field matters, because *multicentric phases mean heightened economic competition*. Such competition puts states at perilous risk. For hegemons, there is the prospect of ultimate decline, as rising contenders nip at their heels and steadily grow in strength. For the rising contenders, there is the prospect that their ascent will be thwarted by their peers, as everyone makes their bids for power. Thus, for both the declining hegemon and the rising contenders, direct imperial aggression becomes the tactic of choice; a means of warding off rivals, tempering the challenge from competitors if not undercutting them, and securing position in the field. In this way, global competitive fields breed imperial aggression.

But what about periods of hegemony, when competition is lessened?

Hegemony and Abatement

Periods of hegemony entail a different global structure than multicentric periods. In hegemonic periods, a rising state emerges typically from the ashes of a world war to maintain a preponderance over the world economy. The global field becomes unipolar: One state commands global economic flows more than any single competitor. We have seen the correlates of this scenario: Both the British and American states during their respective periods of hegemony lessened their direct aggression. Although still imperialistic, they nonetheless tempered their boldness and entered a phase of imperial abatement. They initiated fewer military interventions and slowed their rate of territorial expansion, instead preferring clientelism, financial entanglements, and covert operations. So what is it about hegemonic states that make them less interested in direct imperialism?

The beginnings of an answer can be found if we reconsider Britain's trade policies. The British state took steps to liberalize global trade amid its period of hegemony. Despite the protectionist Corn Law of 1815, the British state nonetheless enacted the Reciprocity of Duties Act (1823) that promoted reciprocal agreements with foreign governments to free up trade. Progress was slow, but these steps demonstrated Britain's willingness to reduce mercantilist restrictions if not eventually abandon them altogether.[55] In the end many restrictions were lifted, as Britain entered into various treaties that reduced discriminatory tariffs and repealed the Corn Laws in 1846. Thus, Britain showed a stronger

---

[55] Irwin (1993); O'Brien and Pigman (1992), p. 94.

desire to end mercantilism during its period of hegemony than during the late eighteenth century. The reason why is informative: British firms and the British state were confident that open markets would be to their benefit. Of course, Britain's industrialization and population growth compelled industry to seek more markets and raw materials, and this was one reason behind liberalization. However, the related push came from British industry's belief that markets and materials would be more easily obtained through liberalization rather than restricted mercantilist markets attendant with colonialism. That belief was premised on the assumption that British capital would benefit most from any such liberalization.[56] Provide an open playing field, and British firms will fare best. Obviously, this was a very different view than those espoused in the eighteenth century, when mercantilism ruled. Mercantilism assumed that tariffs were the best way to serve the interests of capital. But the new view of liberalization was different: It marked a new confidence.

As scholars have argued, the new view and self-confidence became dominant during Britain's period of hegemony because of that hegemony precisely. The self-confidence driving liberalization first emerged among British industrialists and traders who saw monumental success during the Napoleonic Wars. It continued to spread as more and more firms saw increasing successes and looked to fields abroad.[57] British officials and policy makers came around to the notion at the same time.[58] Together they liked liberalization because they knew Britain enjoyed comparative advantage. Dominant already in the economic field, and enjoying the most capital, machinery, and high relative productivity, British firms would out-compete anyone given a level playing field and thus reap the most rewards from an open trading economy.[59] If anything, tariffs would hurt British capital: It would encourage other nations to maintain tariffs, thereby shutting British capital out.

Anticolonialism followed partly from this view. If colonialism meant mercantilism, and if mercantilism hurt rather than helped British capital, it would be better not to bother with the expense of territorial rule. The reality at the time must have given sustenance to this view, for British trade in these years saw as much economic fruit outside of the British empire as within it. By the 1850s, exports to the British formal empire constituted only about 30 percent: The rest went to nominally independent nations, especially the United States,

---

[56] "Britain found no need to strive for preferential access in foreign markets, remaining confident that its comparative advantage in manufactured goods would ensure the success of exporters, provided only that non-discriminatory treatment of its goods abroad was assured." Irwin (1993), p. 94.

[57] See, on the immediate post-1815 period, Hilton (1977). See also the excellent overview in Cain (1999), pp. 38–9.

[58] Platt (1968a), p. 362.

[59] This is an argument made by proponents of the "hegemonic stability" thesis, among many others. See especially Gilpin (1978) and Krasner (1976). Gilpin argues that the strongest countries reap the most benefits from liberalization (see for example Gilpin [1975], p. 84).

Europe, and Latin America.[60] In 1860, only one-fifth of imports came from within the empire.[61] Although trade within the empire was still important, policy makers and businesses alike began to see that trade could flourish even without colonies. Trade needed to expand, but, as the historian Kitson Clark put it long ago, the expansion was not to occur through "force of arms, or the extension of territorial sovereignty," but rather through "the much more subtle weapon of cheapness, the cheapness of the goods produced in Great Britain, a weapon which did not need the might of empire to back it up."[62]

Britain's imperial abatement in the nineteenth century can now be apprehended. Compared to the previous period of ascent or the later period of decline, the threats to British economic power were minimal. Therefore, there was less of a need to seek privileged access to markets or materials through direct imperialism or to spend resources trying to undercut rivals. All that was needed was the open market. This is likely why the British state, by its trade agreements with other states, reduced tariffs even for its colonies: It no longer saw the need for a colonial empire covered under a mercantilist umbrella. Colonies might still be useful, not least for military bases; but they were no longer the only route to economic prosperity. Lord Macauley argued against taking over all of India in 1833 on these grounds exactly. "The mere extent of empire is not necessarily an advantage.... It would be ... far better for us that the people of India ... were ruled by their own kings, but wearing our broadcloth, and working with our cutlery, than ... performing their salaams to English collectors and English magistrates."[63] Hegemony meant comparative advantage. Comparative advantage meant a preference for markets over force and money over territory.

This notion of comparative advantage was articulated by various government offices in London when deciding against new annexations. For example, the British state repeatedly declined opportunities to take Sarawak in the 1850s and 1860s. Although some British firms near Sarawak supported annexation, arguing that it was necessary to fend off the nearby Dutch, British officials in London were not worried. Lord Carnavaron explained that the Dutch need not be feared, because "our freer system of trade might give us some advantages over the Dutch."[64] The Foreign Office concurred, adding that "the Dutch are and must remain too weak to cause us any alarm."[65] Similarly, although British trade with the Niger Delta slowly grew in importance through the 1840s to the 1860s, the British state appointed a consul to the region rather than colonize it. The reason was simply that there was no other European presence in the region, and British trade need not worry about competition.[66] Another example is Fiji.

---

[60] Cain (1999), p. 35.
[61] O'Brien (1988a), p. 167.
[62] Kitson Clark (1967), p. 78. See also Cain (1999), p. 39.
[63] Quoted in Dilke (1890), pp. vii–viii.
[64] Carnavaron, Jan. 25, 1859, FO 12/35.
[65] Wodehouse, August 18, 1860, FO 12/28.
[66] Chamberlain (1988), p. 125.

When the Colonial Office in London was offered by Fijian chiefs to annex Fiji, it turned the offer down, despite rumors that the French might take it instead. Part of the reason was fear of settler–native conflicts (as discussed in Chapter 4), but another was Britain's comparative advantage. Even if France took Fiji, France would not pose an economic threat, but rather a possible boon: Given Britain's position in the region, the French would be forced to import from British sources. "Should she [France] seize the Islands, England would have little cause of inquietude; as in forming her Establishments France would import largely from the English colonies."[67]

None of this is to say that the British state failed to initiate direct imperialism entirely. We have seen in previous chapters that the British state took colonies like Hong Kong and added territory to its domains in India. Yet these acquisitions were fewer in number relative to Britain's previous ascent phase or its later decline phase (both phases of multicentrism). They are exceptions that prove the rule. And their acquisition was not governed by the same forces that propelled expansion in multicentric periods. They were not about obtaining privileged access or undercutting rivals amidst the threat of competition. Hong Kong, Singapore, and the Falkland Islands were taken as trading ports or naval stations so that Britain could enhance existing trade or expand into new areas on which Britain had commercial rather than territorial designs (e.g., China and Latin America). As ports rather than massive territories of land, these were small acquisitions that made larger acquisitions unnecessary. Other acquisitions were governed by a settler-frontier logic. Most of the territories annexed in this time were contiguous with or adjacent to preexisting British settlements, for instance, on the coast of Africa, around India, in Canada, and/or in Australia. These were typically taken at the behest of settlers to protect the integrity of preexisting boundaries against local populations.[68] To be sure, except for areas like India, rival powers were few and far between. As Kennedy puts it, "between 1815 and 1880 much of the British Empire existed in a power-political vacuum. . . . [I]n many parts of the tropics, and for long periods of time, British interests (traders, planters, explorers, missionaries) encountered no foreigners other than the indigenous peoples."[69]

In the absence of competition from serious challengers, the principle of restraint was at work. With economic dominance in the global field and the attendant lack of competition, new territory was not necessary. If anything, colonial expansion or other forms of direct imperialism would upset the status quo from which Britain so benefited. It might incite the anger of other states, delegitimate British hegemony, and invite others to make their own bids. "We have possession," wrote Wellington in 1829, "of nearly every valuable port and colony in the world, and I confess that I am anxious to avoid exciting

---

[67] Smythe Report, 1 May, 1861, CO 83/1.

[68] Darwin (1997), p. 630; Robinson and Gallagher (1961), p. 8. For more on the frontier logic, see Galbraith (1960), McIntyre (1967).

[69] Kennedy (1987), p. 155

the attention and jealousy of other powers by extending our possessions, and setting the example of gratification of a desire to seize more territories."[70] Restraining from territorial aggrandizement was partly performative, aimed at ensuring the existing geopolitical structure and hence the British position in it. In 1857, Lord Palmerston advised against annexing Egypt on these grounds precisely. In his letter to Lord Clarendon, he admitted that "many parts of the world would be better governed by England." However, because Britain's position depended on "the maintenance of the existing balance of power," Britain should be careful not to become "unprovoked aggressors" overseas or acquire African territory: "[L]et us try to improve all those countries by the general influence of our commerce, but let us abstain from a crusade of conquest which would call down upon us the condemnation of all other civilized nations."[71] The same principle animated Secretary of State Aberdeen's position on California in 1841. Sir Thomas Pakenham, minister to Mexico, at that time conveyed an interest in setting up a British colony in California (then part of Mexico). Aberdeen replied that he was "not anxious for the formation of new and distant Colonies, all of which involve heavy direct and still heavier indirect expenditure, besides multiplying the liabilities of misunderstanding and collisions with Foreign Powers.'"[72] In short, rather than upset the system from which they and capitalists benefited, state managers preferred to keep things intact by not seizing new swaths of territory. As long as the British state was on top of the hierarchy with little threat from below, it had an interest in stability and order.

This interest meant not only restraining from territorial aggrandizement; it also meant diplomacy with other states rather than military force. Too much aggression would incite other powers and threaten to overthrow stable relations. This was the approach taken by British officials during the Congress of Vienna at the end of the Napoleonic Wars. Having emerged victorious and comparably unscathed, Britain negotiated a postwar settlement that was aimed at preventing disruptive wars and maintaining a balance of power on the European Continent. Because Britain was the most powerful economically, it stood to gain from this arrangement: If other states agreed to the settlement, direct military intervention and costly war would be unnecessary.[73] The strategy involved buying allies. Britain used subsidies and loans to states like Prussia, Austria, and Sweden – as well as arms and contributions to Spain, Portugal, and Sicily – to help win the war and render them dependent on British good will. The subsidies were known as "Pitt's gold."[74] Yet this form of making alliance was precarious, not to mention expensive. So the British state also

---

[70] Anderson (1986), p. 256.

[71] Palmerston to Clarendon, March 1, 1857, reproduced in Bourne (1970), pp. 333–4.

[72] Aberdeen to Pakenham, December 15, 1841, quoted in Adams (1909), p. 747.

[73] On this strategy and the postwar settlement see Chamberlain (1988), Schroeder (1992), Hobson (2002), pp. 312–14, and Mann (1993), pp. 282–8.

[74] Ikenberry (2001a), pp. 94–5.

strove for cultural hegemony. In the words of G. John Ikenberry, it exercised "strategic restraint" to maintain the status quo.[75] Britain strove to legitimate its dominance and maintain a balance of power on the European Continent by showing that it would use excessive force. This would limit the possibility of future rivalry and hence limit future threats to British hegemony.

Strategic restraint at the Congress of Vienna translated into performative anticolonialism. To show its moderation, Britain deliberately opted against acquiring the former Dutch colonies at the Congress. "I am sure our reputation on the Continent as a feature of our strength, power and confidence," declared Castlereagh, "is of more real value to us than any acquisition thus made."[76] British officials also stood back as various crises broke out across the European Continent, trying not to meddle directly and thereby upset the equilibrium from which Britain so clearly benefited. This "minimalist participation," notes Patrick Karl O'Brien, was meant "to avoid enmity towards the Empire and envy at Britain's huge stake in overseas trade, shipping, and investment." In fact, over the entire period, the only time when British troops again operated on the European Continent was during the Crimean War of 1854–1856. This stands as the exception; for the most part, British power was aimed at "co-opting" other states "into a system for the orderly and predictable conduct of international relations, especially commerce, that could remain efficient for the security of the empire and for the preservation of the dominant role that the British economy had attained in world trade and in servicing the global economy."[77]

Britain's imperial abatement was thus driven by its place within the overarching global field and by that field's very structure. Because Britain was hegemonic, and by the same token because the global field was unipolar with minimal competition, the British state tended toward restraint. Its comparative advantage in the economic field meant that serious competition was absent, and direct imperialism was not necessary for undercutting rivals or gaining privilege. Moreover, Britain's position in the field meant that it had an interest in maintaining the status quo, which in turn meant influencing other states through hidden and subtle exercises of power rather than bold, direct, and provocative imperialism that might mobilize opposition. We now know that it was only when Britain's share of trade was later threatened that this strategy shifted and military aggression or direct rule became more necessary. But generally for the nineteenth century, the British state followed the principle of informal rule when possible and formal rule when necessary (to paraphrase a

---

[75] Ibid., p. 90.

[76] Nicolson ([1946] 2001), p. 99; see also Ikenberry (2001a), p. 98, fn. 50.

[77] O'Brien (2002), p. 11. It is the case, as seen in a previous chapter, that the English state summoned its military might to attack China and threaten South America. But as Kitson Clark notes, in general "these occasions were only the contingent consequences of the movement caused by the ebullient power of a world-wide commerce, which normally did not need the power of empire to secure its entry." See Kitson Clark (1967), p. 78. See also for this point Fieldhouse (1973), p. 94.

famous phrase from Robinson and Gallagher). It only became more necessary during the multicentric phase of intense competition and British decline.[78]

Was America's imperial abatement during its hegemonic phase in the mid-twentieth century governed by the same logic? From a previous chapter, we have already seen that the United States did not seize colonies during its period of hegemonic maturity. Besides turning the former Japanese mandated islands into "strategic trust" territory in the immediate aftermath of the Second World War, it tempered its territorial ambition and preferred informal mechanisms of imperial power. We have also seen that part of the reason for this was the global spread of anticolonial nationalism. Anticolonial nationalism made the costs of recolonization far too high. Still, territorial annexation is not the only expression of direct imperialistic aggression. Besides annexation, the United States might have initiated temporary military occupations or military assaults such as those that proliferated later in the century during America's period of decline. So why were there fewer of those types of actions during the period of U.S. hegemonic maturity?

Part of the answer lies in the rivalry between the United States and USSR during the Cold War. Too much military aggression would anger the Soviets and spark a global confrontation that, given the development of nuclear technology, would be disastrous to everyone. The fear of provoking the Soviets was important to key policy makers of the period, such as Dean Acheson in the State Department, who preferred covert operations for precisely this reason. Covert operations, such as the clandestine activities by the CIA against Communists in Greece in 1947, were meant to fight against Soviet influence without being blatantly aggressive and confrontational.[79] Similarly, President Dwight Eisenhower was reluctant to intervene in Hungary in 1956, despite his talk of "liberating" Eastern Europe from the USSR, because of this same fear of provoking the Soviets.[80]

Yet in itself, the desire to avoid direct confrontation with the USSR does not explain abatement. The 1945 Yalta agreements with Churchill, Stalin, and Roosevelt had specified different spheres of influence: The USSR would have one-third of the globe (much of east of the Oder-Nesse Line in Europe across through China), whereas the United States and its allies would de facto control the rest. This means that the United States could have heightened its imperialistic activity in its own spheres of influence – such as its own hemisphere – with less risk of a hot war. And we know that the American state did indeed heighten its military activity in Central America despite the Cold War: In the 1980s, during America's period of economic decline, the United States invaded Panama and Grenada. So why, during America's period of hegemony were there not more Panamas and Grenadas? Why the relative decrease in imperial aggression?

[78] Robinson and Gallagher (1953).
[79] Isenberg (1989).
[80] Kovrig (1973).

As was the case with Britain in the nineteenth century, part of the answer lies in America's structural position as hegemon and, therefore, America's comparative advantage. From 1948 onward, the United States accounted for a larger proportion of international trade than any other country.[81] Of the world's fifty largest corporations in 1956, forty-two were American.[82] In 1950, no country in the world had a GNP totaling even one-third that of America's.[83] Economically dominant, the United States had fewer economic rivals than in other periods, and American firms as well as the American state fretted less about obtaining privileged access to other countries or regions than they did earlier in the century. As long as doors were kept open through treaties or subsidies, they need not have been forced open by military power.

Due to America's relative economic power after the war, this is exactly what happened. We have already seen that the United States used its economic power after the Second World War to compel the European empires to open their colonies up to American trade. Here it should also be noted that the United States used its economic might to compel Europe itself to be opened up. By conditions attached to various loans and subsidies from 1945 onward, the United States was able to make the dollar supreme and increase trade with Europe.[84] Given the power of its dollar, the American state did not have to employ direct imperialism to open up the world to its economic interests. It could buy it. This repeated what Britain had tried to do during and after the Napoleonic Wars.[85] It is the hegemon's privilege to use money so that direct imperialism would be less necessary. Pitt's gold is the hegemon's gold.

America's economic hegemony also meant that officials and policy makers in Washington had a stronger interest in maintaining rather than altering the status quo from which the United States so benefited. The global order had to be kept intact rather than transformed, if only because U.S. hegemony relied on it. This is how the Cold War fits into the story. The containment policy – first advocated by Dean Acheson to help justify the Korean War and then embedded in the famous National Security Council document 68 (NSC-68) of 1950 – was to let the USSR coexist with the United States because this was deemed the best way to ensure stability.[86] The Yalta agreement of 1945 had expressed the basic

---

[81] Webb and Krasner (1989), pp. 188–9.

[82] Bergesen and Sahoo (1985), pp. 596–7.

[83] Lundestad (1986), p. 264.

[84] The United States encouraged a regional European bloc in the interests of promoting its internal development, which in turn helped increase trade, even as the actual stipulations in the loans did not dismantle tariff barriers against the United States. See Lundestad, 1986 #2468}, pp. 268–9; Gilpin (1971), pp. 411–12; Stein (1984), pp. 377–9.

[85] Ikenberry (2001a), pp. 94–5.

[86] On Acheson and containment compared with other possible routes at the time, see Cumings (1990), II, pp. 3–78 and Messer (1977). For more on the containment strategy and global order, see the seminal works by Gaddis (1982) and Leffler (1992). Gaddis and Leffler differ in their opinions on America's global ambitions: Leffler suggests that America's Cold War containment strategy was essentially about overthrowing the Soviet Union in the end, whereas Gaddis is closer to the view that containment was more about maintaining a bipolar political order.

idea. By Yalta, the Soviets were unofficially granted jurisdiction over the areas essentially occupied by the Red Army already, and the United States was given the rest. This was simply "an agreement on the status quo," as Wallerstein puts it.[87] The agreement had the effect of global stabilization. As both the United States and USSR more or less kept their end of the bargain, overt military aggression would not be necessary for security.[88]

In short, America's hegemonic position gave the American state an interest in the existing geopolitical structure. The status quo was vital for America's own vitality. This was not just a matter of maintaining the peace; it was a matter of maintaining the existing structure of the global hierarchy so that the United States remained at the apex. If the order from which the American economy benefited was unraveled, so might America's economic hegemony. George Kennan neatly summed up the imperative in a foreign policy review by the State Department in 1948: "We have about 50% of the world's wealth but only 6.3% of its population. This disparity is particularly great as between ourselves and the peoples of Asia. In this situation, we cannot fail to be the object of envy and resentment. Our real task in the coming period is to devise a pattern of relationships which will permit us to maintain this position of disparity without positive detriment to our national security."[89]

One result of this search for stability was containment. Another was the Atlantic Charter and then, ultimately, the United Nations. The final and more important result for our purposes was strategic restraint. As for Britain after 1815, so too for the United States: Strategic restraint meant displays of moderation in order to gain the acquiescence of other states. In the case of the United States, strategic restraint was partly directed at the colonial and postcolonial world. Already we have seen that American policy makers were concerned about their prestige in the eyes of the colonial world and the newly independent countries. This concern militated against any American-led recolonization of postcolonial areas. However, the concern over maintaining prestige also prevented the United States from engaging in excessive militaristic aggression. This is why covert action was preferable to overt action: Not only would overt action anger the Soviets, it would incite third-world nationalists and put the global political equilibrium from which the United States benefited at risk.[90]

---

[87] Wallerstein (2002a), p. 62.

[88] The times when it became more necessary were when the ambiguities in the Yalta agreements became manifest, such as during the Korean crisis that led to the Korean War. But this, along with Vietnam, was the exception that proved the rule. To be sure, even those instances when the United States and USSR were unclear on their boundaries – such as the Greek civil war (1946–1949), the Hungarian crisis (1956), the question of Eastern Europe as a whole from 1945–1947 – there was no full-scale conflict. American military power was not used to resolve it. Generally, Yalta worked. See Wallerstein (2006), p. 79.

[89] "Memorandum by the Director of the Policy Planning Staff [Kennan] to the Secretary of State and Under Secretary of State [Lowell]," February 24, 1948, FRUS 1948, I., p. 524; see also Ikenberry (2001a), p. 169.

[90] Rudgers (2000).

The concern over prestige and global stability also explains why the Eisenhower administration was so incensed over the French, British, and Israeli invasion of the Suez Canal in 1956. This is an instance where U.S. interests were threatened and direct imperial aggression could have been used – but was not. The reason why it was not cuts to the heart of our story.

Successive American administrations had not been happy with Egyptian President Gamal Nasser. His decision to nationalize the Suez Canal was a direct challenge to America's influence in the region. But Eisenhower did not command U.S. forces to join the French-British-Israeli invasion. To the contrary, he pulled the invasion back, precisely because he worried about America's loss of prestige and hence, potentially, disequilibrium in the global order. Eisenhower had said in early October of 1956 that direct military action to oust Nasser "could not be taken where there is as much hostility as at present. For a thing like this to be done without inflaming the Arab world, a time free from heated stress holding the world's attention as at present would have to be chosen."[91] Ambassador Jefferson Caffrey had prefigured Eisenhower's views. If Arab nationalists were aroused, he had warned, the Suez would "explode with a loud bang at no distant date, an explosion with a potential chain reaction of occupation, revolution, eventual Commie domination."[92] It is not surprising that, in the wake of the curtailed invasion, the United States chose to handle Nasser through covert operations.[93] Hidden imperialism was preferable to direct imperialism, lest the world mobilize its anger against the American-dominated global order.

Even before the onset of the Cold War and the containment policy, and before the 1956 Suez fiasco, the postwar American state was concerned about displaying restraint in order to maintain the status quo. Here restraint was aimed not at the colonial or postcolonial world, but at its allies. We have seen that British officials from Wellington to Palmerston often militated against new colonial acquisitions on the grounds that it would incite envy or resentment from other states, unwittingly encourage them to also seek colonies, and ultimately threaten the balance of power. The American state did the same in the wake of World War II. When the Truman administration pondered seizing the former Japanese Pacific territories unilaterally after the war, it hesitated because of this very concern. Unilateral seizure would make the United States appear too greedy and set off, as Wm. Roger Louis puts it, "a new scramble for territory."[94] The State Department similarly worried that unilateral seizure of

---

[91] Quoted in Fraser 1992, p.118.
[92] Cairo to State Dept, 30 Nov 1951, FRUS 1951, V, p. 428; see also Lucas (2000), pp. 145–6.
[93] Lucas (2000), p. 152. Louis (1985), p. 414. The subsequent invasion by British and French forces invoked the Eisenhower administration's ire not only because the Americans had not been consulted, but also because the administration feared how the invasion would look to the rest of the world. Dulles hit the nail on the head: The invasion was "nothing but the straight old-fashioned variety of colonialism of the most obvious sort," and this the United States could not abide (ibid., p. 414).
[94] Louis (1978), p. 85.

the islands would invite Britain to reinitiate colonialism in the Middle East and threaten stability there.[95] Acquiring colonies would also undermine America's "moral prestige and political leadership" – as one State Department official put it – and run against "our general security policy."[96] Of course, later, as anticolonial nationalism and the Cold War extended its grip over the world, the United States would also restrain from colonial acquisitions lest third-world nationalists retaliate with ire. But in this immediate postwar period, one of the main worries was that territorial aggrandizement would set off other grabs for power and initiate a chain of destabilizing events, thereby threatening the geopolitical hierarchy upon which American hegemony rested.

Much more could be said about America's period of imperial abatement, but the similarities with the British state in the nineteenth century should be clear by now. As both the American and British states were economically dominant, both were intent on maintaining the status quo. This involved a policy of strategic restraint and therefore an aversion to direct imperialism. Rather than delegitimate their hegemony or upset the existing structure by blatant land grabbing or hasty military assaults, the two hegemonic states tried to cultivate imperial power by more indirect and hidden means.

Finally, understanding this process helps us apprehend the trends in imperial discourse. For both states, self-identification as "empire" was minimized during the hegemony period. This can be seen as part of an attempt to legitimate their global dominance and prevent inciting others. The historian A. P. Thornton's classic study of mid-Victorian British self-conception is telling. "In the view of all Englishmen of substance [in the 1840s and 1850s], whose own idols were progress, Free Trade, and the *pax Britannica*, 'Empire' was a foreign joss, whose worshippers, where they were not simply benighted, were assumed to be the sinister agents of the forces of wrong. Secure in that mid-Victorian power which was based jointly on the buoyancy of her economy and her navy, Great Britain had no need to pursue politics of national self-aggrandisement. Having no need, she had accordingly had no business to seek to do so."[97] This might apply equally well to American denials of empire in the mid-twentieth century.

---

[95] See FRUS 1945, I, pp. 140–1, 198–9; see also Friedman (1995), p. 353.
[96] Brynes quoted in Foltos (1989), p. 330.
[97] Thornton (1959), p. 1.

7

Conclusion

> To an outsider, the fact that America is an empire is the most obvious fact of all.
> – Henry Fairlie (1965)[1]

> The so-called American Empire is in fact a feeble imitation of the Roman, British, and French empires.
> – Arthur Schlesinger, Jr. (2005)[2]

It has become more common to think of the United States as an empire. Although some "empire deniers" persist, they face an increasingly loud chorus of post-revisionist scholars, pundits, and even officials who are willing to entertain the idea that the United States is and always has been imperial.[3] This book joins that chorus, but it has also sought to push further, dig a little deeper, and look more widely. Rather than seeking a warrant to call the United States an empire, this book has put America's imperial formation in comparative light. It has examined differences and similarities between America's imperial practices, forms, and dynamics on the one hand and Britain's imperialism on the other. The United States is and has been an empire; this book has examined its differences and similarities with its predecessor.

To be clear, this book has not been about world powers or "great powers." Empire is not the same thing as a great power. Nor has this book been concerned with every aspect of the two empires or every actor or group involved in the two empires. Such an analysis would hardly be possible in a single volume. Instead, in our search for similarities and differences, we have focused on the imperial policies, modalities, and forms exercised by the imperial state (rather than private corporations or transnational institutions). Furthermore,

---

[1] Fairlie (1965)
[2] Schlesinger (2005), p. 46.
[3] I take the term "empire deniers" from Tomes (2009), p. 538. Historian Charles Maier notes that "empire has displaced civil society as the fashionable political concept for the new decade." Maier (2006), p. 8.

we have covered only those imperial issues summoned by existing exceptionalist claims. Exceptionalism implies that the U.S. colonial empire has been more liberal, benign, and tutelary than other empires. Accordingly, Chapter 2 has tried to assess this claim by examining U.S. colonialisms in Puerto Rico and the Philippines, comparing them with other colonies in the U.S. empire, and comparing them all with Britain's. Similarly, exceptionalist thought suggests that America's nonterritorial imperialism in the twentieth century reflects America's domestic political values. Therefore, Chapters 3 and 4 explored the United States' and Britain's informal imperialism and the forces shaping them. In brief, the focus of this book has been on the exceptionalist themes implicitly and explicitly raised in existing discussions about American empire. The overarching goal of this book has been to assess these exceptionalist themes; to see how far exceptionalism gets us and perhaps look beyond.

The comparative method of the book has been precisely motivated. Rather than arbitrarily comparing the two empires or picking from the archive whatever suits our argument, the exploration has used economic historical phases as a guiding light. We have compared the policies, practices, and forms of the two empires by looking at them at comparable stages in the larger cycle of hegemony: ascent, hegemonic maturity, and decline. This has given some amount of control to an otherwise slippery comparison, enabling us to make sure that our comparative claims about the empires are not spurious. The method carries limitations of course. By using relative economic status in the world system as the guide, the analysis runs the risk of overlooking other important dimensions of the two empires. But the bet is that this comparative method offers greater analytic purchase than otherwise. At the very least, it enables us to better assess existing assertions of American exceptionalism that have not attempted to validate their claims through controlled comparisons.

What, then, does the book tell us of the exceptionalism thesis for understanding American power abroad? The conclusion here is unequivocal. Exceptionalism obscures more than it enlightens. It masks complex histories of imperial power exercised by both the U.S. and British empires. It overlooks important similarities between the two empires and blinds us to localized and sometimes global logics that shape imperial policies, practices, and processes. As both a set of claims about what happened and as explanatory framework, exceptionalism should be put to rest.

As a set of claims, exceptionalist thought has long posited a fundamental break between American and British history: The United States cast off English tyrannical monarchism and set a course for a new anti-imperial, liberal democratic future. Yet we have seen that the United States did not so much break with its English imperial past as it did pick up the mantle. It did so, first, as the original thirteen colonies expanded westward, adopting some of the same imperial tactics and techniques that the British had handed down. It did so again in the late nineteenth century, as it expanded overseas to rule colonies such as Puerto Rico, the Philippines, Guam, and Samoa, sometimes deploying modalities of colonial rule not unlike those of their British peers and, in some cases, modeled directly on them. And it did so again after the Second World War. The American state first outsourced imperial functions to the British state. Then, once the British imperial formation began to fissure under the pressure of global anticolonial movements, the American state took over in the spaces the British empire (and European empires) left behind. To do so, the American state mobilized the very same tactics of informal empire that the British state had deployed in places like Africa and Latin America a century earlier. The United States did not denounce the imperial legacy it inherited; rather, it repeatedly deployed its forms.

We have also seen that the two empires developed similarly over time. Both began as settler empires expanding into contiguous areas. Both then moved farther and farther away from the metropolitan center, constructing administrative colonial empires that ruled a diversity of peoples. As the British empire expanded to Asia and Africa after 1815, it crafted colonial states employing multiple modalities of rule, ranging from assimilation projects to paternalistic protection to sheer repression. Likewise, as America's frontier expansion led to overseas expansion into the Caribbean and the Pacific, the United States crafted colonial regimes exhibiting similar variations in colonial governmentality. Finally, over the longer *dureé*, the American empire reiterated the waves of aggression initiated by its British predecessor. Following the same pattern of extension, abatement, and reassertion, the American empire summoned the tactics of the British empire while also replaying its historical dynamics – and perhaps, too, its foibles and follies. *Plus ça change, plus c'est la meme chose.*

Exceptionalism runs the risk of overlooking these similarities by claiming an essential difference between the American and British empires. It also occludes its own banality. Some historians have insisted that because the United States has produced so much exceptionalist anti-imperial scholarship, it must be intrinsically anti-imperial.[4] Yet this misses the fact that exceptionalist discourse itself is not unique: Britons in the nineteenth century likewise exhibited ambivalence about their empire, if they did not deny its existence entirely. When they did admit of empire, they saw it as uniquely benign and liberal – a distinct empire for liberty (as seen in Chapter 1). Even the historical swings and shifts in exceptionalist discourse are not unique to the American scene. During both states' hegemonic phases, imperial self-identification was much weaker than during the later period associated with the two states' new imperialisms or the earlier period of ascent. Exceptionalist thought in the two empires' hegemonic phases thus extended the imperial states' own historically specific global strategy. Just as the United States during its hegemonic mode preferred informal empire to formal rule and sought to legitimize itself to the world as a benign power, so too did exceptionalism's proponents portray the United States as an anti-imperial force. And just as the British empire in the mid-nineteenth century portrayed itself as a non-empire rooted in free trade rather than mercantilism, so too did many Britons hesitate to recognize the British empire as

4 Suri (2009), p. 531.

an empire proper. Such shifts and cross-imperial comparisons invite us to historicize exceptionalism as a mode of thought. Rather than illuminating truths, exceptionalist thought (whether in its American or British variant) more likely reflects the empire's own shifting self-consciousness – not to mention its strategic public image. According to Karl Marx, bourgeois economics is bourgeois society's understanding of itself. It may be that, likewise, exceptionalist thought is empire's preferred self-apprehension.

None of this is to deny differences between the American and British imperial formations. Some scholars have already probed some differences in the two states' economic hegemonies and military capacities. Renowned historian Paul Kennedy remains amazed that the United States in 2000 accounted for close to 36 percent of world defense spending, far exceeding anything Britain might have mobilized during its heyday. "Nothing has ever existed like this disparity of power; nothing."[5] Still, the concern here is of the two states' imperial policies and practices, not their standing as great powers; and on this count there are differences too. America's approach to some of its colonies, for example, had a much more palpable and consistent tutelary character than Britain's. In Puerto Rico and the Philippines, the United States provided colonial institutions like elections and native offices much more swiftly than in Britain's colonies. Furthermore, after the Second World War and the subsequent acquisition of the former Japanese-mandated territories (current-day Micronesia), the United States did not seize any more colonies. Whereas Britain annexed new territory in the nineteenth century, the United States a century later resorted primarily to military occupations and informal tactics of imperial influence. Compared to Britain's, America's imperial formation since the mid-twentieth century has been much less territorially bound.

These differences cannot be overlooked. Exceptionalist thought surely does not overlook them. It seizes on them to validate its assertions. But let us remember: Difference is not the same thing as exceptionalism. Exceptionalism not only asserts difference; it sees the difference as unrivaled uniqueness – that is, everything else is the same and the United States deviates from that sameness. Furthermore, exceptionalism treats difference as essential, a matter of fundamental quality, not quantity, and explains difference between entities by reference to that essence. In this view, the United States deviates from the sameness – from the general rule – because of its unique national character and institutions.

The differences between the U.S. and British empires that we have found in this book are not of this sort. First, America's liberal governmentality in Puerto Rico and the Philippines was not reflective of an American essence: It was itself an exception in light of America's colonial policies in Guam and Samoa. Second, even America's approach to Puerto Rico and the Philippines was not entirely unrivaled; in comparative perspective, it appears as little else than a more extended form of Britain's preexisting approach to India – a

[5] Kennedy (2002).

matter of degree rather than fundamental kind. In addition, the reason for the tutelage approach in the Philippines and Puerto Rico had less to do with America's inherent character of culture than with preexisting local conditions in the two colonies conjoined with the colonial state's legitimacy imperative. Liberal policies in the colonies reflected the advanced political culture of the local colonial elite rather than the political culture of the United States.

The same goes for the other difference we have found. The American empire's reliance on informal modalities of power after World War II rather than formal colonialism was not determined by America's intrinsic qualities but rather by the qualities of the global field in which it operated. This is probably why the United States is not an exception even on this score: Few if any major states in the entire world have annexed territory in the mid- to late twentieth century.[6] Yet according to exceptionalism's logic, the United States should be the only nonterritorial imperialist. And according to exceptionalism's logic, China's current unwillingness to colonize Africa and its preference for informal methods of imperialism on that continent must mean that it is intrinsically anticolonial, that China's "national character" or "culture" militates against imperialism. It is hard to accept that claim.

Here we arrive at the other aspect of exceptionalism that this book challenges. Exceptionalism falters not only in its descriptive claims about what happened, but also in its explanations. According to exceptionalist thought, what the United States does is determined by what ostensibly it *is*: a benign liberal democracy with a deep anti-imperial tradition. The reason why the United States acts the way it does in the world is because of its so-called national style, its deep values, its constitution, or its culture. Presumably, colonial modes of rule or imperial policies are determined by America's national character, its cultural forms, or the dispositions of imperial personnel.[7] Here, however, the underlying problem with exceptionalism's explanatory regime is starkly disclosed: "methodological nationalism." Exceptionalism explains what the United States does in the world by isolating its "culture," "character," or "institutions" from wider relations, thus explaining outcomes by reference to internal factors alone.[8]

On this count, exceptionalism's mode of explanation bears similarities to traditional "metropolitan-centered" explanations of imperial expansion. Metropolitan-centered explanations explain what empires do in terms of what imperialists do and who they are. They explain colonial policies or imperial projects by reference to events, actors, institutions, or characters in the

---

[6] See data on rates of colonization in the world system in Bergesen and Schoenberg (1980).

[7] This mode of thought thus bears similarity to other arguments regarding "national character," such as the argument first articulated by David Hume who observed that European colonial practices in the Americas reflected each European nation's individual style and culture. Hume said: "the same set of manners will follow a nation, and adhere to them over the whole globe, as well as the same laws and languages. The Spanish, English, French and Dutch colonies are all distinguishable even between the tropics," quoted in Elliot (2006), p. xiv.

[8] On "methodological nationalism," see Wimmer and Schiller (2002) and Chernilo (2006).

imperial nation. They account for imperial dynamics by reference to imperial policy makers; they explain imperial exploitation by reference to metropolitan capitalists' tendencies; they reduce acts of imperial benevolence or liberality to imperial rulers' character or the imperial states' political institutions. They even explain imperial success or failure by reference to imperialists' sole agency. The pro-empire neo-revisionist commentator Niall Ferguson urges Americans to own up to America's imperial tendencies but only so that it might be a better empire. The implicit assumption is that American empire would be successful if only Americans had the proper will and commitment; as if empire succeeds or fails based on the imperialists themselves.[9]

Historians Robinson and Gallagher long ago mounted an assault against such metropolitan-centered thinking. To understand why Britain expanded in the late nineteenth century, they urged, we have to look beyond forces at home and instead attend to dynamics in the periphery where colonization was actually taking place. As opposed to a metrocentric explanation, they proposed an "excentric" one.[10] This was meant for investigating the causes of Britain's new imperialism in the late nineteenth century, but its general principle can be applied to more than just imperial expansion. It can be enlisted to transcend exceptionalism's explanations of imperial forms and practices – as well as its portrayal of empire more broadly.

In explaining what the United States does by reference to a presumably unique American "national character," exceptionalism portrays empires as entities with special characteristics or styles rooted in the imperial nations' values, institutions, and traditions. It thus paints empires as monolithic states whose policies and practices are determined by those essential characteristics. Empires are shaped from within. The evidence marshaled in this book offers a different approach entirely. First, rather than seeing empires as monolithic essences, it seems them as *imperial formations* with potentially conflicting tendencies, tactics and techniques, and multiple modalities of power that do not always add up to a coherent style or singular character. Across the empire at any given point in time, a variety of policies and practices are mobilized; over time they are substituted, replaced, transferred, or modified, and the imperial formation as a whole undergoes shifts, transformations, extensions, and contractions. In both America's colonial empire and Britain's colonial empire, there were a variety of colonial regimes and governmentalities, ranging from paternalistic protection to tutelary assimilation; both imperial states deployed informal mechanisms of influence in other parts of the world; and both states later substituted some direct methods for indirect ones while undergoing various historical waves of aggression in the longer run. One is hard pressed to find homogeneity or national essences here.

Second, rather than seeing empires as shaped only from within, the analysis in this book sees empires as *located in wider global fields of conflict and*

---

[9] Ferguson (2004).
[10] Robinson (1972), Robinson (1986).

competition as they reach across, through, and down to more localized settings of power relations. Embedded in and moving about these fields and power relations, empires are in turn shaped by them. They project their power on a global scale, but adapt their techniques and forms to better suit the global fields they seek to dominate. They rule natives but sometimes also "go native," adapting themselves to local conditions and to the spaces and places they seek to rule – if only to better rule them.[11] And they sometimes shift, redirect, or modify their imperial policies and practices depending on the character of the local fields in which they operate and the place they occupy within those fields. Imperial formations change over time, and their changes depend in part on the dynamics of the wider arena and the imperial states' position in it. To be sure, as seen in Chapter 6, during both their periods of hegemony, the U.S. and British empires preferred "informal" imperialism and adopted seemingly "anti-imperial" promarket stances resulting from their hegemonic status. Here, the two empires did what they did partly because of the wider relations in which they were embedded and, even more importantly, their dominant place within those relations. Sitting at the apex of the global system, they had an interest in abating their aggression and shifting toward informal tactics. The structural position of the empire at the time – not its internal character or culture, its institutions or traditions – helps explain the empires' activities.

In sum, as opposed to methodological nationalism and metropolitan-centered theories, the approach to empire culled from this book emphasizes various scales of determination beyond the imperial nation itself. Exceptionalism's analysis of national essences must be replaced with an analysis of local and global relations.[12]

The point is not to discard metropolitan determinants entirely. Colonial agents overseas will carry some influences with them as they craft policies and strategize on the ground. In the imperial state itself there are a variety of actors, from presidents and prime ministers to parliamentarians and congressmen, judges and jurists – all of whom reside within the metropole, and so will be influenced to some degree by what happens there (including, in some cases, domestic public opinion). Ultimately, imperial policies have to be forged by actors in the metropole.[13] But this book has tried to show that sometimes metropolitan factors in themselves are not determinant; that nonmetropolitan factors must also be taken into account. It has tried to show that sometimes non-metropolitan factors can matter more than domestic forces, if only to influence

---

[11] This might apply not only to the U.S. or British empire, but probably also to other empires as well, from the French to the Ottoman to the Russian. See especially for the Ottoman empire Barkey (2008); for the Russian empire, see Lieven (2002). For an impressive macro comparative view, see Cooper and Burbank (2010).

[12] In social science parlance, the epistemology of exceptionalist thought exemplifies "essentialism," whereas the approach in this book adopts "relationalism." On essentialism versus relationalism in sociology, see Emirbayer (1997).

[13] For an examination of domestic factors shaping foreign policy that does not fall prey to exceptionalist thought, see Zelizer (2010).

exactly what policies and imperial programs actors in the metropole formulate and enact.

The point, then, is not to hastily discount the possibility that metropolitan forces matter. It is to challenge the exceptionalist assumption that those factors amount to a singular essence or character. Rather than a singular political culture or set of monolithic political beliefs and values, it is more likely that the United States, as with Britain before, has had tendencies within it of *both* imperialism and anti-imperialism, of benign posturing and ruthless exploitation, of liberal governmentality and more illiberal tyranny – as well as shades in between. Why one tendency becomes more dominant rather than another, why empires formulate one policy or deploy one modality and not the other – such things are likely the result of a host of factors, rather than just factors within the metropole. In the story told in previous chapters, we have seen some of those factors (not least the particular structure of the field in which the empires happened to be operating and the empires' place in the overarching global structure).

The related point, finally, is not to entirely discount metropolitan determinants, but instead overturn the still-dominant exceptionalist assumption that everything that happens flows outward from the metropole, as if power were only a one-way street, as if empires can be analytically extracted from the spaces they inhabit or the peoples they dominate. Empires might wish for these things. But global structures can overwhelm and alter imperial designs; the agency of subject peoples can thwart, reshape, and transform them too. Our theories should capture this banality of power; they should reflect the messy realities of power's applications.[14] Exceptionalist histories realize in theory what empires wish for in practice. Our theories can and should do better.

Still, if this book offers a critique of exceptionalism and an alternative analytic approach to empire, why bother? Is such a critique of exceptionalism still worth making? The proliferation of empire talk might suggest that exceptionalism as a mode of thought has already reached its limits, that exceptionalism at best is a specter that haunts lesser minds only. Yet the stubborn persistence of exceptionalist themes in some sectors of scholarship suggests otherwise. Even as an increasing number of scholars treat American empire as worthy of examination, skeptics remain.[15] Besides, admitting the existence of American empire does not in itself overthrow exceptionalism as an analytic framework. The notion of an exceptional American empire endures, as does the explanatory regime that lends primacy to metropolitan factors. Exceptionalism remains a deep and powerful mode of thought in scholarly investigation: Even some critics of exceptionalism (and, for that matter, critics of American imperialism) do not always challenge its foundations. For example, some criticisms claim that

[14] On the "banality of power" in the African postcolonial context, see Mbembe (1992).
[15] See, for instance, the refusal to see the United States as an "empire" in Suri (2009); others refuse to stake a claim either way (e.g., Maier [2006]). For a recent reinscription of exceptionalism for understanding U.S. development, see Rauchway (2006).

American imperialism has *not* been benign and virtuous, if only because it was not benign and virtuous in the first place (rather exploitative, racist, and violent), or because true American "ideals" and "character" have been corrupted by imperialism.[16] As the diametric opposite of exceptionalist thought, these criticisms risk carrying its problematic assumption that empires first and foremost express the national character of the metropole or the will of its people. Agency is reserved for the imperialists.

Exceptionalism remains powerful outside scholarship too. Everyday language is filled with talk of an "American way." Perhaps by the same token, exceptionalist themes continue to shape foreign policy. Donald Kagan (Yale historian and formerly of the influential policy group called "Project for the New American Century") insists that "all comparisons between America's current place in the world and anything legitimately called an empire in the past reveal ignorance and confusion about any reasonable meaning of the concept empire."[17] Furthermore, recent U.S. presidents from Reagan to Bush the Elder to Bush the Younger have shown themselves to be believers in American exceptionalism, and their beliefs have probably provided some of the ideological arsenal for American military interventions. At the very least, exceptionalism has underpinned American hubris.[18] "America is a Nation with a mission," declared George W. Bush in his Inaugural Address of 2004, still amidst the second Iraq War, "and that mission comes from our most basic beliefs. We have no desire to dominate, no ambitions of empire." →NO! expanded in M.E. ~~bombing~~

Pundits have wondered whether President Barack Obama is a "post-imperial" president.[19] But we might also wonder: Is he a post-exceptionalist president too? Consider his major speech on foreign affairs, titled "A New Beginning," given in 2009. On the one hand, President Obama reiterates exceptionalist denials of empire: "America is not the crude stereotype of a self-interested empire. The United States has been one of the greatest sources of progress that the world has ever known. We were born out of revolution against an empire. We were founded upon the ideal that all are created equal, and we have shed blood and struggled for centuries to give meaning to those words – within our borders, and around the world." On the other hand, elsewhere in the speech, the president admits to America's role in the overthrow of Iranian

---

[16] William Appleman Williams argues that American foreign policy has been guided by "three ideals": (1) a "humanitarian impulse," (2) "the principle of self-determination," and (3) the idea that foreign societies should "improve their lives." The "tragedy," however, is that American foreign policy has failed to live up to these ideals in practice: "America's humanitarian urge to assist other peoples is undercut – even subverted – by the way it goes about helping them." Williams (1972), pp. 13, 15.

[17] Kagan (2002)

[18] President George W. Bush's speech in 2004 to the Philippine Congress justifying the Iraq War and continued U.S. military support of Manila's campaign against Islamic separatists in the southern Philippines is but one example. On exceptionalism's influence on American human rights policy, see Ignatieff (1995).

[19] Zakaria (2009).

president Mohammed Mosaddiq in 1953. "For many years, Iran has defined itself in part by its opposition to my country, and there is indeed a tumultuous history between us. In the middle of the Cold War, the United States played a role in the overthrow of a democratically elected Iranian government."[20] Here Obama figures as a revisionist exceptionalist, or perhaps even a liberal exceptionalist. By referring to the overthrow in 1953, he admits America's imperial tendencies. Yet he also insists on America's potential for a benevolent imperialism based on America's national character and founding ideals.

President Obama's liberal exceptionalism is strikingly resonant with the exceptionalist discourse seen throughout this book. Also resonant is the fact that his speech was given in Cairo, Egypt. This was where, in 1882, some 20,000 British troops also stood, having mounted an assault on the Suez Canal and seized Cairo. British troops would occupy the country for another seventy-two years. President Obama's speech did not refer to that. Nor did it refer to the fact that Obama would soon call for additional troops to be deployed in Afghanistan where British troops had also been, multiple times. In 1878, for example, just four years before the invasion of Egypt, British commanders led close to 40,000 forces into Afghanistan from three different points, beginning an attack that led to an occupation, an apparent peace, and then an unexpected anti-British uprising that left the British envoy killed. This summoned the return of British forces soon after. Although the British did not remain too long, they did return again to Afghanistan after September 11, 2001, alongside American troops. The world's past and present hegemonic empires have not only been similar, they continue to be conjoined.

But for how long? Britain's imperial determination has already abated. In December 2010, a year after President Obama gave his speech in Cairo, the new British prime minister, David Cameron, vowed not to deploy any more British troops in Afghanistan, thus declaring Britain's imminent withdrawal.[21] Conversely, America's imperial activities persist. As 2010 approached, President Obama vowed to increase the number of American soldiers in Afghanistan. He called upon 21,000 more to join the fight. He also called for enhanced operations in neighboring areas in Pakistan. His justification should be eerily familiar: "[W]e will use all elements of our national power to defeat al Qaeda, and to defend America, our allies, and all who seek a better future. Because the United States of America stands for peace and security, justice and opportunity. That is who we are, and that is what history calls on us to do once more."[22] This marks a persistent if not stubborn empire. It also marks an enduring exceptionalism upon which the sun has not yet set.

[20] The White House Web site names it "A New Beginning." See www.whitehouse.gov/blog/NewBeginning (accessed June 30, 2010).

[21] "David Cameron Signals Afghan Withdrawal," *The Guardian*, December 7, 2010 (http://www.guardian.co.uk/world/2010/dec/07/david-cameron-afghanistan; accessed February 18, 2011).

[22] "Remarks by the President on a New Strategy for Afghanistan and Pakistan," White House Press Release, March 27, 2009, (http://m.whitehouse.gov/the_press_office/Remarks-by-the-President-on-a-New-Strategy-for-Afghanistan-and-Pakistan; accessed February 1, 2011).

This is frightening. If the story in this book tells us something, it is that empires that insist on their exceptionality do not behave well. And self-fashioned exceptional empires that are falling behave worse still. In this sense, our affair in Iraq and Afghanistan may just be a portent. Something more is coming.

Appendix

Notes on Data

Time-series data on British annexations come from the compendium by Stewart (1996). This lists every territory annexed by Britain since 1493 with the initial date of annexation. It also provides brief historical information on each territory. This data is more robust than the data from Henige (1970) that has been typically used in world-system analyses of colonization. Henige lists colonial governors appointed by all states. Scholars have used the data as a rough measure of the year when a new colony was annexed, corresponding with the year when the first colonial governor was appointed. The shortcoming is that the data does not differentiate between territories that are newly acquired and territories that are renamed or reorganized. Alternatively, Stewart's book enables us to ascertain the year when Britain first annexed a territory and thus treat it as a single event. Stewart's book provides the name of each territory and year of founding while providing a brief historical overview. The overview enables the analyst to ascertain whether the territory had been previously colonized by Britain or not. If it had been, it would not be counted in the data as a new colonial annexation. Conversely, Henige's data would include when a colony that has already been taken is simply reorganized or renamed.

Data on British military interventions are compiled from the following sources: (Clowes 1903), (Farmer 1984[1901]), (Harris 1944), (Kohler 1975), and Public Record Office files (ADM 171-1, "Naval General Service Medal 1793–1840"; ADM 171/202: "Naval Medals and Clasps Awarded from 1818 to 1914"). Information from these sources is necessary for supplementing information in traditional war databases such as the Correlates of War data in Singer (1987), which only lists large-scale interstate wars. Because of data limitations, the data begins in 1800 only. "Military intervention" includes small wars, big wars, and troop or naval deployments. Small operations involving slave raiding or infrastructural building are not included. The data is coded to specify the year the intervention began. Each intervention is treated as a single event, so repeated deployments of troops for the same engagement are not added; only the initiation of the event is entered.

For the United States, data on colonial annexations are compiled from Goertz and Diehl (1992), Henige (1970), and Tir et al. (1998). Data on U.S. military interventions come from Collier (1993) and Grimmett (2004). These are lists complied by the State Department and Foreign Affairs and National Defense Division of the Library of Congress. They cover "instances of the use of United States forces abroad" covering, together, the years 1798 to 2004. The list represents "a judgment as to which US armed interventions overseas represented major military actions" and provides, for each action, a date and a very brief description [see (United States Congress Committee on Foreign Affairs 1970), p. 15]. The actions include official and undeclared wars, naval operations and uses of air force, troop deployments and land invasions, and provision of direct military support to other nations. It excludes the operations of the U.S. military in the western frontier. To cover the years prior to 1798, I used various secondary sources. Number of covert operations/subverted elections comes from data in "Basic Statistics for United States Imperialism" at http://www.whatreallyhappened.com/usinterventionism.html (accessed July 18, 2007).

Archives and Abbreviations

BL British Library

BM Bernard Moses Papers, Bancroft Library, University of California at Berkeley

CC Cross Collection: correspondence of Richard Assheton Cross, 1st Viscount Cross as Secretary of State for India, BL

CE Clarence R. Edwards Papers, Massachusetts Historical Society

CO Colonial Office Records, PRO

CP Clarendon Papers, Bodleian Library, Oxford

ERP The Papers of Elihu Root. Library of Congress, Manuscript Division. Washington, DC

FO Foreign Office Records, PRO

FRUS Foreign Relations of the United States, U.S. Department of State, Washington, DC: Government Printing Office

GPR Governor of Puerto Rico

HP Hopkins Papers, Franklin D. Roosevelt Library

MP The Papers of William McKinley. Library of Congress

PP Parliamentary Papers

PRO Public Record Office, UK (Kew)

RP Ripon Papers, "Correspondence on Afghanistan and India: Correspondence with Persons in England," Rare Books & Music Room, BL

USCG United States Consulate General. Hong Kong. USNA

USNA United States National Archives

USWD United States War Department

WP Worcester Philippine Collection, Rare Books and Special Collections, Hatcher Library, University of Michigan, Ann Arbor

References

Abernathy, David B. 2000. *The Dynamics of Global Dominance: European Overseas Empires, 1415–1980*. New Haven, CT: Yale University Press.

Adams, Brooks. 1947 [1900]. *America's Economic Supremacy*. New York and London: Harper & Brothers Publishers.

Adams, Ephraim. 1909. "English Interest in the Annexation of California." *The American Historical Review* 14(4):744–63.

Alexander, Holmes. 1951. "Based on Friendship . . . the American Empire." *Nation's Business* 39:27–9, 70–3.

Ambler, Charles H. 1943. "The Oregon Country, 1810–1830: A Chapter in Territorial Expansion." *The Mississippi Valley Historical Review* 30(1):3–24.

American Samoan Commission. 1931. *The American Samoan Commission Report*. Washington, DC: Government Printing Office.

Anderson, M. S. 1986. *The Ascendancy of Europe, 1815–1914*. New York: Longman.

Anonymous. 1886. *The Strength and Weakness of the British Empire: Dedicated to the Working Men of England*. London: Wyman & Sons.

Armitage, David. 2000. *The Ideological Origins of the British Empire*. Cambridge: Cambridge University Press.

Arrighi, Giovanni. 1994. *The Long Twentieth Century*. London: Verso.

Arrighi, Giovanni. 2002. "The African Crisis: World Systemic and Regional Aspects." *New Left Review* 15(May–June):5–36.

Arrighi, Giovanni, Beverly J. Silver, and Iftikhar Ahmad. 1999. *Chaos and Governance in the Modern World System*. Minneapolis: University of Minnesota Press.

Babb, Sarah. 2009. *The Banks and the Beltway: Three Decades of Washington Politics and World Development*. Chicago: University of Chicago Press.

Bacevich, A. J. 2002. *American Empire: The Realities and Consequences of U.S. Diplomacy*. Cambridge, MA: Harvard University Press.

Bailey, Thomas A. 1939. "Dewey and the Germans at Manila Bay." *American Historical Review* 45(1):59–81.

Bailyn, Bernard. 1965. *The Origins of American Politics*. New York: Alfred A. Knopf.

Bairoch, Paul. 1982. "International Industrialization Levels from 1750 to 1980." *Journal of European Economic History* 11(2):2.

Ball, Durwood. 2002. "By Right of Conquest: Military Government in New Mexico and California, 1846–1851." *Journal of the West* 41(3):8–18.

Balogh, Brian. 2009. *A Government out of Sight*. Cambridge: Cambridge University Press.

Bankoff, Greg. 2002. "Response: A Tale of Two Wars." *Foreign Affairs* 81(6):179–81.

Banks, Wiliam C., and Jeffrey D. Straussman. 1999. "A New Imperial Presidency? Insights from U.S. Involvement in Bosnia." *Political Science Quarterly* 114(2):195–217.

Barkey, Karen. 2008. *Empire of Difference: The Ottomans in Comparative Perspective*. Cambridge: Cambridge University Press.

Battle, Joyce (Ed.). 2003. *Shaking Hands with Saddam Hussein: The US Tilts toward Iraq, 1980–1984*. Washington National Security Archive Electronic Briefing Book No. 82. Washington, DC: National Security Archive.

Baugh, Daniel A. 1994. "Maritime Strength and Atlantic Commerce." Pp. 185–223 in *An Imperial State at War. Britain from 1689 to 1815*, edited by Lawrence Stone. London and New York: Routledge.

Bayly, C. A. 1998. "The First Age of Global Imperialism, c. 1760–1830." *Journal of Imperial and Commonwealth History* 26(2):28–47.

Beeler, John F. 1997. *British Naval Policy in the Gladstone-Disraeli Era, 1866–1890*. Palo Alto, CA: Stanford University Press.

Beers, Henry P. 1944. *Administrative Reference Service Report No. 6. American Naval Occupation and Government of Guam, 1898–1902*. Washington, DC: Office of Records Administration, Administrative Office, Navy Department.

Bell, Philip W. 1952. "Colonialism as a Problem in American Foreign Policy." *World Politics* 5(1):86–109.

Bellamy Foster, John. 2006. "The New Geopolitics of Empire." *Monthly Review* 57(8):1–18.

Bender, Thomas. 2006a. "The American Way of Empire." *World Policy Journal* XXIII(1):45–61.

Bender, Thomas. 2006b. *A Nation among Nations: America's Place in World History*. New York: Hill and Wang.

Berbusse, Edward. 1966. *The United States in Puerto Rico, 1898–1900*. Chapel Hill: University of North Carolina Press.

Bergesen, Albert, and Chintamani Sahoo. 1985. "Evidence of the Decline of American Hegemony in World Production." *Review* 8(4):595–611.

Bergesen, Albert, and Ronald Schoenberg. 1980. "Long Waves of Colonial Expansion and Contraction." Pp. 231–77 in *Studies of the Modern World-System*, edited by Albert Bergesen. New York: Academic Press.

Bergsten, C. Fred, and Institute for International Economics. 2005. *The United States and the World Economy*. Washington, DC: Institute for International Economics.

Bernstein, Michael A. 1994. "Understanding American Economic Decline: The Contours of the Late-Twentieth-Century Experience." Pp. 3–33 in *Understanding American Economic Decline*, edited by Michael A. Bernstein and David E. Adler. Cambridge: Cambridge University Press.

Betts, Raymond. 1961. *Assimilation and Association in French Colonial Theory 1890–1914*. New York: Columbia University Press.

Black, Jeremy. 1986. *Natural and Necessary Enemies: Anglo-French Relations in the Eighteenth Century*. Athens: University of Georgia Press.

Boahen, A. Adu (Ed.). 1990. *Africa under Colonial Domination, 1880–1935*. Berkeley: University of California Press.

Bodelson, C. A. 1968. *Studies in Mid-Victorian Imperialism*. New York: Howard Fertig.

Bombay Public Meeting. 1883. *Report of the proceedings of a public meeting of the inhabitants of Bombay held in the Framji Cowasji Institute on Monday the 27th August, 1883, to vote an address to Major the Hon'ble Sir. E. Baring*. Bombay: Bombay Gazette Steam Press.

Boot, Max. 2003. "Neither New nor Nefarious: The Liberal Empire Strikes Back." *Current History* 102(667):361–66.

Boswell, Terry. 1989. "Colonial Empires and the Capitalist World-Economy: A Time Series Analysis of Colonization, 1640–1960." *American Sociological Review* 54:180–96.

Boswell, Terry. 1995. "Hegemony and Bifurcation Points in World History." *Journal of World-Systems Research* 1(15):1–63.

Boswell, Terry. 2004. "American World Empire or Declining Hegemony." *Journal of World-Systems Research* 10(2):516–24.

Bothwell Gonzalez, Reece B. 1979. *Puerto Rico: Cien Años de Lucha Política*. Rio Piedras: Editorial Universitaria.

Bourne, Kenneth. 1970. *The Foreign Policy of Victorian England, 1830–1902*. Oxford: Clarendon Press.

Bowman, Kirk S. 2001. "The Public Battles over Militarisation and Democracy in Honduras." *Journal of Latin American Studies* 33(3):539–60.

Boyer, William W. 1983. *America's Virgin Islands: A History of Human Rights and Wrongs*. Durham, NC: Carolina Academic Press.

Brands, H. W. 1989. "The Limits of Manipulation: How the United States Didn't Topple Sukarno." *Journal of American History* 76(3):785–808.

Brasted, Howard. 1980. "Indian Nationalist Development and the Influence of Irish Home Rule, 1870–1886." *Modern Asian Studies* 14(1):37–63.

Brenner, Robert. 2002. *The Boom and the Bubble: The U.S. in the World Economy*. London; New York: Verso.

Brewer, Anthony. 1990. *Marxist Theories of Imperialism: A Critical Survey*. London; New York: Routledge.

Brewer, John. 1989. *The Sinews of Power: War, Money and the English State*. New York: Alfred A. Knopf.

Brewer, John. 1994. "The Eighteenth-Century British State: Contexts and Issues." Pp. 52–71 in *An Imperial State at War. Britain from 1689 to 1815, edited by Lawrence Stone. London and New York: Routledge.

Brooks, Philip Coolidge. 1934. "The Pacific Coast's First International Boundary Delineation, 1816–1819." *Pacific Historical Review* 3(1):62–79.

Brown, Ian. 1978. "British Financial Advisers in Siam in the Reign of King Chulalongkorn." *Modern Asian Studies* 12(2):193–215.

Brown, Matthew (Ed.). 2008. *Informal Empire in Latin America: Culture, Commerce and Capital*. Oxford: Blackwell.

Brzezinski, Zbigniew. 1997. "A Geostrategy for Eurasia." *Foreign Affairs* 76(5):50–65.

Brzezinski, Zbigniew. 1998. *The Grand Chessboard: American Primacy and its Geostrategic Imperatives*. New York: Basic Books.

Buckle, George Earl. 1920. *The Life of Benjamin Disraeli*. New York: The MacMillan Company.

Bull, Hedley, and Adam Watson. 1984. "Introduction." Pp. 1–8 in *The Expansion of International Society*, edited by Hedley Bull and Adam Watson. Oxford: Clarendon Press.

Burbank, Jane, and Mark von Hagen (Eds.). 2007. *Russian Empire: Space, People, Power, 1700–1930*. Bloomington: Indiana University Press.

Burnett, Christina Duffy, and Burke Marshall. 2001. *Foreign in a Domestic Sense: Puerto Rico, American Expansion, and the Constitution*. Durham, NC: Duke University Press.

Burns, Sir Alan. 1957. *In Defence of Colonies*. London: George Allen and Unwin Ltd.

Burstein, Andrew. 1999. *Sentimental Democracy*. New York: Hill and Wang.

Cabranes, José. 1979. *Citizenship and the American Empire: Notes on the Legislative History of the United States Citizenship of Puerto Ricans*. New Haven, CT: Yale University Press.

Cain, Peter J. 1985. "J. A. Hobson, Financial Capitalism and Imperialism in Late Victorian and Edwardian England." *Journal of Imperial and Commonwealth History* 8(3):1–27.

Cain, Peter J. 1999. "Economics: The Metropolitan Context." Pp. 31–52 in *The Oxford History of the British Empire: Volume III, The Nineteenth Century*, edited by Andrew Porter. Oxford: Oxford University Press.

Cain, Peter J., and A. G. Hopkins. 1993. *British Imperialism: Innovation and Expansion, 1688–1914*. London: Longman.

Campbell, John C. 1947. *The United States in World Affairs, 1945–1947*. New York: Harper & Brothers.

Carano, Paul, and Pedro C. Sanchez. 1964. *A Complete History of Guam*. Tokyo and Rutland: Charles E. Tuttle Company.

Carpenter, Ted Galen. 1999. "That Was Then, This Is Now: Toward a New NSC-68." *SAIS Review* 19(1):72–84.

Carrión, Arturo Morales. 1983. *Puerto Rico: A Political and Cultural History*. New York: W.W. Norton & Company, Inc.

Carroll, Henry K. 1899a. "How Shall Puerto Rico Be Governed." *The Forum* 28(November):256–7.

Carroll, Henry K. 1899b. *Report on the Island of Porto Rico; Its Population, Civil Government, Commerce, Industries, Productions, Roads, Tariff, and Currency, with recommendations by Henry K. Carroll . . . .* Washington, DC: Government Printing Office.

Carruthers, Susan. 2003. "The Imperial Interrogative: Questioning American Empire." Paper presented at the *Third Drew Colloquium in Transdisciplinary Theological Studies, "An American Empire? Globalization, War, and Religion,"* September 25–27, 2003.

Chakrabarty, Dipesh. 2000. *Provincializing Europe: Postcolonial Thought and Historical Difference*. Princeton, NJ: Princeton University Press.

Chamberlain, Muriel E. 1984. "Imperialism and Social Reform." Pp. 148–67 in *British Imperialism in the Nineteenth Century*, edited by C. C. Eldridge. New York: St. Martin's Press.

Chamberlain, Muriel E. 1988. *'Pax Britannica'? British Foreign Policy 1789–1914*. London: Longman.

Chamberlain, Muriel E. 1999. *The Scramble for Africa*. London: Longman.

Chandler, D. G. 1967. "The Expedition to Abyssinia 1867–8." Pp. 107–59 in *Victorian Military Campaigns*, edited by Brian Bond. London: Hutchinson & Co, Ltd.

Chapman, John K. 1964. *The Career of Arthur Hamilton Gordon*. Toronto: University of Toronto Press.

Chappell, David. 2000. "The Forgotten *Mau*: Anti-Navy Protest in American Samoa, 1920–1935." *Pacific Historical Review* 69(2):217–60.

Chase-Dunn, Christopher, Rebecca Giem, Andrew Jorgenson, Thomas Reifer, John Rogers, and Shoon Lio. 2002. *The Trajectory of the United States in the World-System: A Quantitative Reflection*. The Institute for Research on World-Systems Working Paper #8: http://irows.ucr.edu/papers/irows8/irows8.htm. Accessed December 2003.

Chase-Dunn, Christopher, Andrew K. Jorgenson, Thomas E. Reifer, and Shoon Lio. 2005. "The Trajectory of the United States in the World-System: A Quantitive Reflection." *Sociological Perspectives* 48(2):233–54.

Chatterjee, Partha. 1993. *The Nation and its Fragments*. Princeton, NJ: Princeton University Press.

Chernilo, Daniel. 2006. "Social Theory's Methodological Nationalism." *European Journal of Social Theory* 9(1):5–22.

Chorev, Nitsan. 2007. *Remaking U.S. Trade Policy: From Protectionism to Globalization*. Ithaca, NY: Cornell University Press.

Christopher, Warren. 1995. "Charting a Transatlantic Agenda for the 21st Century: Address at Casa de America, Madrid, 2 June 1995." *US Department of State Dispatch* 6(23):468–70.

Churchill, Bernardita Reyes. 1983. *The Philippine Independence Missions to United States, 1919–1934*. Manila, Philippines: National Historical Institute.

Churchill, Winston. 1906. *Lord Randolph Churchill*. New York: The MacMillan Company.

Ciutâ, Felix. 2006. "What Are We Debating? IR Theory between Empire and the 'Responsible' Hegemon." *International Politics* 43(2):173–96.

Clarke, Jonathan G. 1992. *The Eurocorps: A Fresh Start in Europe (Cato Institute Foreign Policy Briefing No. 21)*. Washington, DC: Cato Institute.

Clowes, W. Laird. 1903. *The Royal Navy, a History from the Earliest Times to Present*. London: Sampson, Low, Marston and Company.

Clymer, Kenton J. 1984. "The Education of William Phillips: Self-Determination and American Policy toward India, 1942–45." *Diplomatic History* 8(1):13–35.

Coats, John. 2008. "Half-Devil and Half-Child: America's War with Terror in the Philippines, 1899–1902." Pp. 181–206 in *Enemies of Humanity: The Nineteenth-Century War on Terrorism*, edited by Isaac Land. New York: Palgrave Macmillan.

Colley, Linda. 2003a. *Britons: Forging the Nation, 1707–1837: With a New Preface by the Author*. London: Pimlico.

Colley, Linda. 2003b. *Captives: Britain, Empire and the World 1600–1850*. London: Pimlico.

Collier, Ellen. 1993. *Instances of the Use of United States Forces Abroad, 1798–1993*. Washington, DC: Government Printing Office.

Committee on Africa, the War, and Peace Aims. 1942. *The Atlantic Charter and Africa from an American Standpoint*. New York: Committee on Africa, the War and Peace Aims.

Conant, Charles. 1898. "The Economic Basis of Imperialism." *North American Review* 167(502):326–40.

Conklin, Alice L. 1998. *A Mission to Civilize: The Republican Idea of Empire in France and West Africa, 1895–1930*. Stanford, CA: Stanford University Press.

Conway, Stephen. 2005. "Continental Connections: Britain and Europe in the Eighteenth Century." *History [Great Britain]* 90(299):353–74.

Cooper, Frederick. 2005. *Colonialism in Question.* Berkeley: University of California Press.

Cooper, Frederick, and Jane Burbank. 2010. *Empires in World History: Power and the Politics of Difference.* Princeton, NJ: Princeton University Press.

Corden, W. Max. 1990. "American Decline and the End of Hegemony." *SAIS Review* 10(2):13–26.

Coronil, Fernando. 2007. "After Empire: Reflections on Imperialism from the Américas." Pp. 241–71 in *Imperial Formations*, edited by Ann Laura Stoler, Carole McGranahan, and Peter C. Perdue. Santa Fe, NM: School for Advanced Research Press.

Cox, L. M. 1917. *The Island of Guam.* Washington, DC: Government Printing Office.

Cramer, Jane. 2006. "'Just Cause' or Just Politics? U.S. Panama Invasion and Standardizing Qualitative Tests for Diversionary War." *Armed Forces & Society* 32(2):178–201.

Crapol, Edward. 1979. "John Quincy Adams and the Monroe Doctrine: Some New Evidence." *Pacific Historical Review* 48(3).

Cromer, Earl of. 1908. *Modern Egypt.* New York: The MacMillan Company.

Cullather, Nick. 1999. *Secret History: The CIA's Classified Account of its Operations in Guatemala, 1952–1954.* Stanford, CA: Stanford University Press.

Cullinane, Michael. 1971. "Implementing the 'New Order': The Structure and Supervision of Local Government during the Taft Era." Pp. 13–76 in *Compadre Colonialism: Studies on the Philippines under American Rule*, edited by Norman Owen. Ann Arbor: Michigan Papers on South and Southeast Asia No. 3.

Cullinane, Michael. 2003. *Ilustrado Politics: Filipino Elite Responses to American Rule, 1898–1908.* Manila: Ateneo de Manila University Press.

Cumings, Bruce. 1990. *The Origins of the Korean War. II. The Roaring of the Cataract 1947–1950.* Princeton, NJ: Princeton University Press.

Cumings, Bruce. 2003. "Is America an Imperial Power?" *Current History* 102: 355–60.

Cumings, Bruce. 2009. *Dominion from Sea to Sea: Pacific Ascendancy and American Power.* New Haven, CT: Yale University Press.

Cumpston, Mary 1961. "Early Indian Nationalists and Their Allies in the British Parliament, 1851–1906." *The English Historical Review* 76(299):279–97.

Cunningham, Hugh. 1971. "Jingoism in 1877–78." *Victorian Studies* XIV:429–53.

Cunningham, Hugh. 1981. "The Language of Patriotism." *History Workshop* XII: 8–83.

Darby, Phillip. 1987. *Three Faces of Imperialism: British and American Approaches to Asia and Africa, 1870–1970.* New Haven, CT: Yale University Press.

Darden, Capt. T. F. 1951. *Historical Sketch of the Naval Administration of the Government of American Samoa.* Washington, DC: Government Printing Office.

Darwin, John. 1997. "Imperialism and the Victorians: The Dynamics of Territorial Expansion." *The English Historical Review* 112(447):614–42.

Darwin, John. 2008. *After Tamerlane: The Global History of Empire since 1405.* New York: Bloomsbury Press.

Darwin, John. 2009. *The Empire Project: The Rise and Fall of the British World-System, 1830–1970.* Cambridge: Cambridge University Press.

Davis, General George W. 1900. *Report of General Davis: Civil Affairs in Puerto Rico, 1899.* Washington, DC: Government Printing Office.

Davis, Lance E., and Robert A. Huttenback. 1988. *Mammon and the Pursuit of Empire.* Cambridge: Cambridge University Press.

Dean, Britten. 1976. "British Informal Empire: The Case of China." *The Journal of Commonwealth & Comparative Politics* 14(1):64–81.

Deming Lewis, Martin. 1962. "One Hundred Million Frenchmen: The 'Assimilation' Theory in French Colonial Policy." *Comparative Studies in Society and History* 4(2):129–53.

Denby, Charles. 1898. "America's Opportunity in Asia." *North American Review* 166(494):32–40.

Dicey, Edward. 1898. "The New American Imperialism." *The Nineteenth Century* 44(September):487–501.

Dietz, James L. 1986. *Economic History of Puerto Rico: Institutional Change and Capitalist Development.* Princeton, NJ: Princeton University Press.

Dike, K. O. 1956. *Trade and Politics in the Niger Delta 1830–85.* Oxford: Clarendon Press.

Dilke, Sir Charles Wentworth. 1890. *Problems of Greater Britain.* London: MacMillan and Co.

Dirom, Alexander. 1828. *Sketches of the State of the British Empire; With Remarks on its Domestic and Foreign Policy, and the Probable Consequences of the Late Transactions with Turkey, for the Liberation of Greece.* Edinburgh: Cadell & Co.

Donnelly, Thomas, Donald Kagan, and Gary Schmitt. 2000. *Rebuilding America's Defenses.* Washington, DC: Project for the New American Century.

Douglas, Ann. 1995. *Terrible Honesty: Mongrel Manhattan in the 1920s.* New York: Farrar, Straus, and Giroux.

Dow, Mark. 1995. "Occupying and Obscuring Haiti." *New Politics* 5(2):12–22.

Dowd, Maureen. 2003. "Hypocrisy and Apple Pie." *New York Times*, April 30, Section A, p. 27.

Doyle, Michael W. 1986. *Empires.* Ithaca, NY; London: Cornell University Press.

Drus, Ethel. 1950. "The Colonial Office and the Annexation of Fiji." *Transactions of the Royal Historical Society* 32:87–110.

Du Boff, Richard. 2003. "U.S. Hegemony: Continuing Decline, Enduring Danger." *Monthly Review* 55(7 (December)):1–15.

DuBois, W.E.B. 1935. "Inter-Racial Implications of the Ethiopian Crisis." *Foreign Affairs* 14(1):82–93.

Duffy, Michael. 1987. *Soldiers, Sugar, and Seapower: The British Expeditions to the West Indies and the War against Revolutionary France.* Oxford: Clarendon Press.

Duffy, Michael. 1998. "World-Wide War and British Expansion, 1793–1815." Pp. 184–207 in *The Oxford History of the British Empire: Volume II, The Eighteenth Century*, edited by P. J. Marshall. Oxford: Oxford University Press.

Duffy Burnett, Christina. 2008. "'They say I am not an American . . .': The Noncitizen National and the Law of American Empire." *Virginia Journal of International Law* 48(4):659–718.

Dulles, Foster Rhea, and Gerald E. Ridinger. 1955. "The Anti-Colonial Policies of Franklin D. Roosevelt." *Political Science Quarterly* 70(1):1–18.

Duus, Peter. 1996. "Imperialism without Colonies: The Vision of a Greater East Asia Co-Prosperity Sphere." *Diplomacy & Statecraft* 7(1):54–72.

Easton, Stewart C. 1964. *The Rise and Fall of Western Colonialism.* New York: Frederick A. Praeger.

Eblen, Jack Ericson. 1968. *The First and Second United States Empires*. Pittsburgh, PA: University of Pittsburgh Press.

Edelstein, Michael. 1982. *Overseas Investment in the Age of High Imperialism: The United Kingdom, 1850–1914*. New York: Columbia University Press.

Eisenstadt, S. N. 1963. *The Political Systems of Empires*. Glencoe, IL: The Free Press.

Eisenstadt, S. N 1968. "Empires." Pp. 41–9 in *International Encyclopedia of the Social Sciences*, edited by David L. Sills. New York: The MacMillan Company & the Free Press.

Eldridge, C. C. 1967. "The Imperialism of the 'Little England Era': The Question of the Annexation of the Fiji Islands, 1858–1861." *The New Zealand Journal of History* 1(2):171–84.

Eldridge, C. C. 1978. *Victorian Imperialism*. Atlantic Highlands: Humanities Press Inc.

Elliot, J. H. 2006. *Empires of the Atlantic World*. New Haven, CT: Yale University Press.

Ellison, Joseph. 1938. *Opening and Penetration of Foreign Influence in Samoa to 1880*. Corvallis: Oregan State College Monographs, Studies in History, No. 1.

Emerson, Rupert. 1947. "American Policy toward Pacific Dependencies." *Pacific Affairs* 20(3):259–75.

Emirbayer, M. 1997. "Manifesto for a Relational Sociology." *American Journal of Sociology* 103(2):281–317.

Enders, Walter, and Todd Sandler. 2000. "Is Transnational Terrorism More Threatening? A Time-Series Investigation." *Journal of Conflict Resolution* 44(3):307–32.

Erman, Sam. 2008. "Meanings of Citizenship in the U.S. Empire: Puerto Rico, Isabel Gonzalez, and the Supreme Court, 1898–1905." *Journal of American Ethnic History* 27(4):http://www.historycooperative.org/journals/jaeh/27.4/erman.html (February 11, 2009).

Etherington, Norman. 1982. "Reconsidering Theories of Imperialism." *History and Theory* 21(1):1–36.

Fairlie, Henry. 1965. "A Cheer for American Imperialism." *New York Times*, July 11, SM7.

Farmer, John S. 1984[1901]. *The Regimental Records of the British Army: A Historical Resume Chronologically Arranged of Titles, Campaigns, Honours, Uniforms, Facings, Badges, Nicknames, etc.* Bristol: Crécy Books.

Fay, C. R. 1940. "The Movement towards Free Trade, 1820–1853." Pp. 388–414 in *The Cambridge History of the British Empire, Volume II: The Growth of the New Empire, 1783–1870*, edited by J. Holland Rose, A. P. Newton, and E. A. Benians. Cambridge: Cambridge University Press.

Federal Party of the Philippine Islands. 1905. *Manifesto of the Federal Party*. Manila: Tip. 'La Democracia.'

Ferguson, Niall. 2004. *Colossus: The Price of America's Empire*. New York: Penguin Press.

Fernandez, Ronald. 1996. *The Disenchanted Island: Puerto Rico and the United States in the Twentieth Century*. Westport, CT: Praeger.

Ferns, H. S. 1953. "Britain's Informal Empire in Argentina, 1806–1914." *Past and Present* 4(November):60–75.

Ferns, H. S. 1960. *Britain and Argentina in the Nineteenth Century*. Oxford: Clarendon Press.

Fieldhouse, D. K. 1973. *Economics and Empire 1830–1914*. London: Cox & Wyman, Ltd.

Fieldhouse, D. K. 1982. *The Colonial Empires: A Comparative Survey from the Eighteenth Century.* London: The MacMillan Press, Ltd.

Fieldhouse, D. K., and Rupert Emerson. 1968. "Colonialism." Pp. 1–12 in *International Encyclopedia of the Social Sciences*, edited by David L. Sills. New York: MacMillan.

Finley, M. I. 1976. "Colonies: An Attempt at a Typology." *Transactions of the Royal Historical Society* 26:167–88.

Fischer, Hannah. 2009. *United States Military Casualty Statistics: Operation Iraqi Freedom and Operation Enduring Freedom.* Washington, DC: Congressional Research Service.

Fletcher, Ian. 2006. *The Waters of Oblivion: The British Invasion of the Rio de la Plata.* Staplehurst: Spellmount.

Flournoy, F. R. 1935. *British Policy towards Morocco in the Age of Palmerston, 1830–1865.* London.

Foltos, Lester J. 1989. "The New Pacific Barrier: America's Search for Security in the Pacific, 1945–47." *Diplomatic History* 33(3):317–42.

Forbes, W. Cameron 1928. *The Philippine Islands.* Boston: Houghton Mifflin Company.

Forbes, W. Cameron. 1945. *The Philippine Islands. Revised Edition.* Cambridge, MA: Harvard University Press.

Foster, John Bellamy. 2006. "The New Geopolitics of Empire." *Monthly Review* 57(6).

Fraser, Cary. 1992. "Understanding American Policy towards the Decolonization of European Empires, 1945–64." *Diplomacy & Statecraft* 3(1):105–25.

French, Willard. 1905. "An Isolated American Island. How We Are Neglecting our Duty to Guam." *Booklover's Magazine* V:369–79.

Friedman, Hal. 1995. "The Limitations of Collective Security: The United States and the Micronesian Trusteeship." *Isla: Journal of Micronesia Studies* 3(2):339–70.

Friend, Theodore. 1963. "American Interests and Philippine Independence, 1932–1933." *Philippine Studies* 11(4):505–23.

Friend, Theodore. 1965. *Between Two Empires. The Ordeal of the Philippines, 1926–1946.* New Haven, CT: Yale University Press.

Fry, Joseph. 1996a. "In Search of an Orderly World: U.S. Imperialism, 1898–1912." Pp. 1–23 in *Modern American Diplomacy*, edited by John M. Carroll and George C. Herring. Lanham, MD: Rowan & Littlefield.

Fry, Joseph A. 1996b. "From Open Door to World Systems: Economic Interpretations of Late Nineteenth Century American Foreign Relations." *Pacific Historical Review* LXV(2):277–303.

Furedi, Frank. 1994. *Colonial Wars and the Politics of Third World Nationalism.* London: I. B. Tauris.

Gaddis, John Lewis. 1982. *Strategies of Containment: A Critical Appraisal of Postwar American National Security Policy.* New York: Oxford University Press.

Galbraith, J. S. 1960. "The 'Turbulent Frontier' as a Factor in British Expansion." *Comparative Studies in Society and History* II(2):150–68.

Galbraith, J. S., and Afaf Lutfi al-Sayyid-Marsot. 1978. "The British Occupation of Egypt: Another View." *International Journal of Middle East Studies* 9(4):471–88.

Gallo, Klaus. 2001. *Great Britain and Argentina: From Invasion to Recognition, 1806–26.* Houndmills: Palgrave.

Gallup, George, and Claude Robinson. 1938. "American Institute of Public Opinion Surveys, 1935–38." *The Public Opinion Quarterly* 2(3):373–98.

Gannon, John C. 2000. *Intelligence Challenges for the New Millennium: A Special Look at Russia and China.* Washington, DC: National Intelligence Council. http://www.dni.gov/nic/speeches_newmillennium.html; accessed November 2, 2009.

Gardner, Lloyd C. 2000. "How We 'Lost' Vietnam, 1940–1954." Pp. 121–39 in *The United States and Decolonization*, edited by David Ryan and Victor Pungong. New York: St. Martin's Press, Inc.

Gatell, Frank Otto. 1960–1961. "The Art of the Possible: Luis Muñoz Rivera and the Puerto Rican Jones Bill." *The Americas* 17(1):1–20.

Gellman, Barton. 1992. "Keeping the U.S. First: Pentagon Would Preclude a Rival Superpower." *Washington Post*, March 11, A1.

Gilboa, Eytan. 1995–1996. "The Panama Invasion Revisited: Lessons for the Use of Force in the Post Cold War Era." *Political Science Quarterly* 110(4):539–62.

Gilchrist, Huntington. 1944. "The Japanese Islands: Annexation or Trusteeship?" *Foreign Affairs* 22(July):635–42.

Gilpin, Robert. 1971. "The Politics of Transnational Economic Relations." *International Organization* 25(3):398–419.

Gilpin, Robert. 1975. *U.S. Power and the Multinational Corporation: The Political Economy of Foreign Direct Investment.* New York: Basic Books.

Gilpin, Robert. 1978. "Economic Interdependence and National Security in Historical Perspective." Pp. 19–66 in *Economic Issues and National Security*, edited by Klaus Knorr and Frank Trager. Lawrence: University Press of Kansas.

Go, Julian. 2004. "'Racism' and Colonialism: Meanings of Difference and Ruling Practices in America's Pacific Empire." *Qualitative Sociology* 27(1):35–58.

Go, Julian. 2007. "The Provinciality of American Empire: 'Liberal Exceptionalism' and US Colonial Rule." *Comparative Studies in Society and History* 49(1):74–108.

Go, Julian. 2008a. *American Empire and the Politics of Meaning: Elite Political Cultures in the Philippines and Puerto Rico during U.S. Colonialism.* Durham, NC: Duke University Press.

Go, Julian. 2008b. "Global Fields and Imperial Forms: Field Theory and the British and American Empires." *Sociological Theory* 26(3):201–29.

Godfrey, John Blennerhassett. 1882. *The Means of Preventing the Downfall of the British Empire.* London: Wyman & Sons.

Goertz, Gary, and Paul F. Diehl. 1992. *Territorial Changes and International Conflict.* London; New York: Routledge.

Goetzmann, William H. 1959. *Army Exploration in the American West, 1803–1863.* New Haven, CT: Yale University Press.

Gómez, Laura E. 2007. *Manifest Destinies: The Making of the Mexican American Race.* New York: New York University.

Gopal, Sarvepalli. 1965. *British Policy in India, 1858–1905.* Cambridge: Cambridge University Press.

Gordon, Arthur. 1883. "Native Councils in Fiji." *Contemporary Review* XLIII(January-June):711–31.

Gordon, Arthur Hamilton. 1897. *Fiji, Records of Private and of Public Life, 1875–1880.* Edinburgh: R. and R. Clark.

Goswami, Manu. 1998. "From Swadeshi to Swaraj: Nation, Economy, and Territory in Colonial South Asia." *Comparative Studies in Society and History* 40(4):609–36.

Gould, Harold. 1974. "The Emergence of Modern Indian Politics: Political Development in Faizabad, Part I: 1884–1935." *Journal of Commonwealth and Comparative Politics* 12(1):20–41.

Governor of Guam. 1901–1941. *Annual Reports of the Governor of Guam*. Washington, DC: Government Printing Office.

Governor of Samoa. 1913. *American Samoa: A General Report by the Governor*. Washington, DC: Government Printing Office.

Governor of Samoa. 1927. *American Samoa: A General Report by the Governor*. Washington, DC: Government Printing Office.

Gowan, Peter. 1999. *Global Gamble: Washington's Faustian Bid for World Dominance*. London: Verso.

Graebner, Norman A. 1983. *Empire on the Pacific: A Study in American Continental Expansion*. Santa Barbara, CA: ABC-Clio.

Grant, Daniel. 1870. *Home Politics, or the Growth of Trade Considered in its Relation to Labor, Pauperism, and Emigration*. London: Longmans, Green, Reader and Dyer.

Gray, J.A.C. 1960. *Amerika Samoa: A History of American Samoa and its United States Naval Administration*. Annapolis, MD: United States Naval Institute.

Greene, Evarts 1898. *The Provincial Governor in the English Colonies of North America*. New York: Longmans, Green, and Co.

Greene, Jack P. 1986. *Peripheries and Center: Constitutional Development in the Extended Polities of the British Empire and the United States, 1607–1788*. Athens: University of Georgia Press.

Greene, Jack P. 1994a. "The Jamaica Privilege Controversy, 1764–66: An Episode in the Process of Constitutional Definition in the Early Modern British Empire." *Journal of Imperial and Commonwealth History* 22(1):16–53.

Greene, Jack P. 1994b. *Negotiated Authorities: Essays in Colonial Political and Constitutional History*. Charlottesville: University Press of Virginia.

Greene, Jack P. 1998. "Empire and Identity from the Glorious Revolution to the American Revolution." Pp. 208–30 in *The Oxford History of the British Empire: Volume II, The Eighteenth Century*, edited by P. J. Marshall. Oxford: Oxford University Press.

Greene, Jack P. 2002. "Transatlantic Colonization and the Redefinition of Empire in the Early Modern Era: The British American Experience." Pp. 267–82 in *Negotiated Empires: Centers and Peripheries in the Americas, 1500–1820*, edited by Christine Daniels and Michael V. Kennedy. New York: Routledge.

Greene, Jack P. (Ed.). 2010. *Exclusionary Empire. English Liberty Overseas, 1600–1900*. Cambridge: Cambridge University Press.

Grimal, Henri. 1978. *Decolonization: The British, French, Dutch, and Belgian Empires, 1919–1963*. Boulder, CO: Lynne Rienner.

Grimmett, Richard F. 2004. *Instances of Use of United States Armed Forces Abroad*, Washington, DC: Congressional Research Service, Foreign Affairs, Defense, and Trade Division.

Grupo de Investigadores Puertorriqueños. 1984. *Breakthrough from Colonialism: An Interdisciplinary Study of Statehood*. Rio Piedras: Editorial de la Universidad de Puerto Rico.

Guha, Ranajit. 1997. *Dominance without Hegemony: History and Power in Colonial India*. Cambridge, MA: Harvard University Press.

Gwertzman, Bernard. 1983. "Steps to the Invasion: No More 'Paper Tiger.'" *New York Times*, October 30, p. 1.

Gwyn, Julian. 1980. "British Government Spending and the North American Colonies 1740–1175." *Journal of Imperial and Commonwealth History* 8(2):74–84.

Haas, Richard. 1999. *Intervention: The Use of American Military Force in the Post-Cold War Period*. Washington, DC: Brookings Institution Press.

Hallward, Peter. 2004. "Option Zero in Haiti." *New Left Review* 27(May-June):23–47.

Hammond, J. L., and M.R.D. Foot. 1953. *Gladstone and Liberalism*. New York: The MacMillan Company.

Hanson, Victor Davis. 2003. "What Empire?" Pp. 146–55 in *The Imperial Tense: Prospects and Problems of American Empire*, edited by Andrew Bacevich. Chicago: Ivan R. Dee.

Harcourt, Freda. 1980. "Disraeli's Imperialism, 1866–1868: A Question of Timing." *The Historical Journal* 23(1):87–109.

Hard, William. 1930. "American Empire." *The Saturday Evening Post* 203(September 20):12–13.

Hardt, Michael, and Antonio Negri. 2001. *Empire*. Cambridge, MA: Harvard University Press.

Harkavy, Robert E. 1982. *Great Power Competition for Overseas Bases: The Geopolitics of Access Diplomacy*. New York: Pergamon Press.

Harling, Philip, and Peter Mandler. 1993. "From 'Fiscal-Military' State to Laissez-Faire State, 1760–1850." *The Journal of British Studies* 32(1):44–70.

Harlow, Vincent T. 1952. *The Founding of the Second British Empire, 1763–1793*. London: Longmans, Green.

Harris, Bob. 1996. "'American Idols': Empire, War, and the Middling Ranks in Mid-Eighteenth-Century Britain." *Past and Present* 150:111–41.

Harris, P. Valentine. 1944. *The British Army Up-to-Date: Campaigns, Regimental Histories, Battle Honours, Badges, etc.* London: George Allen & Unwin.

Hart, Albert Bushnell. 1919. *Actual Government as Applied under American Conditions*. New York: Longmans, Green and Co.

Harvey, David. 2003. *The New Imperialism*. Oxford: Oxford University Press.

Haynes, Douglas E. 1991. *Rhetoric and Ritual in Colonial India: The Shaping of a Public Culture in Surat City, 1852–1928*. Berkeley: University of California Press.

Healy, David. 1970. *U.S. Expansionism: The Imperialist Urge in the 1890s*. Madison: University of Wisconsin Press.

Healy, David. 1988. *Drive to Hegemony: the United States in the Caribbean*. Madison: University of Wisconsin Press.

Henige, David. 1970. *Colonial Governors*. Madison: University of Wisconsin Press.

Heumann, Stefan. 2009. "Tutelary Empire: State- and Nation-Building in the 19th Century United States." Ph.D. dissertation, University of Pennsylvania.

Hietala, Thomas R. 1985. *Manifest Design: Anxious Aggrandizement in Late Jacksonian America*. Ithaca, NY: Cornell University Press.

Hill, Gen. James T. 2003. *Statement before the House Armed Services Committee, U.S. House of Representatives, March 12, 2003*. Washington, DC: Center for International Policy.

Hilton, Boyd. 1977. *Corn, Cash, Commerce: The Economic Policies of the Tory Governments, 1815–1830*. Oxford: Oxford University Press.

Hirsh, M. 2002. "Bush and the World." *Foreign Affairs* 81(5):18–43.

Ho, Engseng. 2004. "Empire through Diasporic Eyes: A View from the Other Boat." *Comparative Studies in Society and History* 46:210–46.

Hobsbawm, E. J. 2003. "United States: Wider Still and Wider." *Le Monde Diplomatique* June.

Hobson, John A. 1902. *Imperialism: A Study*. London: James Nisbet & Co., Limited.

Hobson, John A. 1965 [1902]. *Imperialism: A Study*. Ann Arbor: University of Michigan Press.

Hobson, John M. 2002. "Two Hegemonies or One? A Historical-Sociological Critique of Hegemonic Stability Theory." Pp. 305–25 in *Two Hegemonies: Britain 1846–1914 and the United States 1941–2001*, edited by Patrick Karl O'Brien and Armand Clesse. Aldershot: Ashgate.

Hoffman, Stanley. 1968. "The American Style: Our Past and Our Principles." *Foreign Affairs* 46(2):362–76.

Hofschneider, Penelope Bordallo. 2001. *A Campaign for Political Rights in the Island of Guam, 1899 to 1950*. Saipan: CNMI Division of Historic Preservation.

Hoganson, Kristin. 2000. *Fighting for American Manhood: How Gender Politics Provoked the Spanish-American and Philippine-American Wars*. New Haven, CT: Yale University Press.

Holcombe, Arthur N. 1941. *Dependent Areas in the Post-War World*. Boston: World Peace Foundation.

Holland, R. F. 1985. *European Decolonization, 1918–1981*. New York: St. Martin's Press.

Holt, Jim. 2007. "It's the Oil, Stupid." *The London Review of Books* 29(20):3–4.

Hopkins, A. G. 1968. "Economic Imperialism in West Africa: Lagos, 1880–92." *Economic History Review* 21(3):580–606.

Hopkins, A. G. 2007. "Comparing British and American Empires." *Journal of Global History* 2:395–4040.

Horn, James. 1998. "British Diaspora: Emigration from Britain, 1680–1815." Pp. 28–52 in *The Oxford History of the British Empire: Volume II, The Eighteenth Century*, edited by P. J. Marshall. Oxford: Oxford University Press.

Horowitz, Richard. 1998. "Mandarins and Customs Inspectors: Western Imperialism in Nineteenth Century China Reconsidered." *Papers on Chinese History* 7:41–57.

Howe, Stephen. 1993. *Anticolonialism in British Politics: The Left and the End of Empire 1918–1964*. Oxford: Oxford University Press.

Howe, Stephen. 2002. *Empire: A Very Short Introduction*. Oxford: Oxford University Press.

Howe, Stephen. 2003. "New Empires, New Dilemmas – And Some Old Arguments." *Global Dialogue* 5(1–2):62–3.

Howland, Charles P. 1928. *Survey of American Foreign Relations*. New Haven, CT: Yale University Press.

Hunt, Michael H. 1987. *Ideology and Foreign Policy*. New Haven, CT; London: Yale University Press.

Huntington, Samuel P. 1982. "American Ideals versus American Institutions." *Political Science Quarterly* 97:1–37.

Huntington, Samuel. 1991. *The Third Wave: Democratization in the Late Twentieth Century*. Norman: University of Oklahoma Press.

Hyam, Ronald. 1999. "The Primacy of Geopolitics: The Dynamics of British Imperial Policy, 1763–1963." Pp. 27–52 in *The Statecraft of British Imperialism*, edited by Robert D. King and Robin W. Wilson. London: Frank Cass.

Hyam, Ronald. 2002. *Britain's Imperial Century, 1815–1914: A Study of Empire and Expansion*. London: B. T. Batsford.

Hyam, Ronald, and Ged Martin. 1975. *Reappraisals in British Imperial History*. London: The MacMillan Press Ltd.

Hynes, W. G. 1976. "British Mercantile Attitudes towards Imperial Expansion." *The Historical Journal* 19(4):969–79.

Ide, Henry C. 1897. "Our Interest in Samoa." *North American Review* 165:155–73.

Ignatieff, Michael (Ed.). 1995. *American Exceptionalism and Human Rights*. Princeton, NJ: Princeton University Press.

Ikenberry, G. John. 2001a. *After Victory: Institutions, Strategic Restraint, and the Rebuilding of Order after Major Wars*. Princeton, NJ: Princeton University Press.

Ikenberry, G. John. 2001b. "American Power and the Empire of Capitalist Democracy." Pp. 191–212 in *Empires, Systems and States: Great Transformations in International Politics*, edited by Michael Cox, Ken Booth, and Tim Dunne. Cambridge: Cambridge University Press.

Ikenberry, G. John. 2002. "America's Imperial Ambition." *Foreign Affairs* 81(5):44–60.

Irwin, Douglas 1993. "Multilateral and Bilateral Trade Policies in the World Trading System: An Historical Perspective." Pp. 90–199 in *New Dimensions in Regional Integration*, edited by Jaime de Melo and Arvind Panagariya. Cambridge: Cambridge University Press.

Isenberg, David. 1989. "The Pitfalls of U.S. Covert Operations." The Cato Institute. http://www.cato.org/pub_display.php?pub_id=1645 (accessed June 8, 2011).

Jacobson, Mathew Frye. 1999. "Imperial Amnesia: Teddy Roosevelt, the Philippines, and the Modern Art of Forgetting." *Radical History Review* 73:166–27.

Jessup, Philip. 1938. *Elihu Root*. New York: Dodd, Mead & Company.

Johnson, Richard R. 1998. "Growth and Mastery: British North America, 1690–1748." Pp. 276–99 in *The Oxford History of the British Empire. Volume II, The Eighteenth Century*, edited by P. J. Marshall. Oxford: Oxford University Press.

Johnson, Robert. 2003. *British Imperialism*. Houndmills: Palgrave-Macmillan.

Johnson, Theodore. 1876. *A Physical, Political, Commercial, and Historical Geography of the British Empire with its Colonies and Dependencies*. Manchester: John Heywood.

Judis, John. 2004. "Imperial Amnesia." *Foreign Policy* July/August 2004(143):50–9.

Judt, Tony. 2004. "Dreams of Empire." *New York Review of Books* 51(17):38–41.

Juhasz, Antonia. 2007. "Whose Oil is it Anyway?" *New York Times*, March 13.

Kagan, Donald. 2002. "Reaction to 'Bush's Real Goal in Iraq.'" *The Atlanta Journal and Constitution* (October 6, 2002):http://www.newamericancentury.org/defense-20021006.htm, accessed June 1, 2010.

Kammen, Michael. 1993. "The Problem of American Exceptionalism: A Reconsideration." *American Quarterly* 45(1):1–43.

Kaplan, Amy. 1993. "Left Alone in America." Pp. 3–21 in *Cultures of United States Imperialism*, edited by Amy Kaplan and Donald E. Pease. Durham, NC: Duke University Press.

Kaplan, Amy. 2003. "Violent Belongings and the Question of Empire Today." *American Quarterly* 56(1):1–18.

Kaplan, Amy, and Donald E. Pease (Eds.). 1993. *Cultures of United States Imperialism*. Durham, NC: Duke University Press.

Kaplan, Robert. 2003b. "Supremacy by Stealth." *The Atlantic Monthly* 292(1):66–83.

Karnow, Stanley. 1989. *In Our Image: America's Empire in the Philippines*. New York: Ballatine Books.

Kasaba, Resat. 1992. "Open-Door Treaties: China and the Ottoman Empire Compared." *New Perspectives on Turkey* 7:71–89.

Katznelson, Ira. 2002. "Flexible Capacity: The Military and Early American Statebuilding." Pp. 82–110 in *Shaped by War and Trade: International Influences on American Political Development*, edited by Ira Katznelson and Martin Shefter. Princeton, NJ: Princeton University Press.

Kaufmann, Eric. 1999. "American Exceptionalism Reconsidered: Anglo-Saxon Ethnogenesis in the 'Universal' Nation, 1776–1850." *Journal of American Studies* 33(3):437–57.

Keesing, Felix. 1934. *Modern Samoa: Its Government and Changing Life*. Stanford, CA: Stanford University Press.

Kennedy, Paul. 1975. "Idealists and Realists: British Views of Germany, 1864–1939." *Transactions of the Royal Historical Society* 25:137–56.

Kennedy, Paul. 1981. *The Realities Behind Diplomacy: Background Influences on British External Policy, 1865–1980*. London: George Allen & Unwin.

Kennedy, Paul. 1984. "Continuity and Discontinuity in British Imperialism 1815–1914." Pp. 20–38 in *British Imperialism in the Nineteenth Century*, edited by C. C. Eldridge. New York: St. Martin's Press.

Kennedy, Paul M. 1987. *The Rise and Fall of the Great Powers: Economic Change and Military Conflict from 1500 to 2000*. New York: Random House.

Kennedy, Paul. 2002. "The Eagle has Landed." *Financial Times*, February 1.

Kent, John. 2000. "The United States and the Decolonization of Black Africa, 1945–63." Pp. 168–87 in *The United States and Decolonization*, edited by David Ryan and Victor Pungong. New York: St. Martin's Press.

Kitson Clark, G.S.R. 1967. *An Expanding Society: Britain 1830–1900*. Cambridge: Cambridge University Press.

Kloman, Erasmus H. 1958. "Colonialism and Western Policy." Pp. 360–82 in *The Idea of Colonialism*, edited by Robert Strauz-Hupé and Harry W. Hazard. New York: Frederick A. Praeger, Inc.

Knaplund, Paul. 1961. "Gladstone-Gordon Correspondence, 1851–1896: Selections from the Private Correspondence of a British Prime Minister and a Colonial Governor." *Transactions of the American Philosophical Society* 51(4):1–116.

Knight, Alan. 1999. "Britain and Latin America." Pp. 122–45 in *Oxford History of the British Empire, Volume III, The Nineteenth Century*, edited by Andrew Porter. Oxford: Oxford University Press.

Knox, B. A. 1973. "Reconsidering Mid-Victorian Imperialism." *Journal of Imperial and Commonwealth History* 1(2):155–72.

Knox, B. A. 1984. "British Policy and the Ionian Islands, 1847–1864: Nationalism and Imperial Administration." *English Historical Review* 99(392):503–29.

Koebner, Richard. 1952. "The Emergence of the Concept of Imperialism." *Cambridge Journal* 5(12):726–41.

Koebner, Richard. 1961. *Empire*. Cambridge: Cambridge University Press.

Koebner, Richard, and Helmut Dan Schmidt. 1964. *Imperialism: The Story and Significance of a Political Word, 1840–1960*. Cambridge: Cambridge University Press.

Koehn, Nancy. 1994. *The Power of Commerce. Economy and Governance in the First British Empire*. Ithaca, NY: Cornell University Press.

Koenigsberger, H. G. 1989. "Composite States, Representative Institutions and the American Revolution." *Historical Research* 62(148):135–53.

Koh, Harold Hongju. 2003. "On American Exceptionalism." *Stanford Law Review* 55(5):1479–527.

Kohler, Gernot. 1975. "War, the Nation-State Paradigm, and the Imperialism Paradigm: British War Involvements." *Peace Research* 7(1):31–41.

Kolko, Gabriel. 1988. *Confronting the Third World. United States Foreign Policy 1945–1980*. New York: Pantheon Books.

Kovrig, Bennet. 1973. *The Myth of Liberation: East-Central Europe in U.S. Diplomacy and Politics since 1941*. Baltimore: Johns Hopkins University Press.

Kramer, Paul. 1999. "Making Concessions: Race and Empire Revisited at the Philippine Exposition, St. Louis, 1901–1905." *Radical History Review* 73:74–114.

Kramer, Paul. 2003. "Empires, Exceptions, and Anglo-Saxons: Race and Rule between the British and U.S. Empires, 1880–1910." Pp. 43–91 in *The American Colonial State in the Philippines: Global Perspectives*, edited by Julian Go and Anne Foster. Durham, NC: Duke University Press.

Kramer, Paul. 2006. *The Blood of Government: Race, Empire, the United States, & the Philippines*. Chapel Hill: University of North Carolina Press.

Krasner, Stephen. 1976. "State Power and the Structure of International Trade." *World Politics* 28(3):318–47.

Krasner, Stephen. 1988. "Sovereignty: An Institutional Perspective." *Comparative Political Studies* 21(1):66–94.

Kumar, Krishan. 2010. "Nation-States as Empires, Empires as Nation-States: Two Principles, One Practice?" *Theory and Society* 39:119–43.

Kupchan, Charles. 2003. *The End of the American Era*. New York: Vintage Books.

LaFeber, Walter. 1963. *The New Empire: An Interpretation of American Expansionism, 1860–1898*. Ithaca, NY: Cornell University Press.

LaFeber, Walter. 1989. *The American Age: United States Foreign Policy at Home and Abroad since 1750*. New York: Norton.

Lamar, Howard. 1956. *Dakota Territory, 1861–1889*. New Haven, CT: Yale University Press.

Lambert, Andrew D. 1995. "The Royal Navy, 1856–1914: Deterrence and the Strategy of World Power." Pp. 69–92 in *Navies and Global Defense*, edited by Keith Neilson and Elizabeth Jane Errington. Westport, CT: Praeger.

Layne, Christopher. 1997. "From Preponderance to Offshore Balancing: America's Future Grand Strategy." *International Security* 22(1):86–124.

Layne, Christopher. 2006. *The Peace of Illusions: American Grand Strategy from 1940 to the Present*. Ithaca, NY: Cornell University Press.

Leffler, Melvyn. 1992. *A Preponderance of Power: National Security, the Truman Administration and the Cold War*. Palo Alto, CA: Stanford University Press.

Leibowitz, Arnold H. 1989. *Defining Status: A Comprehensive Analysis of United States Territorial Relations*. Dordrecht; Boston, Norwell, MA, U.S.A.: Nijhoff; Sold and distributed by Kluwer/ Academic Publishers.

Lenin, Vladimir Il. 1939. *Imperialism, the Highest Stage of Capitalism*. New York: International Publishers.

Lenin, V. I. 1964. *Imperialism, The Highest Stage of Capitalism: A Popular Outline*. Moscow: Progress Publishers.

Lenman, Bruce. 1998. "Colonial Wars and Imperial Instability, 1688–1793." Pp. 151–68 in *The Oxford History of the British Empire: Volume II, The Eighteenth Century*, edited by P. J. Marshall. Oxford: Oxford University Press.

Leopold, Richard W. 1966. "The Emergence of America as a World Power: Some Second Thoughts." Pp. 3–34 in *Change and Growth in Twentieth Century America*, edited by John Braeman, Robert H. Bremner, and Everett Walters. New York: Harper and Row.

Lepgold, Joseph, and Timothy McKeown. 1995. "Is American Foreign Policy Exceptional? An Empirical Analysis." *Political Science Quarterly* 110(3):369–84.

Lewis, Gordon K. 1972. *The Virgin Islands: A Caribbean Lilliput*. Evanston, IL: Northwestern University Press.

Library of Congress Federal Research Division. 2005. *Dominican Republic: Country Studies*. Washington, DC: Library of Congress.

Lieven, Dominic. 1999. "Dilemmas of Empire 1850–1918: Power, Territory, Identity." *Journal of Contemporary History* 34(2):163–200.

Lieven, Dominic. 2002. *Empire: The Russian Empire and its Rivals*. New Haven, CT: Yale University Press.

Lieven, Dominic. 2005. "Empire, History and the Contemporary Global Order." *Proceedings of the British Academy* 131(2):127–56.

Limerick, Patricia Nelson. 1988. *The Legacy of Conquest: The Unbroken Past of the American West*. New York: W. W. Norton & Co.

Linn, Brian. 2000. *The Philippine War, 1899–1902*. Lawrence: University Press of Kansas.

Lipset, Seymour M. 1996. *American Exceptionalism: A Double-Edged Sword*. New York: W. W. Norton.

Liska, George. 1978. *Career of Empire: America and Imperial Expansion over Land and Sea*. Baltimore: Johns Hopkins University Press.

Lloyd, Francis, and Charles Tebbitt. 1880. *Extension of Empire, Weakness? Deficits, Ruin? With a Practicable Scheme for the Reconstitution of Asiatic Turkey*. London: C. Kegan Paul & Co.

Lloyd, T. O. 1996. *The British Empire 1558–1995*. Oxford: Oxford University Press.

Louis, William Roger (Ed.). 1976. *Imperialism: The Robinson and Gallagher Controversy*. New York: New Viewpoints.

Louis, William Roger. 1978. *Imperialism at Bay 1941–1945: The United States and the Decolonization of the British Empire*. New York: Oxford University Press.

Louis, William Roger. 1985. "American Anti-Colonialism and the Dissolution of the British Empire." *International Affairs* 61(3):395–420.

Louis, William Roger, and Ronald Robinson. 1994. "The Imperialism of Decolonization." *Journal of Imperial and Commonwealth History* 22(3):462–511.

Lucas, Scott. 2000. "The Limits of Ideology: US Foreign Policy and Arab Nationalism in the Early Cold War." Pp. 140–67 in *The United States and Decolonization*, edited by David Ryan and Victor Pungong. London: MacMillan Press.

Lundestad, Geir. 1986. "Empire by Invitation? The United States and Western Europe, 1945–1952." *Journal of Peace Research* 23(3):263–77.

Lutz, Catherine. 2006. "Empire Is in the Details." *American Ethnologist* 33(4):593–611.

Lynch, Allen. 2002. "Woodrow Wilson and the Principle of 'National Self-Determination': A Reconsideration." *Review of International Studies* 28:419–37.

Lynch, John. 1969. "British Policy and Spanish America, 1783–1808." *Journal of Latin American Studies* 1(1):1–30.

Lynn, Martin. 1982. "Consul and Kings: British Policy, the 'Man on the Spot,' and the Seizure of Lagos, 1851." *Journal of Imperial and Commonwealth History* 10(2):150–67.

Lynn, Martin. 1986. "The 'Imperialism of Free Trade' and the Case of West Africa, c.1830–1870." *Journal of Imperial and Commonwealth History* 15(1):22–40.

Lynn, Martin. 1999. "British Policy, Trade, and Informal Empire in the Mid-Nineteenth Century." Pp. 101–21 in *The Oxford History of the British Empire: Volume III, The Nineteenth Century*, edited by Andrew Porter. Oxford: Oxford University Press.

Macdonald, Douglas J. 1992. *Adventures in Chaos: American Intervention for Reform in the Third World*. Cambridge, MA: Harvard University Press.

MacDonald, Paul K. 2009. "Those who Forget Historiography Are Doomed to Republish It: Empire, Imperialism, and Contemporary Debates about American Power." *Review of International Studies* 35:45–67.

MacKenzie, John M. (Ed.). 1986. *Imperialism and Popular Culture*. Manchester: Manchester University Press.

Maddison, Angus. 2001. *The World Economy: A Millennial Perspective*. Paris: Organisation for Economic Co-Operation and Development.

Madsen, Deborah. 1998. *American Exceptionalism*. Jackson: University of Mississippi Press.

Magdoff, Harry. 1972. "Imperialism without Colonies." Pp. 144–70 in *Studies in the Theory of Imperialism*, edited by Roger Owen and Bob Sutcliffe. London: Longman.

Mahan, Alfred 1902. *Retrospect and Prospect: Studies in International Relations Naval and Political*. Port Washington: Kennikat Press, Inc.

Maier, Charles S. 2006. *Among Empires: American Ascendancy and its Empires*. Cambridge, MA: Harvard University Press.

Majul, Cesar A. 1967. *The Political and Constitutional Ideas of the Philippine Revolution*. Quezon City: University of the Philippines Press.

Mamdani, Mahmood. 1996. *Citizen and Subject: Contemporary Africa and the Legacy of Late Colonialism*. Princeton, NJ: Princeton University Press.

Mandelbaum, Michael. 1988. *The Fate of Nations: The Search for National Security in the Nineteenth and Twentieth Centuries*. Cambridge; New York: Cambridge University Press.

Manegold, Catherine. 1994. "Aristide Picks a Prime Minister with Free-Market Ideas." *New York Times*, October 25, A1.

Manela, Erez. 2006. *The Wilsonian Moment: Self-Determination and the International Origins of Anticolonial Nationalism*. Oxford: Oxford University Press.

Mann, Michael. 1993. *The Sources of Social Power, Volume II. The Rise of Classes and States, 1760–1914*. Cambridge; New York: Cambridge University Press.

Mann, Michael. 2003. *Incoherent Empire*. London; New York: Verso.

Manning, Helen Taft. 1965. "Who Ran the British Empire 1830–1850?" *Journal of British Studies* 5(1):88–121.

Marks, Frederick. 1990. "The CIA and Castillo Armas in Guatemala, 1954: New Clues to an Old Puzzle." *Diplomatic History* 14(1):67–86.

Marshall, P. J. 1998. "Introduction." Pp. 1–27 in *The Oxford History of the British Empire: Volume II, The Eighteenth Century*, edited by P. J. Marshall. Oxford: Oxford University Press.

Marshall, P. J. 2003. "The British State Overseas, 1750–1850." Pp. 171–84 in *Colonial Empires Compared: Britain and the Netherlands, 1750–1850*, edited by Bob Moore and Henk Van Nierop. Aldershot: Ashgate.

Marshall, P. J. 2005. *The Making and Unmaking of Empires: Britain, India, and America c. 1750–1783*. Oxford: Oxford University Press.

Martel, Gordon. 1991. "The Meaning of Power: Rethinking the Decline and Fall of Great Britain." *International History Review* 8(4):662–94.

Martin, Briton. 1967. "Lord Dufferin and the Indian National Congress, 1885–1888." *The Journal of British Studies* 7(1):68–96.

Mathew, W. M. 1968. "The Imperialism of Free Trade: Peru, 1820–70." *The Economic History Review* 21(3):562–79.

Mathur, L. P. 1972. *Lord Ripon's Administration in India.* New Delhi: S. Chand & Co. (Pvt) LTD.

May, Glenn A. 1980. *Social Engineering in the Philippines: The Aims, Execution, and Impact of American Colonial Policy, 1900–1913.* Westport, CT: Greenwood Press.

May, Glenn. 1991. *Battle for Batangas: A Philippine Province at War.* New Haven, CT; London: Yale University Press.

Maynes, Charles W. 1986. "Comments." Pp. 186–9 in *Grenada and Soviet/Cuban Policy,* edited by Jiri Valenta and Herbert J. Ellison. Boulder, CO: Westview Press.

Mbembe, Achille. 1992. "The Banality of Power and the Aesthetics of Vulgarity in the Postcolony." *Public Culture* 4(2):1–30.

McCormick, Thomas J. 1967. *China Market: America's Quest for Informal Empire, 1893–1901.* Chicago: Quadrangle Books.

McCormick, Thomas J. 1995. *America's Half-Century: United States Foreign Policy in the Cold War and After.* Baltimore: Johns Hopkins University Press.

McCormick, Thomas J. 2004. "American Hegemony and European Autonomy, 1989–2003: One Framework for Understanding the War in Iraq." Pp. 75–112 in *The New American Empire,* edited by Lloyd C. Gardner and Marliyn B. Young. New York: The New Press.

McCoy, Alfred, and Ed. C. de Jesus (Eds.). 1982. *Philippine Social History: Global Trade and Local Transformations.* Quezon City: Ateneo de Manila University Press.

McCoy, Alfred W., and Francisco Scarano (Eds.). 2009. *Colonial Crucible: Empire in the Making of the Modern American State.* Madison: University of Wisconsin Press.

McIntyre, W. D. 1960. "Anglo-American Rivalry in the Pacific: The British Annexation of the Fiji Islands in 1874." *Pacific Historical Review* 29(4):361–80.

McIntyre, W. D. 1962. "New Light on Commodore Goodenough's Mission to Fiji 1873–74." *Historical Studies. Australia and New Zealand* 10(39):270–87.

McIntyre, W. D. 1967. *The Imperial Frontier in the Tropics, 1865–75.* London: MacMillan.

McLay, K.A.J. 2006. "Wellsprings of a 'World War': An Early English Attempt to Conquer Canada during King William's War, 1688–97." *Journal of Imperial and Commonwealth History* 34(2):155–75.

McLean, David. 1995. *War, Diplomacy, and Informal Empire: Britain and the Republics of La Plata, 1836–1853.* London: British Academic Press.

McMahon, Robert J. 1989. "Toward a Post-Colonial Order: Truman Administration Policies toward South and Southeast Asia." Pp. 339–66 in *The Truman Presidency,* edited by Michael J. Lacey. Cambridge: Cambridge University Press.

McMahon, Robert J. 1999. *The Limits of Empire: The United States and Southeast Asia since World War II.* New York: Columbia University Press.

McMahon, Robert J. 2001. "The Republic as Empire: American Foreign Policy in the 'American Century.'" Pp. 80–100 in *Perspectives on Modern America,* edited by Harvard Sitkoff. Oxford: Oxford University Press.

McNab, David. 1977. "Herman Merivale and the Native Question, 1837–1861." *Albion: A Quarterly Journal Concerned with British Studies* 9(4):359–84.

Mearsheimer, John, and Stephen M. Walt. 2003. "An Unnecessary War." *Foreign Policy* 134(Jan-Feb):50–9.

Mehta, Uday Singh. 1999. *Liberalism and Empire. A Study in Nineteenth-Century British Liberal Thought.* Chicago: University of Chicago Press.

Meinig, D. W. 1993. *The Shaping of America: A Geographical Perspective on 500 Years of History: Volume 2, Continental America 1800–1867.* New Haven, CT: Yale University Press.

Merrell, James H. 1991. "'The Customes of our Countrey': Indians and Colonists in Early America." Pp. 117–56 in *Strangers within the Realm: Cultural Margins of the First British Empire*, edited by Bernard Bailyn and Philip D. Morgan. Chapel Hill: University of North Carolina Press.

Messer, Robert L. 1977. "Paths Not Taken: The United States Department of State and Alternatives to Containment, 1945–1946." *Diplomatic History* 1(4).

Metcalf, Thomas R. 1964. *The Aftermath of Revolt.* Princeton, NJ: Princeton University Press.

Metcalf, Thomas R. 1994. *Ideologies of the Raj.* Cambridge; New York: Cambridge University Press.

Miller, Rory. 1993. *Britain and Latin America in the Nineteenth and Twentieth Centuries.* London and New York: Longman.

Milner, Clyde A. 1981. "Indulgent Friends and Important Allies: Political Process on the Cis-Mississippi Frontier and Its Aftermath." Pp. 123–48 in *The Frontier in History: North America and Southern Africa Compared*, edited by Howard Lamar and Leonard Thompson. New Haven, CT: Yale University Press.

Modelski, George. 1978. "The Long Cycle of Global Politics and the Nation-State." *Comparative Studies in Society and History* 20(2):214–35.

Modelski, George, and William R. Thompson. 1996. *Leading Sectors and World Powers: The Coevolution of Global Politics and Economics.* Columbia: University of South Carolina Press.

Mommsen, Wolfgang J. 1982. *Theories of Imperialism.* Chicago: University of Chicago Press.

Moore, R. J. 1966. *Liberalism and Indian Politics 1872–1922.* London: Edward Arnold Publishers Ltd.

Moore, Robin. 1999. "Imperial India, 1858–1914." Pp. 422–46 in *The Oxford History of the British Empire: Volume III, The Nineteenth Century*, edited by Andrew Porter. Oxford: Oxford University Press.

Moraes Ruehsen, Moyara de. 1993. "Operation 'Ajax' Revisited: Iran, 1953." *Middle Eastern Studies* 29(3):467–86.

Morley, Morris, and Chris McGillion. 1997. "'Disobedient' Generals and the Politics of Redemocratization: The Clinton Administration and Haiti." *Political Science Quarterly* 112(3):363–84.

Morris, Charles. 1899. *Our Island Empire: A Hand-book of Cuba, Porto Rico, Hawaii, and the Philippine Islands.* Philadelphia: J. B. Lippincott Company.

Morris, Henry C. 1900. *The History of Colonization.* London: MacMillan & Co., LTD.

Morrison, Delesseps. 1965. *Latin American Mission.* New York: Simon and Schuster.

Moses, Bernard. 1905. "Control of Dependencies Inhabited by the Less Developed Races." *University of California Chronicle* 7(2):3–18.

Motyl, Alexander. 2006. "Empire Falls." *Foreign Affairs* July/August:www.foreign affairs.com (accessed August 5, 2007).

Murphy, E. L. 2009. "Women's Anti-Imperialism, The White Man's Burden, and the Philippine-American War." *Gender & Society* 23(2):244–70.

Nardin, Terry, and Kathleen D. Pritchard. 1990. *Ethics and Intervention: The United States in Grenada*. Washington, DC: Institute for the Study of Diplomacy, Georgetown University.

National Intelligence Council. 1997. *Global Trends 2010*. Washington, DC: Government Printing Office.

National Intelligence Council. 2000. *Global Trends 2015*. Washington, DC: Government Printing Office.

National Intelligence Council. 2001. *Russia in the International System*. Washington, DC: Government Printing Office.

Newbury, C. W. 1965. *British Policy towards West Africa: Select Documents 1786–1874*. Oxford: Clarendon Press.

Nicolson, Harold. [1946] 2001. *The Congress of Vienna: A Study in Allied Unity, 1812–1822*. New York: First Grove Press.

Nieves, Juan. 1898. *La Anexion de Puerto Rico*. Ponce, P.R.: Tipografia del "Listin Comercial."

Ninkovich, Frank A. 1999. *The Wilsonian Century: U.S. Foreign Policy since 1900*. Chicago: University of Chicago Press.

Novak, William J. 2008. "The Myth of the 'Weak' American State." *American Historical Review* 113(June):752–72.

O'Brien, Patrick Karl. 1988a. "The Costs and Benefits of British Imperialism 1846–1914." *Past and Present* 120(August):163–200.

O'Brien, Patrick Karl. 1988b. "The Political Economy of British Taxation, 1660–1815." *The Economic History Review* 41(1):1–32.

O'Brien, Patrick Karl. 1998c. "Inseparable Connections: Trade, Economy, Fiscal State, and the Expansion of Empire, 1688–1815." Pp. 53–77 in *The Oxford History of the British Empire: Volume II, The Eighteenth Century*, edited by P. J. Marshall. Oxford: Oxford University Press.

O'Brien, Patrick Karl. 2002. "The Pax Britannica and American Hegemony: Precedent, Antecedent or Just Another History?" Pp. 1–64 in *Two Hegemonies: Britain 1846–1914 and the United States 1941–2001*, edited by Patrick Karl O'Brien and Armand Cleese. Aldershot: Ashgate.

O'Brien, Patrick Karl, and Geoffrey Allen Pigman. 1992. "Free Trade, British Hegemony, and the International Economic Order in the Nineteenth Century." *Review of International Studies* 18:89–113.

An Officer of His Majesty's Navy. 1823. *The true principles of financial, commercial, and political institutions explained in a way to render the same intelligible to all capacities; and applied in such a manner as cannot fail to promote the prosperity and happiness, and adapted to the use of all nations, without deranging the existing institutions of any nation*. Plymouth: E. Nettleton.

O'Gorman, Frank. 1997. *The Long Eighteenth Century: British Political and Social History 1688–1832*. London: Arnold, a member of the Hodder Headline Group.

Olson, Alison Gilbert. 1992. *Making the Empire Work. London and American Interest Groups*. Cambridge: Cambridge University Press.

Onuf, Peter S. 1987. *Statehood and Union: A History of the Northwest Ordinance*. Bloomington: Indiana University Press.

Onuf, Peter S. 2000. *Jefferson's Empire: The Language of American Nationhood.* Charlottesville: University Press of Virginia.

Orchard, John E. 1951. "ECA and the Dependent Territories." *Geographical Review* 41(1):66–87.

Osterhammel, Jurgen. 1999a. "Britain and China, 1842–1914." Pp. 146–69 in *The Oxford History of the British Empire: Volume III, The Nineteenth Century,* edited by Andrew Porter. Oxford: Oxford University Press.

Osterhammel, Jürgen. 1999b. *Colonialism: A Theoretical Overview.* Princeton, NJ: Markus Wiener Publishers.

Owen, Roger. 1972. "Egypt and Europe: From French to British Occupation 1798–1882." Pp. 195–209 in *Studies in the Theory of Imperialism,* edited by Roger Owen and Bob Sutcliffe. London: Longman Group Limited.

Owen, Roger. 1992. "The 1838 Anglo-Turkish Convention: An Overview." *New Perspectives on Turkey* 7:7–14.

Pagden, Anthony. 1995. *Lords of All the World: Ideologies of Empire in Spain, Britain, and France, c. 1500–1800.* New Haven, CT: Yale University Press.

Pagden, Anthony. 2005. "Imperialism, Liberalism, & the Quest for Perpetual Peace." *Daedalus* 134(2):46–57.

Paquette, Gabriel. 2004. "The Image of Imperial Spain in British Political Thought, 1750–1800." *Bulletin of Spanish Studies* 81(2):187–214.

Paredes, Ruby R. 1988. "The Origins of National Politics: Taft and Partido Federal." Pp. 41–69 in *Philippine Colonial Democracy,* edited by Ruby R. Paredes. New Haven, CT: Yale University, Southeast Asia Studies Monograph Series no. 32.

Parker, Jason. 2006. "Cold War II: The Eisenhower Administration, the Bandung Conference, and the Reperiodization of the Postwar Era." *Diplomatic History* 30(5):867–92.

Pelcovits, Nathan. 1948. *Old China Hands and the Foreign Office.* New York: King's Crown Press.

Perez Hattori, Anne. 1995. "Righting Civil Wrongs: The Guam Congress Walkout of 1949." *ISLA: A Journal of Micronesian Studies* 3:1–27.

Perkins, Whitney T. 1962. *Denial of Empire: The United States and Its Dependencies.* Leyden: A. W. Sythoff.

Perkins, Whitney. 1981. *Constraint of Empire. The United States and Caribbean Interventions.* Westport, CT: Greenwood Press.

Peters, Marie. 1993. "The Myth of William Pitt, Earl of Chatham, Great Imperialist: Part One, Pitt and Imperial Expansion 1738–1763." *Journal of Imperial and Commonwealth History* 21(1):31–74.

Pettigrew, Richard F. 1920. *The Course of Empire, an Official Record.* New York: Boni & Liveright.

Pierce, James Oscar. 1903. "The American Empire." *Dial* 34(398):42–4.

Pitts, Jennifer. 2005. *A Turn to Empire: The Rise of Imperial Liberalism in Britain and France.* Princeton, NJ: Princeton University Press.

Platt, D.C.M. 1968a. *Finance, Trade, and Politics in British Foreign Policy.* Oxford: Clarendon Press.

Platt, D.C.M. 1968b. "The Imperialism of Free Trade: Some Reservations." *Economic History Review* 21(2):296–306.

Pocock, J.G.A. 1988. "States, Republics, and Empires: The American Founding in Early Modern Perspective." Pp. 54–77 in *Conceptual Change and the Constitution,* edited by Terence Ball and J.G.A. Pocock. Lawrence: University of Kansas Press.

Pocock, J.G.A. 1995. "Empire, State, and Confederation: The War of American Independence as a Crisis in Multiple Monarchy." Pp. 318–48 in *A Union for Empire*, edited by John Robertson. Cambridge: Cambridge University Press.

Pomeroy, Earl S. 1944. "The American Colonial Office." *The Mississippi Valley Historical Review* 30:521–32.

Pomeroy, Earl S. 1947. *The Territories and the United States 1861–1890*. Philadelphia: University of Pennsylvania Press.

Pomeroy, William J. 1992. *The Philippines: Colonialism, Collaboration, and Resistance.* New York: International Publishers.

Porter, Bernard. 1999. *The Lion's Share: A Short History of British Imperialism, 1850–1995*. London; New York: Longman.

Porter, Bernard. 2004. *The Absent-Minded Imperialists*. Oxford: Oxford University Press.

Porter, Bernard. 2006. *Empire and Superempire: Britain, America, and the World.* New Haven, CT: Yale University Press.

Powell, John Enoch. 1969. *Freedom and Reality*. London: B. T. Batsford Ltd.

Pownall, Thomas. 1766. *The Administration of Colonies*. London: J. Dodsley and J. Walter.

Pratt, E. J. 1931. "Anglo-American Commercial and Political Rivalry on the Plate, 1820–1830." *The Hispanic-American Historical Review* 11(3):302–35.

Pratt, Julius William. 1934. "The Collapse of American Imperialism." *American Mercury* 31(March):269–78.

Pratt, Julius W. 1936. *Expansionists of 1898: The Acquisition of Hawaii and the Spanish Islands*. Baltimore: Johns Hopkins University Press.

Pratt, Julius William. 1950. *America's Colonial Experiment: How the United States Gained, Governed, and in Part Gave away a Colonial Empire.* New York: Prentice-Hall.

Pratt, Julius William. 1958. "Anticolonialism in United States Policy." Pp. 114–51 in *The Idea of Colonialism*, edited by Robert Strauz-Hupé and Harry W. Hazard. New York: Frederick A. Praeger, Inc.

Preston, Antony, and John Major. 1967. *Send a Gunboat! A Study of the Gunboat and its Role in British Policy, 1854–1904*. London: Longmans, Green and Co Ltd.

Price, Jacob M. 1998. "The Imperial Economy." Pp. 78–104 in *The Oxford History of the British Empire: Volume II, The Eighteenth Century*, edited by P. J. Marshall. Oxford: Oxford University Press.

Prucha, Francis Paul. 1994. *American Indian Treaties: The History of a Political Anomaly*. Berkeley: University of California Press.

Quintero Rivera, Ángel. 1981. *Conflictos de Clase y Política en Puerto Rico*. Río Piedras: Ediciones Huracán.

Rahman, Qamrun. 1975. "Official Ideas of Representation in the Local Self-Government Bodies in India in the Late Nineteenth Century." *Journal of the Asiatic Society of Bangladesh* 20(2):53–68.

Rauchway, Eric. 2006. *Blessed among Nations: How the World Made America*. New York: Hill and Wang.

Raustiala, Kal. 2003. "America Abroad: US May Not Be Imperial, but It Does Have an Empire." *International Herald Tribune* (July 2):http://www.iht.com/articles/2003/07/02/edraust_ed3_.php (accessed August 17, 2005).

Ravenal, Earl C. 2009. "What's Empire Got to Do with It? The Derivation of America's Foreign Policy." *Critical Review* 21(1):21–75.

Ricks, Thomas E. 2006. "Biggest Base in Iraq Has Small-Town Feel." *Washington Post*, February 4.

Rivero Méndez, Angel. 1922. *Crónica de la Guerra Hispano Americana en Puerto Rico*. Madrid, Spain: Sucesores de Rivadenyera (S.A.) Artes Gráficas.

Robbins, William G. 1994. *Colony and Empire: The Capitalist Transformation of the American West*. Lawrence: University Press of Kansas.

Robinson, F.C.R. 1971. "Consultation and Control in the United Provinces' Government and its Allies, 1860–1906." *Modern Asian Studies* 5(4):313–36.

Robinson, Ronald. 1972. "Non-European Foundations of European Imperialism: Sketch for a Theory of Collaboration." Pp. 117–40 in *Studies in the Theory of Imperialism*, edited by Roger Owen and Bob Sutcliffe. London: Longman Group Ltd.

Robinson, Ronald. 1986. "The Excentric Idea of Imperialism." Pp. 267–89 in *Imperialism and After: Continuities and Discontinuities*, edited by Wolfgang J. Mommsen and Jurgen Osterhammel. London: Allen & Unwin.

Robinson, Ronald, and John Gallagher. 1953. "The Imperialism of Free Trade." *Economic History Review* 6:1–15.

Robinson, Ronald, and John Gallagher. 1961. *Africa and the Victorians*. New York: St. Martin's Press.

Robinson, William I. 1996. *Promoting Polyarchy: Globalization, US Intervention, and Hegemony*. Cambridge: Cambridge University Press.

Rodgers, Daniel T. 1998. "Exceptionalism." Pp. 21–40 in *Imagined Histories. American Historians Interpret the Past*, edited by Anthony Molho and Gordon S. Wood. Princeton, NJ: Princeton University Press.

Rodgers, Nini. 1984. "The Abyssinian Expedition of 1867–1868: Disraeli's Imperialism or James Murray's War?" *The Historical Journal* 27(1):129–49.

Rodkey, F. S. 1930. "Lord Palmerston and the Rejuvenation of Turkey 1830–1841, 2." *Journal of Modern History* 2(2):193–225.

Rogers, Howard J. (Ed.). 1905. *Congress of Arts and Science: Universal Exposition, St. Louis, 1904*. Boston and New York: Houghton, Mifflin, and Company.

Romahn, Theresa. 2009. "Colonialism and the Campaign Trail: On Kennedy's Algerian Speech and His Bid for the 1960 Democratic Nomination." *Journal of Colonialism and Colonial History* 10(2):1–23.

Ross, Dorothy. 1984. "Historical Consciousness in Nineteenth-Century America." *The American Historical Review* 89(4):909–28.

Rotter, Andrew J. 1984. "The Triangular Route to Vietnam: The United States, Great Britain, and Southeast Asia, 1945–1950." *International History Review* 6(3):404–23.

Routledge, David. 1974. "The Negotiations Leading to the Cession of Fiji, 1874." *Journal of Imperial and Commonwealth History* 2(3):278–93.

Rudgers, David F. 2000. "The Origins of Covert Action." *Journal of Contemporary History* 35(2):249–62.

Safford, W. E. 1903. "Guam and its People." *Annual Report of the Board of Regents of the Smithsonian Institution* 57:493–508.

Sandars, C. T. 2000. *America's Overseas Garrisons: The Leasehold Empire*. Oxford; New York: Oxford University Press.

Schirmer, Daniel B. 1972. *Republic or Empire: American Resistance to the Philippine War*. Cambridge, MA: Schenkman Pub. Co.; distributed by General Learning Press, Morristown, NJ.

Schlesinger, Arthur, Jr. 2005. "The American Empire? Not So Fast." *World Policy Journal* 22(1):43–46.

Schoonover, Thomas D. 1991. *The United States in Central America, 1860–1911: Episodes of Social Imperialism and Imperial Rivalry in the World System*. Durham, NC: Duke University Press.

Schroeder, Paul. 1992. "Did the Vienna Settlement Rest on a Balance of Power?" *American Historical Review* 97(3):683–706.

Schroeder, Paul. 1994. "Historical Reality vs. Neo-Realist Theory." *International Security* 19(1):108–48.

Schroeder, Seaton. 1922. *A Half Century of Naval Service*. New York; London: D. Appleton & Co.

Schurman, Jacob G. 1902. *Philippine Affairs: A Retrospect and Outlook*. New York: Scribner's and Sons.

Schwabe, Klaus. 1986. "The Global Role of the United States and Its Imperial Consequences, 1898–1973." Pp. 13–33 in *Imperialism and After*, edited by Wolfgang J. Mommsen and Jurgen Osterhammel. London: Allen & Unwin.

Scott, David. 1995. "Colonial Governmentality." *Social Text* 43:191–220.

Seal, Anil. 1968. *The Emergence of Indian Nationalism*. Cambridge: Cambridge University Press.

Sebrega, John J. 1986. "The Anticolonial Policies of Franklin D. Roosevelt: A Reappraisal." *Political Science Quarterly* 101(1):65–84.

Seed, Patricia. 1995. *Ceremonies of Possession in Europe's Conquest of the New World, 1492–1640*. Cambridge: Cambridge University Press.

Selfa, Lance. 1999. "The 1991 Gulf War: Establishing a New World Order." *International Socialist Review* 7(Spring).

Seth, Sanjay. 1999. "Rewriting Histories of Nationalism: The Politics of 'Moderate Nationalism' in India, 1870–1905." *The American Historical Review* 104(1):95–116.

Shafer, Byron. 1991. *Is America Different? A New Look at American Exceptionalism*. New York: Oxford University Press.

Shalom, Stephen R. 1980. "Philippine Acceptance of the Bell Trade Act of 1946: A Study of Manipulatory Democracy." *Pacific Historical Review* 49(3):499–517.

Shaw, Angel Velasco, and Luis Francia. 2002. *Vestiges of War: The Philippine-American War and the Aftermath of an Imperial Dream, 1899–1999*. New York: New York University Press.

Sheridan, Richard B. 1998. "The Formation of Caribbean Plantation Society, 1689–1748." Pp. 394–414 in *The Oxford History of the British Empire: Volume II, The Eighteenth Century*, edited by P. J. Marshall. Oxford: Oxford University Press.

Sherwood, Robert E. 1950. *Roosevelt and Hopkins: An Intimate History*. New York: Harper and Brothers.

Shorrock, Tim. 1984. "Reagan: Beating Plowshares into Swords." *Multinational Monitor* 5(1):http://multinationalmonitor.org/hyper/issues/1984/01/review-reagan.html; accessed December 11, 2007.

Short, Giles. 1977. "Blood and Treasure: The Reduction of Lagos." *ANU Historical Journal* 13:11–19.

Sieg, Kent. 1997. "Marshall Green and the Reverse Course in Indonesia, 1965–1966." *American Asian Review* 15(2):101–25.

Simons, Geoff. 1996. *Iraq: From Sumer to Saddam*. New York: St. Martin's Press.

Singer, David. 1987. "Reconstructing the Correlates of War Dataset on Material Capabilities of States, 1816–1985." *International Interactions* 14:115–32.

Skowronek, Stephen. 1982. *Building a New American State: The Expansion of Administrative Capacities, 1877–1920*. New York; Cambridge: Cambridge University Press.

Smith, Ephraim K. 1993. "William McKinley's Enduring Legacy: The Historiographical Debate on the Taking of the Philippine Islands." Pp. 205–49 in *Crucible of Empire. The Spanish-American War & Its Aftermath*, edited by James C. Bradford. Annapolis, MD: Naval Institute Press.

Smith, Gaddis. 1988. "The Two Worlds of Samuel Flagg Bemis." *Diplomatic History* 9(4):295–302.

Smith, Neil. 2003. *American Empire: Roosevelt's Geographer and the Prelude to Globalization*. Berkeley: University of California Press.

Smith, Tony. 1981. *The Pattern of Imperialism: The United States, Great Britain, and the Late-Industrializing World since 1815*. Cambridge; New York: Cambridge University Press.

Smith, Tony. 1994. *America's Mission. The United States and the Worldwide Struggle for Democracy in the Twentieth Century*. Princeton, NJ: Princeton University Press.

Snape, J. 1882. *The Trade of the British Empire: A Lecture Delivered by Mr. Councillor Snape (of Salford) at the Barton-upon-Irwell Conservative Club, Eccles*. Salford: Salford Steam-Printing Company.

Snow, Alpheus. 1902. *The Administration of Dependencies. A Study of the Evolution of the Federal Empire, with Special Reference to American Colonial Problems*. New York: G. P. Putnam's Sons.

Snow, Freeman. 1894. *Treaties and Topics in American Diplomacy*. Boston: Boston Book Company.

Sohmer, Sara. 1984. "Idealism and Pragmatism in Colonial Fiji: Sir Arthur Gordon's Native Rule Policy and the Introduction of Indian Contract Labor." *The Hawaiian Journal of History* 18:140–55.

Sparrow, Bartholomew H. 2005. "Empires External and Internal: Territories, Government Lands, and Federalism in the United States." Pp. 231–49 in *The Louisiana Purchase and American Expansion, 1803–1898*, edited by Sanford Levinson and Bartholomew H. Sparrow. Lanham, MD: Rowman & Littlefield Publishers, Inc.

Sparrow, Bartholomew H. 2006. *The Insular Cases and the Emergence of the American Empire*. Lawrence: University Press of Kansas.

Spencer, Herbert. 1902. *Facts and Comments*. London: Williams & Norgate.

Steel, Ronald. 1995. *Temptations of a Superpower*. Cambridge, MA: Harvard University Press.

Steele, Ian K. 1986. *The English Atlantic: 1675–1740: An Exploration of Communication and Community*. New York: Oxford University Press.

Steele, Ian K. 1998. "The Anointed, the Appointed, and the Elected: Governance of the British Empire, 1689–1784." Pp. 105–27 in *The Oxford History of the British Empire: Volume II, The Eighteenth Century*, edited by P. J. Marshall. Oxford: Oxford University Press.

Stein, Arthur A. 1984. "The Hegemon's Dilemma: Great Britain, the United States, and the International Economic Order." *International Organization* 38(2):355–86.

Steinmetz, George. 2003. "'The Devil's Handwriting': Precolonial Discourse, Ethnographic Acuity, and Cross-Identification in German Colonialism." *Comparative Studies in Society and History* 45(1):41–94.

Steinmetz, George. 2004. "Odious Comparisons: Incommensurability, the Case Study, and 'Small N's' in Sociology." *Sociological Theory* 22(3):371–400.

Steinmetz, George. 2005. "Return to Empire: The New U.S. Imperialism in Comparative Historical Perspective." *Sociological Theory* 23 (4):339–67.

Stephanson, Anders. 1995. *Manifest Destiny*. New York: Hill and Wang.

Stewart, John. 1996. *The British Empire: An Encyclopedia of the Crown's Holdings, 1493 through 1995*. Jefferson, NC: McFarland & Co.

Stoler, Ann Laura (Ed.). 2006. *Haunted by Empire: Geographies of Intimacy in North American History*. Durham, NC: Duke University Press.

Stoler, Ann Laura, Carole McGranahan, and Peter C. Perdue (Eds.). 2007. *Imperial Formations*. Santa Fe, NM: School for Advanced Research Press.

Stone, Lawrence. 1994. "Introduction." Pp. 1–32 in *An Imperial State at War*, edited by Lawrence Stone. London: Routledge.

Strang, David. 1991. "Anomaly and Commonplace in European Political Expansion: Realist and Institutional Accounts." *International Organization* 45(2):143–62.

Strange, Susan. 1987. "The Persistent Myth of Lost Hegemony." *International Organization* 41(4):551–74.

Sturgis, James. 1984. "Britain and the New Imperialism." Pp. 85–105 in *British Imperialism in the Nineteenth Century*, edited by C. C. Eldridge. New York: St. Martin's Press.

Subrahmanyam, Sanjay. 2006. "Imperial and Colonial Encounters: Some Comparative Reflections." Pp. 217–28 in *Lessons of Empire: Imperial Histories and American Power*, edited by Craig Calhoun, Frederick Cooper, and Kevin W. Moore. New York: The New Press.

Suri, Jeremi. 2009. "The Limits of American Empire." Pp. 523–31 in *Colonial Crucible: Empire in the Making of the Modern American State*, edited by Alfred W. McCoy and Francisco A. Scarano. Madison: University of Wisconsin Press.

Suskind, Ron. 2004. "Without a Doubt." *The New York Times Magazine*, October 17, Section 6; Column 1; Magazine Desk; p. 44.

Sylla, Richard. 1996. "Experimental Federalism: The Economics of American Government, 1789–1914." Pp. 483–581 in *The Cambridge History of the United States, Volume II: The Long Nineteenth Century*, edited by Stanley L. Engerman and Robert E. Gallman. Cambridge: Cambridge University Press.

Taft, William H. 1908. *Special Report of Wm. H. Taft Secretary of War to the President on the Philippines*. Washington, DC: Government Printing Office.

Tarrow, Sidney. 1999. "Expanding Paired Comparison: A Modest Proposal." *APSA-CP Newsletter* Summer:9–12.

Thomas, Nicholas. 1994. *Colonialism's Culture: Anthropology, Travel, Government*. Princeton, NJ: Princeton University Press.

Thompson, Lanny. 2010. *Imperial Archipelago: Representation and Rule in the Insular Territories under US Domination after 1898*. Honolulu: University of Hawaii Press.

Thompson, Laura. 1944. "Guam: Study in Military Government." *Far Eastern Survey* 13(16):149–54.

Thompson, William R. 2001. "Martian and Venusian Perspectives on International Relations: Britain as System Leader in the Nineteenth and Twentieth Centuries." Pp. 253–92 in *Bridges and Boundaries: Historians, Political Scientists, and the Study of International Relations*, edited by Colin Elman and Miriam Fendius Elman. Cambridge, MA: MIT Press.

Thornton, A. P. 1959. *The Imperial Idea and its Enemies; A Study in British Power*. London; New York: Macmillan; St. Martin's Press.

Thornton, A. P. 1978. *Imperialism in the Twentieth Century*. London: Macmillan.

Tilley, B. F. 1901. "Development of Our Possessions in Samoa." *The Independent* 53(2745):1601–02.

Tilly, Charles. 1997. "How Empires End." Pp. 1–11 in *After Empire: Multiethnic Societies and Nation-Building*, edited by Karen Barkey and Mark von Hagen. Boulder, CO: Westview Press.

Tinker, Hugh. 1968. *The Foundations of Local Self-Government in India, Pakistan, and Burma*. New York: F. A. Praeger.

Tir, Jaroslav, Philip Schafer, Paul F. Diehl, and Gary Goertz. 1998. "Territorial Changes, 1816–1996." *Conflict Management and Peace Science* 16:89–97.

Tomes, Nancy. 2009. "Crucibles, Capillaries, and Pentimenti: Reflections on Imperial Transformations." Pp. 532–40 in *Colonial Crucible: Empire in the Making of the Modern American State*, edited by Alfred W. McCoy and Francisco A. Scarano. Madison: University of Wisconsin Press.

Tomlins, Christopher. 2001. "The Legal Cartography of Colonization, the Legal Polyphony of Settlement: English Intrusions on the American Mainland in the Seventeenth Century." *Law & Social Inquiry* 26(2):315–72.

Tomlinson, B. R. 1999. "Economics and Empire: The Periphery and the Imperial Economy." Pp. 53–74 in *The Oxford History of the British Empire: Volume III, The Nineteenth Century*, edited by Andrew Porter. Oxford: Oxford University Press.

Trumbull, Robert. 1946. "A Swing around our Pacific 'Empire.'" *New York Times Magazine*, May 19, pp. 13–14.

Tucker, Robert W., and David C. Hendrickson. 1990. *Empire of Liberty: The Statecraft of Thomas Jefferson*. Oxford: Oxford University Press.

Tyler, J. E. 1938. *The Struggle for Imperial Unity (1868–1895)*. London: Longmans, Green and Co.

Tyler, Patrick. 1992. "Excerpts from Pentagon's Plan." *New York Times* March 8, 1992, p. 14.

Tyrrell, Ian. 1991a. "American Exceptionalism in an Age of International History." *American Historical Review* 96(4):1031–55.

Tyrrell, Ian. 1991b. *Woman's World/Woman's Empire: The Woman's Christian Temperance Union in International Perspective*. Chapel Hill: University of North Carolina Press.

United States Bureau of the Census. 1943. *Sixteenth Census of the United States: Territories and Possessions*. Washington, DC: Government Printing Office.

United States Bureau of the Census. 1999. *Statistical Abstract of the United States (119th edition)*. Washington, DC: Government Printing Office.

United States Commission on National Security. 1999. *New World Coming: The United States Commission on National Security in the 21st Century*. Washington, DC: United States Commission on National Security.

United States Congress Committee on Foreign Affairs. 1970. *Background Information on the Use of United States Armed Forces in Foreign Countries*. Washington, DC: Government Printing Office.

United States Congress Committee on International Relations. 1976. *Selected Executive Session Hearings of the Committee, 1943–1950*. Washington, DC: Government Printing Office.

United States Congress Committee on Territories and Insular Possessions. 1928. *American Samoa. Joint Hearings before the Committee on Territories, United States Senate* and Insular Possessions and the Committee on Insular Affairs, House of Representatives. Seventieth Congress, First Session on S. Con. Res. 2. Washington, DC: Government Printing Office.

United States Department of State. 1955. *The Conferences at Malta and Yalta 1945.* Washington, DC: Government Printing Office.

United States House of Representatives Committee on Foreign Affairs. 1917. *Cession of Danish West Indian Islands: Hearings before the Committee on Foreign Affairs.* Washington, DC: Government Printing Office.

United States Major-General Commanding the Army. 1899. *Annual Report of the U.S. Major-General Commanding the Army. 1899. In Three Parts.* Washington, DC: Government Printing Office.

United States Navy Department. 1900. *Annual Reports of the Navy Department for the Year 1900. Report of the Secretary of the Navy. Miscellaneous Reports.* Washington, DC: Government Printing Office.

United States Navy Department. 1901. *Annual Reports of the Navy Department for the Year 1901. Report of the Secretary of the Navy. Miscellaneous Reports. In Two Parts. Part 1.* Washington, DC: Government Printing Office.

United States Navy Department. 1904a. *Annual Reports of the Navy Department for the Year 1904. Report of the Secretary of the Navy. Miscellaneous Reports.* Washington, DC: Government Printing Office.

United States Navy Department. 1904b. *Data Relating to the Island of Guam.* Washington, DC: Government Printing Office.

United States Philippine Commission. 1900. *Report of the [Schurman] Philippine Commission to the President (January 31, 1900).* Washington, DC: Government Printing Office.

United States Philippine Commission. 1901. *Report of the United States Philippine Commission to the Secretary of War for the Period from December 1, 1900 to October 15, 1901.* Washington, DC: Government Printing Office.

United States War Department. 1899. *Annual Reports of the War Department for the Fiscal Year Ended June 30, 1899. Report of the Secretary of War. Miscellaneous Reports.* Washington, DC: Government Printing Office.

Van Alstyne, R. W. 1960. *The Rising American Empire.* Oxford: Basil Blackwell.

Vane, Charles William (Ed.). 1851. *Correspondences, Despatches, and Other Papers of Viscount Castlereagh.* London: William Shoberl.

Venkatarangaiya, M., and M. Pattabhiram (Eds.). 1969. *Local Government in India.* Bombay: Allied Publishers.

Waddell, D.A.G. 1959. "Great Britain and the Bay Islands, 1821–1861." *Historical Journal* 2(1):59–77.

Wald, Priscilla. 1992. "Terms of Assimilation: Legislating Subjectivity in the Emerging Nation." *Boundary* 2 19(3):77–104.

Walker, Eric A. 1943. *The British Empire. Its Structure and Spirit.* London: Oxford University Press.

Wallace, Anthony. 1993. *The Long Bitter Trail: Andrew Jackson and the Indians.* New York: Hill & Wang.

Wallerstein, Immanuel 1974. *The Modern World-System.* New York: Academic Press.

Wallerstein, Immanuel. 1980. *The Modern World-System II: Mercantilism and the Consolidation of the European World-Economy, 1600–1750.* Boston: Academic Press, Inc.

Wallerstein, Immanuel. 1984. "The Three Instances of Hegemony in the History of the Capitalist World Economy." Pp. 100–7 in *Current Issues and Research in Macrosociology*, edited by Gerhard Lenski. Leiden: E. J. Brill.

Wallerstein, Immanuel. 1989. *The Modern World-System III. The Second Era of Great Expansion of the Capitalist World Economy, 1730–1840s*. Boston: Academic Press, Inc.

Wallerstein, Immanuel. 2002a. "The Eagle Has Crash Landed." *Foreign Policy* July/August:60–8.

Wallerstein, Immanuel. 2002b. "Three Hegemonies." Pp. 357–61 in *Two Hegemonies: Britain 1846–1914 and the United States 1941–2001*, edited by Patrick Karl O'Brien and Armand Cleese. Aldershot: Ashgate.

Wallerstein, Immanuel. 2006. "The Curve of American Power." *New Left Review* 40(July-August):77–94.

Ward, J. R. 1998. "The British West Indies in the Age of Abolition, 1748–1815." Pp. 415–39 in *The Oxford History of the British Empire: Volume II, The Eighteenth Century*, edited by P. J. Marshall. Oxford: Oxford University Press.

Watson, Adam. 1992. *The Evolution of International Society*. London and New York: Routledge.

Watson, Michael. 1995. "The British West Indian Legislatures in the Seventeenth and Eighteenth Centuries: An Historiographical Introduction." *Parliamentary History* 14(1):89–98.

Webb, Michael, and Stephen Krasner. 1989. "Hegemonic Stability Theory: An Empirical Assessment." *Review of International Studies* 15(2):183–98.

Webster, Anthony. 2000. "Business and Empire: A Reassessment of the British Conquest of Burma in 1885." *The Historical Journal* 43(4):1003–25.

Webster, Anthony. 2006. *The Debate on the Rise of the British Empire*. Manchester: Manchester University Press.

Weeks, William Earl. 1996. *Building the Continental Empire*. Chicago: Ivan R. Dee.

Weiner, Mark S. 2001. "Teutonic Constitutionalism: The Role of Ethno-Juridical Discourse in the Spanish-American War." Pp. 48–81 in *Foreign in a Domestic Sense*, edited by Christina Duffy Burnett and Burke Marshall. Durham, NC: Duke University Press.

Weis, Michael W. 2001. "The Twilight of Pan-Americanism: The Alliance for Progress, Neo-Colonialism, and Non-Alignment in Brazil, 1961–1964." *International History Review* 23(June):322–44.

Welch, Richard E. 1979. *Response to Imperialism: The United States and the Philippine-American War, 1899–1902*. Chapel Hill: University of North Carolina Press.

Welles, Sumner. 1943. "Text of Address of Sumner Welles Calling for United Use of Force to Preserve World Peace." *New York Times*, October 17, p. 32.

Westad, Odd Arne. 2005. *The Global Cold War: Third World Interventions and the Making of Our Times*. Cambridge: Cambridge University Press.

Wheeler-Bennett, J. W. 1929. "Thirty Years of American-Filipino Relations, 1899–1929." *Journal of the Royal Institute of International Affairs* 8(5):503–21.

White, Richard. 1991. *"It's Your Misfortune and None of My Own": A History of the American West*. Norman: University of Oklahoma Press.

Williams, Daniel R. 1913. *The Odyssey of the Philippine Commission*. Chicago: A. C. McClurg & Co.

Williams, Gary. 2002. "Brief Encounter: Grenadian Prime Minister Maurice Bishop's Visit to Washington." *Journal of Latin American Studies* 34:659–85.

Williams, William Appleman. 1955. "The Frontier Thesis and American Foreign Policy." *Pacific Historical Review* 24:379–95.

Williams, William Appleman. 1969. *The Roots of the Modern American Empire: A Study of the Growth and Shaping of Social Consciousness in a Marketplace Society.* New York: Random House.

Williams, William Appleman. 1972. *The Tragedy of American Diplomacy.* New York: W. W. Norton.

Willoughby, William F. 1905. *Territories and Dependencies of the United States.* New York: The Century Co.

Wilson, Kathleen. 1988. "Empire, Trade, and Popular Politics in Mid-Hanoverian Britain: The Case of Admiral Vernon." *Past and Present* 121:74–109.

Wilson, Kathleen. 1995. *The Sense of the People. Politics, Culture, and Imperialism in England, 1715–1785.* Cambridge: Cambridge University Press.

Wilson, P. W. 1925. "Few Worlds Left for Us to Conquer." *New York Times*, January 4, SM7.

Wilson, Woodrow. 1901. "Democracy and Efficiency." *The Atlantic Monthly* 87: 289–99.

Wiltshire, David. 1978. *The Social and Political Thought of Herbert Spencer.* Oxford: Oxford University Press.

Wimmer, Andreas, and Nina Glick Schiller. 2002. "Methodological Nationalism and Beyond: Nation-State Building, Migration and the Social Sciences." *Global Networks* 2(4):301–34.

Winks, Robin W. 1997. "American Imperialism in Comparative Perspective." Pp. 139–54 in *America Compared*, edited by Carl J. Guarneri. Boston: Houghton Mifflin.

Winn, Peter. 1976. "British Informal Empire in Uruguay in the Nineteenth Century." *Past and Present* 73:100–26.

Wood, Ellen Meiksins. 2003. *Empire of Capital.* London: Verso.

Yasin, Madhvi. 1977. "The Indian Councils Act of 1892: An Analytical Study." *Journal of Indian History* 55(1–2):255–63.

Zakaria, Fareed. 1998. *From Wealth to Power: The Unusual Origins of America's World Role.* Princeton, NJ: Princeton University Press.

Zakaria, Fareed. 2009. "The Post-Imperial Presidency: Realism and Idealism in the Age of Obama." *Newsweek*, December 14, pp. 36, 40.

Zakheim, Dov S. 1986. "The Grenada Operation and Superpower Relations: A Perspective from the Pentagon." Pp. 175–85 in *Grenada and Soviet/Cuban Policy*, edited by Jiri Valenta and Herbert J. Ellison. Boulder, CO: Westview Press.

Zelizer, Julian. 2010. *Arsenal of Democracy.* New York: Basic Books.

Zimmerman, Warren. 2002. *First Great Triumph.* New York: Farrar, Straus and Giroux.

Zolberg, Aristide R. 2002. "International Engagement and American Democracy: A Comparative Perspective." Pp. 24–54 in *Shaped by War and Trade: International Influences on American Political Development*, edited by Ira Katznelson and Martin Shefter. Princeton, NJ: Princeton University Press.

Index

Made in the USA
San Bernardino, CA
19 January 2018